DEAN B. ELLIS LIBRARY
ARKANSAS STATE UNIVERSITY

POVERTY, U. S. A.

THE HISTORICAL RECORD

ADVISORY EDITOR: David J. Rothman
Professor of History, Columbia University

AMERICAN CHARITIES

AMOS G. WARNER

Arno Press & The New York Times
NEW YORK   1971

Reprint Edition 1971 by Arno Press Inc.

Reprinted from a copy in
The University of Illinois Library

LC# 76—137192
ISBN 0—405—03129—7

POVERTY, U.S.A.: THE HISTORICAL RECORD
ISBN for complete set: 0-405-03090-8

Manufactured in the United States of America

LIBRARY OF

ECONOMICS AND POLITICS.

EDITED BY

RICHARD T. ELY, Ph.D., LL.D.

NUMBER FOUR.

AMERICAN CHARITIES

A STUDY
IN
PHILANTHROPY AND ECONOMICS

BY

AMOS G. WARNER, Ph.D.

Professor of Economics and Social Science in the Leland Stanford Junior University; formerly Superintendent of Charities for the District of Columbia, General Agent of the Charity Organization Society of Baltimore; etc.

NEW YORK: 46 East Fourteenth Street
THOMAS Y. CROWELL & CO.
BOSTON: 100 Purchase Street

COPYRIGHT, 1894,
BY
THOMAS Y. CROWELL & CO.

TYPOGRAPHY BY C. J. PETERS & SON,
145 HIGH ST., BOSTON, U.S.A.

DEDICATED
TO
Mr. John Glenn,
CHAIRMAN OF THE EXECUTIVE COMMITTEE OF THE
CHARITY ORGANIZATION SOCIETY
OF BALTIMORE.

"*The subject has great attractions: As science, because it links phenomena to phenomena, and reveals their laws; as philanthropy, because the knowledge of these laws may be used as a weapon to conquer the vice, the crime, the misery which science investigates.*"

RICHARD L. DUGDALE.

TABLE OF CONTENTS.

PART I.—INTRODUCTORY AND THEORETICAL.

CHAPTER.		PAGE.
I.	PHILANTHROPY AND ECONOMICS IN THE PAST	3
II.	CAUSES OF POVERTY	22
III.	PERSONAL CAUSES OF INDIVIDUAL DEGENERATION	59
IV.	SOME OF THE SOCIAL CAUSES OF INDIVIDUAL DEGENERATION	95
V.	CHARITY AS A FACTOR IN HUMAN SELECTION	118

PART II.—THE DEPENDENT CLASSES.

VI.	THE ALMSHOUSE AND ITS INMATES	139
VII.	RELIEF OF THE POOR IN THEIR HOMES	162
VIII.	THE UNEMPLOYED AND THE HOMELESS POOR	177
IX.	DEPENDENT CHILDREN	202
X.	THE DESTITUTE SICK	239
XI.	THE INSANE	260
XII.	THE FEEBLE-MINDED AND ANALOGOUSLY DEGENERATE CLASSES	276
XIII.	FURTHER DIFFERENTIATION AND SUMMARY	293

PART III.—PHILANTHROPIC FINANCIERING.

XIV.	PUBLIC CHARITIES	301
XV.	PRIVATE CHARITIES	315
XVI.	ENDOWMENTS	323
XVII.	PUBLIC SUBSIDIES TO PRIVATE CHARITIES	334

PART IV.—THE SUPERVISION, ORGANIZATION, AND BETTERMENT OF CHARITIES.

CHAPTER.		PAGE.
XVIII.	SUPERVISORY AGENCIES	357
XIX.	THE ORGANIZATION OF CHARITIES	372
XX.	CERTAIN HOPEFUL TENDENCIES	394

APPENDIX.

INDEX	411
BIBLIOGRAPHICAL INDEX	421

PART I.

INTRODUCTORY AND THEORETICAL.

PART I.
INTRODUCTORY AND THEORETICAL.

CHAPTER I.
PHILANTHROPY AND ECONOMICS IN THE PAST.

[On ancient and church charity, see Crooker's brief and sketchy account in " Problems in American Society " (Boston, 1889); Uhlhorn, " Christian Charity in the Ancient Church " (translated from the German, Edinburgh, 1883); " Die Christliche Liebesthätigkeit im Mittelalter " (Stuttgart, 1884); and " Die Christliche Liebesthätigkeit seit der Reformation " (Stuttgart, 1890); also a brief survey by the same writer in the article, "Armenwesen; Geschichte," in *Handwörterbuch der Staatswissenschaften*. The most available work from the Catholic standpoint is Cardinal Baluffi's " The Charity of the Church a Proof of her Divinity " (translated from the Italian, Dublin, 1885). Brace's " Gesta Christi " is good but not critical. Lecky, "History of European Morals," has a good chapter on Charity. Ashley, " Economic History " (New York, 1893), Book II., chap. v., gives the best critical view of Middle Age charity in England; it is preceded by an account of authorities. Eden's " State of the Poor " (1797) is a monumental work, but practically inaccessible to American readers. The economists who have discussed the problems of pauperism at most length are Malthus, Chalmers, and Fawcett; see also a vigorous chapter in Walker's larger text-book. Goschen's address on " Ethics and Economics " describes fairly well the necessity economists are under of reckoning with altruism as a constant force. On the same point see Dargun, " Egoismus und Altruismus in der Nationalökonomie " (Leipzig, 1885). Most of the recent dictionaries of political economy contain articles on poor-laws, pauperism, etc.]

THE science of political economy, as we know it, is hardly more than a century old; while the art of aiding the poor has been practised from time immemorial.

When the patriarch Job was justifying himself, he spoke of his work for the unfortunate in language which is still considered suitable for describing an ideal philanthropist, and which in part is now used as a motto by several charity organization societies.[1] Before Christianity was a power, and far beyond the influence of the Hebrew faith, the instinct of sympathy for those in distress had prompted to kindly acts which philosophers commended and religious leaders enjoined. An imposing array of texts exhorting to charity, and prescribing the methods of it, can be gleaned from the pagan writers of antiquity by any one willing to take the trouble to collect them, or to quote them from the stock writers on the subject. The beggar is known to almost all literatures with which we are acquainted; and where beggars are, there must also be those that give. In China, long before the Christian era, there were "refuges for the aged and sick poor, free schools for poor children, free eating-houses for wearied laborers, associations for the distribution of second-hand clothing, and societies for paying the expenses of marriage and burial among the poor."[2]

Intermittently from the first, the altruistic instinct

---

[1] "When the ear heard me, then it blessed me; and when the eye saw me, it gave witness to me: because I delivered the poor that cried, and the fatherless, and him that had none to help him. The blessing of him that was ready to perish came upon me: and I caused the widow's heart to sing for joy. . . . I was eyes to the blind, and feet was I to the lame. I was a father to the poor: and the cause which I knew not I searched out."

[2] See Crooker, "Problems in American Society," chapter on "Scientific Charity," for this and other references to antiquity. In the opening pages of the chapter cited, Mr. Crooker has "surveyed mankind from China to Peru," and found symptoms of active benevolence among all peoples sufficiently civilized to have left a literature behind them.

seems to have been re-enforced, or its acts counterfeited, by egoistic instincts, originating in educational, or political, or religious considerations. The first of these subsidiary motives was doubtless the weakest of the three. The desire to promote self-culture by development of the benevolent impulses is largely a modern form of selfishness, and yet we find traces of it among the ancients.

Formerly, as now, political considerations frequently led to acts of charity when the motive was absent. Free or greatly cheapened corn for the Roman people was nominally but rendering to them what was their own. In fact, it was a mischievous gratuity; and while sympathy for the people undoubtedly actuated many who favored the largesses, yet the efficient cause of their continual increase was political self-seeking.[1] So the legislation for the better care of exposed infants, and for the support of young women with children (Puellae Faustinianae) of the later Roman Empire resulted partly from sympathy for the unfortunates, and largely from a wish to fill up the depleted ranks of the Roman and Italian population.

The commonest and most powerful incentive to benevolence has been everywhere and at all times that supplied by religion. Any impulse or habit that is for the good of the race is likely in the course of time to be fixed and intensified by religious sanctions. Almost all customs, including the organization of the family and of

---

[1] The indiscriminate granting of pensions to the Union soldiers of the Civil War results from the same mixed motives, among which political considerations are the final and efficient cause of mischievously reckless disbursements.

the government, and even habits of dress, diet, and cleanliness, have been thus confirmed. For present purposes we need not bother ourselves with teleological considerations, nor inquire whether the useful impulses and habits originated in a divine command supernaturally revealed, or whether they had their origin in spontaneous variation or rational adaptation, and were then seized upon, and perpetuated by the religious instincts. To whatever source we may trace the sentiment of pity and the desire to relieve the destitute, it certainly had not been in existence long, before its cultivation was enjoined by religious authority.

Religion, however, like the subsidiary motives based on educational or political considerations, has too frequently substituted self-seeking for self-sacrifice as the motive power in aiding the poor. Mr. Crooker well says that the charity of antiquity was very largely "a means of obtaining merit." "The riches of the infinite God," says the Vendidad, "will be bestowed upon him who relieves the poor;" or, according to a Hindu epic, "He who giveth without stint food to a fatigued wayfarer, never seen before, obtaineth merit that is great." It was when Job was justifying himself that he enumerated his works of mercy. While rewards were offered for benevolent work, on the other hand punishments were promised for hardheartedness. The grim threat of the Talmud, "The house that does not open to the poor shall open to the physician," is typical of many passages that might be quoted from the earlier religious writings. Under the influence of such threats or of more direct ones, believers felt constrained to aid the poor for purely selfish reasons, to do some overt act that seemed to have been prescribed, in order that it might be accounted to them for righteousness. Subjectively considered, the act itself was not one of charity but of penance; its motive was not a desire to aid the distressed, but to propitiate a more or less unreasonable deity or fate.

The influence of religion upon the benevolent instincts of man can be studied in nearly all its phases in the history of charities administered by the Christian church; and in that history can be traced the power of an accepted theology both to exalt and to degrade the charitable impulse. While the antiquarian may be able to point out many traces of active benevolence before the Christian era, while there is much genuine philanthropy outside of Christianity, and while it may even be said that the church of the present day that administers its charities most wisely is not Christian at all, but Jewish,—it yet remains true that charity, as we know it, gets its chief religious authority and incentive from Him who gave as the summary of all the law and prophets the co-ordinate commands to love God and to love our neighbor, and who, in explaining these commands, pronounced the parable of the Good Samaritan. At first, Christianity brought to the world a purified and ennobled charity, a love of fellow men very different from the semi-selfish motives that prompted to prayer, penance, and almsgiving as means to a common end — that of securing divine favor. The early diaconate seems to have been a satisfactory way of organizing what is now called "friendly visiting."

But with success came degeneration; as the church became an institution administering progressively large revenues, its service of the poor degenerated, partly from worldliness, and partly from "other-worldliness." The former cause of degeneracy, that which came from overt worldliness, and led to the misapplication of revenues designed for the relief of the poor, sometimes attained great proportions, and was a tendency that honest ecclesiastics found it necessary to fight continually. But such palpable evils wrought little harm, as compared with the dry rot of spiritual selfishness, which caused charity to degenerate into almsgiving for the benefit of the one who gave. The doctrine of Augustine, which he taught only with qualifications, that "alms have power to extinguish and expiate sin," became the motive power in the charities of the Middle Ages. Gifts to the church for charitable purposes became merely a method of securing a satisfactory balance on the books of the recording angel, a way of getting out of purgatory or of getting others out — "a species of fire insurance." [1] As an agent for securing gifts both of property and of personal service the church was almost incredibly successful. If the devotion of material wealth to the relief of the poor could alone have cured destitution, it would have been cured. But we are all familiar with the disastrous results that followed so much indiscriminate giving. A rich church among a multitude of poor, which Emming-

---

[1] In a lecture on "The Evolution of Charities," delivered before the Brooklyn Ethical Association, the writer quoted this phrase in much the same connection. In the discussion which followed, Mr. Bolton Hall said that people of the present day do not give to the poor for the purpose of "fire insurance," mainly, perhaps, because they have ceased to believe in the fire. He further suggested that nowadays men may be suspected of giving away as "cyclone insurance" part of the wealth which they have unfairly won.

haus declares to have been always the ecclesiastical ideal, did not prove a satisfactory arrangement. When Hubert-Valleroux, in discussing the rural charities of France, shows that all the great charitable institutions of that country originally owed their existence to the influence of Christianity through the church, he is historically correct. But when he makes this statement of fact the basis of plea for the non-intervention of the state in the present administration of charitable institutions, he is wrong; for the history of charitable institutions shows that, while they originated through the influence of the church, it was also through ecclesiastical influence that they degenerated and became mischievous. The state interfered for many reasons, some of them certainly unworthy; but one sufficient cause was everywhere present — ecclesiastical mismanagement, and the necessity the community was under to protect itself from the spreading disease of pauperism. "In no case," says Lecky, "was the abolition of monasteries effected in a more indefensible manner than in England, but the transfer of property, that was once employed in a great measure in charity, to the courtiers of King Henry, was ultimately a benefit to the English poor; for no misapplication of this property by private persons could produce as much evil as an unrestrained monasticism."[1]

In almost every European country, the state first tried to stop beggary and vagabondage by repressive measures, and only when these failed was obliged to assail the evil at one of its sources by taking charge of relief work. This work was taken in hand by the state in Scandinavia at a very early period, in England at the

[1] "History of European Morals," vol. ii., pp. 94-5.

time of the Reformation, in France at the time of the Revolution, and in Italy within the last few years. In Germany, Luther suggested that the church and state should work together to root out beggary, and to lessen as much as possible the misery caused by destitution and disease. The religious wars that followed the Reformation in that country interfered with the immediate transfer of relief work to the state. "The Protestant authorities," says Emminghaus, "were not more prudent than their predecessors where valuable property of the church for the benefit of the poor remained; and wherever the care of the poor was still in ecclesiastical hands, the only alteration in the way in which it was conducted arose from the fact that the church had less abundant means at its disposal. But," he adds, "this fact alone may be considered a great gain, for abundance of means is the greatest danger of all in the relief of the poor." [1]

From what has been said regarding the failure of the church as an almoner, it must not be inferred that its influence was wholly perverse and mischievous. On the contrary, even Lecky, whose opinion as to the good effects of the secularization of the monastic properties in England has been already noticed, says that "the value of Catholic services in alleviating pain and sickness and the more exceptional forms of suffering can never be overrated;" and even in the field of charity he says that "we must not forget the benefits resulting, if not to the sufferer, at least to the donor. Charitable habits, even when formed in the first instance from selfish motives, even when so misdirected as to be positively injurious to the recipient, rarely fail to exercise a sof-

[1] "Poor Relief in Different Parts of Europe," p. 13.

tening and purifying influence on character. All through the darkest period of the Middle Ages, amid ferocity and fanaticism and brutality, we may trace the subduing influence of Catholic charity, blending strangely with every excess of violence and every outburst of persecution." [1] In fact, the church educated the community up to a point where it insisted that a large amount of relief work must be done, and only in attempting to administer large funds did the ecclesiastical machinery work badly and break down. It was right that the state should undertake relief work, but that relief work, and the great access of sympathy for our fellow-men which compelled it, would never have existed except for the influence of the church.

Improvements usually improve things but little at first, and the change from ecclesiastical administration of relief work to administration by the state hardly seemed for a time to be an improvement at all. We have heard of the failure of the English poor-law almost as much as we have heard of the failure of the monastic system of poor-relief. The break-down of public charities has come from time to time in various parts of Europe; and as it is a matter primarily of administration, we must expect to be constantly reminded of the aphorism that "whatever is best administered is best."

Turning now to consider more directly the influence of economic philosophy upon charitable enterprises, we find that many early writers dealt with the subject of poor relief in its economic aspects before political economy was recognized as a distinct science. Defoe, for example, wrote a paper on "Giving Alms no Charity," in which he said that the reason why so many pretend

[1] "History of European Morals," vol. ii., p. 95.

to want work is that they can live so well with the pretence of wanting work.

Among the earliest writers who treated of this subject, and whose works have been collected as those of economists, Ricci should have a place. He wrote a book on the reform of the institutions of charity in Modena, published in 1787. The author called attention to the gigantic development of mendicancy in Italy, tracing it to the excessive charity of the people, and seemed to regard "as an evil all charity which sprang from religious motives, and was greater than would spring from the unaided instincts of man."[1] This appeal to a natural man back of the actual man influenced by religion and law, marks Ricci as one moved by the spirit of the times which immediately preceded the French Revolution. This time-spirit influenced the relief of the poor in two ways; one through politics, and one through economics or political economy. Liberty and equality were the two words which represented the regnant ideas of the times. The religious dogma of the brotherhood of man was paralleled by the political dogma of the equality of man, and the result was a tendency to relieve distress with greater promptness and completeness. The revolutionary governments of France guaranteed to all not only opportunities to work, but security against starvation, and the facile manner in which the state in that country still assumes the care of abandoned infants, perhaps shows the influence of such philosophers as Rousseau, who believed that children should be raised by the state, and who gladly turned over his own children to be brought up

[1] Cited by Lecky, vol. ii., p. 98.

by that agency. Indirectly and by unseen ways it is probable that the same belief in the political dogma of the equality of men influenced the administration of the English poor-law, until it culminated in the great abuses which compelled the reforms of 1834. But "equality" was not the first word in the sociological creed of the revolutionary period from 1789 to 1848. The first word was "liberty." And while this word was constantly used by the politicians, the group of men who stood most consistently for it in industrial affairs were the students of the new-born science of political economy. They thought that a man ought not only to be left free by government to succeed and be happy, but also to fail and suffer.[1]

For some time the economists had little to say regarding the relief of the poor, though the subject was mentioned by several of the early writers, including Sir James Steuart and Adam Smith; and others took up the subject of the English poor-laws. It received very full mention, however, in Malthus's work on the "Principle of Population," where he gave two chapters to the English poor-law and two other excellent ones to the consideration of certain proposals for improving the condition of the poor. Many of the extracts from chapter nine of the second edition of his work might serve as mottoes for modern charity organization societies. It would not, however, be expedient to use them, since people have insisted on connecting with the name of this English clergyman so much that is brutal and ma-

[1] Turgot is an exception to this statement, which is, in fact, more nearly true of many of the followers of the early economists than of the economists themselves.

terialistic and hopeless. As a matter of fact, he does not deprecate the exercise of charity, and would even give to it a much broader field than that accorded by Mr. Spencer in his latest work; but he calls attention to the fact that there is no direction in which human ingenuity has been more exerted than in the endeavor to ameliorate the condition of the poor, and that there is certainly none in which it has so completely failed. "There is no subject," he further adds, " to which general principles have been so seldom applied; and yet, in the whole compass of human knowledge, I doubt if there be one in which it is so dangerous to lose sight of them, because the partial and immediate effects of a particular mode of giving assistance are so often directly opposite to the general and permanent effects." [1]

Among the economists of the first quarter of this century, Whately and Chalmers dealt quite extensively with the poor-law and the problems of poor-relief. Chalmers re-enforced his teachings in this matter by doing away with public relief of the poor in his parish, and providing for their care entirely through voluntary contributions. He believed that all public relief of the poor was bad; and, besides what is contained in his political economy, he wrote upon the subject at length in the three volumes which appear under the title of "The Christian and Civic Economy of Large Towns."

It was in the second quarter of the century that the economists and philanthropists were to come into most direct collision. They joined issues on two questions, and the victors in one case were vanquished in the other. Curiously enough, each party was defeated on

[1] Principle of Population, 2d ed., p. 583.

the ground that seemed especially to belong to itself.
The economists won in the fight for the reform of the
poor-laws, and the philanthropists won in the fight for
the protection of women and children in the mines and
factories of England. The English economists of the
time had had excellent opportunities for saying "Don't."
In their contention for the limitation of the poor-law
relief, and their contention for a repeal of the corn-
laws, they rendered great services to English industry
by simply abolishing governmental interference. It is
therefore not strange that they should have been inclined
to go to the extreme in thinking that government could
never interfere without doing more harm than good.

The English poor-law, before its reform in 1834, is
used by General Walker to point the moral that while
"the legislator may think it hard that his power for
good is so closely restricted, he has no reason to complain of any limits upon his power for evil." Describing the operations of the act, General Walker says that
" All its details were unnecessarily bad. The condition
of the person who threw himself flat upon public charity
was better than that of the laborer who struggled on to
preserve his manhood in self-support. The disposition
to labor was cut up by the roots. All restraints upon
increase of population disappeared under a premium
upon births. Self-respect and social decency vanished
before a money premium on bastardy." Professor Senior
was an active member of the commission of inquiry
regarding the operations of the poor-law, and for
some time the reports of the poor-law commission were
written in line with the views of the economists. It
was while reviewing these reports that Carlyle charac-

terized political economy as "the dismal science." He thus summarizes the teachings of the economists as evidenced in the reports. "Ours is a world requiring only to be well let alone. Scramble along, thou insane scramble of a world; thou art all right and shalt scramble even so. And whoever in the press is trodden down has only to lie there and be trampled broad:— such at bottom seems to be the chief social principle, if principle it have, which the poor-law amendment act has the merit of courageously asserting, in opposition to many things." But however true or false may have been the principle upon which the economists of the time worked, they were right in standing out for the restriction and modification of public poor-relief. The laxness that, as we have already intimated, may have come in part from the humanitarian bearings of the doctrine of political equality, was checked because it proved to be mischievous in practice.

In the other struggle of the same period, that for factory legislation, the economists and philanthropists were distinctly opposed; but this time it was the economists that were deservedly beaten. The issue involved the welfare of three hundred thousand operatives, male and female, in the factories of England, and of forty thousand children under thirteen years of age. The question was complicated with many political considerations, and perhaps was championed by the conservatives not so much because the country gentlemen sympathized with the mill-hands, as because it seemed a method by which they could get even with the representatives of the manufacturing towns for the repeal of the corn-laws. Lord Ashley, afterwards the Earl of Shaftesbury, is acknowledged on all hands to have been the leader in the fight for the protection of the operatives. His motives, while bitterly impugned at the time, are now acknowledged by all to have been of the purest, the motive power in his life-work being sincerest sympathy with all who suffered. He was called a humanity-monger, and it was said that no practical man agreed with him. Cobden, in a private letter, sneered at his "canting." Senior, Cobden, and Miss Martineau, among the economists, supplied the scientific weapons of offence and defence for such men as John Bright and Gladstone and Peel and Lord Brougham among the politicians. A majority of economists, both in and out of Parliament, were against the factory acts. Indeed, nearly all the arguing that was done on economic grounds was against the acts. As Jeans observes, in a paper which, curiously enough, is the Cobden prize essay for 1891, "Lord Shaftesbury and his opponents played a veritable game of cross questions. They attacked him, for instance, with the threatened ruin of English trade, and the pauperization of the working-class. And he would reply by pointing to the great sanitary or moral or religious benefits which must accrue."[1] As the Earl of Shaftesbury himself says, "To practical prophecies of overthrow of trade, of ruin to the operatives themselves, I could only oppose 'humanity' and general principles."[2] Sir John Russell is said to have been converted to support the acts, not by labored arguments, but by being induced to walk back and forth in his parlor for a time over a track similar to that which many of the child

---

[1] "Factory Act Legislation," p. 20.
[2] Hodder, "Life of Shaftesbury," vol. ii., p. 209.

operatives had to travel for twelve or more hours a day. Shaftesbury's speech of May, 1847, and Macaulay's speech on the ten-hour bill, gave evidence of what a strong case might have been made out for the acts on economic grounds;[1] but these were almost the only examples of such argumentation. It was sympathy for the operatives, not an appreciation of the good results to be got for English industry by the factory acts, that secured their passage. As the Encyclopædia Britannica puts it, "they were passed in the name of the moral and physical health of the community." Professor Fawcett, as late as 1878, opposed from his seat in Parliament that part of the consolidated factory acts intended to protect adult women operatives.

But at the present time there is substantial agreement among economists that factory legislation might have been defended on strictly economic grounds. Macaulay's position was well taken. Factory legislation, instead of ruining British industry, re-established its foundations. Some of the parliamentary opponents of the early bills voted for the later ones, and, in publicly recanting, expressly said that they had been misled by the economists and "the gentlemen from Lancashire." The debt owing to the economists for the reform of the poor-laws, the philanthropists had paid.

The experience of England in these two matters very well illustrates the interaction of sense and sympathy in the direction of human affairs. The discussions in

---

[1] The key-note of Macaulay's telling speech is struck in this sentence from it: "Never will I believe that what makes a population stronger and healthier and wiser and better can ultimately make it poorer." — *Speeches*, vol. ii., p. 28.

the houses of parliament, between the so-called "humanity-mongers" and the students of the so-called "dismal science," have their counterpart in the opposing considerations which suggest themselves to every thinking man who tries to aid the poor. If our instincts were all healthy, or our intellects all perfect, we could rely upon either side of our nature without fear of blundering. But, as in the case of English legislation first one party blundered and then the other, so each man, in threading his way along the devious paths of conduct, must sometimes put rational restraints upon his emotions, and at other times must be content to let "his instincts save him from his intelligence." This principle, which holds in national and personal affairs, holds also in the formulation of a true social philosophy. Such a philosophy must recognize that the instincts of men very commonly have their origin or their justification in race-experience, and that they are sometimes a more trustworthy guide than reasoning which is conceivably inaccurate, or which may be based on information which is possibly incomplete.

If economics has had some influence on philanthropy, the philanthropic instincts of men are finally coming to have some influence in compelling the broadening of the science. They dominate too much legislation and the using of too much wealth to be left out of account in the science of wealth. As we have seen, they are not only powerful, but at times indispensably helpful; and, even if it were possible to ignore them, it would be unwise to do so.

For two or three decades that branch of social philosophy known as political economy seemed bound, so far as England was concerned, to discredit itself by not recognizing this truth. Its teachings were too final and dogmatic to be influential or even true. From 1850 to 1880, Cromwell's exhortation to the theologians of his time might properly have been addressed to the English economists: "In the bowels of the Lord, I beseech you, brethren, consider it possible that you may be mistaken!" Indeed, equivalent exhortations were addressed to them, but without effect. In the United States a few professors of political economy echoed or attacked Manchestrian economics. For the most part, however, they had no influence. This country was too young to bother with industrial science. Its resources seemed to be so inexhaustible that no thought was given to conserving them. Least of all was it imagined that we need give serious attention to the matter of poor-relief. It was intimated or asserted that we were quarantined against poverty and distress by our glorious Constitution and Declaration of Independence. Not twenty-five years ago a writer in the New York *Nation*, when reviewing a work on French charities, half apologized for treating such a subject; but suggested in extenuation that, *if* we should ever have to organize a system of charities, French experience might be a useful guide.

At the present time, however, both in England and in this country, political economy is itself again. Its latest pronouncements give evidence of a scientific modesty which augurs future usefulness. In Marshall's "Principles of Economics" and Goschen's recent address as President of the British Economic Association, "altruism" receives not only respectful but quite extended treatment. On this side the Atlantic the renaissance in economics came even earlier than in England, and in many schools it has dealt more directly with the problems of philanthropology than has been the case in England. Outside of Germany, and with the exception of Chalmers' lectures, the economists have seldom said anything that could be of direct and positive use to philanthropists. Their lessons on this subject have all been negative. But in American colleges within the last ten years, many lectures have been given and some courses offered, in which the attempt has been to do constructive work in studying the economic aspects of altruism. "Philanthropy as a failure" is not the only aspect of philanthropy that the modern professor of political economy feels called upon to treat. People are tired of the gospel of inaction, and the teacher has been compelled to heed their demand for guidance in the doing of constructive work. Students must be trained in a more generous political economy than that of Senior and Miss Martineau, if they are to make this study, as many American students now desire to do, part of their preparation for becoming the paid employees of benevolent organizations. They and many others wish to study a system of economics that may be constructively useful in the betterment of charities. There is no doubt that the science itself will be improved by being broadened to meet the demand.

CHAPTER II.

CAUSES OF POVERTY.

[There are few publications based on an inductive study of the causes of poverty. The best are those by Charles Booth, "Labour and Life of the People," vol. i., particularly part I., chap. v. (1st ed. 1891); "Pauperism, a Picture" (1892). German official tables are most conveniently assembled in Böhmert's "Armenwesen in 77 deutschen Städten" (1886). The best study of an American almshouse population is that contained in the Tenth Annual Report of the New York State Board of Charities. The Annual Reports of the Pennsylvania Board of Public Charities contain a tolerably careful analysis of the causes of poverty for each year. Wines, "Causes of Pauperism and Crime," N. C. C. (1886), pp. 207-14, is mainly negative in its conclusions. The sources chiefly consulted in the preparation of the present chapter have been the Reports of the Charity Organization Societies of the United States, and the unpublished case schedules prepared by the societies of New York, Boston, and Baltimore.]

THREE tolerably distinct methods have been employed by those students of the social sciences who have sought to ascertain the causes of poverty. First, there are those deductive or philosophical thinkers, who, from the well-known facts of social organization, have sought to deduce the causes tending to poverty, as a systematic writer on pathology seeks to set forth the inherent characteristics of the bodily organism which tend to make disease likely or inevitable. Secondly, there are those who study the classes not yet pauperized, to determine by induction what forces are tending to crowd individuals downward across the pauper line, as the health officer of a city might undertake, by an examination of the drainage system, or an analysis of the water or food supply, to ascertain the causes of disease in a given locality. Thirdly, there are those who make an inductive study of concrete masses of pauperism, usually separating the mass into its individual units, seeking to ascertain in a large number of particular cases what causes have operated to bring about destitution. This work resembles that of the practising physician, endeavoring to ascertain the causes of sickness by a careful diagnosis of the cases under his care.

Examples of the philosophical or deductive method are found in the writings of men like Malthus, or Karl Marx, or Henry George, who, while they describe actual conditions at great length, still make the philosophical reasoning which is the heart of their work antecedent to their facts. Their facts are given by way of illustration rather than of proof. Writers of this class are prone to think that they can find some single underlying cause of all the misery and destitution that exist. The three names just mentioned recall three explanations of poverty, each alleged to be universal, and the three mutually exclusive. Malthus was too wise a man to put forth his principle of population as an all-sufficient explanation of distress; but his followers have not been so wise. It has been a fundamental thought in the writings of many economists that poverty exists mainly, if not entirely, because population tends to increase faster than food supply. All other causes are held to contribute to this, or to be derived from this. The pressure of population against the means of subsistence is held to guarantee that there shall always be a vast number of persons who can just manage to live miserably.

A rise of wages will promote early marriages and rapid increase among laborers, until population is again checked by over-crowding and consequent misery and death. So wise a man as John Stuart Mill allowed his economic philosophy to be overshadowed by this idea.

Mr. Henry George, as is well known, ridicules the Malthusian explanation of poverty, and offers an all-sufficient explanation of his own, which is, substantially, that poverty exists, on the one hand, because the landlord receives in rent so large a share of the annual product; on the other, because private property in land encourages the withholding of natural resources from use, the owners waiting to obtain an unearned increment. The owner of land receiving wealth without labor to an increasing extent with the development of society, there must be an increasing number of those who labor but receive little or nothing.

Opposed to both these explanations of the existence of poverty, is that of the socialists, who follow for the most part Karl Marx's analysis of capitalistic production. Reduced to a sentence by Dr. Aveling, this explanation of poverty may be stated by saying that labor is "paid for, but not paid." The consumer pays enough for the product to remunerate the laborer, but the capitalist retains all except what will barely suffice to keep the laborer alive.

No one who has studied carefully modern industrial society can doubt, I think, that each one of these explanations explains much; that each one of these causes is efficient in producing a very considerable amount of destitution. But neither can it be doubted that no one of them, nor all three of them together, can be taken as an all-sufficient explanation of the existence of poverty. Suppose a second Robinson Crusoe on a desert island under exactly the same material conditions as the friend of our childhood; suppose he spent his time in distilling some kind of liquor, and subsequently getting drunk; suppose he allowed his mind to wander in dreamy and enervating revery upon debasing subjects; suppose that in consequence of these habits he neglected his work, did not plant his crops at the right time, and failed to catch fish when they were plentiful. Manifestly he would become poor and miserable; might become diseased from having insufficient food, and finally die in abject want. Poverty in such a supposititious case could not be traced to the fact that an employer had cheated the laborer of wages honestly earned; or to the fact that a landlord had robbed him by exacting rent; nor could it be traced to an excessive increase of population.

An explanation of the poverty of our second Crusoe might be offered promptly by one who approaches sociology from the standpoint of theology. Ministers frequently inform us that all poverty comes primarily from vice and immorality, — " Seek ye first the kingdom of God and his righteousness; and all these things shall be added unto you." They quote David as saying, "I have been young, and now am old; yet have I not seen the righteous forsaken, nor his seed begging bread." The temperance lecturer specializes upon the preacher's theory, and assures us that ninety-nine per cent of all poverty comes from the abuse of intoxicants. The propagandist of the White Cross League tells us that it is undoubtedly the abuse of the sexual nature that leads to most of the social degradation and consequent poverty of our times. These different students of social science, if such they may be called, all say that what Crusoe No. 2 needed to make him prosperous, was moral reformation or spiritual regeneration.

But manifestly if Crusoe No. 2 had simply lacked judgment or skill, he might have become poor, although thoroughly pious and moral. If he had built a canoe that would not float, or a cave that crumbled in and injured him, or constructed a summer-house that he did not need, or had not the ingenuity to devise tools for his varied purposes, he might have failed to secure the necessaries of life, and have died in miserable destitution.

Now, if all these various causes are conceivably operative in the case of an isolated person, it is manifest that in actual industrial society as now organized, where the individual suffers not only from his own mistakes and defects, but also from the mistakes and defects of a large number of other people, the causes of destitution must be indefinitely numerous and complicated; and the man who comes to us saying that he has found one single cause discredits himself as promptly as the physician who announces that he has found a single universal and all-sufficient explanation of bodily disease.

The second class of investigators, those who study inductively the operation of poverty-begetting causes among the relatively well-to-do, are more numerous at the present time than ever before. The best example of such work is probably that of Mr. Charles Booth in his "Labour and Life of the People." Almost all the reports of our labor statisticians, the works on occupational mortality and morbidity, and in fact everything of a descriptive nature that has been written about modern industrial society, can be used in this second method of seeking for the causes of poverty. We shall find that many causes can be studied best, and some only, by this method.

The third method of seeking for causes of poverty, that of case-counting, or the inductive study of concrete masses of poverty and pauperism, is the one with which we are specially concerned in this chapter. It is the one most likely to suggest itself to a student who is brought in contact with relief work, and many have expected from it much greater and more definite results than it is likely to yield. Its limitations suggest themselves, if we reflect on the analogy of the physician standing by the sick-bed, and trying to learn the cause of disease from an examination of the patient only. He may learn the immediate or exciting cause or causes of sickness; but back of these are the remoter causes, which can only be learned by other methods of investigation. This will become clear if we glance at the analysis on the following page of the causes of poverty. It is not intended to be complete, but only to give in general outline a map of the field upon which we are to enter. It is a field where explorers have often wandered aimlessly from jungle to jungle, and from one impassable obstacle to another, or have travelled in profitless circles, simply because they failed to take the general survey before plunging into the thicket of details. The analysis given was derived from something more than a philosophical study of the subject. It was elaborated while the author was general agent of the Charity Organization Society of Baltimore, and its adequacy was then tested by continual reference to concrete cases of destitution.

ANALYSIS OF THE CAUSES OF POVERTY.

SUBJECTIVE.

Characteristics.
1. Undervitalization and indolence.
2. Lubricity.
3. Specific disease.
4. Lack of judgment.
5. Unhealthy appetites.

Habits producing and produced by the above.
1. Shiftlessness.
2. Self-abuse and sexual excess.
3. Abuse of stimulants and narcotics.
4. Unhealthy diet.
5. Disregard of family ties.

OBJECTIVE.

1. Inadequate natural resources.
2. Bad climatic conditions.
3. Defective sanitation, etc.
4. Evil associations and surroundings.
5. Defective legislation and defective judicial and punitive machinery.
6. Misdirected or inadequate education.
7. *Bad industrial conditions.
    a. Variations in value of money.
    b. Changes in trade.
    c. Excessive or ill-managed taxation.
    d. Emergencies unprovided for.
    e. Undue power of class over class.
    f. Immobility of labor.
8. Unwise philanthropy.

A statistical analysis of a concrete mass of poverty or pauperism will probably give more light concerning the subjective causes of poverty than the objective causes. In dealing with individuals, their character is apt to be more studied than their environment. Even when environment is the primary cause of poverty, the immediate cause or co-ordinate result, is often deterioration of character. Sickness is more obvious than bad sanitation; laziness than a malarial atmosphere; inefficiency than a defective educational system. The one who attempts the analysis of cases is apt to be confused by the fact that under the operation of exactly similar general causes, some families are destitute and some are not. One man is able to secure an adequate income under the most adverse circumstances, — bad climate, bad housing, bad taxing, no opportunities for education, etc. Another man, under exactly the same conditions, will become destitute, and the observer puts down as the final and determining cause something in the physique or character of the latter person. The ministers and charity agents who come most immediately in contact with the poor are very prone to take short-sighted views of the causes of poverty. On the other hand, as we have seen, those who study the question from a philosophical standpoint are apt to lay too much stress on the influence of institutions or environment. The questions of character are very far from insignificant; and until it is possible to trace character to its source more fully than any one can pretend to do at present, we shall have need to study character as a cause of the failure of the individual.

The results to be obtained from an investigation conducted on the case-counting principle will manifestly vary much according to the particular class of destitute persons investigated. To count the cases of those who simply apply for relief will give different results from an investigation of the inmates of an almshouse. To study a group of distinctly pauper families having close inter-relations will give different results from an inquiry about all the poor in a given locality. To study in a locality where all the deaf and dumb, the blind, the feeble-minded, and the insane have previously been taken to institutions, will, of course, give different results from those in a locality where these classes are still mingled with the population. If the cases be those of persons who have merely applied for relief, the first thing to be ascertained is how many of these applicants really ought to have material relief of any sort. The following table gives the returns in 27,961 cases of applicants for relief who were investigated by the Charity Organization Societies in 1887.

TABLE I.

Worthy of continuous relief	2,888, or 10.3 per cent.
Worthy of temporary relief	7,451, or 26.6 per cent.
Need work rather than relief	11,280, or 40.4 per cent.
Unworthy of relief	6,342, or 22.7 per cent.

It will be noticed that more than 22 per cent of the applicants were held to be "unworthy"[1] of relief. Commenting upon this table, Mr. Kellogg, who submitted the report containing it to the Conference, says that among all the societies of the country "there is a notable unity of opinion that only from thirty-one to thirty-seven per cent, or, say one-third, of the cases actually treated, were in need of that material assistance for which no offices of friendly counsel or restraint could compensate. The logical application of this generalization to the whole country is that two-thirds of its real or simulated destitution could be wiped out by a more perfect

---

[1] The term "unworthy" was subsequently dropped, as it did not express what was meant. It carried an implication of ill desert, which was not intended, and which was frequently misleading.

CAUSES OF POVERTY. 31

adjustment of the supply and demand for labor, and a more vigorous and enlightened police administration." An exacter view of the same thing may be obtained if we consider the statistics of some of the better organized charity organization societies in the large cities only, and especially the tables for recent years, when a fuller classification is used. For this purpose are given the returns from Baltimore, Boston, and New York, presenting percentages as well as absolute numbers. (See Table II.) It will be seen that in the summary for the four cities it was held that over 35 per cent of the cases should have work rather than relief; 9.1 per cent should have no relief; 5.8 per cent should be disciplined; 7.42 per cent should have visitation and advice only; and that only about 42.64 per cent needed direct relief of any sort.[1]

The Charity Organization Societies of the United States, represented in the National Conference of Charities and Corrections held in Buffalo in 1888, agreed upon a schedule of causes of poverty to be used by all the societies. It was further agreed to give in these tables only the chief cause of destitution, and not the tributary causes. The schedule as drawn was based partly upon one already elaborated by the Buffalo Society, which that society had used in tabulating the results reached by an investigation of 6,197 cases that had come under its care during the ten years 1878–87. The table of the Buffalo Society is herewith reproduced on page 33.

---

[1] In cases where work or discipline was the most desirable thing, if this could not be furnished, it might be necessary to resort to relief as a makeshift. That this will be done too often is the leading danger of **relief work**.

TABLE II.

DECISIONS IN THE CASES OF 8,294 APPLICANTS FOR RELIEF.

SHOULD HAVE	BALTIMORE. 1892.		BALTIMORE. 1893.		BOSTON. 1891.		BOSTON. 1892.		NEW YORK. 1891.		NEW YORK. 1892.		TOTAL.	
	No.	%	No.	%	No.	%	No.	%	No.	%	No.	%	No.	%
Continuous Relief*	42	5.43	18	2.21	76	7	87	7	50	3.36	60	2.15	333	4.01
Intermittent Relief	43	5.56	40	4.93	49	4	39	3	21	1.41	36	1.29	228	2.75
Temporary Relief	171	22.12	251	30.94	278	24	314	25	262	17.60	434	15.57	1710	20.63
Work rather than Relief	173	22.38	211	26.01	267	23	292	23	683	45.87	1289	46.26	2915	35.06
Indoor Relief	115	14.90	88	10.85	88	8	113	9	166	11.15	380	13.57	950	11.57
Transportation	24	3.10	34	4.16	33	2	33	3	70	4.70	111	3.96	305	3.68
Visitation and advice only	89	11.50	66	8.14	110	9	138	11	70	4.70	143	5.13	616	7.42
Discipline	38	4.91	33	4.25	84	7	76	6	90	6.04	161	5.78	482	5.81
No Relief	78	10.09	70	8.63	188	16	170	13	77	5.17	172	6.17	755	9.10
TOTAL	773		811		1173		1262		1489		2786		8,294	

* Relief for more than two years.

TABLE III.
Causes of Poverty in Buffalo.

	1878-9	1880	1881	1882	1883	1884	1885	1886	1887	Total.	%
Lack of Employment	162	62	72	235	186	316	550	169	121	1,873	30.2
Sickness	116	73	145	156	181	162	172	120	143	1,268	20.5
Accident	20	14	17	17	32	26	51	14	17	208	3.4
Insanity of bread-winner	3	6	5	3	5	3	14	8	4	51	.8
Insufficient earnings	97	48	86	74	32	22	35	33	24	451	7.3
No male support	33	26	44	37	25	21	15	65	131	397	6.4
Imprison. of bread-winner	8	11	15	15	7	14	6	14	18	108	1.7
Intemperance	127	81	81	101	72	69	44	84	41	700	11.3
Shiftlessness	83	40	74	69	64	37	18	50	5	440	7.1
Physical defects	78	41	121	76	44	38	55	45	27	525	8.4
No cause *	36	17	17	21	28	13	12	32		176	2.9
Total number of cases	763	419	677	804	676	721	972	634	531	6,197	100

* Cause undetermined.

The question most commonly in the minds of those who undertake to investigate the causes of poverty by a system of case-counting is this: Is poverty a misfortune or a fault? No full answer to the question can probably be worked out by scientific methods, but the question is so frequently asked that it seems worth while to ascertain what light a case-counting investigation of poverty can throw upon it. With this end in view, I have arranged a table giving a comparison of the results reached by German investigators, by Mr. Charles Booth, and by the American Charity Organization Societies, grouping the specified causes of poverty under three main heads: first, those indicating misconduct; second, those indicating misfortune; and third, those not classified, or unknown. (See Table IV.)

The first duty of one presenting such a table as this is to indicate clearly what it does not show. It deals, as already indicated, only with the exciting causes of poverty; and yet this fact is not kept clearly in mind, even by careful workers. Mr. Booth, for instance, includes "pauper association and heredity" in this list of causes; and the American societies include "nature and location of abode." Both of these are by their nature predisposing causes, rather than immediate or exciting causes; and it is confusing to mix the two. Secondly, many of the persons whose cases are here tabulated have been, as Mr. Booth says, the foot-ball of all the causes in the list. Under such circumstances to pick out one cause, and call it the most important, is a purely arbitrary proceeding. Any one of the causes might have been inadequate to produce pauperism had not others co-operated with it. A man

TABLE IV.

Causes of Poverty as Determined by Case-Counting

REPORT FROM	AGENCY OR PERSON RESPONSIBLE FOR THE REPORT.	YEAR OR YEARS.	CAUSES INDICATING MISCONDUCT.														LACK OF NORMAL SUPPORT.										CAUSES INDICATING MATTERS OF EMPLOYMENT.								CAUSES INDICATING		
			Drink.		Immorality.		Laziness.		Shiftlessness and Inefficiency.(a)		Crime and Dishonesty.		Roving Disposition.(f)		Total.		Imprisonment of Breadwinner.		Orphans and Abandoned Children.		Neglect by Relatives.		No Male Support.(c)		Lack of Employment.(b)		Insufficient Employment.		Poorly Paid Employment.		Unhealthy or Dangerous Employment.	
			No.	%	No.	%	No.	%	No.	%	No.	%	No.	%	No.	%	No.	%	No.	%	No.	%	No.	%	No.	%	No.	%	No.	%	No.	%
BALTIMORE.	Charity Organization Society.	1890-91	62	9.0	..	..	..	..	97	14.0	5	.7	9	1.4	173	25.1	..	..	2	.4	14	2.0	28	4.0	90	13.0	55	8.0	41	6.0	3	.4
		1891-92	49	7.1	..	..	..	..	83	12.0	7	1.0	10	1.4	149	21.5	3	.4	10	1.4	10	1.4	35	5.0	83	12.0	63	9.1	28	4.0	2	.3
BOSTON.	Associated Charities.	1890-91	190	19.2	..	..	..	..	75½	7.6	14½	1.5	6	.6	286	28.9	16½	1.6	5	.5	8	.8	71	7.2	139½	14.1	59½	6.0	5	.5	6	.7
		1891-92	239	21.9	..	..	..	..	75½	6.9	15	1.4	12	1.1	341½	31.4	19	1.7	12	1.0	12	1.0	52	4.8	156	14.3	55½	5.0	14	1.3	1	.1
BUFFALO.	Charity Organization Society.	1878-87	700	11.6	..	..	..	..	440	7.3	..	..	..	..	1140	18.9	108	1.8	..	..	..	..	397	6.6	1873	31.1	..	..	451	7.5	..	..
		1888-89	44	8.9	..	..	..	..	18	3.6	..	..	..	..	62	12.5	11	2.2	..	..	..	..	74	14.9	135	27.2	..	..	43	8.7	..	..
		1889-90	28	4.9	..	..	..	..	33	5.7	..	..	..	..	61	10.6	14	2.4	..	..	..	..	77	13.4	187	32.5	..	..	38	6.6	..	..
		1890-91	32	5.7	..	..	..	..	10	1.8	..	..	1	.2	42	7.5	10	1.9	..	..	..	..	109	19.4	150	26.8	..	..	39	7.0	..	..
		1891-92	47	8.1	..	..	..	..	20	3.4	2	.3	..	..	70	12.0	11	1.9	..	..	..	..	87	15.0	127½	21.9	33	5.7	2	.3	..	..
CINCINNATI.	Associated Charities.	1890-91	288	13.3	..	..	..	..	290	13.3	15	.7	113	5.2	706	32.5	6	.3	11	.5	23	1.1	155	7.1	211	9.7	54	2.5	19	.9	4	.2
		1891-92	246	9.2	..	..	..	..	334	12.5	80	3.0	145	5.4	805	30.1	32	1.2	44	1.6	13	.5	190	7.1	302	11.3	317	11.9	200	7.5	21	.8
NEW YORK CITY.	Charity Organization Society.	1891	151	10.7	..	..	..	..	102	7.2	20	1.4	46	3.3	319	22.6	8	.6	2	.1	7	.5	102	7.2	409	29.0	86	6.1	35	2.5	..	..
STEPNEY.	Charles Booth.	....	80	12.6	16	2.5	12	1.9	32	5.1	..	..	..	..	140	22.1	..	..	..	..	..	..	29	4.6	28	4.4	..	..	..	..	..	..
ST. PANCRAS.	Charles Booth.	....	161	21.9	51	6.9	78	10.6	21	2.8	..	..	..	..	311	42.2	..	..	..	..	..	..	21	2.8	16	2.2	..	..	..	..	..	..
76 GERMAN CITIES.	Böhmert.	....	1262	1.3	..	..	..	..	..	..	..	..	1300	1.4	2562	2.7	1619	1.7	5337	5.6	610	.6	2427	2.5	11,991	12.5	..	..	..	..	..	..

(a) Includes Mr. Booth's headings, "Extravagance" and "Incapacity," "Temper," etc.
(b) Includes, for the English tables, "Trade Misfortune." For German, An examination of the cases classed by Mr. Booth under the latter heading shows that it is more properly placed as above than it would be elsewhere. Earnings."
(c) Includes "Death of Husband" and "Desertion."

		MISFORTUNE — Matters of Personal Capacity													NOT CLASSIFIED										
		Ignorance of English		Accident		Sickness or Death in Family		Physical Defect		Insanity (d)		Old Age		Total		Large Family (e)		Nature of Abode		Pauper Associates and Heredity		Other or Unknown		Total		Total
		No.	%	No.	%	No.	%	No.	%	No.	%	No.	%	No.	%	No.	%	No.	%	No.	%	No.	%	No.	%	No.
		2	.4	28	4.0	134	19.5	35	5.0	4	.6	35	5.0	471	68.3	31	4.5	5	.7	..	..	10	1.5	46	6.7	690
		..	..	28	4.0	146	21.0	49	7.1	7	1.0	49	7.1	513	73.8	14	2.0	3	.4	..	..	16	2.3	33	4.7	695
		6½	.7	35½	3.6	229½	23.2	24½	2.5	7	.7	38	3.8	651	65.7	5½	.6	3	.3	..	..	45½	4.5	54	5.4	991
		10	.9	25	2.3	271½	24.9	25	2.3	7	.6	47	4.4	707	64.7	4	.4	..	..	..	..	39	3.5	43	3.9	1092
		..	..	208	3.5	1268	21.1	525	8.7	51	.8	..	..	4881	81.1	..	..	..	..	..	..	..	..	..	..	6021
		..	..	23	4.6	113	22.7	33	6.6	3	.6	..	..	435	87.5	..	..	..	..	..	..	..	..	..	..	497
		..	..	29	5.0	137	23.8	30	5.2	3	.5	..	..	515	89.4	..	..	..	..	..	..	..	..	..	..	576
		..	..	31	5.5	147	26.2	28	5.0	4	.7	..	..	518	92.5	..	..	..	..	..	..	..	..	..	..	560
		1	.2	26	4.5	171½	29.5	6	1.0	10	1.8	21	3.6	496	85.4	1	.2	13	2.2	..	..	1	.2	15	2.6	581
		23	1.1	49	2.3	337	15.5	38	1.7	13	.6	66	3.0	1009	46.4	69	3.2	35	1.6	..	..	355	16.3	459	21.1	2174
		16	.6	62	2.3	389	14.6	86	3.2	19	.7	83	3.1	1774	66.4	84	3.1	7	.3	..	..	..	..	91	3.4	2670
		5	.4	47	3.3	261	18.5	39	2.7	10	.7	47	3.3	1058	74.9	8	.6	7	.5	..	..	20	1.4	35	2.5	1412
		..	..	30	4.7	169	26.7	..	..	11	1.7	208	32.8	475	74.9	..	..	..	..	7	1.1	12	1.9	19	3.0	634
		..	..	19	2.6	152	20.7	..	..	32	4.3	172	23.4	412	56.0	..	..	..	..	13	1.8	..	..	13	1.8	736
		..	..	1100	1.1	43,747	45.8	2325	2.4	3406	3.4	15,086	15.8	87,648	91.4	4774	5.0	..	..	..	..	861	.9	5635	5.9	95,845

(d) Includes "Mental Derangement."
(e) Includes from German tables "Grosse Kinderzahl," "Vorhandensein mehrerer Kinder."
(f) Includes from German tables "Laziness and Shiftlessness," "Arbeitsscheu."

Table, "Small

is drunk and breaks his leg; is the cause "accident" or "drink"? When this question was submitted to a group of charity organization workers, it was very promptly answered by two of them; but their answers were different. A man has been shiftless all his life, and is now old; is the cause of poverty shiftlessness or old age? A man is out of work because he is lazy and inefficient. One has to know him quite well before they can be sure that laziness is the cause. Perhaps there is hardly a case in the whole seven thousand where destitution has resulted from a single cause.

The writer was so thoroughly convinced of this that, at the Conference of Charities at Buffalo, when the first of the cause schedules was adopted, he tried to have the societies directed to consider the influences resulting in destitution in each case as making up ten units, and indicate the relative force of each cause by a proportionate number of units. This would serve to show the grouping of the causes. The chief cause could be indicated in each case, and also the contributory causes. The system was rejected as too complicated; and after the writer tried to have the agents of a single society, that of Baltimore, use it in making their reports to the central office, he concluded that possibly the objection was valid. Yet if the requisite amount of skill and care were used, it would give valuable results. In a different way Mr. Booth has endeavored to tabulate contributory causes in studying pauperism at Stepney and St. Pancras; and, as indicating the character of results to be got from this kind of tabulation, his table of the causes of Stepney pauperism is here given. (See Table V., p. 36.)

TABLE V.

Principal Causes of Pauperism at Stepney.

(Adapted from Booth's "Pauperism and the Endowment of Old Age," p. 10.)

PRINCIPAL OR OBVIOUS CAUSES.	MALES.	FEMALES.	TOTAL.	PER CENT.	CONTRIBUTORY CAUSES.			
					DRINK.	PAUPER ASSO. AND HEREDITY.	SICKNESS.	OLD AGE.
1. Drink	53	27	80	12.6		23	11	11
2. Immorality	6	10	16	2.5	3	3	3	1
3. Laziness	10	2	12	1.9	6	5	1	3
4. Incapacity, Temper, etc.	17	7	24	3.8	4	5	2	6
5. Extravagance	7	1	8	1.3	4	2		3
6. Lack of Work or Trade Misfortune	26	2	28	4.4	4		5	13
7. Accident	25	5	30	4.7	4	2	1	14
8. Death of Husband		26	26	4.1	3	2	10	8
9. Desertion		3	3	.5	3		1	1
10. Mental Derangement	3	8	11	1.7	1	2		2
11. Sickness	98	71	169	26.7	24	38	5	41
12. Old Age	113	95	208	32.8	22	18	44	
13. Paup. Asso. and Heredity	6	1	7	1.1	1		2	2
14. Other Causes	9	3	12	1.9	6	6	2	2
TOTAL	373	261	634	100	85	106	87	107
Total for causes 1-5, "Misconduct"	93	47	140	22.1	17	38	17	24
Total for causes 6-12, "Misfortune"	265	210	475	74.9	61	62	66	79

CAUSES OF POVERTY. 37

The impossibility of giving an accurate statistical description of the facts is still clearer when we try to separate the causes indicating misconduct from those indicating misfortune. Back of disease may be either misconduct or misfortune. The imprisonment of the bread-winner indicates misconduct on his part, but may only indicate misfortune on the part of wife and children. The same is true in the case of abandoned children and neglect by relatives. This particular classification is made in deference to popular inquiry only. In the writer's opinion its chief value consists in showing how little it is worth.

But after all possible allowance has been made for the "personal equation" of the investigator, and for all the inevitable inconclusiveness of the figures, there is a residuum of information to be got from the tables. They give, as well as such statistics can, the conclusions reached by those who are studying pauperism at first hand. If the figures furnished by all the investigators were added together into one great total, and this only were put before him, the author would indeed hesitate to base any conclusions whatever upon it. But when it is found that different investigators, at different times, in different places, reach conclusions which, while varying in many and often inexplicable ways, are yet in agreement as regards certain important facts, we can but think that the figures to some extent reflect actual conditions. It will be noticed that these tables are not totalized, and that for many cities the figures for different years are not combined. They were left separate in order that their consistency might be tested by comparison.

Considering at present only the figures for American cities presented in Table IV., we notice first that the percentages for all causes indicating misconduct vary only between 10 and 32. The most important of the individual causes here grouped is "drink." The percentage for this cause averages about 10, going as low as 4.9 one year in Buffalo, and as high as 21.9 one year in Boston. Nearly but not quite so important as drink is "shiftlessness and inefficiency." It goes as low as 1.8 one year in Buffalo, and as high as 14 per cent one year in Baltimore. For the American societies, this heading is taken to include "laziness." The other causes grouped in this section of the table are insignificant, so far as the figures reveal their importance.

The "causes indicating misfortune" are regrouped under three heads; first, those showing lack of normal support; second, matters of employment, and third, matters of personal capacity. The most important of those in the first group is "no male support," which has a tolerably constant influence, ranging from 4 to 19.4 per cent. The high percentage under this cause at Buffalo and the corresponding small percentage of cases attributable to "misconduct" causes in the same place is perhaps owing in part to the fact that a much larger proportion of the cases investigated by the Buffalo society are those of persons receiving public relief than with the other societies. It may be noted that the percentages under "no male support," which includes "desertion" and "death of husband," are tolerably constant, even when the view is extended to Germany and England.

The causes grouped under the heading "matters of employment" account for somewhat more than a third of the destitution dealt with by the American societies. The percentage is given lowest for Cincinnati, being there about 14 per cent; but all the percentages for this city are too low for fair comparison, since 16.3 per cent of the cases are included under the heading "others or unknown." The highest percentage under "matters of employment" is Buffalo, where it reaches in one year nearly 40 per cent. No one well acquainted with the cases with which the Charity Organization Societies deal can at all doubt that most of those whose poverty is said to result from lack of employment are somehow and to some extent incapable or unreliable. If one wanted thoroughly efficient help, male or female, he would hardly expect to find it among the "out-of-works" with whom the charitable societies deal. Back of the cause "lack of work," ordinarily and in ordinary times, will be found some perversion of character, or some limitation of capacity.

Under "matters of personal capacity," "accident" and "physical defect" exert a minor but quite constant influence, the former somewhat greater than the latter. The constancy of their influence can be traced even in the European figures. "Old age" was at first not included by the American societies among the causes of poverty; and this, together with the fact that the percentage of influence now accorded it is so small, may be attributed to the fact that the American societies are dealing with people who are, for the most part, still struggling against pauperism, or are at any rate still mixed with the ordinary population of the cities in which they live. The results in studying these classes must manifestly differ from those got by a study of confirmed pauperism inside of institutions.

So far as these tables show, the most constant cause of poverty everywhere, at all times, and according to all investigators, is "sickness." In both American and English experience, the percentage attributable to this cause sinks but once slightly below 15, and never quite reaches 30. The average is between 20 and 25. This is one of the most significant facts brought out by these tables. It was not one which the author anticipated when the collection of statistics began; and yet it has been confirmed and re-confirmed in so many ways, that the conclusion seems inevitable that the figures set forth real and important facts. Personal acquaintance with the destitute classes has further convinced him that most of the causes of poverty result from or result in a weakened physical and mental constitution, often merging into actual disease.[1]

Nearly all of the causes named might furthermore be grouped under the general heading "incapacity." Six of them avowedly belong there. The six which we have tabulated as indicating misconduct can be so classed if we are willing to include under the term infirmities of character as well as of body. The causes which indicate lack of normal support may also be said to show that the dependents are personally incapable of self-support, and that, through fault or misfortune on the part of their natural guardians, they have been left to themselves. The four causes grouped as "matters of

---

[1] How this confirms conclusions previously reached by Dugdale will be noted later on.

employment" would seem at first to be of a different nature, and to indicate that capable persons may suffer from enforced idleness to the extent of becoming paupers. There are, of course, such instances; but, as already noted, those who have undertaken the work of finding employment for the unemployed, and who are intimately acquainted with the people about whom information is given in these tables, know that most of those out of employment are not capable in any complete sense of the term. They may be able-bodied, but they are not able-minded. They may lack one thing or another, but they almost always lack something; it may be skill, or strength, or judgment, or reliability, or even temper. For the faithful and efficient there is work in all ordinary times. Often the incapacity seems to consist in nothing more than a lack of ingenuity, which prevents the person from fitting himself into the industries of the time. Give him a set task requiring little skill, and he will do it gladly. But such set tasks are very few in modern industry, and the result is that the individual is unemployed.

The English and German figures made a part of Table IV. are not readily comparable with the American statistics, and yet there are enough points of similarity to make some comparison useful. The essential differences can for the most part be accounted for by the difference in the type of pauperism studied. The great majority of the German and all of the English cases are those of inmates of institutions. The cases at Stepney are examples of chronic pauperism to a greater extent than any group in the American Charity Organization Society tables. At St. Pancras the pauperism is still more definitely fixed and hopeless. The German figures are the only ones covering all the official relief work of a large number of cities. The writer knows so little of the methods of German relieving officers that it is perhaps dangerous to venture an opinion; but we might explain the very high percentage attributable to sickness, and the very low percentage attributable to drink, on the assumption that they are strict in their methods of granting relief, and disinclined to relieve those who because of drunkenness deserve punishment. This percentage is so unexpectedly low that Böhmert discusses it at some length. He points out that drink is a predisposing cause in many cases where the immediate cause is lack of work, accident, sickness, imprisonment, abandonment of children, etc.[1] Böhmert makes a further analysis of the causes, indicating that about 7.54 per cent of the cases may be held to be destitute through misconduct, though he puts little reliance upon this conclusion.[2] As bearing in some sort upon the same point, his table of the causes of poverty in the cases of over 13,000 children is interesting. His table of percentages is shown on opposite page.

Commenting on these percentages, Dr. Böhmert says that, if we group together causes 4, 5, 6, 8, and 9, it appears that more than one-fourth of the dependent children are dependent through the fault of their parents or other guardians.

The American figures that can be most profitably compared with the German and English tables are those collected by the New York State Board of Charities,

---

[1] "Armenwesen in 77 deutschen Städten," p. 114.
[2] *Ib.* p. 115.

CAUSES OF POVERTY.

TABLE VI.

DEPENDENT CHILDREN (13,252) IN GERMAN CITIES.

(Böhmert, pp. 115-116, and 127-128.)

CAUSE OF POVERTY.	PER CENT.
1. Orphanage	38.75
2. Lack of Work on Part of Guardian	14.99
3. Sickness, etc.	11.88
4. Abandoned by Guardian	11.66
5. Imprisonment of Guardian	4.70
6. Taken by Courts from Abusive or Neglectful Guardian	4.50
7. Sickness of Guardian	4.34
8. Laziness of Guardian	3.49
9. Drunkenness of Guardian	1.54
10. Mental or Physical Defect of Guardian	1.74
11. Deaf and Dumb	.56
12. Large Family of Guardian	.35
13. Accident to Child or Guardian	.37
14. Pauper Burials	.18
15. Blindness	.16
16. Cripples	.05
17. Advanced Age of Guardian	.04
18. Other Causes	.70

embodying the result of an investigation regarding the inmates of all the almshouses of that State in 1874 and 1875. The number of almshouse inmates was 12,614, embracing at that time a considerable number of children, lunatics, and others since removed to special institutions. The length of time that a large number of persons had been inmates of the almshouses made an inquiry into the remote causes of dependency impracticable. The table of immediate or existing causes is as follows:[1]

[1] Tenth Annual Report State Board of Charities, New York, p. 109.

TABLE VII.

Existing Causes of Dependence, N. Y. Almshouse Inmates.

1874–75.	NUMBER.	PER CENT.
1. Homeless Children (illegitimate)	312	2.47
2. Homeless Children (abandoned)	432	3.42
3. Homeless Children (by death of father)	277	2.20
4. Homeless Children (by death of mother)	154	1.22
5. Homeless Children (by death of both parents)	107	.85
6. Homeless Children (by pauperism of parents)	674	5.34
7. Homeless Children (by imprison. of parents)	74	.59
8. Homeless Women (abandoned by husbands)	204	1.62
9. Homeless Women (by death of husband)	74	.59
10. Old and Destitute	2,081	16.50
11. Permanently Diseased	795	6.31
12. Temporarily Diseased	463	3.68
13. Crippled	240	1.90
14. Deformed	17	.13
15. Blind	303	2.40
16. Deaf Mutes	29	.23
17. Insane	4,047	32.08
18. Idiots	580	4.60
19. Epileptics	268	2.12
20. Paralytics	322	2.55
21. Feeble Minded	394	3.12
22. Vagrant and Idle	767	6.08
Total	12,614	100

Two facts are brought out prominently by the general character of this table; one is the tendency of

	NUMBER.	PER CENT.
Shiftlessness and inefficiency (22)	767	6.1
Imprisonment of bread-winner (7)	74	.6
Orphans and Abandoned Children (1-6)	1,956	15.5
No male support (8-9)	278	2.2
Sickness (11, 12, 20)	1,580	12.5
Physical defect (13-16)	589	4.7
Insanity (17, 18, 19, 21)	5,289	41.9
Old Age (10)	2,081	16.5
Total	12,614	100

TABLE VIII.

		AMERICAN.		GERMAN.		COLORED.		IRISH.		ENGLISH.		FRENCH.		RUSSIAN AND POLISH.		SPANISH.		ITALIAN.		SCANDINAVIAN.		OTHER COUNTRIES.		TOTAL.	
		No.	%	No.	%	No.	%	No.	%	No.	%	No.	%	No.	%	No.	%	No.	%	No.	%	No.	%	No.	%
INDICATING MISCONDUCT.	Drink	409	15.14	66	7.83	34	6.23	433	23.62	107	16.93	11	9.25	5	3.24	. .	. .	6	5.60	3	9.09	30	14.21	1104	15.28
	Immorality	17	.63	1	.11	5	.91	5	.27	2	.31	. .	. .	. .	. .	. .	. .	. .	. .	. .	. .	2	.94	32	.44
	Shiftlessness and Inefficiency	248	9.19	63	7.48	31	5.68	106	5.78	45	7.12	7	5.88	11	7.09	4	10.00	9	8.41	2	6.06	17	8.05	543	7.51
	Crime and Dishonesty	20	.74	4	.47	4	.73	7	.38	7	1.10	3	2.52	. .	. .	1	2.50	3	2.80	. .	. .	. .	. .	49	.68
	Roving Disposition	44	1.63	8	.95	1	.18	7	.38	16	2.53	1	.84	2	1.29	. .	. .	1	.93	. .	. .	6	2.84	86	1.19
INDICATING MISFORTUNE. LACK OF NORMAL SUPPORT.	Imprisonment of Bread-winner	18	.66	1	.11	2	.36	22	1.20	8	1.26	1	.84	. .	. .	. .	. .	1	.93	1	3.03	1	.47	55	.76
	Orphans and Abandoned Children	10	.37	. .	. .	2	.36	7	.38	4	.63	. .	. .	2	1.29	. .	. .	. .	. .	. .	. .	. .	. .	25	.34
	Neglect by Relatives	24	.88	7	.83	7	1.28	7	.38	8	1.26	1	.84	10	6.45	1	2.50	1	.93	. .	. .	. .	. .	66	.91
	No Male Support	111	4.11	36	4.27	16	2.93	93	5.07	20	3.16	6	5.05	10	6.45	2	5.00	7	6.54	2	6.06	8	3.79	311	4.30
MATTERS OF EMPLOYMENT.	Lack of Employment	663	24.57	242	28.62	95	17.42	346	18.87	156	24.68	32	26.89	37	23.87	5	12.50	33	30.85	14	42.42	51	24.17	1674	23.16
	Insufficient Employment	179	6.63	64	7.60	47	8.62	117	6.38	30	4.74	12	10.08	7	4.51	. .	. .	6	5.60	3	9.09	6	2.84	471	6.51
	Poorly Paid Employment	56	2.07	22	2.61	5	.91	15	.81	9	1.42	3	2.52	3	1.93	6	15.00	5	4.67	. .	. .	7	3.31	131	1.81
	Unhealthy and Dangerous Employ.	3	.11	2	.23	1	.18	1	.05	. .	. .	. .	. .	. .	. .	. .	. .	. .	. .	. .	. .	. .	. .	7	.09
MATTERS OF PERSONAL CAPACITY.	Ignorance of English	. .	. .	4	.47	. .	. .	1	.05	. .	. .	2	1.68	6	3.87	5	12.50	4	3.75	. .	. .	8	3.79	30	.41
	Accident	72	2.66	30	3.56	8	1.46	57	3.10	17	2.69	3	2.52	6	3.87	. .	. .	4	3.75	1	3.03	9	4.26	207	2.86
	Sickness or Death in Family	548	20.31	193	22.92	216	39.63	363	19.80	145	22.94	21	17.65	39	25.16	13	32.50	18	16.82	4	12.12	49	23.22	1609	22.27
	Physical Defects	92	3.40	40	4.73	30	5.49	64	3.49	11	1.74	9	7.56	10	6.45	1	2.50	3	2.80	2	6.06	5	2.37	267	3.69
	Insanity	25	.92	6	.71	. .	. .	17	.91	8	1.26	1	.84	1	.64	. .	. .	. .	. .	. .	. .	4	1.89	62	.85
	Old Age	76	2.81	23	2.73	25	4.57	128	6.97	23	3.63	4	3.36	1	.64	1	2.50	3	2.80	1	3.03	4	1.89	289	4.00
NOT CLASSIFIED.	Large Family	14	.51	10	1.18	3	.55	16	.87	5	.79	. .	. .	3	1.93	1	2.50	1	.93	. .	. .	. .	. .	53	.73
	Nature of Abode	2	.07	1	.11	1	.18	1	.05	3	.47	1	.84	. .	. .	. .	. .	. .	. .	. .	. .	. .	. .	9	.12
	Other, or Unknown	67	2.58	29	3.44	12	2.19	20	1.09	8	1.26	1	.84	2	1.29	. .	. .	2	1.87	. .	. .	4	1.89	145	2.00
	TOTAL	2698		842		545		1833		632		119		155		40		107		33		211		7225	

CAUSES OF POVERTY.   45

statistics based on case-counting to degenerate into mere description of the personal characteristics or condition of dependents, and the other is the tendency of drink as a cause of pauperism to disappear when we study chiefly chronic cases of long standing. In this table of "existing causes" it is not mentioned at all, its results only being registered.

By the courtesy of the General Secretaries of the Charity Organization Societies of Baltimore, New Haven, and New York, and of the Associated Charities of Boston, original schedules regarding somewhat more than eight thousand cases of destitution investigated by these societies were furnished for the present work. With the separate cases at hand, it was possible to recombine the facts so as to get much information not obtainable from the published reports.

As the first question popularly asked regarding the causes of poverty would probably be whether poverty indicates misconduct or misfortune, so the second would probably be: What are the indications as to the tendency of different nationalities or races to become poor?

For the purpose of finding what answer could be obtained to this question, Table VIII. was prepared, giving the facts regarding 7,225 American cases. They are classified horizontally according to the causes of poverty, the causes being grouped as in Table IV., and vertically according to nationality.

Of the Americans, Germans, Colored, Irish, and English, there are enough cases in each column to make the percentages tolerably trustworthy; while of the French, Polish, Spanish, Italian, Scandinavian, and "other countries," the numbers are too small to make the relative figures of much value, consequently only the former are discussed.

As to "drink," we find a general average of 15.28 per cent. The Americans are slightly below, and the English slightly above, this average. The Germans are far below it, 7.83 per cent, and the Colored still farther, 6.23 per cent. The Irish, on the other hand, have a larger percentage under this head than any other nationality, 23.62. In "shiftlessness and inefficiency" the Americans lead all other well represented nationalities, having here a percentage of 9.19, as against an average of 7.51. The Irish here fall much below the average, 5.78 per cent. Totalizing the percentages for "causes indicating misconduct," we get a general average of 25.10; the Irish lead with 30.43, and the English and American come next with 27.99 and 27.33 respectively. The Germans are far below the average with 16.84 per cent, and the Colored the lowest of all with 13.73. These relative positions are not changed if we include the cases coming under the first three causes put down as "indicating misfortune." These causes, namely, "imprisonment of bread-winner," "orphans and abandoned children," and "neglect by relatives," may be taken to indicate misconduct on the part of the natural guardians of minors or feeble persons, and so may be properly added to the causes indicating misconduct. The number of orphans who are such through misfortune may be held to be balanced by the number of deserted wives who come under the class "no male support," the last named heading not being anywhere reckoned as indicating misconduct. The percentages, when the three causes named are added, run as follows: Irish, 32.39; English, 31.14; Americans, 29.24; Germans, 17.78; Colored, 15.73. In no nationality, therefore, does the number of cases of destitution held to result from causes indicating misconduct reach one-third of the total.

"Matters of employment" vary less in relative importance as between the different nationalities, and the same is true of "accident" and "physical defect." Under the very important heading of "sickness" we find one decided variation. The average for this cause is 22.27 per cent, and all the largely represented nationalities conform quite closely to this average with one exception; the cases of colored people show a percentage for sickness of 39.63, a rate that comes near to being the double of the average, and is the double of the percentage for this cause among the Irish.

Those who know the colored people only casually or by hearsay may be surprised to find the misconduct causes running so low among them, while sickness as a cause is of greater relative importance than in any other nationality. But to one who has worked in Baltimore or Washington it seems a natural result, and indeed a confirmation of the reliability of the statistics. The colored people are weak physically, become sick easily, and often die almost without visible resistance to disease. At the same time they have a dread of being assisted, especially when they think an institution will be recommended; and this, together with a certain apathy, will often induce them to endure great privations rather than ask for help. Besides this, there are many associations among them for mutual help, and the criminal and semi-criminal men have a brutal way of making their women support them. That the percentage for "lack of work," 17.42, is the lowest, and that for "insufficient employment" is the highest, under these two heads, perhaps reflects their hand-to-mouth way of working at odd jobs, rather than taking steady work.

But one must hesitate to put much weight upon a general average of this kind, and the constituent elements of the table have therefore been given separately; that is, for each city a table like this one has been made out. The purpose of this is to find how far the differences we have noted between the nationalities are constant for different places and according to different observers. It would occupy too much space to reproduce all of these four large tables; so from them have been abstracted the more important results which are embodied in Table IX., on opposite page.

In the matter of drink, we see that the nationalities keep the same relative positions everywhere as in the summary; and in every case sickness is of greater relative importance among colored people than among any others. On the other hand, the indication of Table VIII. that a larger proportion of Americans are destitute because of "shiftlessness and inefficiency" than in any other nationality, is confirmed by the experience of New York and New Haven, but not by that of Boston and Baltimore. On the whole, however, there are no astounding variations in the special tables that need destroy our confidence in the general average. The similarities are sufficiently constant; so that if a new table were given the writer, like Table VIII., but in which the numbers and per cents were re-arranged, and the headings of the lines and columns left blank, he should ex-

CAUSES OF POVERTY.

TABLE IX.

CAUSES.	NEW YORK.		BOSTON.		BALTIMORE.		NEW HAVEN.	
	No.	%	No.	%	No.	%	No.	%
AMERICANS (White).								
Matters of Employment .	391	39.49	137	21.33	363	36.74	10	12.50
Sickness . . .	165	16.66	163	25.38	203	20.54	17	21.25
Drink	155	15.65	141	21.96	100	10.12	13	16.25
Shiftlessness and Inefficiency . .	73	7.37	48	7.47	112	11.33	15	18.75
All causes . . .	990	37.17	642	30.93	988	48.38	80	17.93
COLORED.								
Matters of Employment .	19	35.18	24	17.39	96	29.62	9	30.00
Sickness . . .	20	37.03	63	45.65	126	38.88	7	23.33
Drink	4	7.40	11	7.97	16	4.93	3	10.00
Shiftlessness and Inefficiency . .	3	5.55	6	4.34	21	6.48	1	3.33
All causes . . .	54	2.02	138	6.65	324	15.86	30	6.72
GERMAN.								
Matters of Employment .	161	44.10	12	20.33	141	35.60	16	50.00
Sickness . . .	87	23.83	14	23.72	85	21.46	7	21.87
Drink	22	6.02	9	15.25	32	8.08	3	9.37
Shiftlessness and Inefficiency . .	18	4.93	9	15.25	36	9.09		
All causes . . .	365	13.70	59	2.84	396	19.39	32	7.17

TABLE IX. — *Concluded.*

CAUSES.	IRISH.							
	NEW YORK.		BOSTON.		BALTIMORE.		NEW HAVEN.	
	No.	%	No.	%	No.	%	No.	%
Matters of Employment	263	37.04	107	16.41	58	27.75	51	19.46
Sickness	130	18.30	151	23.15	36	17.22	46	17.55
Drink	133	18.73	217	33.28	37	17.70	46	17.55
Shiftlessness and Inefficiency	41	5.77	29	4.44	27	12.91	9	3.43
All causes	710	26.66	652	31.42	209	10.23	262	58.74
ALL NATIONALITIES.								
Matters of Employment	1059	39.76	414	19.95	707	34.62	103	23.09
Sickness	507	19.03	543	26.16	470	23.01	89	19.95
Drink	364	13.66	475	22.89	196	9.59	69	15.47
Shiftlessness and Inefficiency	170	6.38	142	6.84	204	9.99	27	6.05
All causes	2663		2075		2042		446	

pect to be able to write in the names of the leading causes and of the leading nationalities without serious error.

A classification in Table X. of 4,176 Boston and New York cases according to the number of persons in a family, and by nationality, confirms the indication of Table IV., that large families is a relatively unimportant cause of destitution.

TABLE X.

Boston and New York.

Number in Family.	American.		Colored.		English.		French.		German.		Italian.		Irish.		Polish and Russian.		Scandinavian.		Other Countries.		Total.	
	No.	%	No.	%	No.	%	No.	%	No.	%	No.	%	No.	%	No.	%	No.	%	No.	%	No.	%
1	202	14.81	31	16.14	87	17.54	8	10.38	45	12.06	8	7.33	203	15.77	6	4.68	4	18.18	16	12.40	610	14.60
2	285	20.90	52	27.08	95	19.15	17	22.07	65	17.42	12	11.00	247	19.19	11	8.59	3	13.63	19	14.72	806	19.30
3	240	17.61	44	22.91	87	17.54	18	23.36	66	17.69	15	13.76	233	18.10	25	19.53	6	27.26	28	21.70	762	18.24
4	243	17.82	26	13.54	93	18.75	14	18.18	57	15.28	20	18.34	199	15.46	16	12.50	5	22.72	23	17.82	696	16.66
5	158	11.59	15	7.81	64	12.90	10	13.00	65	17.42	21	19.26	165	12.82	23	17.96	3	13.63	18	13.95	542	12.97
6	108	7.90	15	7.81	30	6.06	2	2.59	31	8.31	11	10.09	103	8.00	12	9.37	. . .	. . .	13	10.07	325	7.78
7	77	5.64	6	3.12	19	3.83	6	7.78	20	5.36	17	15.59	73	5.67	14	10.93	1	4.54	8	6.20	241	5.77
8	33	2.34	1	.52	12	2.45	1	1.29	9	2.41	3	2.75	39	3.03	13	10.15	. . .	. . .	3	2.32	114	2.72
9	11	.80	1	.52	3	.60	1	1.29	7	1.87	2	1.83	18	1.39	4	3.12	. . .	. . .	1	.77	48	1.14
10	5	.46	. . .	. . .	3	.60	. . .	. . .	3	.80	. . .	. . .	6	.46	3	2.34	. . .	. . .	. . .	. . .	20	.47
11	1	.08	. . .	. . .	. . .	. . .	. . .	. . .	3	.80	. . .	. . .	1	.07	1	.78	. . .	. . .	. . .	. . .	6	.14
12	. . .	. . .	. . .	. . .	3	.60	. . .	. . .	2	.53	. . .	. . .	. . .	. . .	. . .	. . .	. . .	. . .	. . .	. . .	5	.11
13	. . .	. . .	1	.52	. . .	. . .	. . .	. . .	. . .	. . .	. . .	. . .	. . .	. . .	. . .	. . .	. . .	. . .	. . .	. . .	1	.02
Total	1,363		192		496		77		373		109		1,287		128		22		129		4,176	

Unmarried persons with no one dependent upon them are not included in this table. The "families" of only one person are either widows or widowers. The largest single family is found among the colored people; but the largest proportion of relatively large families, say those numbering from five to nine persons each, is found among the Italians and the Poles and Russians. The families of paupers or semi-paupers usually average smaller than those of the population as a whole, partly because the number among classes degenerate enough to be dependent is not as large as is ordinarily supposed, partly because of a high infant mortality, and partly because the families of these classes tend to disintegrate rapidly, children drifting away from parents, and aged parents in their turn being shaken off by adult children.[1] The "family," therefore, which applies for relief is often only the fragment of a family.

Tables XI. and XII. give classifications of applicants for relief by marital condition and nationality.

Of those applying to the charity organization societies, about half are married people living together, and about one-half the remainder, or one-quarter of the whole, are widows. Deserted wives make up about 7 per cent of the total. The difference in the work of different societies is the principal thing reflected by the fact that "single men" make up 20 per cent of the applicants in New York, or over 13 per cent in New Haven, while in other places this category is

---

[1] A young woman graduate student who is making a study of women paupers in San Francisco finds that many of the old women in the almshouse actually do not remember how many children they have had, or what has become of them.

TABLE XII.

	NEW YORK.		BOSTON.		BALTIMORE.		NEW HAVEN.		TOTAL.	
	No.	%	No.	%	No.	%	No.	%	No.	%
Married	1,229	43.3	1,177	49.2	1,208	53.7	209	37.9	3,823	47.7
Widows	565	20.0	601	25.1	580	25.8	157	28.5	1,903	23.7
Deserted Wives	137	4.8	221	9.3	180	8.0	17	3.1	555	6.9
Single Women	120	4.2	152	6.4	127	5.6	47	8.7	446	5.6
Deserted Husbands and Widowers	205	7.2	89	3.7	50	2.2	40	7.3	384	4.8
Single Men	563	19.9	118	4.9	95	4.2	75	13.4	851	10.6
Orphans	4	.1	10	.4	3	.1	6	1.1	23	.3
Divorced	10	.4	12	.5	7	.3	.	.	29	.4
Miscellaneous	3	.1	11	.5	.	.	.	.	14	.2
TOTAL	2,836		2,392		2,250		551		8,028	

TABLE XI.

	AMERICAN.		GERMAN.		COLORED.		IRISH.		ENGLISH.		FRENCH.		POLISH AND RUSSIAN.		ITALIAN.		SPANISH.		SCAN-DINAVIAN.		OTHER COUNTRIES.		TOTAL.	
	No.	%	No.	%	No.	%	No.	%	No.	%	No.	%	No.	%	No.	%	No.	%	No.	%	No.	%	No.	%
Married	1379	46.63	570	58.40	271	44.20	902	44.00	318	45.82	74	55.65	110	62.50	71	60.68	19	46.34	9	24.32	100	42.75	3823	47.62
Widows	654	22.11	176	18.03	187	30.50	610	29.75	153	22.04	29	21.80	17	9.65	26	22.22	12	29.26	3	8.10	36	15.38	1903	23.70
Deserted Wives	207	7.00	54	5.53	52	8.48	123	6.00	54	7.78	9	6.76	27	15.34	7	5.98	3	7.31	5	13.51	14	5.98	555	6.91
Single Women	186	6.29	22	2.25	48	7.83	133	6.48	32	4.61	5	3.75	1	.56	2	1.70	5	12.19	. .	. .	12	5.12	446	5.55
Deserted husbands and Widowers	145	4.90	50	5.12	24	3.91	98	4.78	33	4.75	6	4.51	4	2.27	5	4.27	. .	. .	7	18.91	12	5.12	384	4.78
Single men	353	11.93	99	10.15	31	5.05	170	8.29	93	13.40	10	7.51	16	9.09	6	5.12	2	4.87	12	32.45	59	25.21	851	10.60
Orphans	15	.50	. .	. .	. .	. .	5	.24	2	.28	. .	. .	1	.56	. .	. .	. .	. .	. .	. .	. .	. .	23	.28
Divorced	13	.43	4	.41	. .	. .	5	.24	5	.72	. .	. .	. .	. .	. .	. .	. .	. .	1	2.70	1	.42	29	.36
Miscellaneous	5	.16	1	.10	. .	. .	4	.19	4	.57	. .	. .	. .	. .	. .	. .	. .	. .	. .	. .	. .	. .	14	.17
TOTAL	2957		976		613		2050		694		133		176		117		41		37		234		8028	

relatively unimportant. The classification of nationality does not seem to yield many results that are at once important and reliable. The proportion of "deserted wives" among the colored people might have been expected to exceed the average under that head more than it does. As a rule, the white Americans exceed the average more under this heading than the colored. The average of all nationalities and all cities is 6.91 per cent, which may be considered large by those unacquainted with the modern urban population, but it is lower than many of the charity organization workers expected to find it.

Table XIII. shows for the four cities the percentage of native white, colored, and foreign born among the population as a whole, and among those who applied to the charity organization societies in these cities. It will be noted that the proportion of applicants who are foreign born is considerably larger than of the population as a whole.

A matter which is not brought out by the tables thus far given, but which is well shown by the collateral investigations of the different agencies, is the large number of children either dragged into pauperism by the destitution of their parents or entirely abandoned by the latter. In the investigations of almshouse pauperism, of course, this is not brought out, as the children have been put in other institutions, and are beyond the view of the investigator. But in the American experience, where the cases are studied as they cross this pauper line, the large number of children is striking. Out of 4,310 persons dealt with by the New York C. O. S. in 1891, over 40 (40.8) per cent, or 1,762, were under 14.

TABLE XIII.

LOCALITY.	NATIVE WHITE.				COLORED.				FOREIGN.				TOTAL.		
	POPULATION.		APPLICANTS.		POPULATION.		APPLICANTS.		POPULATION.		APPLICANTS.		POPULATION.	APPLICANTS.	
	No.	%	No.	% OF TOTAL.	No.	%	No.	% OF TOTAL.	No.	%	No.	% OF TOTAL.	No.	No.	% OF POPULATION.
New York	851,757	56.21	1053	37.12	23,601	1.55	57	2.00	639,943	42.23	1726	60.86	1,515,301	2836	.18
Boston	282,180	62.91	727	30.40	8125	1.81	164	6.85	158,172	35.25	1500	62.73	448,477	2391	.53
Baltimore	298,332	68.55	1072	47.64	67,104	15.45	348	15.46	69,003	15.86	830	36.88	434,439	2250	.51
New Haven	55,871	68.7	105	19.05	2433	3.00	45	8.16	22,994	27.05	401	72.77	81,298	551	.67
TOTAL	1,488,140		2957	36.83	101,263		613	7.63	890,112		4458	55.53	2,479,515	8028	.32

In Boston, out of 3,972 individuals dealt with, over 42 (42.5) per cent were under 14 years of age. In Buffalo, out of 2,515 individuals, over 48 (48.3) per cent were under 14 years of age. In Baltimore the percentage of those under 14 years of age drops to a little less than 16 (15.8); but, on the whole, it may be concluded that, while the leading cause of confirmed pauperism, as investigated by Mr. Booth in England, is the weakness of old age, the leading cause of incipient pauperism, as investigated by the American Charity Organization Societies, is the weakness of childhood.

Taking this in connection with the large percentage of pauperism which is constantly and everywhere attributed to sickness and physical defect, and we have a striking confirmation of the conclusion reached by Dugdale in his study of the Jukes. He says: —

"1. Pauperism is an indication of weakness of some kind, either youth, disease, old age, injury, or, for women, childbirth.

"2. Hereditary pauperism rests chiefly upon disease in some form, tends to terminate in extinction, and may be called the sociological aspect of physical degeneration."

We find, phrasing our conclusions in medical terms, that the commonest exciting cause of the poverty that approaches pauperism is incapacity, resulting in most chronic cases from sickness or other degenerate and degenerating conditions. Weakness of some sort is the most typical characteristic of the destitute classes. The predisposing causes of this degeneration and weakness are next to be sought for. A physician turns from diagnosing a case to inquire for predisposing causes, first in the habits and heredity of the individual, and secondly in the nature of his occupation, or other conditions of life. If we assume, as is roughly true, that the forces which tend to break down the physical man, and bring about the the various forms of degeneration, are those which are pushing him towards death, we may present them graphically by a modification of a diagram used by

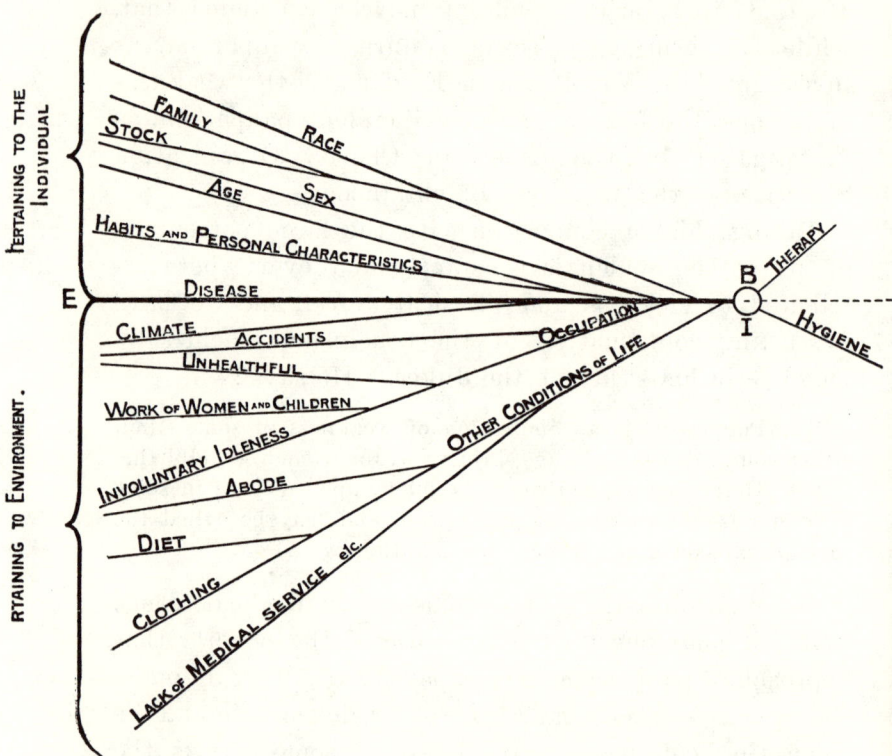

Dr. J. S. Billings in the Cartwright lectures delivered before the Alumni Association of the College of Physicians and Surgeons of New York.[1]

[1] "On Vital and Medical Statistics." Printed in *Medical Record* of Nov. 30, Dec. 7 and 14, 1889. The diagram referred to is on p. 37 of the reprinted copy of the lectures.

Let the point B represent birth, and the point D represent death. The individual I passes to the right along the line ED at a rate proportionate to the progressive exhaustion of his vital energies. The forces which retard his movement are grouped under the two heads, therapy and hygiene. The forces which accelerate it are grouped under two main heads; one, those pertaining to the individual; the other, those pertaining to the environment. The most constant force in producing the incapacity from which pauperism results we have found to be disease, which is placed accordingly in the middle position among the forces tending towards death. In Chapter III. we will consider some of the predisposing causes of disease and of other forms of degeneration which pertain to the individual; and in the succeeding chapter some of those which pertain to environment. It is an inquiry fraught with great difficulties; and, before entering upon it, the author cannot forbear quoting and applying to this subject the words with which Dr. Billings closed the course of lectures already mentioned:—

"In studying medical and vital statistics one is somewhat in the position of a man on the deck of a large Atlantic steamer, out of sight of land and gazing on the troubled ocean. He sees many waves, large and small, apparently moving in very different directions; and it is not until he has, by careful examination and repeated comparison, learned to distinguish the ripples due to the wind now blowing, the larger cross seas resulting from forces which were acting a few hours before, and the long, rolling swells which indicate, to some extent, the direction of force of the tempest of yesterday, that he can begin to understand the roll of the ship on which he stands; while to appreciate the force and direction of the great current which is sweeping with it all the troubled water and the ship itself requires skilled observation with special instruments, and the use of charts which embody the experience of hundreds of voyages. So, also, in viewing the records of human life, disease, and death, the variations which are at first most perceptible are often those which are most superficial, and which give little or no indication of the magnitude and direction of the great masses beneath."

CHAPTER III.

PERSONAL CAUSES OF INDIVIDUAL DEGENERATION.

[DRINK: The best available works of a semi-medical character are, Wilson, "Drunkenness;" Kerr, "Inebriety." On the social influence of drink, Patten, "Economic Basis of Prohibition," in "Annals American Academy," vol. ii., p. 59 ff.; also works named under other heads in this and following chapter. Of literature circulated by active temperance organizations may be mentioned, Pitman, "Alcohol and the State;" Gustafsen, "The Foundation of Death;" "Cyclopædia of Temperance, Prohibition," etc.; "Annual Addresses" of President Willard, of the W. C. T. U.; and among periodicals the *Voice* and the *Union Signal*. PERVERSION OF SEXUAL INSTINCT: Amos, "State Regulation of Vice;" Acton, "Prostitution;" Scott, "A State Iniquity;" Stead, "Josephine Butler;" Leffingwell, "Illegitimacy." HEREDITY: Weismann, "Heredity, and other essays;" Galton, "Hereditary Genius" and "Inquiries into Human Faculty;" Strahan, "Marriage and Disease;" Bell, "Memoir upon the Formation of a Deaf Variety of the Human Race." On all the three special topics named: Dugdale, "The Jukes" (Putnams), invaluable to a special student, the completest study of a distinctly pauper family extant; a supplementary study by Mr. Dugdale, "Hereditary Pauperism," N. C. C., 1877, pp. 81-95, is valuable. Of equal value, though not equally accessible, is Dr. Howe's report on the "Causes of Idiocy in Massachusetts" (1848). McCulloch's "Tribe of Ishmael" is accompanied by an interesting chart of relationship among pauper families, but the facts are arranged for popular rather than for scientific use. Supplementary to this is Wright, "Marriage Relations in the Tribe of Ishmael," N. C. C., 1891, pp. 435-7. Booth, "Pauperism," etc., affords a convenient study of English cases. MacDonald, "Abnormal Man" (U.S. Bureau of Education), contains a very large bibliography, ostensibly classified, but still hard to use.]

OF the causes which pertain to the individual and tend to produce degeneration, we have said in the preceding chapter all that there is space to say regarding disease, age, sex, and race. There remain to be considered in the present chapter personal habits and characteristics, and the influence of stock and family through heredity; that is, the characteristics and habits of the individual himself which render him incapable or likely to become so; first, as to their nature, and, finally, as to their origin. In other words, having advanced from the effect, poverty, to the exciting cause, incapacity, we proceed from that to the predisposing causes.

It is to bad habits that the ordinary observer attributes a large part of the misery of the world; and, as immediate causes of degeneration, they undoubtedly have great influence.

·Intemperance, meaning by this the abuse of alcoholic drinks, is commonly believed to be a very important cause of pauperism. It is held to be the predisposing cause back of sickness, back of insanity, back of crime. Probably nothing in the tables of the causes of poverty, as ascertained by case-counting, will more surprise the average reader than the fact that intemperance is held to be the chief cause in only from one-fifteenth to one-fifth of the cases, and that where an attempt is made to learn in how many cases it had a contributory influence, its presence cannot be traced at all in more than 28.1 per cent of the cases. It will be remembered that the Ishmaelites, as a rule, were temperate; and Mr. Dugdale did not consider intemperance the fundamental vice of the Jukes.

The scientific study of inebriety has only recently been entered upon, and this chiefly from the medical standpoint. In all the great mass of literature bearing upon the social influence of intemperance, very few conclusions are stated which are based upon inductions sufficiently wide to be final. An examination of the scattered material at hand, however, serves to explain the difference between popular impressions on the subject, and the conclusions reached by the statistical studies of pauperism. The ravages of intemperance are most plainly to be traced in classes distinctly above the pauper class. It is among artisans and those capable of earning good wages that the most money is spent for alcohol, and the most vitality burnt out by it. The man that has become a pauper does not find it easy, for one thing, to get liquor; and his vitality is apt to be so low that the exhilaration to be had from alcohol is not as much craved as by one with greater remaining strength. This does not correspond to the conclusion reached by Dugdale, who thought that drunkenness was usually the result of exhaustion rather than the cause of it, and that intemperance usually appeared in an individual subsequent to licentiousness and ill-health, and that its cause is antecedent hereditary or induced physical exhaustion. It is suggested, as an hypothesis which would reconcile the facts given by Mr. Dugdale[1] with others which have been observed, that intemperance is most likely to develop in persons of considerable natural strength who have become exhausted by vice, or overwork, or conditions of work or life that tend to undermine the health. This hypothesis would fit the cases detailed by Mr. Dugdale, though not that part of his conclusion which attributes drunkenness to hereditary exhaustion. By this hypothesis, intense work, irregular work, bad air, either in the home or workshop, inadequate or ill-prepared food, as well as the exhaustion

[1] "Jukes," pp. 40, 41, and 93.

resulting from vice, would tend to produce intemperance; while at the same time it would account for the fact that the most degenerate stock is not intemperate, and that frequently we cannot trace intemperance as a direct cause of pauperism in any considerable proportion of cases. In passing through the wards of an almshouse, the writer has frequently been surprised at the number of inmates who were said to have been temperate, and of whom the statement was apparently true. On the other hand, on learning the habits of laboring people, and especially those of skilled artisans, he has frequently been surprised at the enormously heavy handicap of dissipation which many of the men were carrying.

W. Bevan Lewis, who writes in the *Fortnightly* for September, 1893, on "The Conditions of Crime," finds that, territorially, crime rather than pauperism seems to accompany drunkenness. He concludes, however, that drunkenness "makes itself felt in the development of epileptic offspring amongst the non-criminal community, in the moral obtuseness and degradation of such subjects, in the frequency of imbecile or idiot offspring, and peculiar *epileptoid* states of mind." This confirms the conclusion reached by Dr. S. G. Howe, in his well-known study of the causes of idiocy in Massachusetts.[1] The habits of one or both parents of 300 idiots having been learned, 145 of the children were found to be the progeny of habitual drunkards. Dr. Kerr calls attention to the following facts: —

"That the impairment of the bodily or mental faculties arises from the intemperance of one or both heads of the family, is

---

[1] Report to the Legislature, 1848, and subsequent reports and pamphlets.

demonstrated by the healthfulness and intellectual vigor of children born while the parents were temperate, contrasted with the sickliness and mental feebleness of their brothers and sisters born after the same parent or parents became intemperate. In one case, there were first a son and daughter, both excellent specimens, mental and physical, of vigorous humanity. After the birth of the daughter the father fell into habits of dissipation, and rapidly became a habitual drunkard. He had four children after his declension into insobriety. Of these, one was defective in mind, and the remainder were complete idiots." [1]

"A striking illustration of the part played by drunkenness in the production of idiocy is to be found in Norway. In that country, in 1825, the spirit duty was removed, and, consequently, intemperance at once began to increase alarmingly among the people. The result — or rather one of the results — of this was, that during the first ten years following this regrettable event, insanity increased among the Norwegians by 50 per cent. This was, perhaps, to be expected under the circumstances ; but no one anticipated that the increase of congenital idiocy among the children born during the same decennial period would amount, as it did, to 150 per cent." [2]

An inquiry concerning the inmates of almost any orphan asylum will confirm the implications of the foregoing observations. As one matron said when asked about two children under her care, "Well, they are like a good many others here. Both parents were drunkards, and the children somehow do not seem to be up to par."

Irrespective of transmitted tendencies to degeneration, the children of drunken parents fare badly because of neglect and privation. Whether the mother herself drinks, or is merely linked to a drunken husband, her life during the period of gestation is almost inevitably

[1] Kerr, "Inebriety," 2d ed., p. 160.
[2] S. A. K. Strahan, "Marriage and Disease," p. 124.

such as endangers the well-being of the child. The fact that, when a large part of the family income goes for liquor, other branches of expenditure must be curtailed, is so obvious that it only needs to be mentioned. Moreover, the irrational and often brutal treatment received by children of the intemperate makes right development almost impossible for them. One fact brought out by the statistics of the Registrar General of England may be given as showing in an extreme instance the perils attending child life when parents drink: A much larger number of children are suffocated in bed on the nights of Saturday and holidays than on other nights of the week. This prompt extinguishing of infant life is hardly a greater misfortune than for the child to grow up with irrational guidance and the evil example of drunken parents.

"Typically the action induced in the brain [by alcohol] is of the nature of a progressive paralysis, beginning with the *highest level* and its most delicate functions, and spreading gradually downward through the lower. Moral qualities and the higher processes of intelligence are, therefore, first invaded."[1] Children growing up under the influence of parents subject to such degeneration are not likely to develop the higher qualities at all, since the development of such qualities comes very largely from imitation.[2] The utter lack of foresight, and the

---

[1] Wilson, "Drunkenness," pp. 15–16.

[2] Prof. G. Stanley Hall cites the following from Principal Russell's collection of observations which indicates the influence of imitation in the formation of bad habits: "Boy, Irish, *ae.* 7. Stood drinking water at a sink with his back to other people. Was making believe to be drinking in a saloon with his feet crossed, and remarking on the quality of the drink to an imaginary bar-keeper. Paid imaginary money and received imaginary change." — *Forum*, vol. xvi., p. 431.

CAUSES OF INDIVIDUAL DEGENERATION. 65

impossibility of postponing present gratification for the sake of future gain is one of the pronounced characteristics of the drunkard, and is also common among the distinctly pauper class.

It has been repeatedly pointed out that the latest social development, especially in the United States, tends to separate the community into two classes, — the total abstainers and the hard drinkers. The tenser nervous organization of the modern man is in a state of less stable equilibrium than that of his progenitors, who lived largely out of doors, used their muscles in heavy work, ate large quantities of coarse food, and drank large quantities of mildly alcoholic liquor.[1] In America, climatic conditions intensify the tendency indicated. A dry atmosphere, and extremes of heat and cold, produce nervous diseases unknown to European medical practice, or, at least, known here in advance of their appearance in Europe.[2] It is a matter of common observation that the children of European immigrants usually drink either less or more than their parents, and those who drink resort to the stronger liquors.

The general conclusion regarding drink as a cause of poverty is sufficiently well formulated by Mr. Booth:[3] "Of drink in all its combinations, adding to every trouble, undermining every effort after good, destroying the home, and cursing the young lives of the children, the stories tell enough. It does not stand as apparent

---

[1] See on this and following points, Simon N. Patten, "The Economic Basis of Prohibition," Annals of Am. Acad. of Pol. and Soc. Science, vol. ii., p. 59 *et seq.* An able article.

[2] See Beard, "Physical Future of the American People," *Atlantic Monthly Magazine*, vol. xliii., p. 718.

[3] "Pauperism," pp. 140-141.

chief cause in as many cases as sickness and old age; but, if it were not for drink, sickness and old age could be better met." Mr. Booth's conclusions were reached by a study of concrete masses of pauperism, and yet they serve equally well to express the results reached by the study of inebriety as a disease. It is at once an effect and cause, a symptom and a source of degeneration.

In the tables of the causes of poverty, the column next to the one giving the percentages for intemperance gives the number of cases in which poverty has been traced directly to "immorality." This term is here used to stand for sexual licentiousness, or other perversion of the sexual instinct. The small number of cases of poverty directly attributable to this factor in no wise reflects its importance as either a direct or a predisposing cause of destitution. Careful observers believe it to be a more constant and fundamental cause of degeneration than intemperance.[1] It certainly effects degeneration of a more or less pronounced type in a much larger number of persons. It persists almost to the end in the most degenerate stock, while at the same time it is operative among the healthier classes. A reference to the accounts quoted later on, describing the habits of the Rooneys, the Jukes, and the Ishmaels, will show that in these distinctly pauper families sexual vice plays a part in degradation more important than intemperance. The medical profession has given us even less of scientific

---

[1] Mr. Booth speaks of intemperance as the most prolific of all the causes of poverty; but, so far as his publications show, he has not studied with much thoroughness the influence of sexual immorality as a cause of pauperism.

CAUSES OF INDIVIDUAL DEGENERATION. 67

exposition of the degeneration which results from perversion of the sexual instincts, than of that which comes from the abuse of stimulants and narcotics. The changes which must undoubtedly take place in the structure of the nervous and circulatory systems, as a consequence of self-abuse or sexual excess, have not been sufficiently studied. Venereal disease has been treated at length, but the effect upon the physical and mental man of vice as vice has been neglected. The great bulk of literature existing upon the subject is simply the output of advertising quacks.

And yet the effect of lubricity as such is appreciated to be an evil, and we condemn without hesitation such plans as those once put forward by Annie Besant for limiting population by mechanical appliances for preventing conception. It is felt at once that a sparse population which is vicious may be more miserable than a comparatively dense one which is moral. If, while limiting population, we promote sensuality, we do more harm than good. Anything which encourages sexual excess promotes misery. Mrs. Besant has herself acknowledged this by withdrawing her book from publication. She says that the remedy proposed was materialistic, and she withdraws the book because she no longer accepts materialism. In this she is consistent; but even a well-reasoned materialism might surely have shown that her "remedy" for misery would probably produce more misery than it cured. ("If we consider man merely as a machine . . . let us not forget what a piece of mechanism he is.")

No boy among boys, or man among men, can have failed to have evidence thrust upon him showing that a very great amount of vitality is burnt out by the fires of lust. Among the rougher classes of day laborers upon railroads, in quarries, and even upon the farms, the whole undercurrent of thought, so far as conversation gives evidence of it, is thoroughly base and degrading. In several cases that the author investigated carefully, inefficiency certainly resulted from the constant preoccupation of the mind with sensual imaginings. At the present day, a given amount of such preoccupation will diminish a man's industrial efficiency more than ever before, because of the increasing importance of the mental element in all work. If a man has brute strength, he can shovel dirt quite passably, even though his thoughts are elsewhere. But most of the occupations of the present require alertness and sustained attention. Personal acquaintance with railroad day laborers, and others of a similar class, convinces the writer that they are very commonly kept from rising in the industrial scale by their sensuality, and that it is this and the resulting degeneration that finally convert many of them into lazy vagabonds. The inherent uncleanness of their minds prevents them from rising above the rank of day laborers, and finally incapacitates them even for that position. It may also be suggested that the modern man has a stronger imagination than the man of a few hundred years ago, and that sensuality destroys him the more rapidly. A highly developed nervous system makes him a more powerful man, if it is properly used, but it enables him to destroy himself more promptly if that be his tendency.

In addition to the direct effect of the perversion of the sexual instincts must be reckoned the ravages of venereal disease. Among the degraded class it is ac-

CAUSES OF INDIVIDUAL DEGENERATION. 69

counted a mark of manliness to have had syphilis until exposure to it is no longer dangerous. From twenty-five to thirty per cent of the Juke family were tainted with it. "Significant as are these aggregate figures, they are weak as compared with the lesson which is pointed when we analyze the lines along which this disease runs, and note its devastation of individual careers, and its pauperizing influence on successive generations." It is this disease co-operating with drunkenness that finally brings the prostitute and her consort through the hospital to the almshouse. There are probably few almshouses in the country where some of the inmates are not paupers in part because of its effects upon them; it is not easy to visit a foundling hospital of any size, or a children's hospital where this disease is not especially excluded, without finding children in bitter and hopeless misery because of congenital syphilis. The doctors administer remedies which give temporary relief, but the doctors themselves often express a belief that the best thing that can be hoped for such children is an early death.

Surgeons who have a large practice among those affected with this disease frequently advocate the state regulation of vice as a means of checking its spread. Some half-way experiments in this direction have been made by American cities. In England a desire to keep the soldiers of Her Majesty's army in a condition fit for service led to the passage of the Contagious Diseases Acts in 1866, which provided for the official medical examination of prostitutes. Proposals to extend the system so as to "protect" the civil population brought the whole policy of state regulation of vice under discussion, and after a most bitter agitation the Acts were repealed in 1877. This experiment seemed to confirm the contention that state regulation of vice tends so to promote vice that the end sought is defeated. Syphilis exists and spreads because of promiscuous sexual intercourse, and anything that makes the latter more common tends to disseminate the former. The surgeons had erred by taking a too limited view of the matter; and their mechanical remedy re-enforced the moral causes of disease, which they had shortsightedly ignored. Physicians are quite inclined to insist upon a recognition of the physical basis of pauperism, and the average person would pay more attention to them were they themselves more willing to reckon with all the moral causes of disease.

As in the case of the sister vice, intemperance, the effect of sexual immorality is to bring unhealthy children into the world, to cause many of them to be neglected so that early death results,[1] and finally to provide for those that survive an environment that all but insures their degradation.

Taking the Jukes as typical of degeneration at its worst, we find Dugdale's summary of their habits, and of the results of their habits, to be confirmatory of all other evidence obtainable upon the subject: "Fornica-

[1] In twelve urban districts in England, 1871-5, the mortality was, for legitimate children, 192 per 1,000 births; for illegitimate children, 388 per 1,000 births. In Glasgow, 1873-5 the figures stood, legitimate, 152; illegitimate, 286. Newsholme, "Elements of Vital Statistics," p. 108. Leffingwell, "Illegitimacy," pp. 70-2 gives figures to similar purpose. He also calls attention to the fact, p. 73, that a study of coronors' inquests held upon children under one year of age shows that illegitimate children are "more than four times as liable to 'accident' as their legitimate kindred."

tion, either consanguineous or not, is the backbone of their habits, flanked on the one side by pauperism, on the other by crime. The secondary features are prostitution, with its complement of bastardy, and its resultant, neglected and miseducated childhood ; exhaustion, with its complement, intemperance, and its resultant, unbalanced minds; and disease, with its complement, extinction." [1]

After drink-crave and sensuality, we might enumerate a large number of characteristics or habits which result from and result in a tendency to degenerate. On the side of appetites would be the craving for opium, and for various kinds of unwholesome food. On the side of defects, would be all those sufficiently pronounced to have been enumerated in the table of causes, and in addition the mental incapacity to judge wisely in the ordinary business affairs of life. This last is one of the most vexatious causes of poverty with which the ordinary friendly visitor for a charity organization society has to deal. It sometimes manifests itself in the form of extravagance, but oftener in pure blundering, which does not even bring the satisfaction of temporary indulgence. "Against stupidity the gods themselves are powerless." A proverbial saying, which has a very direct bearing on the subject, asserts that "Poor folks have poor ways." This cause is generally operative ; yet writers upon social pathology seldom give it distinct treatment, apparently thinking that it is an individual and not a social phenomenon. The social results of it, however, are not to be ignored. The development of modern industries puts upon the judgment of individuals an ever increas-

[1] "Jukes," p. 13.

ing burden. The breaking down of the barriers of custom, the rapid changes in the methods of industry, the increasing amount of purchasing to be done to obtain family supplies, the increased need of wise bargaining in the selling of services, the extension of the borrowing habit both for good and evil, these and a hundred other features of modern industry, tend to add to sobriety and industry as prerequisites of industrial success, a further requisite — that of good judgment, and a judgment that acts not only surely but promptly. From the proprietary farmer all the way down to the disease burdened man who decides whether or not he will go to a hospital, mistaken judgments are constantly pushing people towards and across the pauper line. One of the commonest mistakes is an utter failure to appreciate in advance the burden of a debt at compound interest. The chattel mortgage shark, the pawnbroker, and the "instalment plan" houses thrive because of this failure.[1]

The only remaining characteristic to which special reference need here be made is that of laziness. Philosophers of the Benjamin Franklin type find in this the cause of nearly all destitution. Yet, in so far as it has a physical basis in undervitalization, it is hardly to be cured by exhortation or even by hunger, any more than intemperance can under similar circumstances be so cured. Frequently what appears to the pushing citizen to be laziness is only the result of general incompetence, which the subject does not consciously recognize as existing, but which checks any ambition to do by a

[1] See Chap. IV., and reference there given to Hobson, for a brief description of the way in which industry has developed so as to render certain individuals incapable.

premonition of failure. The weightiest charge which many contented and discontented vagabonds might bring against the modern industrial organization is that they have become what they are through the effect of involuntary idleness; for idleness, voluntary or involuntary, tends to produce a degeneration, physical, mental, and moral, which perpetuates the condition that begets it.

The old economists sought to starve everybody back into habits of work and thrift; but starvation as a remedy for idleness is a medicine which the community is not willing to have administered in large doses, and even laziness is an evil which we must assail in its causes. The cause may be unwise coddling of the individual, but it may not.

Thus far we have not needed to inquire whether the evil propensities and bad habits which result in degeneration have come through free choice on the part of the individual, or have been the result of foreordination in the theological or the scientific sense of the term. We have been concerned simply with their interactions and their effects. Ignoring all discussion as to the freedom of the will in any absolute sense of the term, it is our present business to trace causes just as far as they are found to be traceable. As an insurance company is justified in refusing to take a risk upon the life of a man who comes of a sickly family, or is engaged in some peculiarly dangerous occupation, so the student of social science is justified in concluding that certain influences of heredity and environment have an influence upon the character of the individual that is often manifest, and that is frequently to some extent measurable. In the one calculation relating to the longevity of an individual, and in the other relating to the character and career of an individual, there is always an uncertainty, but there is also a very constant element of probability.

From the time of birth, or even from the time of conception, the characteristics of race and of sex are fixed; and these are not without influence on the industrial history of the individual, as our tables show. In addition to this the transmission of a tendency to suffer from some specific disease such as gout, or consumption, or scrofula, or insanity, is very generally recognized. Observations more than ordinarily careful show that more varieties of bodily and mental weakness are transmitted from parent to child than is ordinarily supposed. Beyond this, occult characteristics tending to inefficiency or absolute pauperism, are undoubtedly transmitted, although their exact nature, either in parent or child, cannot be ascertained and described. The proof is that the child follows by some secret but almost irresistible propulsion the history of the parent. The transmission of hereditary tendencies to degeneration can be most easily traced where some palpable defect is the result and evidence of degeneration. In his "Memoir upon the Formation of a Deaf Variety of the Human Race," Professor Alexander Graham Bell has collected with thoroughness and caution the facts available for this country, which show the transmissible character of deafness.[1] It has been shown by three different investigators that where two persons born deaf marry, about one-third of the

---

[1] The author has incorporated the more important conclusions reached in this Memoir in "Marriage; An Address to the Deaf," published by the Volta Bureau, Washington, D.C.

CAUSES OF INDIVIDUAL DEGENERATION. 75

children are born deaf.[1] The difference between different classes of deaf persons in the tendency to transmit deafness is shown in the following table:[2] —

TABLE XIV.

CLASSES.	NUMBER OF FAMILIES.	NUMBER OF DEAF CHILDREN.	PERCENTAGE (No. of Deaf Children to Every 100 Families).
CLASS 1. Not born deaf; no deaf relatives	363	17	4.7
CLASS 2. Not born deaf; deaf relatives	53	5	9.4
CLASS 3. Born deaf; no deaf relatives	130	15	11.5
CLASS 4. Born deaf; deaf relatives	230	41	17.8

The classification of this table is based upon information regarding one parent in each case.

On page 25 of the "Memoir" is given a much more detailed statement of the same facts, from which Professor Bell draws the conclusion that "A hereditary tendency towards deafness, as indicated by the possession of deaf relatives, is a most important element in determining the production of deaf offspring. . . . · It may even be a more important element than the mere fact of congenital deafness in one or both of the parents." The following diagram of "The Brown Family of Henniker, New Hampshire," from page 28 of the "Memoir," is given,

---

[1] "Marriage," pp. 4 and 5; "Memoir," chap. iii., giving tables and detailed statements.
[2] "Marriage," Table III., p. 8.

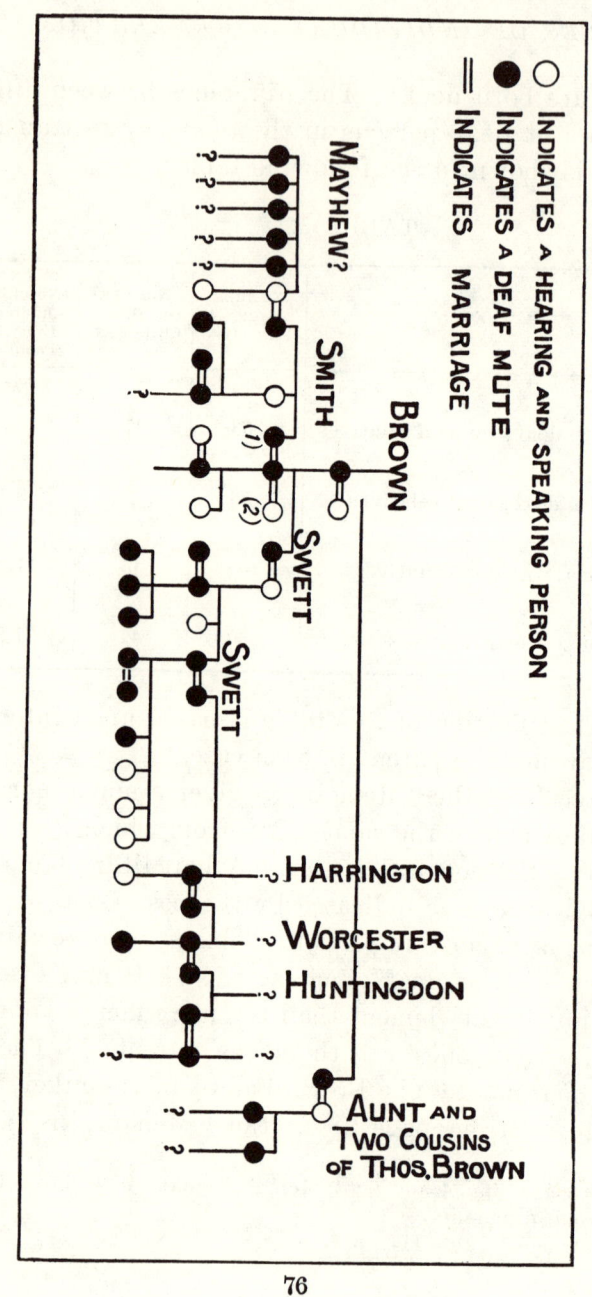

as showing at a glance the extent to which deafness prevails in certain families.

Professor Bell calls attention to the fact that lack of information leads to an under statement rather than an over statement in both the diagrams and the tables.

In his work on "Marriage and Disease," Dr. Strahan has given striking instances of the hereditary transmission of disease tendencies. He enumerates certain diseases which, in his opinion, spring from degeneration, and shows how a tendency to degenerate may result in one case in drunkenness; in another in deaf-mutism; in another in consumption; in another in insanity or imbecility. He quotes authorities to show that the ratio of blindness among deaf-mutes is fourteen and a half times as great as among the whole population; while idiocy, the deepest of all forms of degeneration, is forty-three times as great among these unfortunates as among the general population.[1] In his opinion the intermarriage of deaf-mutes or other defectives will not result in the formation of a deaf variety of the human race, but rather in the extinction of the degenerate stock.[2] The more important diseases transmissible by inheritance which he regards at once as results, evidences, and causes of degeneration, are insanity, imbecility, epilepsy, drunkenness, deaf-mutism, blindness, cancer, scrofula, tubercular disease, gout, rheumatism, and instinctive criminality. While he has not marshalled the statistics which might be given to show the

[1] "Marriage and Disease," p. 169.
[2] Congenital deafness is not the simple absence of one of the senses which is not absolutely necessary for life; it is a sign of a general decay, which, if deepened by intermarriage, must soon reach the necessarily fatal type and extinguish the family. — *Ib.* p. 171.

common dependence of the diseases upon general degeneration, yet his diagrams and statements of family history abundantly prove the interdependence of these diseases, or of many of them, and establishes beyond question the fact that they are frequently transmitted by inheritance.[1]

In his investigation of the causes of idiocy in Massachusetts, Dr. S. G. Howe had careful inquiries made regarding the influence of heredity. The facts most pertinent at this stage of the inquiry are grouped in the table on opposite page.

When we turn from the palpably defective to measure as accurately as may be the influence of heredity upon the failure of apparently normal individuals to keep themselves self-dependent, the difficulties are much increased. It has been remarked[2] that the only experiments which would allow us to test fully the influence of heredity in determining the character of individuals, must be made in the cases of infants whose parentage is known and who have been adopted into good homes. The child who is born in an almshouse and grows up there is almost always a pauper, and would probably be so regardless of its heredity, though in such cases the latter agency usually re-enforces the influence of environment. The child that grows up in an infant asylum or orphans' home has a most imperfect opportunity for right development, and the original possibilities of its nature are but faintly reflected by its career. With a

---

[1] Boies, in his work on "Prisoners and Paupers," pp. 281-2, has reproduced eight of Strahan's diagrams of families.

[2] By Mr. Homer Folks of New York State Charities Aid Association.

TABLE XV.

Hereditary Tendencies apparently affecting Idiocy in Massachusetts.

	Congenital Idiocy.	Idiocy Supervened.	Total.
Idiotic persons who are known to be of decidedly scrofulous families	355	64	419
Idiotic persons whose parents were known to be habitual drunkards	99	15	114
Idiotic persons some of whose near relatives are idiotic or insane	177	34	211
Idiotic persons whose parents were known to be neither very scrofulous nor very intemperate . .	5	5	10
Idiotic persons who have 1 near relative idiotic . .	44	5	49
Idiotic persons who have 2 near relatives idiotic .	8	1	9
Idiotic persons who have 3 near relatives idiotic .	5	1	6
Idiotic persons who have 4 near relatives idiotic .	3	1	4
Idiotic persons who have 5 near relatives idiotic .	6	. .	6
Idiotic persons who have 10 near relatives idiotic .	3	. .	3
Idiotic persons who have 19 near relatives idiotic .	1	. .	1
Idiotic persons one or both of whose parents were idiotic or insane	. .	. .	50
Idiotic persons who are parents	. .	. .	21
Idiotic persons whose parents were advised to marry on account of ill-health	12	. .	12
Families where the parents of idiotic persons are near relatives	17	. .	17
Of these families,— 6 have 1 idiotic child each. 2 have 2 idiotic children each. 3 have 3 idiotic children each. 5 have 4 idiotic children each. 1 has 5 idiotic children. Average idiotic persons in each of these 17 families .	3	. .	3

TABLE XV. — *Concluded.*

	Congenital Idiocy.	Idiocy Supervened.	Total.
Parents who have 2 idiotic children	43	2	45
Parents who have 3 idiotic children	10	3	13
Parents who have 4 idiotic children	8	. .	8
Parents who have 5 idiotic children	1	. .	1
Parents who have 7 idiotic children	1	. .	1
Parents who have 9 idiotic children	1	. .	1
Parents who have 11 idiotic children	. .	1	1
Number of families in which *all* the children of one marriage were idiotic or very puny, while those of another marriage, by the surviving *healthy* parent with a healthy person, were sound in body and mind	. .	. .	15

From Howe's Report, 1848, p. 45 of Tables.

child boarded out in a private family, or given to foster parents, while still an infant, the conditions of life are better, and more might be inferred could we compare its characteristics with those of its parents. But usually the facts regarding the parents are matters of inference rather than knowledge, and foster parents are inclined to fix as deep a gulf of ignorance as possible between the child and its progenitors. It is likely that some time the records of such societies as the Massachusetts or Pennsylvania Children's Aid Society, or of such public officials as the Massachusetts State Board of Lunacy and Charity, will give us useful data. They search out as carefully as possible all the facts regarding the antecedents of the children coming under their care. Even the youngest infants are at once boarded out and their subsequent development watched and recorded.¹

Galton has cited the case of D'Alembert, who was a foundling, and put out to nurse as a pauper baby to the wife of a poor glazier: —

"The child's indomitable tendency to the higher studies could not be repressed by his foster-mother's ridicule and dissuasion, nor by the taunts of his schoolfellows, nor by the discouragements of his schoolmaster, who was incapable of appreciating him, nor even by the reiterated, deep disappointment of finding that his ideas, which he knew to be original, were not novel, but long previously discovered by others. Of course we should expect a boy of his kind to undergo ten or more years of apparently hopeless strife, but we should equally expect him to succeed at last; and D'Alembert did succeed in attaining the first rank of celebrity by the time he was twenty-four." ²

Galton has not many examples of this sort to fortify his belief that "if the eminent men of any period had been changelings when babies, a very fair proportion of those who survived, and retained their health up to fifty years of age, would, notwithstanding their altered circumstances, have equally risen to eminence." ³ Mr. Ritchie, in commenting on this opinion, suggests that while it might be true that restless, energetic natures, like D'Alembert or Lord Brougham, would make their way up in spite of all obstacles, it may be doubted if such would be the case with a nature like that of Charles Darwin. He suggests that under many cir-

¹ Mr. C. L. Brace, the elder, has given some facts regarding the outcome of the children placed by the New York Children's Aid Society which are of interest, but too general to be conclusive. See "Baltimore Conference on Charities," 1887, pp. 107-09.

² Francis Galton, "Hereditary Genius," pp. 43-44.

³ "Hereditary Genius," p. 38.

cumstances the struggle for existence may be so severe that strength is exhausted, even in the man of ability.[1]

Satisfactory experiments with infants of known descent not having been conducted with sufficient care, or in sufficient number, to warrant any final conclusions as to the force of heredity in pushing the individual away from pauperism or towards it, two other methods of observation, less conclusive but more practicable, have been resorted to. The first is to study the family relations of a large number of conspicuously successful or unsuccessful persons, and learn as far as possible what influence heredity has had in bringing about success or failure. The second method is to study the careers of all the children of a family whose members are in general conspicuous for success or failure, in order to see whether or not the manifest tendency can be accounted for by the influence of environment. This second method is, of course, for the most part only a way of checking the results obtained by the first. As examples of the first we may summarize the investigations of Galton regarding relationships of the English judges, (*b*) Booth's summary of the " Stories of Stepney Pauperism," (*c*) the investigation of the almshouse population of New York; and as illustrating the results to be got by the second method, some account is given of the study of the Jukes of New York, and the Ishmaelites of Indiana.

Mr. Galton undertook a study of the English judges between the accession of Charles II. and the year 1864. He found that a very large number of these men were

---

[1] "Darwinism and Politics," p. 51.

related one to another, and an analysis of the facts showed that a very eminent man was more likely to have eminent relations than one who had attained a less degree of success. Out of the 286 judges, more than one in every nine had been either father, son, or brother to another judge, and the other high legal relationships had been even more numerous. " There cannot remain a doubt," he says, " but that the peculiar type of ability that is necessary to a judge is often transmitted by descent." [1]

As showing the possibilities of the persistence of capacity in certain families, the following is inserted from Galton's works: —

" The names of North and Montagu, among the judges, introduce us to a remarkable breed of eminent men, set forth at length in the genealogical tree of the Montagus, and again that of the Sydneys (see the chapter on ' Literary Men'), to whose natural history — if the expression be permitted — a few pages may be profitably assigned. There is hardly a name in those pedigrees which is not more than ordinarily eminent: many are illustrious. They are closely tied together in their kinship, and they extend through ten generations. The main roots of this diffused ability lie in the families of Sydney and Montagu, and, in a lesser degree, in that of North.

" The Sydney blood — I mean that of the descendants of Sir William Sydney and his wife — had extraordinary influence in two different combinations. First with the Dudleys, producing in the first generation, Sir Philip Sydney and his eminent brother and sister; in the second generation, at least one eminent man; and in the third generation, Algernon Sydney with his able brother and much-be-praised sister. The second combination of the Sydney blood was with the Harringtons, producing in the first generation a literary peer, and Elizabeth, the mother of the

[1] Page 69.

large and most remarkable family that forms the chief feature of my genealogical table.

"The Montagu blood, as represented by Sir Edward, who died in the Tower, 1644, is derived from three distant sources. His great-grandfather (*g*F.) was Sir John Finnieux, Chief Justice of the King's Bench; his grandfather (g.) was John Roper, Attorney General to Henry VIII.; and his father — by far the most eminent of the three — was Sir Edward Montagu, Chief Justice of the King's Bench. Sir Edward Montagu, son of the Chief Justice, married Elizabeth Harrington, of whom I have just spoken, and had a large family, who in themselves and in their descendants became most remarkable. To mention only the titles they won: in the first generation they obtained two peerages, the earldom of Manchester and the barony of Montagu; in the second they obtained two more, the earldon of Sandwich and the barony of Capel; in the third five more, the dukedom of Montagu, earldoms of Halifax and of Essex, the barony of Guilford, and a new barony of Capel (second creation); in the fourth one more, the dukedom of Manchester (the Premier in 1701); in the fifth one more, the earldom of Guilford. The second Earl of Guilford, the Premier of George III. (best known as Lord North), was in the sixth generation." ("Hereditary Genius," pp. 70-72.)

In contrast with this, the following pages are reproduced from Mr. Booth's " Stories of Stepney Pauperism."

"Martin Rooney, aged 85, now in Bromley Workhouse, married Eliza King, and this family has been prolific in paupers.

"First there is Mary Rooney, the wife of Martin's brother James, who was deserted by him in 1867, and has had relief in various forms since, including residence in the sick asylum for several years. She also applied on behalf of her married daughter, Mrs. Wilson, and her son Michael appears on the books; but with this branch we do not go at present beyond the second generation.

"The old man Martin, who is now blind, applied for admission in 1878. His wife was then in hospital, having broken her leg when intoxicated. He had been a dock laborer, and had received £21 from the company on breaking a leg in 1857. He was ad-

CAUSES OF INDIVIDUAL DEGENERATION. 85

mitted to Poplar Workhouse. A month later his wife, who is twenty-four years his junior, came out of hospital, and was also admitted. The relieving officer makes a note that he does not know a more drunken, disreputable family than this one. He has seen the woman 'beastly drunk' at all times of the day. From this time the old man remains in the house; but the woman goes out several times, and when out was more than once seen in the streets in a drunken condition. She works sometimes at the lead-works, sleeping occasionally with her sons, at other times in various places — water-closets, on stairs, etc. When her son Patrick was sent to prison for two months she went into the house. In 1888 she absconded, but in March, 1889, applied for re-admission; she had fallen down and cut her face on the Saturday night before.

"This couple had three children, Patrick, James, and Bridget. Patrick, born in 1853, by trade a stevedore, is now in Poplar Workhouse. He was living with his mother in 1886, and she made application for medical attendance for him. He was suffering from rheumatism. He became worse, and was sent to the sick asylum; was discharged, and again admitted a month or two later. Next year he was sent to Bromley Workhouse. He bears a bad character, and was in prison two months in 1888, and had one month in 1889 for attempting to steal some ropes. On coming out of prison he again applied for admission to the workhouse, and was sent to Poplar. He had a bad leg. He got work on the day he was discharged from the sick asylum, injured his leg, and was re-admitted to workhouse. He served fourteen or fifteen years in the Royal Marines, and was discharged in 1885 for striking a petty officer. He was for this sentenced to six months' imprisonment by court-martial.

"James, the second son, is a laborer, not married. He used to live with a woman named O'Reill, but left her, or she him, and is at present living with another woman.

"Bridget, the eldest, born in 1847, married John Murdock, a bricklayer's laborer, eight years older than herself, and there are four children, all boys. Murdock deserted his wife several times, and has been sent to prison for it. She in turn left him in 1877, and has been living with another man since. After this he was in Bromley House with the children. The two eldest were emigrated to Canada in 1880. The man's sister married Richard Bardsley, whose mother, a widow, is living at Bromley, and whose brother and brother's wife both had relief there." [1]

The study of the inmates of the almshouses of New York, made by representatives of the State Board of Charities in the early seventies, included an examination of 12,614 persons in those institutions. At that time many insane and many children and many of the defective classes were still in the local almshouses. In the rural communities it was found possible to get information as to the relationships of these persons with tolerable fulness, while in the cities little could be learned bearing upon the subject. Of course the classes under investigation are those where the ties of relationship are peculiarly loose and untraceable, and yet it was found possible to collect very conclusive facts as to the influence of heredity in perpetuating pauperism. Of the whole number of persons examined, it was ascertained that 397, or nearly 3.15 per cent, were the offspring of pauper fathers; 1,361, or 10.79 per cent, of pauper mothers. The dependence dated back to the third generation in 55 cases on the paternal, and 92 cases on the maternal side. 1,122 had (living or dead) pauper brothers; 951, pauper sisters; 143, pauper uncles; and 133, pauper aunts.

10,161 different families were represented. The total number of persons in these families, including three generations (living and dead) who were known to have been dependent upon public charity was 14,901. The total

---

[1] "Pauperism," pp. 14-5. There is about twice as much more description of individuals belonging to this stock, and pages 18-43 are filled with accounts of similar families.

number of the insane in the same families (living and dead), 4,968; the total number of idiots in the same families (living and dead), 844; and the total number of inebriates in the same families (living and dead), 8,863. The number of heads of families in the poorhouses at the time of inquiry, consisting of both parents, was 2,746; these were said to have in all 7,040 living children. The condition of these children was stated to be as follows : in poorhouses, 1,010; in asylums, 149; in hospitals, 2; in refuges, 29; in prisons and penitentaries, 9; bound out, 346; self-supporting, 4,586; condition unascertained, 909. Thus about 22 per cent of the children of poorhouse parents were found to be of the dependent or delinquent classes. Taking only those whose condition was ascertained, the percentage of those who were a charge upon the public rises to a little more than 25. It should also be noted that a considerable number of those self-dependent at the time would probably with advancing years become public charges; and while some of those in a condition of dependency would perhaps eventually become self-supporting, they would hardly become so as a permanent thing. It is doubtful if half these children would get through life without some taint of dependency.

The suggestion at once occurs to anyone who reviews these facts, that environment may have had as much to do as heredity with the success of the successful, and the failure of those who fail. The sons of the influential classes grow up under conditions which favor their education and advancement, while the children of the pauper, born in the poorhouse or the slums, are foredoomed by the conditions under which they grow up to pauperism. The only way of learning how much force should be given to these considerations is to make a careful analysis of the successful and the unsuccessful families, and to see whether individuals descended from these families, but placed under conditions different from those surrounding the family, nevertheless work out careers analogous to those of their relatives. Mr. Galton has pursued this second method of investigation with apparent care, and proves to his own satisfaction that individuals of successful families are successful by virtue of inherent capacity, and only secondarily by virtue of their opportunities. Mr. Booth has also analyzed the returns regarding Stepney pauperism, and puts pauper association and heredity together as a contributory cause in 106 cases out of 634. His uniting of the two causes in the table reflects the difficulty there is of disassociating the two. In the New York investigation no direct attempt was made to trace out the careers of individuals descended from pauper stock who had yet escaped from pauperism. But two elaborate investigations have been conducted in the United States regarding the life-histories of individuals descended from distinctly pauper families. The first of these included doubtless many of the same individuals, or their progenitors, that were found in the New York almshouses in 1870.

The investigation referred to is the well-known one conducted by Mr. Dugdale concerning the family of the Jukes.[1] The facts regarding this family were so thor-

[1] The report in which the results of this study are embodied has been published by Putnams in "Questions of the Day" series. The best summary for present purposes is Mr. Dugdale's paper on "Hereditary Pauperism," read at the National Conference of Charities in 1877, see pp. 81-95.

oughly worked out that it has become a stock example of the influence of heredity as a factor in crime and pauperism, and exaggerated stories are current as to the number of criminals descended from the woman spoken of by Mr. Dugdale as Ada Juke, but better known as Margaret, the Mother of Criminals. Mr. Charles L. Brace has said that twenty-seven of her descendants were prosecuted by one attorney; one judge stated that he had sentenced sixty-nine of them, and six hundred are estimated to have been tried by law.[1] Mr. Dugdale's tables of ascertained facts, however, while not disproving these statements, do not contain a verification of them. The family has been traced back to a man whom Dugdale calls Max, a descendant of the early Dutch settlers, born between the years 1720 and 1740. He is described as a hunter and fisher, a hard drinker, jolly and companionable, averse to steady toil, working hard by spurts and idling by turns, becoming blind in his old age, and entailing his blindness upon his children and grandchildren. Two of his sons married two of the Juke sisters, of whom there were six in all. The progeny of five of them have been traced with more or less exactness through five generations. The number of descendants registered includes 540 individuals who were related by blood to the Jukes, and 169 connected with the family by marriage or cohabitation, in all 709 persons of all ages, alive and dead. The aggregate of this lineage reaches, says Mr. Dugdale, probably 1,200 persons, but the dispersions that have occurred at different times have prevented the following up and enumeration of many of the lateral branches. They grew up in the

[1] Baltimore Conference on Charities, p. 107.

rural districts of New York, and out-door life probably aided the degenerate stock to resist the tendencies to extinction. The family, as indicated by the statement of its origin, may be considered distinctly American.

The genealogical tables given by Mr. Dugdale, together with a description of the family in his text, would make it possible to reproduce a description of the individuals and their degenerate condition, of still more hideous particularity than that employed in describing the Rooney family and its connections; but for present purposes a statistical summary of the facts will throw more light upon the problems of heredity.

In the subsidiary tables given by Mr. Dugdale, it is shown that, whether we consider pauperism, or crime, or harlotry, or prostitution, this family has produced a number of dependents and delinquents out of all proportion to the numbers of individuals it has contributed to the population. For instance, in table six, relative to pauperism, which deals only with the cases of ascertained dependence in the Juke family, it is shown that pauperism is nearly seven times as common in this family as in the population of the State at large; but a closer analysis of the tables gives still more striking confirmation of the tendency of heredity as compared with environment. Mr. Dugdale classes under the head of X all families not related to the Jukes who married into the last-named family. It is found that if we take people of the Juke blood simply, pauperism is 7.37 times as common among them as in the population as a whole; while if we take X blood only, that is, those families that married into the Juke family, we find pauperism to be only 4.89 times as common as in the population as a

TABLE XVI.

Statistical Summary of the "Jukes."

(From Dugdale, Jukes, p. 69.)

	Total No. in Generation.	Parentage by Sex.			Marriageable Age.	Unmarried Adults.	Married.	Had Bastards Before Marriage.	Had Bastards After Marriage.	Prostitutes.	Unascertained.	Barren Persons.	Kept Brothels.	Syphilis.	Property.		Pauperism.				Crime.		
		Total Each Sex.	Legitimate.	Illegitimate.											Acquired.	Lost.	Outdoor Relief, No. of Persons.	No. of Years.	Almshouse, No. of Persons.	No. of Years.	No. of Persons.	No. of Years.	No. of Offenses.
2d Gen. Juke women	5	5	1	.	5	.	5	3	.	.	.	.	.	.	.	.	.	.	.	.	.	.	.
X men	5	5	2	.	5	.	5	.	.	.	.	.	.	.	.	.	.	.	.	.	.	.	.
3d Gen. Juke women	34	16	15	1	16	2	13	1	1	3	1	5	5	.	1	.	3	20	2	2	.	.	.
X women	16	7	3	.	7	.	4	.	.	3	1	.	1	.	.	.	1	23	.	.	.	.	.
Juke men	.	18	12	6	18	.	11	.	.	4	5	4	1	1	4	1	6	54	3	6	1	1	1
X men	.	9	.	2	9	.	5	.	.	4	.	.	3	1	1	1	2	14	3	5	2	3	2
4th Gen. Juke women	117	46	38	.	39	6	26	6	8	12	.	3	5	12	1	.	18	122	7	7	5	1	7
X women	25	6	1	25	.	15	3	.	4	6	4	1	7	.	.	8	53	3	3	2	½	2
Juke men	.	57	46	3	54	5	22	.	.	4	23	7	1	6	5	3	19	129	8	12	12	11	15
X men	59	34	5	1	34	.	19	.	.	15	.	1	3	2	2	1	11	50	3	3	10	13	11
5th Gen. Juke women	224	119	94	17	90	10	37	6	3	36	7	5	5	25	.	.	24	100	12	18	9	¼	15
X women	.	33	4	2	33	.	15	2	1	14	4	4	.	2	.	.	11	49	2	4	1	¼	1
Juke men	.	102	70	20	69	14	21	.	.	12	22	7	1	7	5	1	25	87	11	21	18	72	41
X men	84	51	11	3	51	.	26	.	.	14	11	6	2	4	3	1	14	33	3	.	12	8	16
6th Gen. Juke women	152	63	33	13	12	8	2	2	.	2	.	.	1	1	.	.	.	.	.	.	2	½	2
X women	.	2	4	.	1	.	1	1	.	.	1	.	.	.	.	.	.	.	.	.	.	.	.
Juke men	.	48	27	20	2	1	1	.	.	1	.	.	.	.	.	.	3	.	.	.	.	.	.
X men	5	3	.	.	3	.	2	.	.	.	1	.	2	.	.	.	.	.	7	7	2	6½	2
7th Gen. Juke women	8	3	1	2	.	.	.	.	.	.	.	.	.	.	.	.	.	.	.	.	.	.	.
Juke men	.	.	.	.	.	.	.	.	.	.	.	.	.	.	.	.	.	.	.	.	.	.	.
Tot. Gen. Juke women	252	182	33	162	26	83	18	12	53	8	13	11	37	1	.	45	242	24	35	16	1¼	24
X women	67	13	3	67	.	35	6	1	21	12	8	1	9	.	.	20	125	5	7	3	¾	3
Juke men	225	155	49	143	20	55	.	.	20	50	18	1	14	14	5	50	270	29	46	33	89½	59
X men	102	18	6	102	.	57	.	.	34	19	7	5	7	7	3	27	97	6	8	24	24	29
Juke blood	540	477	337	82	305	46	138	18	12	73	58	31	12	51	15	5	95	512	53	81	49	91½	83
X blood	169	169	31	9	169	.	92	6	1	55	23	15	6	16	7	3	47	222	11	15	27	24¾	32
Grand Total	709	645	368	91	474	46	230	24	13	128	81	46	18	67	22	8	142	734	64	96	76	116	115

CAUSES OF INDIVIDUAL DEGENERATION. 91

whole. In the matter of harlotry, 52.40 per cent of the adult women of Juke blood are found to have been harlots, while but 41.76 per cent of the women of the X blood were found to be such. Turning to the matter of crime, it is found that within the family itself, there are some distinctly criminal, and some distinctly pauper strains. Intermarriage between people of the Juke blood, that is, breeding within the family, intensified the tendency to pauperism, while marriage with non-related stocks usually resulted in a larger proportion of criminals among the descendants. This last is probably to be accounted for by the greater constitutional vigor that resulted from marriage with non-related groups. As pauperism rests upon weakness of some sort, the tendency to degenerative diseases, as the result of in-and-in breeding, readily accounts for the access of pauperism in the consanguineous lines.

As to environment, it can be said that the family lived at a time and in a State when success was entirely possible, and when many of those with whom the Juke family came in contact were constantly succeeding. At the same time, the "tendency of heredity is to produce an environment which perpetuates that heredity."[1] The child born on the roadside or in the poor-house comes up under conditions that make progressive degeneracy of the individual likely. The licentious parent is an example which greatly aids in fixing habits of debauchery in the child. Yet, this being true, it is still remarkable that, under environments substantially the same, we are able to trace distinctly different tendencies in those of Juke blood and of X blood, and even between the different strains of the family itself.

[1] Page 65.

Leaving the basis of ascertained fact, Mr. Dugdale tries to calculate the cost to society of the entire family of the Jukes, assuming that they number about twelve hundred persons of characters similar to the careers of those he has ascertained. He estimates that in seventy-five years the family cost the community over a million and a quarter of dollars, without reckoning the cash paid for whiskey, or taking into account the entailment of pauperism, crime, and disease of the survivors in succeeding generations.[1]

The second investigation of a group of pauper relatives is that conducted by the late Oscar C. McCulloch of Indianapolis. It was suggested by Mr. Dugdale's study of the Jukes, and modelled in some sort after that study, but it has not the scientific accuracy or completeness of its model. While it includes a larger group of families, and while the elaborate chart of relationships is new of its kind, and gives a striking first impression of the ganglionic nexus of pauper families underlying the self-dependent population of Indianapolis and vicinity, yet it is not possible to put one's finger on the specific facts which would most aid us in forming definite conclusions. The facts as to relationships have been gathered regarding a group comprising 250 families, and 1692 individuals. Out of this number 121 are known to have been prostitutes. The members of the family are licentious and generally diseased, but usually not intemperate. The children often die young. At times three-fourths of the inmates of the city hospital of Indianapolis are said to belong to this family group. In reply to a definite question as to

[1] Pages 69-70.

CAUSES OF INDIVIDUAL DEGENERATION. 93

whether or not any individuals belonging to this group are ever successful and independent, Mr. McCulloch says, "I know of but one who has escaped and is to-day an honorable man. I have tried again and again to lift them, but they sink back; they are a decaying stock; they cannot longer live self-dependent. The children reappear with the old basket. The girl begins the life of prostitution, and is soon seen with her own illegitimate child."[1] "Each child tends to the same life, reverts when taken out."[2]

[1] N.C.C., 1888, p. 159.
[2] Ib. p. 158. The following descriptive passages from Mr. McCulloch's paper may be given as affording a more definite impression of the character of the " Ishmaelites."

"In the fall of 1877 I visited a case of extreme destitution. There were gathered in one room, without fire, an old blind woman, a man, his wife and one child, his sister and two children. A half-bed was all the furnishing — no chair, table, or cooking utensils. I provided for their immediate wants, and then looked into the records of the township trustee. I found that I had touched a family known as the Ishmaels, which had a pauper history of several generations, and so intermarried with others as to form a pauper ganglion of several hundreds.

"Members of this extensive group have had a pauper record in Indianapolis since 1840. They have been in the almshouse, the House of Refuge, the Woman's Reformatory, the penitentiaries, and have received continuous aid from the township. The Ishmaels are intermarried with 250 other families of similar habits and tendencies. In the family history are murders, a large number of illegitimacies, and out of the 1,692 individuals whose cases have been investigated, 121 are known to have been prostitutes. The members of the family are generally diseased. The children often die young. They live by petty stealing, begging, ash-gathering. In summer they "gypsy," or travel in wagons east or west. We hear of them in Illinois about Decatur, and in Ohio about Columbus. In the fall they return. They have been known to live in hollow trees on the river-bottoms, or in empty houses. Strangely enough they are not intemperate. The individuals already traced are over five thousand, interwoven by descent and marriage. They underrun society like devil-grass.

While the facts with which we must deal in studying the influence of heredity on pauperism are often elusive and ambiguous, yet from what has been said it is manifest that there are strong hereditary tendencies making for individual success or failure. Could there be, without encouraging pauperism, a business company to insure people against it, its representatives would inquire about an applicant's family as particularly as about his financial and physical condition, and scions of many stocks would be considered " very undesirable risks."

Pick up one and the whole 5,000 would be drawn up. The women beg and send the children around to beg. They make their eyes sore with vitriol. In my own experience I have seen three generations of beggars among them. I was with a great-grandmother on her death-bed. She had been taken sick on the annual gypsying, was deserted at a little town because sick; shipped into the city; sent to the county asylum; at last brought to the miserable home to die. One evening I was called to marry a couple. I found them in one small room with two beds. In all, eleven people lived it. The bride was dressing, the groom washing. Another member of the family filled a coal-oil lamp while burning. The groom offered to haul ashes for the fee. Soon after, I asked one of the family how they were getting on. 'Oh, Elisha don't live with her any more.' 'Why?' 'Her other husband came back, and she went to him. That made Elisha mad, and he left her.' Elisha died in the pest-house. A mother and two girls present that night were killed by the cars." See further Mr. J. F. Wright's account of "Marriage Relationships in the Tribe of Ishmael," N.C.C., 1890, pp. 435-37.

CHAPTER IV.

SOME OF THE SOCIAL CAUSES OF INDIVIDUAL DEGENERATION.

[Farr, " Vital Statistics " (1885) is a collection of the " Reports and Writings of Dr. Farr," of use chiefly to specialists. Newsholme, " Elements of Vital Statistics " (3d. ed., 1892) is the best and most available presentation of this subject. Billings, " On Vital and Medical Statistics " (*Medical Record*, Nov. 30, Dec. 7 and 14, 1889) is a very useful summary by the man who has had charge of the vital statistics of the Tenth and Eleventh Censuses. Arlidge, "The Hygiene, Diseases, and Mortality of Occupation " (1892), is late, complete, and satisfactory, altogether a splendid contribution to public or preventive medicine. See also Nash, " The Home Office and the Deadly Trades," *Fortnightly Review*, Feb., 1893. Marx, " Capital," gives much useful material, easily separated from his particular explanation of causes. The best work on occupational morbidity for this country is probably that of the N. J. Bureau of Statistics of Labor, 1889, 1890, and 1891, " Health and Trade Life of Workmen." On the industrial status of low-skilled labor, see among others, Hobson, " Problems of Poverty," and Booth, " Labour and Life of the People," 1891.]

IF it were planned to give any complete view of the social and industrial influences which tend to push down the individual financially as well as physically, it would be necessary to review nearly the whole of political economy, descriptive and theoretical; but we are to concern ourselves at present merely with those extrinsic influences which tend to cause incapacity and degeneration in the individual. We must therefore pass by without consideration all the poverty begetting causes that reside in the fluctuation of the purchasing power of money, although many concrete examples could be given of families pushed from the propertied class even across the pauper line by this influence. Neither can we concern ourselves with those changes in industry which have displaced large numbers of individuals, although presumably benefiting the community as a whole, and even laborers as a class. Neither can we take up the undue power of class over class, either of employer over employed, or of organized over unorganized labor. Indirectly, of course, this power of class over class does result in conditions which tend to degenerate the individual, consequently, it will be touched upon; but our view for the most part is limited to the direct influence of occupation and conditions of life upon health, character, and capacity.

At the same time, we cannot but note in passing, that if the conditions and character of working-men have tended to depress many of them below the standard of efficiency which permits them to be useful, it is also true that the standard of efficiency has risen, or perhaps we should say changed, so that the man who would once have been useful can no longer find a place. In the development of modern industry, a vast amount of heavy work is accomplished by the free use of capital, machinery taking the place of men. Man as a source of mechanical energy at the present time is therefore a cumbrous and uneconomical tool, costing much to produce, much to keep in repair, and not nearly so adaptable in many lines as machinery. Hood's workman, who could say, —

> "No alms I ask, give me my task,
> Here are the arm, the leg,
> The strength, the sinews of a man,
> To work and not to beg,"

might at the present time be compelled to ask alms because the strength and sinews of a man are at discount in the modern labor market, and there is wanted the skill, intelligence, and adaptibility of a man in order that he may be useful.[1]

Along with this tendency of machinery to take work away from the merely strong has come the formation of trades unions, so that now, as Hobson puts it, the laborers must either "organize or starve."[2] The development of modern industry has forced higher organization; and just as Franklin said to the thirteen colonies, so now the conditions of industry say to the laborer, "join or die." Those who in consequence of conditions or character cannot organize, and who for the most part belong to the ranks of low-skilled labor, find it constantly more and more difficult to maintain themselves. While at the start they may have possessed a degree of efficiency that formerly would have won them place and living, they are now unable to get work, and through involuntary idleness their incapacity is intensified and perpetuated.

1. The most palpable means by which occupation lessens the capacity of the individual is accident. The industry in which this palpable thing is most obvious is that of transportation, and no country in the world offers more illustrations of such injury to railroad employees than the United States. There were killed on the rail-

---

[1] On the manner in which machinery has taken heavy work away from men, see particularly Hermann, "Economische Fragen und Probleme der Gegenwart."

[2] "Problems of Poverty," p. 225. This and the following pages contain a wonderfully clear and concise account of the status of low-skilled labor in modern industry.

roads of the United States during the year ending June 30, 1892, 2,554 employees, and 28,268 were injured; that is, one employee for every 322 men at work in this industry was killed, and one injured for every 29 men in the employ of the railways. In the case of trainmen, the statistics for the same year show that there was one man killed for every 113 of this class of employees, and one was injured for every 10. The accidents were most numerous in the districts where the railroads are run most cheaply and are least expensively built. In the States of Virginia, North Carolina, and South Carolina, one trainman was killed for every 33 men in employment, and one injured for every 6 employees. In the Middle Southern States the proportion was equally high.[1] Many of these cases were probably provided for by benefit associations maintained by the men or by the relief work of the companies; but such relief is always partial and temporary, and of course makes no atonement to the industry of the country as a whole for the amount of personal capacity destroyed. It would not usually be easy to trace pauperism in a given case to an accident on a railroad, although the author has himself been called to deal with some cases of destitution resulting directly from such accidents; but frequently pauperism does not result until years afterwards, when a widowed mother has broken down in the attempt to support her family, or when some aged or incapable relative has been turned adrift from the incapacity of the family to maintain him longer.

[1] Report of the Statistician of the Interstate Commerce Commission, 1892, pp. 68 and 78.

The transportation industry is but the most conspicuous example of the destruction of personal capacity that comes from accidents, many of which are preventable; and the tendency of legislation to protect factory operatives, miners, and all engaged in exposed trades, from gratuitous harm due to preventable accidents, is one that should be wisely furthered.

2. There is a destruction of personal capacity and a strong tendency to degeneration in a large number of occupations because of the disease-begetting conditions that surround the work. Much more has been done in England and European countries in searching out the source of diseases that have their origin in occupation than in this country. From the time Ramazzini published his memorable work, "De Morbis Artificum Diatriba," in the latter part of the seventeenth century, to Dr. Arlidge's lectures and subsequent volume on "The Diseases of Occupations," published in 1892, there has been a series of careful and helpful studies of the disease-engendering conditions of trades and professions. A good example of official work in this line is contained in an Appendix by Dr. Greenhow to the Third Report of the Medical Officer of the English Privy Council, 1860, "A Report on Districts with Excessive Mortality from Lung Diseases." [1]

In this country, curiously enough, very few of our labor bureaus have investigated this feature of the conditions of labor. The best work thus far done is probably that of the New Jersey Bureau of Labor Statistics, published in its Annual Reports for 1889, 1890, and 1891. The effect of occupation upon the health and

[1] See pp. 193-94.

duration of the trade life of workmen is traced in three industries — pottery, hat-making, and glass-blowing. As specimens of the facts brought to light by the investigation of these trades may be cited that of pot-makers, who prepare the pots in which the raw material for glass is melted. These pots are made of fine clay, which requires a great deal of care in its preparation, involving grinding, pulverizing the dry clay, its mixture, and tempering. Little attention has been paid to the improvement of the machinery in use and the buildings in which these processes are conducted, so as to keep the workmen from inhaling the dust. As a consequence, from ten to fifteen years is about the length of time a man can work at the trade continuously in health. "The writer has witnessed the decline of three generations of pot-makers within the past forty years." [1]

The description of the conditions of work for the hatters, prepared by a physician for the New Jersey State Board of Health, is given in the Report of the Labor Bureau, and a table which shows that of 240 sizers or makers, 76 have catarrh; 44 have rheumatism; 41 have coughs; 17 have had "the shakes"; 13 now have "the shakes"; 12 constantly catch cold because of sudden changes of temperature; 7 complain of dyspepsia; 200 use stimulants and tobacco.[2]

In these three industries, as in others, it is found that the men themselves are recklessly indifferent to the healthfulness of the conditions under which they work.

[1] Annual Report of the Bureau of Labor Statistics of New Jersey, 1889, p. 35.

[2] Ib., p. 36. The last item regarding the use of stimulants and tobacco indicates the interaction of occupational and personal influences in producing degeneration.

SOCIAL CAUSES OF DEGENERATION. 101

They will strike against a very small reduction of wages, but rarely or never for improved sanitation. It is this indifference that has made it necessary for the State to interfere and fix the plane of competition, below which employers are not allowed to go, nor workmen to permit themselves to be employed. The cheaper way to get a wise and capable generation of laborers is to educate the men to something better, rather than to allow the unwise stock to exterminate itself.

3. Turning from the countless preventable causes of disease that exist in the various occupations from unsanitary surroundings, there is one force which tends constantly to individual degeneration and race deterioration. This is the improper employment of women and children. It has been more dwelt upon by writers on political economy, and the agitation for the factory acts has brought it more prominently before the public than many of the others; but it is so fundamental and so entirely mischievous that it cannot be passed without mention. An English writer, Dr. Rentoul, gives the following sketch of women's work and its influence on their character and physique: —

"Suppose that a girl at the age of thirteen to sixteen is placed in one of the Lancashire mills, and is fed on stewed tea, bread, and occasionally badly cooked meat and fish. How can she, with such surroundings, develop into a healthy woman ? Her pale, bloodless, colorless face shows she is bordering on the first stage of consumption. In a few years she is engaged. Married on a Saturday, she returns to work on the following Monday. After some time a baby is about to be born, and she leaves the mill just when labor compels her, but no sooner. She must return to the factory in a few days, else her place will be filled by some one else. Consequently, she has to forsake her infant. It is given out to some nurse or baby farmer, the mother paying from four to six shillings per week towards its support. It is 'taken care of' by a girl eight or ten years of age, fed on unsuitable foods, drugged with 'soothing syrups,' and probably insured in a burial club. Now, what are the products of this system which demands such continuous labor? Only ruin — ruin to the health of the girl, woman, and mother; ruin to her babe denied the food nature intended for its use; ruin to all home comforts — for all the family beyond the children are in the mill — and ruin to the young husband. The human animal may be the cheapest in to-day's market, and have less attention than that given to the brute creation; still, if such a condition be allowed to continue, the country at large must soon feel the evil results which spring from so unnatural a condition. It may seem strange that during the siege of Paris, while the general mortality was doubled, the infant mortality was reduced by about forty per cent. This was owing to the fact that the mothers, having to stay at home, had sufficient time to nurse their infants. A similar experience was recorded during the cotton famine in Lancashire." [1]

The statements regarding experience in Paris and Lancashire, which are presumably correct, give the most striking evidence of the evils resulting from the employment of married women.[2]

4. A common cause of degeneration is enforced idleness, coming from the necessities of variable seasons, or from the spasmodic nature of modern industry, or from the inclination of employing companies, as in many of the bituminous coal regions, to keep a large number of

[1] "The Dignity of Woman's Health," p. 122-24.
[2] The best and most accessible reference on child labor in the United States is to be found in the two articles by Willoughby and De Grafenried in Publications American Economic Association, vol. v., pp. 229–271. Probably the best argument for the Factory Acts within brief compass is Macaulay's speech on the Ten Hours' Bill, " Speeches," vol. ii., pp. 7-30. See also Jeans, " Factory Legislation," and Jevons, " The State in Relation to Labor."

men partially employed, rather than a small number occupied all the time. Every great industrial crisis like that through which we have been passing during the present year leaves behind it a legacy of individual degeneration and personal unthrift, which tends to sink more and more those who have not girded themselves to improve through adversity instead of being depressed by it.

5. Another way of finding out the influence of occupation upon health is by a study of mortality statistics, especially of occupational mortality and morbidity. It is generally recognized that there is a higher death rate among laboring classes than among the well-to-do, but a careful search among statistics collected by American bureaus of labor and for the Federal census shows that we have no vital statistics that are a safe guide in considering occupational mortality. In some states, as Massachusetts and Michigan, there is a register of the occupation of decedents, which makes it possible to get an average age at death in different occupations; but this is an unsafe guide. The Massachusetts statistics, as cited by Royce, show that the average age at death of farmers is 65.19 years, which is the highest average in any occupation. The average age at death among male factory operatives is 38.92, and of female operatives only 27.98, which is the lowest average on the list. Next to female operatives in lowness of average come carvers, 33.84; plumbers, 35.43; and glass-blowers, 37.81. While such a table doubtless indicates something as to the respective healthfulness of the sixty-nine occupations to which it relates, yet the figures are often misleading. This results from the fact that a person frequently

changes his occupation before death. Thus, if we were to take the average age of students at death it would be very low; but this would not prove that it was unhealthful to be a student, but only that nearly all students are comparatively young — those that die included. The average age at death of judges must manifestly be greater than that of lawyers, irrespective of the healthfulness of the two occupations. The average age at death of almshouse paupers would be very high. In the case of female operatives the low average is no doubt partly due to the fact that many women leave the mills after the cares of a family come to them, and if they die in extreme old age as the mothers of families, their early service in the mills is forgotten; whereas, if they had died young, while in the mills, their cases would have helped to keep down the average age at death of female operatives.

The only conclusive way to study occupational mortality is to secure the number dying during one year in a given occupation at a given age out of 1,000 engaged in that occupation of the same age. Taking certain statistics on this point given by Josef Körösi, the eminent statistician of Budapesth, the derivative table on opposite page is prepared.

This derivative table shows that if we start at the age of 25 with 1,000 persons of each class, there will be living at the end of 35 years, of the merchants, 567; of the tailors, 421; of the shoemakers, 376; of the servants, 290; and of the day laborers, only 253.

During this time the total number of years of life lived by the merchants was 28,501.23, and by the day laborers only 22,317. But worse than this, of the

SOCIAL CAUSES OF DEGENERATION.

TABLE XVII.

Mortality and Morbidity in Five Occupations.[1]

Occupation.	No. Living at 25.	No. Living at 60.	Years of Life, 25-60.	Years of Health, 25-60.	Years of Sickness 25-60.	Ratio of Health to Sickness.
Merchants . .	1,000	587.7	28,501.23	27,676.63	824.6	33.5 : 1
Tailors . . .	1,000	421.2	25,673.45	24,515.91	1,157.5	21.1 : 1
Shoemakers .	1,000	376.2	23,872.38	22,624.78	1,247.6	18.2 : 1
Servants . . .	1,000	290.2	22,416.92	20,997.32	1,419.6	14.7 : 1
Day Laborers .	1,000	253.3	22,317.04	20,823.64	1,493.4	13.9 : 1

years of life falling to the lot of the day laborer, 1,493 will be years of sickness, while of the years of life lived by the merchants only 824 will be years of sickness.[2] Or to state the same thing in another way, the merchant will have $33\frac{1}{2}$ years in which to provide for one of sickness, while the day laborer will have only 13.9 years of health in which to provide for one of sickness.

[1] Josef Körösi, Mitteilungen über Individuale Mortalitäts — Beobachtungen, Budapesth, 1876, p. 26. Following is the original table:

Occupation.	Living.	Dead.	Total.
Merchants	20,725	462	21,187
Tailors	12,090	294	12,384
Shoemakers	9,372	286	9,658
Servants	8,754	313	9,067
Day Laborers	17,931	790	18,721
All five classes	68,872	2,145	71,017

[2] This is on the estimate commonly accepted by statisticians, that in a given population there are two years of sickness for each death.

It is not improbable these figures exaggerate the difference between the two occupations, and too much reliance should not be placed on them; but at the same time they have some value, and help us to understand how it is that sickness is held to be the cause of so much pauperism.

Dr. Farr, in his work on "Vital Statistics," gives the following table as to the mortality at six age-periods in certain occupations: —

TABLE XVIII.

MORTALITY PER 1,000 LIVING AT SIX AGE-PERIODS.[1]

\multicolumn{8}{c}{AGES.}							
25.	35 —	OCCUPATION.	45 —	55 —	65 —	75.
10.15	8.64	Farmer	11.09	24.90	55.30	148.02
9.12	10.59	Shoemaker . . .	15.03	28.69	65.05	164.46
7.97	10.56	Weaver	15.37	32.99	74.59	173.08
7.63	10.46	Grocer	15.79	22.65	49.72	124.57
8.12	12.40	Blacksmith . . .	16.51	37.24	74.43	167.10
9.45	10.32	Carpenter	16.67	29.66	65.86	142.86
11.63	14.15	Tailor	16.74	28.18	76.47	155.28
9.79	12.52	Laborer	17.30	29.20	67.90	173.94
8.49	11.35	Miner	20.15	34.50	80.51	178.67
7.59	14.75	Baker	21.21	33.01	66.78	150.66
11.30	16.53	Butcher	23.10	41.49	66.47	154.49
13.83	20.45	Innkeeper	28.34	38.97	81.51	180.84
9.48	12.36	All England . . .	17.87	30.31	63.96	140.55

[1] William Farr, "Vital Statistics," p. 397. The several classes are arranged in the order of the mortality at the age (45-55).

SOCIAL CAUSES OF DEGENERATION.

TABLE XIX.

NUMBER LIVING AT STATED AGES OUT OF 1,000 LIVING AT AGE 25.[1]

	AGES.			
	35.	45.	55.	60.
Farmer	898.5	821.19	730.06	639.54
Shoemaker	908.8	812.45	690.65	591.64
Weaver	920.3	822.78	696.04	581.20
Grocer	923.7	826.68	696.02	617.38
Blacksmith	918.8	804.84	672.02	547.02
Carpenter	905.5	812.18	676.58	576.38
Tailor	883.7	758.17	631.58	544.10
Laborer	902.1	789.35	652.85	557.51
Miner	915.1	810.79	646.97	535.69
Baker	924.1	787.35	620.51	518.04
Butcher	887.0	740.64	569.47	451.41
Innkeeper	861.7	684.99	491.13	395.38

[1] Based on table given by William Farr, "Vital Statistics," p. 397.

The death-rates based on the English experience are here lower than those given by Körösi, and the indicated relative healthfulness of the trades is not the same. According to this calculation, which is based upon very wide inductions, the most unhealthful business is that of an innkeeper, or, as we would say, of saloon-keeper. This illustrates again the interaction of personal and occupational causes of degeneration. Next to this comes the business of the butcher, and so on up, the most healthful occupation being that of the farmer. Dr. Farr makes an examination of the conditions in several occupations, the results of which are presumably reflected by the statistics given.[1]

The table on opposite page is reproduced from Newsholme's "Vital Statistics." [2]

The comparative mortality figure in the last column indicates how many deaths occur out of the same number in the given occupation as in the number of the average population in which 1,000 deaths occur. Thus, in the average population, 1,000 annual deaths occur per 64,641 males, ages 25 to 65, of whom 41,920 were under and 22,721 were over 45 years of age. The figure for clergymen, 556, represents the mean mortality of the clergy between 25 and 65, as compared with the mortality of all males of similar ages in England and Wales. It will be seen that the highest comparative mortality figure is found again among innkeepers, or hotel-keepers and their servants, and next among the general laborers of London. Dr. Newsholme thoroughly analyzes these

---

[1] Dr. Farr's work on occupational mortality begins with a study of the mortality of kings; that is, he examines the length of the reigns of elective and hereditary princes in order to determine, not exactly the relative healthfulness of this calling, but the probable average duration of life in remote periods. Of the thirty-four English sovereigns, ten died violent deaths, two died in battle, three by accident, one was publicly executed, four were assassinated by other sovereigns. Their lives averaged eleven years shorter than they should have been according to the rate of mortality prevalent among people generally in the present century. While this "business" was especially exposed to violence, it is undoubtedly true that the violence of the times affected the death-rate in all classes, and the longer average of modern life is partly due to the cessation of constant wars and turbulence. "Vital Statistics," pp. 392-93.

[2] A. Newsholme, "Vital Statistics," pp. 156-57.

TABLE XX.

Death-Rates of Males, 25–65 Years of Age, in Different Occupations in 1860–61–1871, and in 1880–82, and their Comparative Mortality Figures in 1880–82.

OCCUPATION.	Mean Annual Death-Rates Per 1,000 Living.				Comparative Mortality Figure.
	1860-1-1871.		1880-1-2.		1880-2
	Years of Age.		Years of Age.		Age.
	25-45.	45-65.	25-45.	45-65.	25-65.
All Males	11.27	23.98	10.16	25.27	1,000
Occupied Males	. . . .	. . . .	9.71	24.63	967
Unoccupied Males	. . . .	. . . .	32.43	36.20	2,182
Males in Selected Healthy Districts	. . . .	. . . .	8.47	19.74	804
Clergyman, Priest, Minister . .	5.96	17.31	4.64	15.93	556
Gardener, Nurseryman	6.74	17.54	5.52	16.19	599
Farmer, Grazier	7.66	17.32	6.09	16.53	631
Laborer in agricultural counties .	. . . .	. . . .	7.13	17.68	701
Schoolmaster, Teacher	9.82	23.56	6.41	19.98	719
Grocer	9.49	17.05	8.00	19.16	771
Fisherman	11.26	15.84	8.32	19.74	797
Carpenter, Joiner	9.44	21.36	7.77	21.74	820
Bookseller, Stationer	10.84	21.36	8.53	20.57	825
Barrister, Solicitor	9.87	22.97	7.54	23.13	842
Draper and Manchester Warehouseman	14.34	26.33	9.70	20.96	883
Groom, Domestic, Coachman . .	. . . .	. . . .	8.53	23.28	887
Coal Miners (six districts) . . .	. . . .	. . . .	7.64	25.11	891
Plasterer, Whitewasher	9.50	27.90	7.79	25.07	896
Watch- and Clockmaker . . .	10.78	24.90	9.26	22.64	903
Tanner, Fellmonger	10.43	26.57	7.97	25.37	911
Shoemaker	10.39	22.30	9.31	23.36	921

TABLE XX. — *Continued.*

OCCUPATION.	Mean Annual Death-Rates Per 1,000 Living.				Comparative Mortality Figure.
	1860-1-1871.		1880-1-2.		1880-2
	Years of Age.		Years of Age.		Age.
	25-45.	45-65.	25-45.	45-65.	25-65.
Artist, Engraver, Sculptor, Architect.	11.73	22.91	8.39	25.07	921
Commercial Traveller	12.28	29.00	9.04	25.03	948
Corn Miller	9.32	26.65	8.40	26.62	957
Baker, Confectioner,	10.72	26.39	8.70	26.12	958
Builder, Mason, Bricklayer	11.43	27.16	9.25	25.59	969
Blacksmith	10.07	23.88	9.29	25.67	973
Commercial Clerk, insurance service	14.28	28.88	10.48	24.49	996
Tobacconist	13.19	21.76	11.14	23.46	1,000
Chemist, Druggist	13.92	23.56	10.58	25.16	1,015
Tailor	12.92	24.79	10.73	26.47	1,051
Printer	13.02	29.38	11.12	26.60	1,071
Wool, Worsted Manufacture (West Riding)	...	...	9.71	27.50	1,032
Cotton, Linen Manufacture (Lancashire)	...	...	9.99	29.44	1,088
Physician, Surgeon, General Practitioner.	13.81	24.55	11.57	28.03	1,122
Law Clerk	18.75	37.05	10.77	30.79	1,151
Butcher	13.19	28.37	12.16	29.08	1,170
Glass Manufacturer	13.19	29.32	11.21	31.71	1,190
Plumber, Painter, Glazier	12.48	34.66	11.07	32.49	1,202
Cutler, Scissors, Needle, Saw, Toolmaker	11.88	32.74	11.71	34.42	1,273
Carter, Carrier, Hauler	...	...	12.52	33.00	1,275
Bargeman, Lighterman, Waterman.	14.99	30.78	14.25	31.13	1,305
Musician, Music Master	18.94	34.76	13.78	32.39	1,314

SOCIAL CAUSES OF DEGENERATION.

TABLE XX. — *Concluded.*

OCCUPATION.	MEAN ANNUAL DEATH-RATES PER 1,000 LIVING.				COMPARATIVE MORTALITY FIGURE.
	1860-1-1871.		1880-1-2.		1880-2
	YEARS OF AGE.		YEARS OF AGE.		AGE.
	25-45.	45-65.	25-45.	45-65.	25-65.
Hairdresser	15.11	30.10	13.64	33.25	1,327
Brewer	19.26	36.86	13.90	34.25	1,361
Cab, Omnibus Service	15.94	35.28	15.39	36.83	1,482
Chimney-sweep	17.53	42.87	13.73	41.54	1,519
Innkeeper, Publican	18.01	34.14	18.02	33.68	1,521
Messenger, Porter, Watchman	. . .	. . .	17.07	37.37	1,565
Filemaker	16.27	42.30	15.29	45.14	1,667
Earthenware Manufacturer	12.59	41.75	13.70	51.39	1,742
Miner (Cornwall)	11.94	41.73	14.77	53.69	1,839
Costermonger, Hawker, Street Seller	20.09	37.82	20.26	45.33	1,879
General Laborer (London)	18.35	40.64	20.62	50.85	2,020
Inn, Hotel, Servant	21.91	42.19	22.63	55.30	2,205

figures to see how far the causes of the facts can be traced. The mortality in a given occupation may be high, not because the occupation is unhealthful, but because persons of poor health are likely to resort to it.

But the entire story regarding the degenerative influences brought to bear upon the weaker classes of the community is not brought out by the study of occupational mortality. We must turn to the matter of class mortality in order to obtain this. In occupational mortality we deal only with the diseases and deaths of adults, whereas in class mortality we deal also with the diseases and deaths of minors and of incapable members of the families. In his work on "The Rate of Mortality, etc., in the Upper and Professional Classes," Mr. Charles Ansell, Jr., gives [1] the following figures: —

TABLE XXI.

Out of 100,000 Born Alive there will be Living	End First Year.	Age of 15.	Age of 60.
Peerage Families	93,038	85,890	51,166
"Upper Class experience"	91,955	83,392	53,398
"Clergy Children"	91,667	79,536	....
"English Life Tables"	85,051	68,456	36,983
"Carlisle Table"	84,610	63,000	36,430

That is, out of a hundred thousand children born in the upper classes, nearly ten thousand more will reach the age of fifteen than in the population at large. The influences which induce a higher rate of mortality among the lower classes are given by Ansell as follows: —

PHYSICAL.
1. Food insufficient in quantity and improper as to kind.
2. Deficiency of warm clothing.
3. Want or delay of medical attendance in illness.
4. Crowded and unhealthy dwellings.
5. Neglect on the part of parents (especially when the mother is at work).

[1] Table II. of work cited.

MORAL.
1. Illegitimacy.
2. Children being a burden upon or considered as such by their parents.
3. Parents having a direct pecuniary interest in the death of their children.

For our purpose perhaps the most convenient class-mortality statistics are those prepared by Dr. Grimshaw, Registrar-General of Ireland, giving the experience in Dublin for the four years 1883 to 1886, which will be found on the following page.

Commenting on these tables, Dr. Grimshaw says, "In the column referring to children under five years of age, the rates per 1,000 are found to be in the professional class, 20.52; middle, 58.25; artisan class, 69.05; general service and pauper class, 108.73."[1] The death-rates are such as to give a specially high percentage of persons under fifteen in the second and third classes.[2] The death-rate of children under five years of age is so excessive in Class IV. that the percentage of persons under fifteen is there not up to the average.

Now, let us notice how heavy a burden the condition of things here indicated imposes upon Classes III., IV., and V., as compared with Classes I. and II. Pressure is brought to bear upon the poor, and especially upon Class III. in a fourfold way. First, the number under fifteen years of age, and therefore of non-producers, is relatively high; second, the expense of a disproportionately large number of deaths is imposed upon the poor;

---

[1] British Medical Journal, vol. ii., 1887, p. 341.
[2] This fact appears in the table giving the numbers in each class by age-periods.

TABLE XXII.[1]

Annual Rate of Mortality per 1,000, Dublin, 1883–6.

Occupation or Social Position.	AGE.					
	All Ages.	0.	5.	20.	40.	60 and Upwards.
All Persons —						
Years of life	1,406,124					
Deaths	39,476					
Rate per 1,000	28.07	81.43	8.84	13.30	29.38	90.85
I. — Professional and Independent Classes —						
Years of life	122,198					
Deaths	1,857					
Rate per 1,000	15.20	20.52	2.94	6.26	12.97	51.67
II.— Middle Class —						
Years of life	230,212					
Deaths	6,034					
Rate per 1,000	26.21	58.25	7.99	13.85	29.74	157.36
III. — Artisans Class and Petty Shopkeepers —						
Years of life	430,493					
Deaths	9,902					
Rate per 1,000	23.00	69.05	8.67	11.41	23.62	61.65
IV.— General Service Class, incl. Workhouse Inmates—						
Years of life	623,221					
Deaths	21,683					
Rate per 1,000	34.79	108.73	10.38	15.45	36.93	108.37

[1] Reproduced by Billings, "Vital Statistics," p. 24.

third, the amount of sickness is disproportionately large; and, fourth, the number of births is larger than in the upper classes. Let us see what effects these influences will have upon a population of 1,000 in each class:—

TABLE XXIII.

BURDENS AND BURDEN-BEARING POWER OF 1,000 PERSONS IN VARIOUS CLASSES, POPULATION OF DUBLIN.

CLASS.	NO. OF PERSONS UNDER 15.	PERSONS OVER 15.	DEATHS.	YEARS OF SICKNESS.	YEARS OF HEALTH FOR PERSONS OVER 15.	RATIO OF SICKNESS TO EFFECTIVE HEALTH.
I.	229	771	15.20	30.40	746.5	1 : 24.5
II.	300	700	26.21	52.42	663.3	1 : 12.6
III.	322	678	23.00	46.00	645.6	1 : 14
IV. and V.	277	723	37.79	75.58	665.5	1 : 08.8

By "effective health," as used in the table, is meant the health of persons fifteen years of age or over, that is, of persons capable of doing something for their own support, and possibly for the care of relatives. It will seem from the table regarding burdens and burden-bearing power, that in Class I. there will be one year of sickness to 24.5 of effective health; in Class II. one to 12.6; in Class III. one to 14; and in Classes IV. and V. one to 8.8. Thus we have some explanation of how the high death-rate among the unfortunate classes operates to impose burdens that crush them.

There are too many assumptions involved in the derivative tables given to make it possible to consider the results reached entirely accurate, but in their general outline the figures doubtless reflect the actual situation. The fundamental and well-ascertained fact upon which all the conclusions are based is the high death-rate among the poorer classes; and, as just indicated, all that these derivative tables do is to show how and to what extent this high death-rate imposes disproportionally heavy burdens upon the poor.

It is an obvious thing that this study of mortality and morbidity reflects the results not only of the influence of environment upon individuals, but also the character of the individuals themselves. The mortality in a given class or occupation may be high either because the conditions of life are unhealthful, or because there has been selected into it unhealthy persons, or the two influences may co-operate.

We found that disease produces poverty, and we now find that poverty produces disease; that poverty comes from degeneration and incapacity, and now that degeneration and incapacity come from poverty. Yet it is not without benefit that we trace the whole dismal round of this vicious circle, for it well illustrates the interaction of social forces. A produces B, and B reacts to increase A. In biblical phrase, "The destruction of the poor is their poverty." The "unfit" aid in accomplishing their own extermination. But in tracing the long circle about which we have travelled, there have been many contributory forces added from time to time which are distinctly preventable, especially those pertaining to occupation, and many of those pertaining to the manner of living, concerning which we have said but little. Now, whenever a gratuitous cause of degeneration is introduced, there is introduced a cause of poverty which may be eliminated. A man who could have been a useful member of society, being forced by an occupational accident or disease into the vicious circle where incapacity and bad conditions interact, it is almost impossible for him to get back to the ascending grade. The helpful results of our study should be to renew the search for the preventable causes of degeneration, and to re-instil a consciousness of the necessity of improving both character and conditions, if the poor and incapable are to be turned from degeneration toward betterment.

CHAPTER V.

CHARITY AS A FACTOR IN HUMAN SELECTION.

[There is almost no literature bearing directly upon the subject of this chapter. The following treat it more or less incidentally: Malthus, "Principle of Population," 2d ed., Book IV., especially chaps. ix.-x.; Ritchie, "Pauperism in the Light of the Theory of Natural Selection" (Proceedings, Sec. VII., Congress of Charities, Chicago, 1893); Mrs. Lowell, "One Means of Preventing Pauperism" (N. C. C. 1879, pp. 189-200); Bell, "Memoir," especially chap. vi., "Upon the Causes which determine the Selection of the Deaf by the Deaf in Marriage"; Boies, "Prisoners and Paupers," chap. xv. Most of what the present writer said on the subject in a paper read before the Brooklyn Ethical Association on " The Evolution of Charities " is reproduced in the present chapter. Works dealing with selective processes among human beings are: Spencer, "Biology" (concluding chapters); also, " Negative Beneficence and Positive Beneficence;" Wallace, "Human Selection" (*Popular Science Monthly*, Vol. 38, pp. 93 ff.); Ammon, "Die Natürliche Auslese beim Menschen" (Jena, 1893), a detailed study of the selective processes found to be operating in Baden; Ward, "Psychic Factors of Civilization," Part III. On the transmission of acquired traits, see Weismann, "Heredity," and a great mass of controversial literature in the reviews and elsewhere.]

THE influence of charity in the natural history of mankind has operated in such diverse ways that many have doubted whether its influence was for good or for evil.[1]

---

[1] "I wish the art of benefiting men had kept pace with the art of destroying them; for, though war has become slow, philanthropy has remained hasty. The most melancholy of human reflections, perhaps, is that on the whole it is a question whether the benevolence of mankind does most good or harm. Great good, no doubt, philanthropy does, but then it also does great evil; it augments so much vice, it multiplies so much suffering, it brings to life such great populations

We hear it spoken of as promoting the survival of the unfit, and frequent intimations are made that its interference with the struggle for existence is essentially pernicious. Spencer's dictum that the ultimate result of shielding people from the consequences of their folly is to fill the world with fools, appears to some to justify unmitigated hard-heartedness. Our analysis of the causes of poverty must, however, make it clear that there is a possibility of almost unmixed helpfulness in charity in the future, whatever have been the results in the past. The children of misfortune can be rescued from distress, without enabling the children of degradation to "be fruitful and multiply."[1] In fact, to prevent the one result is as much the work of charity as to promote the other. When charity is willing to canvass the remote results of its activity, it may be of use not only to individuals but to the race.

The question of heredity is at bottom a biological question; and it is decidedly annoying that, just when we most desire certainty, biologists should be able to supply us with little but controverted speculations. After many

to suffer and to be vicious, that it is open to argument whether it be, or be not, an evil to the world; and this is entirely because excellent people fancy that they can do much by rapid action, that they will most benefit the world when they most relieve their own feelings, that, as soon as an evil is seen, "something" ought to be done to stay and prevent it. One may incline to hope that the balance of good over evil is in favor of benevolence; one can hardly bear to think that it is not so; but, anyhow, it is certain that there is a most heavy debit of evil, and that this burden might almost all have been spared us if philanthropists, as well as others, had not inherited from their barbarous forefathers a wild passion for instant action." Bagehot's Works, vol. iv., p. 556.

[1] See McCulloch, N. C. C., 1888, p. 154.

books have been written to explain how acquired characteristics are transmitted from parent to offspring, Professor Weismann steps out of his laboratory to deny that we have any proof that they are so transmitted. He defends his denial so shrewdly that the authors of some of the books referred to accept his view of the matter. This doubt pulverizes the foundations of nearly all that has been written of late on heredity, and of an especially large proportion of what has been written on heredity in its bearing on social life and development.

If acquired characteristics be inherited, then we have a chance permanently to improve the race independently of selection, by seeing to it that individuals acquire characteristics that it is desirable for them to transmit. But Weismann prevents our assuming, that, by improving the environment and training the individuals, we can thereby permanently improve the stock. Change of environment and special training affect only the individual; the progeny are uninfluenced by the life history of the parent. We are thus more in the dark than was for a time supposed as to the causes of variation. According to the new theory those causes are beyond our reach, and beyond our knowledge; all that we can do for the improvement of the race is to make the most possible of each individual, and, by some system of rational selection, see to it that the essentially unfit have every facility for becoming extinct. Wallace, who is inclined to think that Weismann's point is proved, suggests that if we were to take two herds of wild horses, and attempt to develop runners from one by selection without training, and from the other by training without selection, there can be no doubt that the former method would be the surest and most expeditious. Some have felt that if acquired characteristics be not inherited, the outlook for the improvement of the human race is very hopeless, since it would seem to be nature's policy to induce variations blindly, and then to weed out those individuals and strains that prove unsatisfactory. A continuous, though fortuitous, supply of the unfit would constantly be brought to birth only to be exterminated. Suspend the selective processes, and, according to Weismann, the race would not only cease to improve, but would certainly and at once begin to degenerate. Our only hope for the permanent improvement of the human stock would then seem to be through exercising an influence upon the selective processes.[1]

With the tendency which now seems to be manifest to think that Weismann has not finally made his point, at least in so far as it applies to heredity among the higher animals, we can return to the earlier, and perhaps more encouraging view, if we will; but, at the same time, the illustration suggested by Wallace must convince us that selection is a far more important factor in race improvement than the training which can be given by the most carefully adjusted environment. At the present time perhaps the best working hypothesis is to assume that Weismann is right, but remember that, whatever environment cannot do for the race, it is conceded that it is unquestionably in the highest degree important for the individual. Weismann himself shows that many of the resemblances of children to parents, which we have

[1] Kidd's "Social Evolution" is based on the hypothesis that Weismann's opinions on this point are correct; all of Spencer's social philosophy is based on the opposite assumption.

attributed to heredity, are merely the result of early environment on offspring. This has been already dwelt upon in the chapter on the personal causes of degeneration. It should also be remembered that among the higher animals, and especially among human beings, the individual is more plastic than in the lower orders; his life history, and especially the history of his very early life, has more influence upon his character. Therefore, while we must give attention to selection, we cannot conclude that certain families are degenerate and essentially unfit to survive until we have given their offspring the very best opportunities for right development. I would say, then, that to assume Weismann to be right — acquired characteristics to be not transmitted — is possibly the safest working hypothesis, because, on the one hand, it does not limit our efforts to improve environment, while, on the other hand, it gives us a sharp realization of the importance of selection, a factor which we are otherwise prone to forget or to undervalue. In other words, the charitable activity which would be essential to right doing if acquired characteristics are not transmitted, will also be the wisest method of procedure if they are. We may suspend our judgment, but need not suspend our work, while the biologists are debating the point.

To whatever extent heredity may be ascertained to be a factor in determining character and the consequent career, substantially to that extent the problem of preventing the suffering that comes from destitution is a question of human selection. The term "human selection" is used advisedly, and to describe something entirely different from that which is ordinarily understood by "natural selection." Among human beings certain highly developed but often not ineradicable instincts form part of the selective forces, and reason comes in to adapt both natural forces and animal instincts in the farther modification of the selective processes. Many who pride themselves on being scientific and logical talk about letting "natural selection" take its course, as though nature was a Something apart from man, to which he must submit, but which he might not modify. Now, either man is a part of nature, or he is not. If he is, then his benevolent instincts are as "natural" as his predatory instincts; his reasoned mastery of natural forces is as "natural" as the forces themselves. If by "nature" we mean something apart from man, then "natural selection" is not only a harsh but also an unduly long and expensive way of improving the species. It is efficient, but its next most striking characteristic is its enormous wastefulness. A hundred different characteristics may be essential to the survival of a given organism under given conditions, and to fail in one essential is as surely fatal as to fail at all. For a defect in any one of many even temporary essentials the punishment of nature is death. She makes no exception in order to save for future usefulness those who are unable to cope with local and temporary conditions, but who may be very "fit" from the standpoint of race improvement.

The method of nonsentient nature for improving a species is to make a large number of experimental variations, and then to exterminate those individuals who vary unfavorably. Among men, however, natural selection, in the sense in which that term would be applied to the killing off of young oak-trees, is very much modified by the two important factors already mentioned, which are commonly overlooked. One is the instincts of man, and the other his reasoning powers. The best example of the first is the parental instinct, which causes the parent to stand between the offspring and the remorseless operations of nonsentient nature. An example of rational selection is seen when a state enacts laws against murder, or endeavors to establish any other rule of justice than that of the strongest; when it drains a malarial swamp, or provides for sanitary inspection in order to lower the death-rate; whenever, in short, any action is taken for the set purpose of effecting the death-rate, or the birth-rate, or of promoting the public health. Mr. Ritchie has reminded us that if we are to let purely "natural" selection do its perfect work, we must abolish marriage laws and all laws relative to the inheritance of property. Instinctive selection is a step toward something better than natural selection, something more economical of time and energy and life; but the advance is still made blindly, with many halts and retrogressions and excursions into no-thoroughfares. The excessive development of the sexual instinct, which at one time is necessary to the survival and dominance of the race, may at another destroy the welfare of the race which it once promoted. It must then be dominated by reason or by other instincts, or the race will disappear. It is a very characteristic proceeding on the part of "nature" to exterminate one race because it does not possess a certain instinct, and another because it does possess that same instinct. The instinct of the fighter, once necessary to preserve him in the rude struggles of the time, may at another time bring about a "social reaction" which hangs the combative individual

CHARITY IN HUMAN SELECTION. 125

as a murderer. The instinctive impulse to aid the destitute and to keep the poor from starving, which results in more economical evolution at one time, may at another be the agent which wastefully prolongs the existence of those who are unfit from the standpoint of race improvement.

Rational selection at first, and at its poorest, is only a shade better than instinctive selection. Indeed, in cases of definite blundering it may have worse results than instinctive selection. It is hard to tell in any given case how far we should allow our reason to dominate our impulses. But it is manifest that rational selection, at its best, and in its possibilities, is the superior of the other two forms; and those races will eventually survive which practise it most constantly and most wisely. This indicates what is the simple truth, that rational selection is but a part, a form, of "natural selection," could we but understand the latter term in its broadest sense. It has been used otherwise so long, that, for the purposes of this volume, we will understand natural selection to mean that selection which results from the operation of the forces of nonsentient nature; instinctive selection that which results from the operation of inborn instincts, or incidentally from rational acts designed to accomplish other ends; and rational selection that which results from conscious human effort to modify the selective processes. "Human selection" includes all three, being made up of the total of the selective forces operating upon the human species.

Benevolence has usually been an instinct only, and has operated on the plane of instinctive selection. On the whole, we may conclude that even so it has introduced some improvements into human selection, made that selection less wasteful, and reached results with less expenditure of energy and life; that its services to the species in keeping those who were " fit," from the standpoint of race improvement, from being crushed by temporary and local conditions, overbalance its tendency to keep the essentially " unfit " in existence.

The most obvious result of charity as a selective force has been to lengthen the lives of the individuals cared for. There are many who believe it to be in and of itself a uniformly desirable result. They hold that no spark of human life can be extinguished without greater indirect loss than the direct gain which comes in freedom from the necessity of supporting the individual. They would care with all tenderness for the most misshapen physically and morally, until death could no longer be postponed. As the author has stood by the beds of consumptive or syphilitic children, he has wondered if it was a kindness to keep life in the gasping, pain-racked body. Cure was out of the question so far as medical science now knows, and one wonders why days of pain should be added to days of pain. The same questions recur as one passes through the incurable wards of an almshouse, especially as one studies the cases of the cancer-patients. The answer of religion to such questions is easy, and it seems very sure that without religious incentive we should not have entertained our present views regarding the sanctity of human life. But now that the feeling is developed, even science can explain in some sort how it is expedient that it should exist. We cannot extinguish or in any wise connive at the extinction of human life without injury to all the instincts and sensibilities that render it possible for us to live together with our fellows in civilized society. When a man, fond of hearing himself talk, advocated the immediate massacre of all Indians as the best way of solving the Indian problem, he was asked what effect he thought such a proceeding would have upon the relations of employers and employees, and upon the industrial relations of people in general. Even he did not fail to realize that it would not pay to be brutal. The imaginary hospital official whose work the colored people frequently believe it to be to shorten the agonies of the dying by hastening death, would be justified in such work neither by philanthropy nor economics, by science no more than by religion. Frequently, however, physicians and matrons and superintendents become so callous to suffering, and so worn out by overstrain, that they almost connive at the extinction of human life. For instance, in the case of a child beyond hope of cure, suffering from hydrocephalus, only the most constant attention to every circumstance of his life could keep him alive. Finally the matron somewhat relaxed her vigilance in seeing that he was properly cared for, and indigestion carried him off. This failure to do all that is conceivably possible to combat disease is common in many institutions, usually without any consciousness of a willingness to facilitate death, but none the less with a latent feeling that possibly those that die are happier than those that live. All such neglect of duty is a coming short of the highest ideal of philanthropy, no less than of religion. While physicians may sometimes be justified in chloroforming a monstrous birth, and while, far off, philosophers think they see the coming of a day when we may have legal suicides, and when we can take human life because we are pitiful, and not because we are selfish,[1] yet for the present it must be held that science justifies and philanthropy corroborates Christianity in holding that each spark of human life must be conserved in all tenderness and with all care.[2]

Another reason why it is expedient to care for all that suffer is that eventually this policy compels us to search for causes of degeneration and suffering. By assuming the burden of protection we give bonds for our final interest in prevention. Could we cheaply rid ourselves of incapables, and close our hearts to the appeal of distress, we might never have the compulsion put upon us of seeking out the wiser plans, which may eventually give us a more uniformly healthy race. Some talk as though extermination would be a remedy for pauperism. Possibly, but it would be a costly remedy biologically; and if we allow our instincts to compel us to forego the use of it, we shall eventually find something better. In view of our present slowness in resorting to wise preventive measures this may seem almost like an unsubstantial refinement; but there are already indications that, as the burden gets heavier, the search for causes and the use of prophylactics will be pushed.[3]

The influence of charity in diminishing the death-rate

---

[1] Cf. views of Felix Adler.

[2] On the powerful and pervasive influence of the altruism born of Christianity upon social and industrial development, see Kidd, "Social Evolution."

[3] "The State, assuming her highest function of protection, obtains at last her authority for prevention. Not until she assumes one will she be able to carry out the other." Dr. Kerlin, N. C. C., 1884, p. 263.

CHARITY IN HUMAN SELECTION. 129

has probably had much to do with the increase in the proportion of insane and feeble-minded persons to the total proportion. The propagation of insanity by enabling the mentally diseased to become parents will be considered later. The mere lengthening of the lives of lunatics greatly increases their absolute and relative numbers. This is one of the most conspicuous, though possibly not one of the most important, effects that the death-delaying influence of charity has upon the average quality of population.

While the intended and usual effect of charity is to diminish the death-rate, mistaken or badly administered charities may have exactly the opposite result. An unclean hospital may result in the death of an undue number of the sick brought to it. In one maternity hospital the death-rate rose as high as two women for each five confinements. Previous to and during the sixties, European experience in maternity hospitals gave a mortality rate of about one death to twenty-nine confinements. In some large hospitals it was as high as one in seven. It is only recently that hospital service has become better than home service in this branch of medical practice.[1] Undoubtedly the actual result of many foundling hospitals is to kill more infants than would meet death did such hospitals not exist. The death-rate is fearfully high; sometimes 97 per cent of the children fail to reach the age of three years; and in such circumstances the results ought to be pleasing to the most uncompromising advocate of the extermination of the "unfit." Few realize how almost impossible it is to raise babies by wholesale. Many who support chari-

[1] See Farr, " Vital Statistics," pp. 273 ff.

ties designed to save infant life might conclude, if they studied all the facts, that they were contributing to its destruction.

The influence of charity upon the death-rate can be traced with comparative ease, though not with anything like exactness. Its influence on the birth-rate is much more obscure. Long before natural selection was discussed under that name, Chalmers called attention to the fact that the relief of the poor from public funds resulted in taking money from the thrifty and giving it to the thriftless. Apparently the last possibility in the way of contributing to the survival of the unfit was reached in the administration of the unreformed English poor-law which has been already referred to. The additional allowance per child was then so large as to make it pecuniarily profitable to have them. As the allowance for illegitimate children was somewhat larger than for those born in wedlock, a premium was put upon illegitimacy. The demonstration was then complete, that a population might be ruined by the charity-induced propagation of the unfit, and that the influence of charity upon the birth-rate is a factor to be reckoned with. A system of charity which might be admissible, could it be applied to an existing generation alone, is wholly inadmissible if it multiplies the number of dependents in succeeding generations. Both Mr. Dugdale and Mr. McCulloch found that the pauper families they investigated got permission to live from the lavish giving of public out-door relief, supplemented by indiscriminate giving on the part of individuals.

In the worst managed almshouses, there is sometimes not adequate means of separating the sexes, and the breeding of paupers goes on upon the premises.[1] Formal marriages between almshouse paupers have very frequently received the sanction of both church and state. A much commoner abuse, as we shall find when we come to study these institutions, — one, in fact, from which few American almshouses are free, — is the facility with which the dissolute and diseased can go there until sufficiently recuperated to be able to have children and then discharge themselves. The doors of the hospitals and almshouses swing freely both ways, and the result is a succession of children, especially from half-witted women. These persons would have been able to have no children or few if left entirely without help, and would have been allowed to have none at all had they been properly taken care of.[2] It is coming to be seen that the feeble-minded (a much larger class than many suppose) must have custodial care through life.

While the infant death-rate is known to be increased through institutions that receive without question all children brought to them, it is more of a question, or at least one that is more difficult to answer definitely, whether or not their influence tends to increase the number of illegitimate and abandoned infants. Lax morals and open foundling hospitals usually are found together; but it is not so easy to demonstrate the causal influence of the institutions in producing laxness of morals, though that they have such an influence is usually believed. The extreme facility and secrecy with which a child could be disposed of to French foundling

[1] See as typical, Reports of the Maryland Lunacy Commission ; 2d, p. 24; 3d, p. 4; 4th, p. 8; 8th, p. 38.

[2] See Chap. VI. p. 154. Also Mrs. Lowell's "One Means of Preventing Pauperism," N. C. C., 1879.

hospitals of the older type is alleged to have had this result. The author's own observation leads him to think that foundling hospitals of the kind usual in America, because of the high death-rate already mentioned, tend to exterminate rather than to multiply the progeny of unfit stock.

A distinct influence upon the quantity and quality of the population is had by those institutions that bring defectives together to be trained, and after training them for self-support, encourage them to marry and to intermarry. This is, of course, most noticeable with the deaf because of the nature of their defect. It does not by any means incapacitate them for self-support, while at the same time it makes the companionship of deaf with deaf especially congenial. The congregate system of education of the deaf has brought them together in a way calculated to promote extensive acquaintance, and sign language tends to make them a peculiar people. It thus comes about that the institutions for the education of the deaf become very definite factors in promoting the propagation of deaf-mutism through inheritance. The latest educational tendency, and one favored by Dr. Howe, is to abandon the sign language to a considerable extent, and to encourage as far as possible the education of the deaf in day schools. This tends to assimilate them with the ordinary population, and their defect is more likely to prove a bar to marriage than under the conditions of boarding-schools.

In general it may be said that the managers of charitable institutions are too prone to encourage marriage among the dependent and defective classes. They feel that a single life is necessarily hard and unhappy, tempting to illicit sexual intercourse. With the thought of promoting to the greatest extent the happiness of the individual with whom they deal, they encourage the satisfaction, through marriage, of the sexual appetite, as they would satisfy the craving for food. The duty of being childless is not one that they try to impose upon dependents. Ritchie suggests as a possible beginning of the work of making the definition of a *mésalliance* scientific, that all persons receiving a marriage license should be required to present a medical certificate giving evidence of freedom from a hereditary tendency to insanity.[1] Experiments along the lines indicated by this suggestion are very desirable.

Members of the medical profession frequently recommend castration as a punishment for certain offences, and as a method of treatment for "sexual perverts." Boies' recent work on "Prisoners and Paupers" culminates in this recommendation. While advances in modern surgery make this a comparatively safe and painless operation, it is doubtful if it will be permitted by modern communities. At least they will have to be very much advanced beyond the present stage of opinion before it will be permitted. It is likely to be introduced first as a curative treatment in the cases of the insane and the feeble-minded. Dr. Kerlin, in addressing the Association of Medical Officers of Institutions for the Feeble-Minded, said: "While considering the help that advanced surgery is to give us, I will refer to a conviction that I have that life-long salutary results to many of our boys and girls would be realized if before adolescence the procreative organs

---

[1] "Pauperism in the Light of the Theory of Natural Selection."

were removed. My experience extends to only a single case to confirm this conviction; but when I consider the great benefit that this young woman has received, the entire arrest of an epileptic tendency, as well as the removal of inordinate desires which made her an offence to the community; when I see the tranquil, well-ordered life she is leading, her usefulness and industry in the circle in which she moves, and know that surgery has been her salvation from vice and degradation, I am deeply thankful to the benevolent lady whose loyalty to science and comprehensive charity made this operation possible." "Whose state," he asks further on, " shall be the first to legalize oöphorectomy and orchitomia for the relief and cure of radical depravity?"[1] Whenever, as in the case cited, it appears that these operations can be performed with benefit to the individual, public opinion will doubtless sanction them even now; and the result of such experimentation may ultimately be to extend their use very widely in the treatment of the diseased and criminal classes. To argue for the introduction of such methods on grounds of social selfishness will not be the best way to hasten their introduction.

Pending such experimentation, the sterilizing of the essentially unfit who may be dependents, seems likely to be carried forward by the humaner methods of sequestration, and of custodial care through life. It is partly the purpose of this book to indicate what is doing and what can be done in this line, in dealing with the various classes of dependents. The permanent isolation of the essentially unfit has commended itself to men as different as Ruskin and General Booth, and the

[1] Report, 1892, pp. 277-8.

wiser administration of charitable and penal institutions which shall make this possible, seems to be the outgrowth of tendencies already existing, and to be a reform for which the public is already in part prepared.

Certain it is, that while charity may not cease to shield the children of misfortune, it must, to an ever increasing extent, reckon with the laws of heredity, and do what it can to check the spreading curse of race deterioration. The desire to prevent suffering must extend to the desire to prevent the suffering of unborn generations.

PART II.

THE DEPENDENT CLASSES.

PART II.

THE DEPENDENT CLASSES.

CHAPTER VI.

THE ALMSHOUSE AND ITS INMATES.

[Eleventh Census, Bulletins Nos. 90 and 154, gives the statistics most completely; these will soon be superseded by the final report. All the reports of the State Boards of Charities contain valuable descriptive material; see especially those cited below. The completest description of the almshouse population of an entire State is to be found in the 10th Report of the New York State Board of Charities. For detailed accounts of particular almshouses, see "Out-Door Alms of the Town of Hartford" (Hartford, Conn., 1891); "Report on Public Institutions" (Boston, Document 192, 1892). The former Board of Charities and Reform of Wisconsin published a number of useful pamphlets on the construction and management of county poor-houses. Some of the valuable papers on the subject submitted to the National Conference of Charities and Corrections are the following: Brinkerhoff, "Infirmary Building," 1879, pp. 104–114; A. O. Wright, "Employment in Poor Houses," 1889, pp. 197–203; H. H. Giles, "Location, Construction, and Management of Poor-Houses," 1884, pp. 295–300; F. B. Sanborn, "Management of Almshouses in New England," 1884, pp. 300–306.]

THE almshouse is the fundamental institution in American poor relief. It cares for all the abjectly destitute not otherwise provided for. Its shelter is the guarantee against starvation which the State offers to all, no matter how unfortunate or degraded. Consequently the inmates of the almshouses are often the most sodden driftwood from the social wreckage of the time. It is ordinarily a depressing experience to visit an almshouse, and accordingly we find it an institution that even the benevolent willingly forget. In many of the country almshouses no clergyman comes the year around; and no friendly visitor appears to encourage the superintendent to be faithful, or to bring to light abuses that may exist. Yet, since the institution is so fundamental, and since the number of its inmates is necessarily considerable, it may be doubted whether a more profitable work can easily be found than that for right organization and proper management of almshouses. The benevolent too frequently hurry away to make excellent provision for certain classes, while the maladministration of the local almshouse leaves a large assortment of destitute people under evil conditions.[1]

In New England, except New Hampshire, where there are both county and town institutions, the town (township) is the local political unit to which the care of the poor is entrusted, and the almshouse is accordingly managed by the town officers. In the other states the almshouse is usually a county institution. "It is not uncommon for several townships or counties to form

[1] Many attempts have been made to avoid the stigma attaching to the almshouse by changing its name. "Almshouse" itself, although thought to be a better term than "poor-house" or the English "workhouse," has in its turn degenerated, so that in many States the term "County Infirmary," or "County Home," is substituted. But an almshouse by any other name is much the same institution; and to call it a "home" or "retreat" will no more remove the disgrace of inmateship, than it will remove the "institution smell" from the suds-soaked floors of the building. The "stigma," whatever it may be, comes primarily from the average character of the inmates, and secondarily, from the character and want of skill of the officers in charge.

themselves into an association, and establish what is called an "association or district almshouse."[1] A low per capita expenditure for maintenance usually results from having a large institution with many inmates; but a small institution may also be economically managed if properly located on a farm, and under an efficient superintendent.

In 1880 there were 66,203 inmates of almshouses in the United States, or one almshouse pauper to 758 inhabitants; in 1890 there were 73,045 almshouse inmates, or one to 857 inhabitants.[2] The decrease in proportion to population does not indicate a general diminution of pauperism, but merely that a historical development, already in progress, has been continued. When the work of relief is first begun by the newly formed political units of an American settlement, it is usual to board out such dependents as must be supported entirely. Farmers or others are paid to care for old people, for imbeciles, and even for sick persons who have no homes of their own. Chiefly with a view to providing a place for the better care of the dependent sick, especially incurable cases, and also to economy, a public almshouse is established. During the first stage of its development, it acts as the charitable catch-all for the community. Idiots, epileptics, incurables, incompetents, the aged, abandoned children, foundlings, women for confinement, and a considerable number of the insane, the blind, and the deaf and dumb are all dumped together into some old farmhouse that has been bought by the authorities, and put to this use. The public then

---

[1] Census Bulletin, No. 90, p. 3.
[2] Bulletin, Eleventh Census, No. 90, p. 3.

goes on its way, and thinks as little about the institution as possible, only grumbling annually at the expenses perhaps, when it happens to review public accounts.

In some populous cities the almshouses are hardly more than enlarged specimens of this same type. The different classes of dependents are still assembled in one great institution, and the public assumes it has discharged its whole duty by giving enough food and fuel to keep the individuals that make up the incongruous mass from hunger and cold.

The defective classes of teachable age, the deaf, the dumb, and the blind, were the first to be drafted off to educational institutions, usually supported by the State. Next an effort was made to have the State take care of the insane. This is now usually done so far as the acute insane are concerned, but the great expense of providing for the increasing numbers of the chronic insane has led to a suspension of their transfer from the almshouses to specialized asylums. The movement for State educational institutions for the feeble-minded has only recently made much headway, and the custodial care of feeble-minded adults in special institutions is not yet attained in more than one or two States. The first special public institution for epileptics has recently been founded in Ohio.

It was early seen that a sure way to train up paupers was to rear children in almshouses. Their mimetic tendencies and the utter lack of education, or of anything to stimulate ambition or provoke energy, guaranteed their ruin. The placing them out by the local poor-law officers gave very unsatisfactory results, as they were spoiled by the time they were old enough to do anything, and the class of people applying for them at the almshouse seldom wanted them for purposes other than service. There was consequently much agitation and some legislation to get children out of the almshouses, either into special institutions, public or private, or into suitable homes.

This differentiation of charitable work has left the old, the infirm, the decrepit, and the chronic invalids and paupers for the almshouse of the present time. A comparison of the figures of the Tenth Census with those of the Eleventh will show this change in progress, and indicate how far it has gone. The average age of almshouse paupers in 1880 was 45.1 years. In 1890 it was 51.03. The average age is lowest in the South Atlantic and the South Central divisions, where differentiation is least advanced, and highest in the Western division, where, as a rule, it is most advanced. In the far West one-half of all the almshouse paupers are between 60 and 80 years of age.[1]

The number of children in almshouses under ten years of age in 1880 and 1890 by geographical divisions is shown in the table on opposite page.[2]

It appears that the largest proportion of children, relatively though not absolutely, at both dates, was found in the South Atlantic and South Central divisions, and the smallest in the Western. In all the divisions, how-

[1] Census Bulletin, 154, pp. 1 and 5. For Census purposes the United States are arranged in the following groups: North Atlantic Division, Me., N.H., Vt., Mass., R.I., Ct., N.Y., N.J., Penn.; South Atlantic Division, Del., Md., D.C., Va., W.V., N.C., S.C., Ga., Fla.; North Central Division, O., Ind., Ill., Mich., Wis., Minn., Ia., Mo., N.D., S.D., Nebr., Kan.; South Central Division, Ky., Tenn., Ala., Miss., La., Tex., Ark.; Western Division, Mont., Wyo., Col., N.M., Ariz., Utah, Nev., Idaho, Wash., Or., Calif.

[2] Arranged from tables in Census Bulletin 154, p.4.

TABLE XXIV.

CHILDREN UNDER TEN YEARS OF AGE IN ALMSHOUSES.

	YEAR.	UNITED STATES.	NORTH ATLANTIC DIVISION.	SOUTH ATLANTIC DIVISION.	NORTH CENTRAL DIVISION.	SOUTH CENTRAL DIVISION.	WESTERN DIVISION.
NUMBER.	1880	6,902	3,021	933	2,358	517	73
	1890	4,338	1,654	779	1,375	492	38
NUMBER PER 1,000,000 INMATES.	1880	104,255	89,028	133,763	119,025	140,642	40,376
	1890	60,499	53,867	97,472	54,822	101,443	12,358

ever, there was a marked decrease in both the proportionate and absolute number of children in almshouses. Many who have been interested in the agitation for the removal of children from these institutions will be disappointed at finding that 4,338 are still so cared for — or rather so neglected. But it should be noted that of this number 793 are under one year of age, and 380 more are under two. The large number under one year of age indicates that many almshouses serve also the purpose of maternity hospitals, and that the children are not retained there after one or two years of age. On the whole, the showing of progress is satisfactory. In those communities where the burden of pauperism is light the proportion of almshouse inmates who are children is large, indicating that this is a condition of things that is tolerated in communities where relief work, because of its small volume, or for other reasons, has not drawn the interested attention of the community. A comparison

THE ALMSHOUSE AND ITS INMATES. 145

of the following table with the one just given will make this point clear: —

TABLE XXV.

PAUPERS IN ALMSHOUSES, 1880 AND 1890.

GEOGRAPHICAL DIVISIONS.	1880.			1890.		
	POPULATION.	PAUPERS.	PAUPERS PER MILLION OF POPULATION.	POPULATION.	PAUPERS.	PAUPERS PER MILLION OF POPULATION.
North Atlantic .	33,507,407	33,933	2,339	17,401,545	31,143	1,790
South Atlantic .	7,597,197	6,975	918	8,857,920	8,100	914
North Central .	17,364,111	19,811	1,141	22,362,279	25,615	1,145
South Central .	8,919,371	3,676	412	10,972,893	5,049	460
Western . . .	1,767,697	1,808	1,023	3,027,613	3,138	1,036
United States .	50,155,783	66,203	1,320	62,622,250	73,045	1,166

As to other classes of dependents in process of removal from almshouses, the figures are not given in a way to make results equally determinable, but in general it may be inferred that the decrease in the proportionate almshouse population comes not from a diminution of pauperism, but rather from the differentiation described. From other sources it is known that expenditures for relief work are in no wise falling off in the North Atlantic division, and yet this is the only section showing an important decrease in almshouse population, both absolutely and relatively to population. It is also the section where the differentiation of charitable functions has been most rapid.

If we attempt to look past the statistics and get a completer view of these more than seventy thousand people in the almshouses of the United States, we can find much material in the reports of the State Boards of Charities. Probably the completest picture of an American almshouse population ever presented was that set forth, statistically and otherwise, by the New York State Board of Charities in response to a legislative resolution passed in May, 1873. It was the beginning of differentiation in that State, and gave the basis for the agitation which resulted in removing the children from New York almshouses, and has finally brought about the removal of the insane from those institutions.

In tables on pp. 99-107 of the Tenth Annual Report of the State Board are given the leading statistical facts regarding the 12,614 inmates. They should be studied in connection with Table VII., already presented in Chapter II., of the existing causes of dependence among this same population. It will be seen by consulting the tables referred to, that, of the total, 422 were born in the almshouses, and of the remainder, 1,650 were admitted when less than ten years old. At the time of examination, nearly thirteen per cent were under ten years of age, and almost exactly the same proportion was over seventy. From the body of the Report,[1] it is learned that 3,085 of the inmates had been in the almshouses less than one year, while 38 persons had been inmates more than forty years. The average time of previous dependence for all inmates amounted to 4.88 years, not including time when they had been public charges in other institutions, or as out-door paupers.

[1] Page 103.

This gives a total of 61,595 years of almshouse care for the benefit of the persons examined. Estimating the number of temperate and intemperate persons from those whose habits were ascertained, it was concluded that 84.36 per cent of the males, and 41.97 of the females, over sixteen years of age, were intemperate. Among the insane the percentages were 79.21 and 21.44 respectively. Of the parents of the insane, reckoning, however, from a much smaller basis of exact information, it was estimated that 45.59 per cent of the fathers and 17.72 per cent of the mothers were intemperate. As to the prospects of the inmates some day becoming independent, the following conclusions, based on a very careful study of each case, were reached ;[1]

	NUMBER.	PERCENTAGE.
Permanently dependent	8,145	64.57
Will probably recover	1,116	8.85
May recover under proper training	1,379	10.93
Future doubtful	1,974	15.65

" In all the poor-houses were found, at the time of examination, more or less inmates whose ancestors were paupers, and who also had, living or dead, other near pauper relatives. The information upon this subject was obtained with considerable fulness in the rural counties, where the history of pauper families was generally well known to the officers and others assisting in the examination. In the cities, however, but little could be learned bearing upon the subject."[2]

The report farther says that the popular impression that the almshouses of the State give shelter to persons who, through misfortune in business or otherwise, have fallen from high estate, is not borne out by the facts. But few of the inmates had ever owned property to any

[1] Page 110.   [2] Page 107. See above, Ch. III, p. 86.

considerable extent. While an exceptional case was found occasionally, the mass confessed to idle and shiftless habits in early life.[1]

[1] Pages 106-07. On the other hand, the almshouses of California, and especially the San Francisco almshouse, have sheltered an unusually large number of persons of formerly high industrial and social standing and wealth. Though few in proportion to the total number of inmates, they are numerous as compared with Eastern institutions of the kind. Doubtless they were capable persons; but in a new country, and amidst a chaotic population, they risked all and lost. Some are no longer even respectable.

Nothing answers so well to bring the character of the inmates before those unfamiliar with almshouses as a detailed account of the inmates of some one institution. For this purpose an average county is selected, Chenango, N.Y. See Tenth Report, pp. 128-29.

"A man fifty-one years old, vagrant and idle, recently admitted, had a pauper sister; a man aged twenty-one years, illegitimate and an idiot, thirteen years in the State Idiot Asylum, mother licentious and dissolute; a boy thirteen years old, with congenital deformity of the lower extremities, is bright and intelligent, but entirely helpless, parents said to be temperate and respectable; an idiot, male, aged thirty-six years, thirty years an inmate, and said to be illegitimate; a girl aged sixteen years, born in the poor-house of an adjoining county, committed to this house as a vagrant at the age of fourteen years, offers but little hope of reformation; a girl eighteen years old, was thrown into the fire when an infant by her mother, who was at the time intoxicated, and sent to the poor-house, where she has since remained, is badly deformed in the face and probably without remedy; a woman aged thirty-four years and feeble-minded, has a pauper brother, but no information obtained as to her parentage; a girl fourteen years old, remarkably intelligent, two months an inmate, confirmed in habits of vagrancy and vice, and said to have been neglected in early childhood, father intemperate; a man aged forty-eight years, unknown in the county, committed on account of sickness, is believed to have been guilty of criminal practices, and probably has been in State prison; an unmarried girl, seventeen years old, fairly intelligent, recently admitted, was orphaned at the age of twelve years, since which time she has been homeless and at service; a woman, said to be one hundred and two years old, and twelve years an inmate, parentage and habits of early life unascertained; a single woman aged eighty-six years, of New England parentage, twelve

THE ALMSHOUSE AND ITS INMATES. 149

The committee appointed by the town of Hartford, Conn., to report upon out-door relief in that place, made a careful examination of the almshouse and its inmates. They found that a considerable number of the insane and imbecile were kept there under very unsatisfactory conditions, also some children suffering from paralysis or other incurable disease. The committee were at first shocked to find that some wards of the building were used as a prison to which police-court cases were sent. It seemed distressing that the "worthy poor" should be put in the same building with criminals. Further inquiry, however, showed that of the two hundred and twenty-nine adult inmates of the almshouse proper, all but nine had probably been intemperate, and that a very large proportion of them had been sentenced for crimes or misdemeanors at some time in their career. It was also found that the most notorious police-court recidivists were most likely to be or to have been in the almshouse.[1] This was an unusually bad showing, but most communities would be surprised to learn how

years in the house, is temperate, fairly intelligent and respectable, the last of her family generation, and a fair type of some twenty other inmates; an idiot boy thirteen years old, five years an inmate, is filthy and beastly in his habits, and the father said to have been grossly intemperate; a vagrant boy thirteen years old, admitted at the age of seven years, placed afterwards in an asylum, but returned to the house; an epileptic girl aged nineteen years, recently admitted, father intemperate; an insane woman fifty years old, once at the State asylum, and fourteen years an inmate of the house, abandoned by her husband, and hopelessly incurable; another insane woman, also fourteen years an inmate, after treatment at the State asylum, and likewise deserted by her husband; and a widowed woman eight years insane, two years at the State asylum, no other insanity in her family'

[1] Report of Committee, pp. xlii–xlv.

large a proportion of the inmates of their respective almshouses have been through a long experience in the police-court and jail. In San Francisco, the jail, the hospital, and the almshouse is each, in turn, the resort of the typical inmate. They come to the latter to recuperate so long as any vitality remains, and finally return there to die, when completely wrecked by dissipation and irregular living. The women are much completer wrecks than the men, because prostitution gives the idle and vicious an alternative career until the last.[1]

The disgrace that attaches to almshouse relief will not be lifted until differentiation has been carried a step farther, and there is some classification of inmates on the basis of character as disclosed in individual and family history. Reformatory institutions to which habitual drunkards, prostitutes, and other misdemeanants can be sent, and in which they must remain until reformation or death supervenes, would relieve the almshouse of many inmates, and the worthy poor of a very considerable portion of the disgrace which attaches to going there.

Of the almshouse abuses which result from the mistakes or wrong-doing of individual officials we shall say but little. Among them may be enumerated dishonest or wasteful management of the funds; culpable stinginess on the part of the appropriating power, resulting in inadequate or unhealthful food, lack of proper buildings, heating apparatus, clothing, and so forth; insanitary conditions, including dirt and vermin; and finally,

---

[1] Another factor is that women of good character are less likely than men to drift far away from all relatives, and relatives are also less likely to refuse to support them.

THE ALMSHOUSE AND ITS INMATES. 151

actual cruelty, resulting from either brutality or neglect on the part of the officials in charge. Few understand how easy it is for an official in charge of the utterly helpless to do cruel things without intentional cruelty. In the rural districts especially, abuses are apt to arise because so few persons concern themselves with the institution. The superintendent has dreary work, small pay, and practically no general recognition of his services, whether they be good or bad. A sensitive, high-minded, ambitious man is not likely to apply for or accept such a place. The incumbent is, therefore, almost of necessity a tolerably stolid, unsympathetic person, and one who has not been very successful in other lines. The officials under whom he works send to him a miscellaneous assortment of the diseased, defective, and incapable, but do not give him the proper facilities for providing for these various classes. They cut his appropriations to the lowest possible point, and he fears that any vigorous protest would lose him the place. He therefore concludes that he may as well get along as best he can, since to object would only bring some more docile man into his place. On the other hand, most of the inmates with whom he has to deal are bad-tempered, unreasonable, and inveterately querulous. They would complain no matter what might be done for them; and he gradually acts on the unrecognized impression that it does not matter what is done for them — that anything is good enough for them. He becomes brutal unconsciously, and almost in self-defence. After a few years he does, without question, things that would have seemed absolutely awful to him when he first entered on his duties. No influential person reviews and criticises his conduct, and he not unnaturally settles into the conviction that he is managing the almshouse as well as the community cares to have it managed. One can but sympathize with such an official, even when very grave abuses have grown up under his management.

There are, however, certain characteristics of our American almshouse administration which beget evil results, even when capable and conscientious officials are in charge. Among the evils of systemic origin for which the legislature or the community itself is responsible, one has just been indicated, — the neglect of the almshouse and its management by the general public.

Probably a majority of the grave evils which could be charged at the present time to the American almshouse have their origin in a lack of proper classification of inmates. Classification is of two kinds, that which takes selected cases out of the almshouses altogether and puts them in specialized institutions, and that which groups properly those that remain in the almshouse. The former has already been discussed at length, and existing faults arise chiefly from the fact that many of the States have not kept pace with the march of opinion among specialists. As regards the insane, for instance, many States have entered upon a policy of State care, and then failed to make appropriations large enough to carry out such a policy. The result has been that, after some State institutions were built, a large number of insane still remain in the local almshouses, because the special institutions are overcrowded and can receive no more. This is practically the situation in Illinois. In California the State has provided accommodations for six thousand insane, but the lunacy commissioners frequently refuse to adjudge an almshouse inmate insane, because the State institutions are so overcrowded that they say he is better left in the almshouse.[1]

In the main it may be said that, wherever the blind, the deaf and dumb, the insane, epileptics, idiots, the feeble-minded, and children are left in the local almshouse, grave abuses are sure to result, unless there is very efficient supervision; and even then the condition of affairs must be far from satisfactory.

Classification inside the almshouse is easy in proportion as the drafting off of special cases to special institutions has been practised; but it is always important, and in some of its branches calls for constant care and readjustment. 1. The separation of the sexes. In small institutions their constant and complete separation involves practical difficulties, and occasionally a hideous condition of affairs is brought to light. 2. Classification by color, resulting in almost duplicate institutions. 3. Isolation of defectives. It is partly because this separation is so frequently out of the question that they ought not to be here huddled together. 4. Special provision for the sick. From one-tenth to one-half the inmates are often practically bedridden. A special ward for syphilitics is often necessary, even in small institutions. Cancer patients must be isolated because of the offensive nature of their malady; and, in view of recent evidence as to the origin of consumption, those suffering with this disease ought also to be separated from the others.

---

[1] For illustrations of abuses resulting from almshouse care of the insane, see Report of the Illinois State Board of Public Charities for 1890, p. 104.

5. Classification by age. This is especially necessary where there are children, but is usually not practised. Young vagabonds and loafers drift into almshouses during the winter, and those who are virtually boys give themselves over for instruction in the arts of vice to the old and decaying devotees of sensuality.[1] 6. Classification according to character for reasons indicated in discussing classification on the basis of age. This is usually not attempted, and can only be carried out profitably where the matron or superintendent has great tact, patience, and ingenuity. In the San Francisco almshouse, instead of wards they have a large number of rooms — a form of construction which under the ordinary official would be very undesirable, but which has here been used to good purpose to give the self-respecting and improvable cases a semi-privacy which they value.[2]

[1] "Before the demand for reform was made, several hundred men were herded together in the basement of the almshouse in what was known as 'Congress Hall.' There the brutal and the weak, the young and the old, the vicious and the simply unfortunate, were crowded together in the way most favorable to moral decomposition and to the destruction of all self-respect." Report on the Charities of Baltimore, published in the proceedings of a local conference on charities, 1887, p. 142.

[2] This institution is in charge of Mr. and Mrs. P. L. Weaver. The latter is a sister of the late General Armstrong of Hampton School, and the missionary spirit is strong within her. Especially on the women's side her methods of classification have wrought notable results. Those who are ambitious in a way, and anxious to keep their rooms in good order, are grouped in the rooms along one corridor, while certain women who have no ambition and no willingness to do anything unless compelled to it, have rooms along another corridor. The inmates themselves have called the first "Grand Hall," and the second "Pauper Alley." Women of one of these localities are disinclined to associate with those of the other. In filling the various rooms, constant effort is necessary to adapt properly the dispositions of the

THE ALMSHOUSE AND ITS INMATES. 155

The second great evil which springs, not from the character of the officials, but from the nature of our almshouse organization, is laxness regarding admission and discharge of inmates. Since every person is entitled to be saved from starvation and death from exposure, and as that is nearly all that the almshouse does for its beneficiaries, anyone that wills to claim its shelter can have it. On the other hand, as it is not a penal institution, and as it is to the interest of no one to have persons stay there who can support themselves outside, an inmate wishing to discharge himself is allowed to do so. The average almshouse official regards the justification of our laxness indicated above as entirely conclusive. Whatever official or board may have the legal right of admitting or discharging inmates, the right of applicants to be admitted or discharged is regarded as inalienable. The door swings, accordingly, outward or inward with the greatest ease. Even the unduly lax rules regarding detention enforced in the English workhouse are unknown with us.

The results of this apparently defensible practice are thoroughly bad. Of the abuses to which it gives rise we may mention as first and least the support by the county of persons having pensions or property, or rela-

several occupants. Mrs. Weaver at one time had quite a number of inmates with whom no one wished to room to provide for, because they were such terrific snorers. They were not even congenial associates for each other. She finally hit on the device of putting a snorer in a room with a woman who was hard of hearing. This plan worked admirably. This almost absurd illustration shows what inventiveness and constant personal attention are necessary in order to fit the inmates of an institution properly together. The method ordinarily is to suppress the individualities of the inmates, and to coerce them into living side by side in long wards.

tives able to support them. In some States, even where it is found after death that an almshouse inmate had considerable property, no attempt is made to recoup the county or town for the outlay.[1] A second and more serious abuse is the making of the almshouse a winter resort for tramps, and a place where the drunkard and the prostitute can recuperate between debauches. The Hartford Committee thus describes the life of drunken almshouse recidivists : —

"They present themselves, or are brought, not infrequently ragged, filthy, shoeless, shivering with incipient delirium, at the office of the selectmen, receive a card, and are transported to the almshouse. There they are bathed, clad in a new suit, if necessary sent to the infirmary, carefully nursed out of their delirium, fed when convalescent upon whiskey and milk. A few days' work follow, prolonged into weeks, perhaps, if it be midwinter ; only a few of those who can get away staying during the summer. The work, otherwise beyond their impaired forces, is made bearable, it may be, by occasional stimulants. Presently — and it is never long delayed — comes the drawing toward the old life ; there is nothing to restrain them, and the bird has flown. Almost before his absence has been well noted, he is back again. The new suit has been pawned, or reduced to rags and filth by two or three days' debauch, and there follows bath, a second suit, more whiskey and milk, a feeble attempt at work, another flight, another debauch, a third application for ticket at the halls of record, — and so on in a vicious circle as unending as the patience of the first selectman and the indifference of the Hartford tax-payer." [2]

This description is in general terms, but particular instances are given. One woman came and went thir-

[1] A number of San Francisco misers have had themselves supported at the almshouse.
[2] Report, pp. xiv, xvi.

THE ALMSHOUSE AND ITS INMATES. 157

teen times in twenty-two and one-half months. A man who went and came at pleasure had allotted to him, in the course of two years and seventeen days, clothing which at wholesale prices amounted in value to $85.28. Two pages of the Report are filled with an itemized account of this clothing. The man was receiving during all this time a pension of $8.00 per month from the Federal government. In some institutions inmates are given passes for ten days or more.[1]

The final and worst result of permitting the destitute to admit and discharge themselves at will is that it enables the dissolute and degenerate to have offspring "after their kind." The results are most manifest in the cases of feeble-minded women.[2] Mr. Charles Booth gives an instance of an English woman who in a little

[1] See comments of a special committee appointed by the mayor of Boston to inspect the Public Institutions ; Report, June, 1892, p. 40.

[2] From the same Report, pp. 28-29, the following is taken : —

Facts concerning Fifty-six Women who were in the Home for Paupers in 1891, who had Illegitimate Children, many of them born in the Home.

  3 had been in Deer Island, drunkards.
  1 had been in Deer Island, drunkard, prostitute, specific disease, very bad woman.
  1 had been in Deer Island, prostitute.
  3   "   "   specific disease.
  2   "   "
  6 were drunkards.
  3 had specific disease.
  2 had three children each, and were feeble-minded.
  3   "   "   "   prostitutes.
  1   "   "
  1 had four children, had been at Deer Island, had specific disease, prostitute, and drunkard.
  1 had two children.
29 had one child each ; nothing further was known.

more than eight years presented the rural workhouse at Ashby-de-la-Zouch with five illegitimate children. In

RECORD OF THE LIVES OF TWO OF THE ABOVE WOMEN.

A.

(H. P. *stands for Home for Paupers — almshouse;* M. S. H., *Marcella-street Home — for children.*)

1885	Mar.	Admitted to H. P. Aged 32.
"	Sept. 12	Admitted to H. P. Baby A born October at H. P.
"	Nov. 17	Discharged from H. P.
"	Nov. 18	Admitted to H. P.
1886	April 30	Discharged from H. P.
"	July 26	Admitted to H. P.
1887	Mar. 12	Discharged from H. P. Baby A placed at M. S. H.
"	Nov. 7	Admitted to H. P.
1888	Mar. 8	Admitted to H. P. Baby B born at H. P.
1889	April 17	Discharged from H. P. Baby B placed in M. S. H.
1890	Sept. 29	Admitted to H. P.
1891	Jan. 19	Baby C born at H. P.
1892	Mar.	Admitted to H. P.
"	April 23	Baby C placed in M. S. H.
"	" 2	Discharged from H. P.

B. — (*A Woman Thirty-four Years Old, feeble-minded.*)

1886	Oct. 13	Admitted to H. P.
"	Dec.	Baby A born in H. P.
1888	Aug. 15	Admitted to H. P.
"	Nov.	Baby B born in H. P.
1890		Baby A placed in M. S. H.
"	Mar. 17	Admitted to H. P.
"	June	Baby B placed in M. S. H.
1891	Sept.	Baby C born.
		Married.
1892	April	Admitted to H. P. Expecting confinement.

"These two young women, one of whom is now at liberty on the city streets, have cost the city for the board of their five illegitimate children, still at Marcella-street Home, the sum of $1,855.53. Two of these children are defective and will long be a care to the city. Women like these have no will-power of their own; they need restraint for their own good. They are too weak to withstand temptation, and should not thus needlessly be allowed to walk into it."

the workhouse this woman was capable and industrious, and a good nurse.[1] After numerous examples in her paper entitled "One Means of Preventing Pauperism," Mrs. Lowell says: "I speak chiefly of women, because they form the visible links in the direful chain of hereditary pauperism and disease; but it must not be forgotten that the treatment here prescribed for them [indeterminate sentence to reformatory institutions] should also be applied to the reformation of the men, whose evil propensities are likewise handed down from one generation to another."[2]

A third very prevalent evil in the management of American almshouses is lack of a work-test, and a failure to enforce proper discipline among the inmates. This is placed among the evils of systemic origin because, while in some places an energetic and specially capable official may overcome all obstacles and enforce discipline and compel work, yet such an undertaking is usually discouraged, or at least not encouraged, by the authorities, and the sentiment of the community and the nature of legislation are usually such as to make this course difficult.

In small rural communities an almshouse is sometimes self-supporting. This usually means that the county or town owns a farm of moderate size, and that a thoroughly good farmer has been employed as superintendent. As a rule, not more than twenty per cent of the expenses of an almshouse can be defrayed by the work of the inmates. Often certain classes of the insane are the most efficient workers, and their presence in the almshouse contributes much towards making it self-supporting. But many of them are incapacitated by disease

[1] "Pauperism," etc., pp. 117–18. [2] N. C. C., 1879, p. 195.

or old age for any work at all. Under the average superintendent, as a rule, it costs more to set the inmates of an almshouse to work than their work is worth. That is, a given number of inmates can be supported more cheaply in idleness than when they are put to work. It is for this reason that the labor in the English "workhouse" has degenerated so persistently into mere task-work.

The advantage to the management in obliging all inmates capable of doing anything to work consists in the deterrent influence of this policy upon would-be applicants. It is the surest and most commendable deterrent known. Its influence is especially valuable in preventing tramps from using the institution as a winter clubhouse. The Mayor of Baltimore complains repeatedly that tramps from all over the United States come there to winter in the almshouse, because it has the reputation of being especially comfortable. Tramps would not gravitate there very fast if they knew that they would merely obtain a chance to work hard for board and lodging during the winter. In most almshouses the main part of the work that can be offered to men is on a farm or in the garden. This kind of work is unavailable in the winter, just at the time when a rigid work-test is most essential. The number of women inmates is relatively so few that usually they can find sufficient employment in taking care of the house and in doing the laundry-work and sewing. In many institutions no inmate is required to work unless he is willing to do so. Some superintendents seem to think it the height of brutality to ask an inmate to do anything against his will. As much service as can be utilized is usually obtained (from the inmates) by offering extra rations of food and tobacco.

From the side of the inmates, work for all is desirable because they are happier for having it. About the only happy persons one finds in an almshouse are those who are occupied. Idleness conduces to restlessness, sensuality, bad temper, and various forms of nervous disorder. In almshouses, as well as in prisons, insane asylums, and other kinds of institutions, discipline is doubly hard when the inmates are idle. That idleness in and of itself brings misery can be seen by any one who passes through one of our Soldiers' Homes, especially the magnificent one for soldiers of the regular army at Washington. So well is this fact now ascertained that special societies are formed in the large cities for giving employment to the inmates of the great public institutions. There ought to be similar societies, or at least similar work done, in our rural communities; if it accomplished nothing else, it would at least interest some of the influential classes in the neglected institutions of the locality.

If there could be in American almshouses thorough investigation of all applicants for admission and all applications for dismissal, if within the institution there could be a thorough classification, thorough discipline, and an intelligent and kindly application of the work-test to all capable of doing anything at all, there would be no danger that almshouses would be overcrowded; while at the same time they would afford cleanly and honorable relief to the real children of misfortune. After some centuries of experiment, England has not realized this ideal, and we are very far from doing so; but it must be realized before the basis of our system of public and private charities can be considered sound.

CHAPTER VII.

RELIEF OF THE POOR IN THEIR HOMES.

[Fowle, " The Poor Law " (London, 1890), gives a comprehensive and satisfactory review of English poor-law experience. The most accessible documents regarding the reform of the English Poor Law in 1834 are " Extracts from the Information Received as to the Administration and Operation of the Poor Laws " (London, 1833), and " Report of the Poor Law Commissioners " (London, 1834). Reports of the State Boards of Charities of Pennsylvania and of New York contain very good statistics. Low, N. C. C., 1879, pp. 200–210, describes Brooklyn's experience; N. C. C., 1881, pp. 144–154, he contributes a paper on the general subject. Mrs. C. R. Lowell has written much and effectively against the system, see N. C. C., 1890, pp. 81–91, and Committee Report to New York State Board of Charities, 1884; both are reprinted. A symposium on the subject, N. C. C., 1891, pp. 28–49. Sanborn in favor of the system, N. C. C., 1890, pp. 73–80. Descriptions of out-door relief in particular places are given of Brookline by Joseph Lee, *State Charities Record*, April, 1892 (same experience, Mrs. Codman, N. C. C., 1891, pp. 46–49); of Hartford, Conn., by a committee reporting " On the Advisability of Establishing a Workhouse," 1887. The last two are also of general interest, giving data gathered from many places and times.]

THERE are absolutely no reliable statistics of out-door relief in the United States as a whole. The census figures of 1880 are avowedly incomplete, and those of 1890 cannot be expected to be much better. Out-door relief in the United States is given by county and township officials; and from its nature the book-keeping is likely to be even more faulty, especially as to the number of persons aided, than is that of almshouses. In addition to this, out-door relief does not have the same meaning in different places and according to different laws. In England it usually means all relief that is given outside of the workhouse. The indigent insane, consequently, who are relieved in special institutions, are classed among those receiving out-door relief, though, as Mr. Sanborn suggests, if anybody is in-doors, it is apt to be the indigent insane. The same policy is followed in the United States, where English precedents have obtained. For instance, in Massachusetts what is called "State out-door relief" is given very largely to cases of the sick poor chargeable to the State, who are placed in hospitals, and their expenses defrayed from the funds at the disposal of the State Board of Lunacy and Charity. Cases of dangerous disease are also provided for under the same heading; and, finally, the administrative expenses of the department are reckoned in with the amount spent for out-door relief; consequently, only a small modicum of the expenditure really goes in temporary aid to the poor in their own homes.[1] Those who dispute about the advisability of out-door relief often confuse themselves and each other by sometimes including and sometimes excluding such relief when given from private funds. Unless otherwise specified, the term out-door relief, as used in this chapter and volume, will mean the relief given from public funds to the poor in their homes, not including medical relief.

The most available summary of pauperism in a given State is perhaps that of Joseph Lee on Out-door Relief in Massachusetts. A map giving a comparison of

[1] See Report of State Board of Lunacy and Charity, 1893, pp. 38–41.

in-door and out-door relief by towns in the State of Massachusetts is reproduced herewith : —

As nearly as can be gathered, the amount of out-door relief in six States, where the facts are readily available, is as follows : —

TABLE XXVI.

OUT-DOOR RELIEF IN SIX STATES.

STATE.	YEAR.	NUMBER RELIEVED.	EXPENSE.	POPULATION, 1890.	REFERENCE.
Pennsylvania . .	1892.	25,029	a $474,347.78	5,258,014	Report State Board, p. 349, Causes, 368.
New York .	End Sept. 30, 1892.	131,439	681,934.99	5,997,853	*Ib.*, p. 57.
Michigan .	1889.	39,115	420,829.13	2,093,889	*Ib.*, p. 118.
Ohio . .	1891.	67,927	442,282.51	3,672,316	*Ib.*, p. 7 and p. 523.
Wisconsin	End March 30, 1892.	4,492	148,691.45	1,686,880	*Ib.*, p. 375.
California	1893.	. . .	b 304,790.00	1,208,130	Unpublished thesis, by R. C. Root.
TOTAL . .	. . .	293,031	$2,472,875.86	19,917,082	

a Includes $3,416.84 for transportation.
b Estimated for about half the counties.

The reports of the State Boards of Charity are furthermore likely to be especially inaccurate regarding local affairs.

In most of the Western States, as, for instance, in California, there is no State official to whom the county and township authorities are called upon to report.

RELIEF OF THE POOR IN THEIR HOMES. 165

They publish no annual accounts, except such as may be found in the local papers annually or semi-annually; and those who have undertaken to study the problem of out-door relief in these States have had to get their facts by personal visits or correspondence with the local officials.[1] The Southern States seldom give out-door relief.

The whole problem of out-door relief has been worked up statistically and otherwise with special thoroughness for the two towns of Hartford and New Haven. In Hartford it was found that with a population of about 45,000 the net expense for all relief was $93,344.73; the gross expense for out-door relief was $40,372.84, or 90 cents per capita.[2]

Mr. Sanborn and others would dissent from the statement made at the beginning of the preceding chapter that the almshouse is the fundamental institution in the

---

[1] This has been the experience of Professor C. R. Henderson of the University of Chicago, who undertook to prepare a paper on the history of out-door relief in the United States for the Conference of Charities of 1894. He obligingly favored me with an opportunity to consult his paper before its appearance in print. The best statistics that he was able to gather were confessedly fragmentary and unreliable."

[2] See Tables, p. 1, of Report of Hartford Committee on Out-door Relief. In England the report is made on the total number of persons receiving in-door and out-door relief on particular days, — on the last day of each week for London. The papers consequently give to the public a tolerably accurate account of the extent of pauperism at any given time. The *Weekly London Times* contains statistics of metropolitan pauperism, in-door and out-door, each week. The number of out-door paupers in England on the first day of July, 1890, was 507,689. (Booth's "Pauperism," p. 163.) This return for a single day, of course does not show fully the number of persons relieved in the course of a year, but it is the best system of return where it is desired to avoid duplicates. The date selected also is not one at which the number of dependent persons would be the greatest.

relief of the poor. They would say that the system of relieving the poor should be founded upon family relief, or what is generally called out-door relief, that is, the relief of the poor in their own homes. They point to the fact that this is one of the kindliest, and may be one of the cheapest, forms of alleviating distress, especially incipient distress, and say that only after a case has been found to belong to some special class, requiring institutional care, should it be passed on to the limitations of institution life. On the other hand, there are those who believe it to the interests of the poor and of the whole community to demand the total abolition of out-door relief; who point again and again to the English experience under an unreformed poor-law before 1834, and to the many disastrous experiments in out-door relief in this country.

The following may be mentioned as the principal reasons assigned by those who believe in the maintenance of out-door relief as a fundamental part of the relieving system : —

1. It is believed to be kindly. The poor person is not separated from relatives and friends, families are not broken up, and the receipt of relief is not as conspicuous and consequently as disgraceful as it is where resort must be had to an institution.

2. It is apparently economical. Many families can almost support themselves, and it seems folly to dismember them and place the children in refuges or board them in private families, and compel the adults to resort to the poorhouse, when a little relief given in the home would keep the family together and enable them to make part of their support by ordinary methods. Those who

receive out-door relief receive usually less than it would cost to maintain the same number of persons in the almshouse.

3. There are not institutions enough. The demand for relief always keeps considerably in advance of the supply; and it would be uneconomical, and in fact impossible, to have buildings enough to accommodate all who should be relieved from time to time. Especially in the winter months, a large number of persons need relieving for a short time; and if the almshouses were large enough to accommodate them during the winter, there would be great buildings vacant during the summer.

This gives certainly a good *prima facie* case for the retention of a certain amount of out-door relief. On the other side the following considerations are urged: —

1. It increases the number of applicants, because it is less manifestly disgraceful than the in-door system, and is much more pleasant to receive for other obvious reasons. The saving in cost for a single person supported is more than made up by the additional number of persons that will claim to require relief. It is a sufficiently pleasant form of being relieved, so that if no requirement except indigency is made, a large number of persons will become duly indigent in order to qualify for the receipt of alms.

2. It is urged that out-door relief is undesirable, because it requires an amount of discrimination between cases that is practically impossible where the work is done by public officials. It has long been a principle that any work was suitable for a government to do in proportion as it could be reduced to a routine and done in a semi-mechanical way. As the work of giving out-

door relief cannot be done in this semi-mechanical way, it is unsuitable for public officials to undertake.

3. It is urged that corruption of politics results from the system, and that, in fact, the whole tone of the population is lowered where this form of relief is given. In many cases, it is unworthy motives favoring the retention of the system that makes it difficult to secure its abolition.

4. Where out-door relief has been given lavishly, as in England at some times and places, it has simply resulted in reducing the rate of wages, the amount given in relief being reckoned on as a possible resource, so that the employee would accept lower wages than would otherwise have been possible.

Those who favor the system of out-door relief usually argue upon theory, or draw their facts from rural communities where the problems are comparatively simple, and where abuses are readily checked.

On the other hand, the opposers of the system deal mainly with facts, and these facts very largely gleaned from the administration of out-door relief in large cities.

The most instructive experiments that have been made in this matter in the United States have consisted chiefly in cutting off peremptorily the supply of out-door relief. The two stock cases of this sort are Brooklyn and Philadelphia. The first was reported to the National Conference of Charities in 1879 by Seth Low, under whose administration as mayor the change had been accomplished. The account of this experiment is given in Mr. Low's own words:—

"Out-door relief, so-called, began in Brooklyn in 1851-52. For the year ending July 31, 1852, the number of people helped was

RELIEF OF THE POOR IN THEIR HOMES 169

6,754, at a cost of $7,139.99. With some variations this had grown in 1864 to 20,743 persons helped, at a cost of $25,921.47. In 1865 the general demoralization which set in after the war placed a corrupt man in charge of the poor-funds, and the figures bear witness to the result. From that moment bad became worse uninterruptedly. In 1865, while only 1,500 more people were helped than in 1864, it cost the county $72,708.97, against $25,921.47 in 1864, an increase of $46,000 in a single year. In 1877 help was given to 46,350 persons, or nearly one-tenth of the population, at a cost of $141,207.35. For the six years from 1872 to 1877, an average of 35,109 were helped at an average cost of $114,943.72. The total outlay for this period of six years by Kings County for out-door relief alone was $689,662.35. To such an item at last had grown the kindly and apparently harmless thing. The population of Kings County is estimated in round numbers to have been in 1852, 150,000; in 1864, 320,000; in 1877, 550,000.

"The system had become furthermore a sore on the body politic. The friends of politicians received help whether needy or not, and so the system was perpetuated. Families with voters were the first served. The 'out-door relief' appropriations became a vast political corruption fund. Large numbers of the population were taught to rely on the county help, and sought it for no other reason than that the county gave it. One woman received help under nine different names. Many sold what they received. Men came from the country every autumn to live at the expense of the city during the winter, because the city was offering a premium to the idle to come there and live in idleness. The poor did not get the chief benefit of increased appropriations. Most of it went to underlings connected with the work of distribution. In every way, and in every direction, the effect was hopelessly bad.

"In 1875 the Commissioners of Charity employed paid visitors to investigate the cases of applicants for relief; and it cost sixty cents to distribute every dollar's worth of food or fuel. This was so monstrous that public clamor compelled a change. In 1876 the visiting system was abandoned, and all applicants were compelled to take oath that they were paupers. As may be imagined, the result was horrible. Moreover, many who lived in New York availed themselves of such easy opportunity to be fed by Brooklyn.

. . . .

"In 1877 a committee of volunteer visitors was organized, who agreed to investigate the cases of all applicants for relief. Their services, fortunately, were accepted by the Charity Commissioners. These visitors were not given power to control the distribution of relief, but could only report. They did not directly accomplish much. But they saw thoroughly the working of the system, and came to the conclusion that 'out-door relief' could not be administered by the county so as to be worth giving. The following year, 1878, the volunteer visitors so reported to the Charity Commissioners and to the Board of Supervisors. The visitors said, however, that as out-door relief had been given for so long, and many of the poor had been educated, in a sense, to depend upon such help, they would continue to visit for that year also, provided nothing should be distributed excepting coal. The visitors suggested that the year following even coal might properly be withheld. . . . Long attention to the subject had convinced some that 'out-door relief,' on the part of the county, was not legal under the laws of the State. At this crisis, through friends in the Board of Supervisors, the question of legality was referred to the counsel of the board.

"The opinion of counsel was delivered at a meeting of the Board of Supervisors, held Jan. 31, 1878. It was to the effect that, in the absence of special laws authorizing it, the system of out-door relief was contrary to the general poor-law of the State of New York. This opinion prevented an appropriation for out-door relief in Kings County during the last winter, 1878–79. Many anticipated great and unusual suffering among the poor by consequence. The testimony of the private relief associations, and of many who give much time personally to visiting among the poor, is all to the same effect. The poor have suffered less this winter in Brooklyn than either last year or the winter before. The saving in the interests of morality cannot be expressed in money."[1]

[1] National Conference of Charities, 1879, pp. 202–04.

Philadelphia in 1879 had a similar experience. The amount distributed in out-door relief in 1875, also in 1876, was $82,000, and in 1879, $66,000. The supply of relief was then cut off peremptorily; and while the secretary of the Society for Organizing Charity reports that there was for a time a somewhat greater pressure upon private relieving agencies, the pressure soon passed away, and the demand for relief was not greater than it had been, while the population of the almshouse decreased, even in the face of the increasing population of the city.

The only suggestion that has ever been made as to evil results from the experiment in Brooklyn, is that the number of dependent children increased after out-door relief had ceased to be given. But the number of dependent children also increased in other parts of New York, where no change in out-door relief administration had occurred, indicating that it was a change in the laws affecting dependency among children that produced the increase. I have never heard of any well-authenticated instance where out-door relief was stopped and where the population of the public charitable institutions subsequently increased. In other words, as administered in the United States, it is found apparently, that out-door relief educates more people for the almshouse than it keeps out of it, and that therefore it is neither economical nor kindly.[1]

[1] Almost the only report that has been made in favor of out-door relief was that of the Committee of the Boston Overseers of the Poor in 1888; but a report by the committee in favor of the system was said to be a foregone conclusion, and certainly the facts adduced do not in any obvious degree support their conclusions. A correspondent of *The Boston Herald*, Aug. 14, 1888, apropos of their report, gives an anal-

An example of out-door relief at its best, but still held to be injudicious and harmful, is found in the village of Brookline, a suburb of Boston. The administration of relief had there been in the hands of certain women trustees, who gave out-door relief with a work-test during a series of years; but on the erection of an almshouse the expenses for the relief of the poor greatly diminished without hardship to the dependents, on whom the effects of the change were said to be good. Previous to 1883 the overseers of Brookline were giving full or partial support to 150 persons, exclusive of the insane. These were warned three months in advance that no pauper rent would be paid after May 1st, but that the almshouse would be open to any one needing shelter. On the 1st of May, 22 adults and 7 families, numbering 33 persons, became self-supporting; 10 adults and 9 families, consisting of 39 persons, assumed the payment of their own rent, asking only partial support from the town, and in no case was the offer of the almshouse accepted. The total expenditure for poor relief for the town fell from $8,487.50 in 1882, to $7,794.49 in 1883, and has never gone back to the old figure, although the population has increased more than 3,000. Besides, the charge for the care of the insane, a class independent of the out-door system, has been heavy, and in the total expenditures for the support of the poor, five per cent interest on the cost of the almshouse was included. The total cost of caring for the poor in 1893

ysis of 73 cases that have been relieved with more or less regularity by the Overseers of the Poor from 1883 to 1888; and the conclusion reached on the basis of the facts ascertained was that out-door relief as there administered was a bad thing for the community.

was $7,218.28.[1] Mrs. Codman says: "I have no hesitation in saying that the whole tone of the population has been raised, and that to 'come upon the town,' at one time regarded as the natural and proper thing to be done, is now looked upon as a disgrace. As a proof of this, it has several times happened that when, through illness or temporary disability, relief has been given to a family, on the coming of better times the amount of that relief has been voluntarily paid back into the town treasury, in order to escape the stigma of the name of pauper. Self-respect and independence have been encouraged, and the race of paupers within our limits has very nearly disappeared." [2]

In Wisconsin it has repeatedly been the case that, when an almshouse was built, the expense for poor relief decreased by half, and the moral tone of the community improved.[3]

Both Dugdale and McCulloch held out-door relief to be largely responsible for the persistence of the pauper families they studied.[4]

It may be that the system of out-door relief is especially difficult to administer under the county system of local

[1] Pamphlet by Joyce, pp. 3-5.

[2] Mrs. Codman, N. C. C., 1891, p. 49. It should be said that Brookline is a thriving and fashionable residence suburb of Boston, and the character of the population added from year to year has not been such as to lead one to expect a proportionate increase of pauperism.

[3] Rep. of State Board of Control, 1892, p. 374.

[4] Dugdale comments as follows: "Lavish public charity becoming a custom, it is manifest that certain families receiving help generation after generation will display a persistence of dependence identical in form to that produced by hereditary pauperism from physical degeneration, but entirely different in nature, and as easy to suppress as true hereditary pauperism is difficult to control." (N. C. C., 1877, p. 94.)

government. In the smaller townships the officials are measurably well acquainted with the people, at least until the population becomes dense, and the people scrutinize public expenditures quite carefully. Under the county system, until the population is large enough to compel the employment of special officials, the writing of orders for out-door relief is frequently left to the individual supervisors or commissioners. As a rule, each one attends to all applications from the district from which he is elected, and the approval of the entire board is a mere formality. The payments are sometimes made in money, sometimes in orders on stores, and sometimes relief is given in goods purchased by the authorities under contract. Obviously this latter method lends itself least readily to abuse. Where orders are given on stores, the goods selected by the beneficiary are often absurdly unsuitable to his condition,[1] and in the state of California such orders are frequently traded for liquor.

On the whole, it must be admitted that the advisability of giving out-door relief is a question of administration. Under the Elberfeld system in Germany, and with the great care exercised by the *Bureaux de Bienfaisance* of France, it has been successful. But it must be remembered that the people of the United States have a larger share of administrative awkwardness than any other civilized population. Nearly all the experiences in this country indicate that out-door relief is a source of corruption to politics, of expense to the community, and of

[1] See Hartford Report, pp. xix, xx, and Table VII. On 594 orders, 132 articles were drawn, among which were canned lobster, green pease, pie, pineapple, canned salmon, and tobacco. There was also some evidence that the orders were used in trade and payment of debts.

RELIEF OF THE POOR IN THEIR HOMES. 175

degradation and increased pauperization to the poor. Whether at its worst or at its best, it has not been found a satisfactory method of relieving distress. In the new communities of the West it has seemed to be almost necessary; but it is always to be watched with care, to be kept at a minimum, and in large cities to be definitely prohibited.

Finally something must be said regarding private our-door relief.

In all large centres of population, there are certain societies, which, together with the churches and private individuals, do a considerable amount of relief-work. These agencies dispense an amount which is not large, as compared with public expenditures for the relief of the poor, but which is sufficient to accomplish a great deal of good or a great deal of evil in the populations among which it is scattered. Those who, like Mrs. Lowell and others, insist that public out-door relief should be abolished, believe in this extension of private associations to care for the cases to whom the alternative of going to the almshouse would be an unmerited hardship. They insist that the private associations are more economical, and more discriminating, and since their treasuries are not replenished from the proceeds of taxation, but from free-will offerings, the poor cannot make demands upon them as of right. The experience of Chalmers is constantly pointed to as showing that public relief can be swept away entirely, and private benevolence take its place. While those who would imitate him would not go as far as he did, they do ask for the substitution of private for public out-door relief. For the present, under existing conditions, in the United States, their case apparently is well made out. It is undoubtedly true that private associations are best fitted to deal with incipient dependency. But it should not be forgotten that private charities are just as open to abuse as public ones, though not to exactly the same abuses. In places where the State has relegated much of the work of relieving the poor to private benevolence, and especially to the church, abuses have grown up of as great magnitude as those that preceded the reform of the English poor-law in 1834. In Italy, where, until recently, the church administered vast relief-funds, those who wish to reform the system of relieving the poor are said to look with envy upon the English system of out-door relief as forming a rational and modifiable basis for charities.[1] At Elberfeld also the present excellent public system originated in a break-down of the private system. There is a possibility of success or failure by either method; but experience seems to indicate that in the United States, at the present time, private is much safer and more helpful than public out-door relief, and indeed that the latter should usually be discontinued.

[1] As good an economist as Professor Alfred Marshall believes that the English system of out-door relief may be modified and made useful, and that this should be done rather than that the system should be swept away. Mr. Bosanquet, of the Charity Organization Society of London, doubts his conclusions, and thinks that the conditions of 1834 were not temporary, but that the conclusion then reached by the Charity Commissioners, that out-door relief should be abolished *in toto*, still holds. (See *Economic Journal*, vol. ii., pp. 186–191, and for Mr. Bosanquet's reply, and Professor Marshall's rejoinder, ib., pp. 369–379.)

CHAPTER VIII.

THE UNEMPLOYED AND THE HOMELESS POOR.

[The completest work is the Report of the English Board of Trade-Labor Department, on "Agencies and Methods for dealing with the Unemployed," 438 pages, indexed (London, 1893). On non-employment in the United States, see Mass. Bureau of Labor, 1879 and 1887; Ohio Bureau of Labor, 1890, 1891, 1893; National Bureau of Labor, First Report, pp. 64-66, and 242-244. On the situation in the United States during the winter of 1893-4, see *Review of Reviews*, Jan., Feb., and March, 1894; and two articles by Closson in *Quarterly Journal of Economics*, Jan. and July, 1894. On vagrancy and relief in work, see Special Consular Reports, " Vagrancy and Public Charities in Foreign Countries " (Washington, 1892); Ribton-Turner, "History of Vagrants and Vagrancy" (London, 1887); Booth's "Darkest England;" "The Homeless Poor of London" (Charitable Organization Society, 1891); for the United States, McCook, *Forum*, Aug., 1893, "A Tramp Census and its Revelations;" J. Flynt, *Century*, March and Feb., 1894, "The City Tramp," "The Tramp at Home;" First Indiana State Conference of Charities, 1890, pp. 34-53; "Relief in Work," N. C. C., 1892 — same papers in *Charities Review*, vol. ii. No. 1; Buzelle, "Some Uses of Relief in Work," *Charities Review*, vol. i., pp. 257-262; Mrs. Lowell and Dr. Abbott, *Forum*, Feb., 1894; Mrs. Lowell and A. F. White, International Congress of Charities, 1893, volume on Organization of Charities, pp. 77-98. On German and Dutch experiments, see references in succeeding foot-note.]

IN all times of industrial depression the number of the unemployed is greatly exaggerated. During the depression of 1873-78 it was alleged that there were 300,000 mechanics out of employment in Massachusetts; and the statement went unchallenged for more than a year, while figures then available would have shown that there were only 318,000 men in the State engaged in mechanical pursuits.[1] The investigation conducted about that time by the Massachusetts State Bureau of Labor indicated the number of unemployed mechanics to be less than 30,000. During the present depression the Governor of Oregon makes the assertion that two-thirds of the workmen in that State are unemployed, and one-third of them have no adequate means of support. Mr. Closson suggests that probably this statement, rather than one-third of the workmen, has no adequate support.

During the depression of 1882 to 1885, it is estimated that about 1,000,000 men were idle; during the recent depression, following the crisis of 1893, the trade-union estimates put the number at about 4,500,000; more conservative estimates at about 1,000,000. Returns made to *Bradstreet's*, the results of which were published Dec. 23, 1893, show that in 119 cities 801,055 men, with about 1,956,110 persons dependent upon them, were out of employment. Carlos C. Closson, investigating the matter while preparing a paper published in the *Quarterly Journal of Economics,* found in sixty cities 523,080 idle men, an estimate sufficiently close to *Bradstreet's* return for the same cities to make it probable that these figures actually reflect the facts.

The most careful investigation made in this country regarding enforced idleness was probably that conducted by the Massachusetts Bureau of Labor during the depression of 1885. There were during that year, in Massachusetts, 816,470 persons engaged in gainful occupations; of these, 241,589 were unemployed during part of the year. The time lost, if we consider only the prin-

[1] First Report of United States Bureau of Labor.

cipal occupation of each individual, was 82,744 years; but many persons, when unable to work at their principal occupation, had some subsidiary work. Making the proper deductions for the time thus put in, the net absolute loss of working-time amounted to 78,717.76 years. If this loss were averaged among all persons engaged in gainful occupations, it would amount to 1.16 months for each person. Averaged, however, among those only who lost a certain amount of time, the loss per man was 3.91 months. While these figures indicate a state of things much less dismal than would be inferred from exaggerated statements noted above, yet the actual loss is sufficiently great. When the Eleventh Census was taken, it was attempted to ascertain the amount of time lost during the census year. The returns of this investigation, which would be especially interesting as being obtained for the whole country during a normal year, are not yet available.

Until there is more discrimination between the different classes of the unemployed, all statistics regarding them must be somewhat ambiguous. The Labour Department of the English Board of Trade has published a report on "Agencies and Methods for Dealing with the Unemployed" which specifies four tolerably distinct classes, composing what is usually thought of as a single class. First, there are those who, being engaged for short periods only, have finished one job and not yet entered on another. Their loss of time is spoken of as mere "leakage." Second, there are those who belong to trades in which the volume of work fluctuates, because of seasonal changes, most commonly during a year, but sometimes during longer periods, as in the ship-building trades, and sometimes during periods of less than a year. Third, there are members of various trades who are economically superfluous. This may come from too many learning such trades, from changes in trade processes, from local shifting of industries, etc. Fourth, there are those who cannot get work because they are below the standard of efficiency usual in their trades.[1]

"One of the most serious features of the situation is the fact that want of employment and casual employment have themselves a powerful tendency to produce inefficiency, both by the physical deterioration due to insufficient nourishment, and the moral deterioration which often results from want of regular work."[2] The best 1,000 unemployed members of a given group of trades at any given time are less efficient, whether from physical, moral, or intellectual defects, than the worst 1,000 who are in actual employment at the same time. To a very large extent, manifestly, the problem is an industrial and not a charitable one. It is only when non-employment results in destitution that its treatment is germane to our present purposes.

The most difficult problem in the whole realm of poor-relief is this of providing for the unemployed. England has worked at it intermittently from the time of Elizabeth, when one of the primitive acts of the English poor-law provided for "setting the poor on work," and authorized the collection of rates for that purpose. So far as it concerns the relief of the resident poor, it was indirectly treated under the head of out-door relief.

---

[1] Report, 1893, pp. 9-11.
[2] Labour Department of the English Board of Trade on Agencies and Methods for Dealing with Unemployed, Report, 1893, p. 12.

This present chapter passes from my hand in March, 1894, when special relief-work for the unemployed is being carried forward on a scale never before known or needed in this country. It is therefore not possible to give the results of this emergency work. The general principles which have been worked out elsewhere through a long series of similar experiences may be summarized as follows: 1. Relief in work should be given by substantially the same methods as other relief, that is, after careful investigation of individual cases. Indiscriminate giving of relief in work by public authorities not connected with the poor-law administration is demoralizing. 2. The work should be real work, and as productive as possible. So far as it is used as a test, it is better if it can be continuous for each individual for a considerable time. 3. Whenever public authorities or private persons see an opportunity to do at unusually low rates, because of the hard times, work that needs doing, they ought to push such work on business and not relief principles, and in the general following of this policy is to be found a radical remedy for trade depression.

The present chapter is concerned especially with the problem of the homeless poor as a constant factor in the administration of charities. The question of how to deal with the tramp is said to be of especial urgency in every locality in the United States with which I am at all acquainted. From Boston to San Francisco, and from St. Paul to New Orleans, complaints come of a number of tramps which is alleged to be "especially" large in each case.

One might think from Professor McCook's articles

that Hartford, Conn., had an "especially" large number of tramps; and one would reach the same conclusion regarding Indiana by reading the report of their State Conference of Charities. If we turn to New York, we find that city also cursed with an "especially" large number of tramps, who fill the station-houses, the free lodging-houses, the insanitary cheap lodging-houses, while the Children's Aid Society finds use for all its six well-equipped lodging-houses for homeless children. In England it was estimated years ago that there were 30,000 persons continually on the tramp; and General Booth estimated the number of the homeless for the United Kingdom at 165,000. A pamphlet of a hundred and fifty pages, published by the Charity Organization Society of London, giving the results of an investigation regarding the homeless poor of that city, shows this estimate to be too high, but also shows the problem to be sufficiently urgent there. If we cross the English Channel and go to Germany, we find there also the same complaint of an extraordinary number of wandering beggars. The estimates of the actual number vary from 40,000 to 200,000. A great system of friendly inns and provident woodyards, and a system of labor colonies which can provide for 2,500 men, has there been established to provide for them. The same complaint of the curse of vagrancy comes from Russia, and the consular report on vagrancy shows that it prevails almost everywhere.

If, instead of extending our inquiries geographically, we had extended them historically, we should have found the same complaint of an exceptionally large number of wandering beggars made in nearly every age of which we have record; and it has been suggested that if, just as we look for proto-martyrs, we should look for the proto-tramp, we should find him near the beginning of history in the person of Cain. And yet it cannot be asserted that even in the domain of trampery there is nothing new under the sun. New means of cheap transportation, and the consequent break-down of the passport system and of settlement laws, have given a new character to vagabondage, as the march of the Coxey armies shows. It is increasingly easy for men to get away from their duties to families and neighbors, and it is getting to be easier to wander than to work. "Mobility of labor" is a good thing, but it is having some unfortunate results.

There are four tolerably distinct ways in which various communities in the United States have tried to deal with the homeless and wandering poor. The first and favorite way is to get rid of them as promptly as possible by sending them on. Nearly every large town makes an appropriation for the transportation of paupers, and the poor-law officers of rural communities also devote some money to the same purpose. Such funds are frequently spent without any adequate investigation. The officials having authority simply consider whether it will be cheaper to ship a given person to a place where he says he wishes to go, or to take care of him. Formerly there was in Baltimore a fund, which was disbursed under the authority of the mayor's private secretary, who was bound by the rule that transportation could be furnished only to the next large city. If a person wished to go to New York, Baltimore gave him a ticket to Philadelphia, and expected him to be forwarded from there by the mayor of Philadelphia. A large number were sent in the same way to Washington. The excuse for this was that Washington sent a large number to Baltimore, and it was only fair to get even.[1]

[1] A woman, shortly to be confined, said she had friends in Louisville, Ky. The route from Baltimore to Louisville over the Pennsylvania road is via Harrisburg. The mayor's secretary accordingly gave her a ticket to Harrisburg. When she had gone as far as that ticket would take her, she was farther from her destination than ever. Through the influence of the Charity Organization Society the mayor's rules in dispensing this fund have since been changed. All cases are now investigated by the society. The result of the change in policy is described and illustrated in the following extract from the confidential circular issued by the society: "Our society makes careful inquiry into each application for a free pass, and in 1891 the city was saved 55 per cent of the fund through our investigations. The mayor's secretary, Colonel Love, does not hesitate to say, however, that with the remaining 45 per cent he was enabled to do far more good than ever before, that he has sent deserving applicants longer distances to places where it was proved they would be better off than in Baltimore, and has discountenanced, on the other hand, any tendency to unburden on neighboring cities a pauper population not their own.

"The other cities do not always return the compliment. York, Pa., furnished transportation to Baltimore last year for a whole family of paupers, and gave them a letter of recommendation besides to the charitable people of our city. A few months ago a poor, battered-looking woman came to us from the City Hall, asking transportation to Washington. She had come down on a free pass from York, and said that some one should be assassinated if she did not get to Washington that day. Gradually our agent succeeded in pacifying her and in gathering together fragments of her story. She had left her home in New Mexico four months before with $10 to pay her way to Washington, intending to check there a deep-laid conspiracy against her property. She had been in almost every city of any size between New Mexico and Maryland, had been sent sometimes forward and sometimes backward, had been aided by ladies' relief societies, by churches, and by public officials, who had shown a willingness to do anything save take the pains to find out what was the right thing to do.

"With difficulty we learned the name of her married daughter, and

UNEMPLOYED AND HOMELESS POOR. 185

The conditions in the smaller cities as regards wandering mendicants are very well reflected by the discussion of the matter which took place at the First Indiana State Conference of Charities. The superintendents of the county asylums met and discussed a paper on travelling mendicants, and compared their experience in dealing with this class. It transpired that most of the county asylums or poor-houses fitted up a room or rooms where tramps were lodged, and that they were given shelter and food with, or more commonly without, a work-test, but that, above all things, the effort was made to induce them to move on. The trustees' office at Fort Wayne reported $231.65 spent for railroad fares, or an average of $69\frac{1}{2}$ cents per person railroaded out of that place. Trustees from other districts admitted that they did the

wrote to her and to the Land Office in Washington. We found a quiet lodging-house for the woman until we could hear from the daughter, feeling that her mind was not sufficiently affected to warrant placing her in confinement. She was very restless, quarrelled with the landlady after four days, and, begging a dollar from some charitable (?) person, slipped off to Washington. We wrote to Washington at once, but it was too late; the district police had furnished her with transportation to Bellaire, Ohio, because she asked for it. One would be puzzled to know the principle underlying the action of Washington police in furnishing transportation, unless it be the principle of Caliban, —

'Let twenty pass, and stone the twenty-first,
Loving not, hating not, just choosing so.'

The next day we received a letter from the daughter, who had been nearly crazed by her mother's mysterious disappearance. The first news in four months had come from Baltimore; and she urged us to keep her mother, who had no business in Washington, until she could raise money enough to return her. This was impossible. We replied, urging her to telegraph Bellaire and a place in Michigan which the woman had announced as her destination; but when we last heard, no clew to her whereabouts had been found."

same thing. When they met in this conference and compared notes, it was apparent that they were making a mistake, and a reform was begun forthwith. Unfortunately, in most of the States such conferences have not been held.

The obvious objection to this manner of providing for the homeless poor is that it does not provide for them; it is simply a way of shifting burdens from one community to another. But each community, while recognizing this fact, thinks itself bound to keep up the foolish work, so that it may not serve as the dumping-ground for the poor of all the adjacent communities.

The second way of dealing with the homeless poor is to punish them as misdemeanants — " vag 'em," as the police say; that is, arrest them as vagrants, and commit them to the jail and workhouse. This is the old English method of dealing with what were called " sturdy beggars." But in the early days it was not a comfortable jail to which tramps were committed, and wanderers who could give no account of themselves were flogged out of the boundaries of the parish in which they were apprehended. They were also liable to be branded, have their ears cut off, or be treated in some similar fashion which would now be regarded as barbarous.

In 1879 Connecticut passed a law providing that every tramp should be punished by imprisonment in the State prison for not more than one year. Soon after this law went into effect it seemed to have been a complete success. The number of lodgers in the Hartford police-station fell off from 85 to 130 to from 3 to 5. The chief of police of New Haven said that the law had been the means of driving from the city a class of criminals who went around begging for the sake of stealing. "There is no begging from door to door as formerly," he reported. The rural authorities were equally well pleased, and for a time it seemed as though the one thing needful for the cure of trampery had been found. Latterly, however, there have been no convictions under this law, and the old order of things has returned. It gives a very good illustration of what repressive legislation can and cannot accomplish in this matter. The method, if rigidly applied, may cause tramps to disappear for a time; but there is always a doubt in the minds of the community as to whether or not many cases of honest destitution are not dealt with too harshly. Such stringent laws are very apt to become dead-letters, and the evil at which they were aimed flourishes while they are in abeyance.

A third very common way of dealing with the homeless poor is to give them indiscriminately the relief they ask. If a man rings the door-bell, and asks for food, give him some; if he asks for the price of a night's lodging, let him have it; if men apply for lodgings at the station-house, fit up a room and let them fill it as full as they can fill it and still live; start a free lodging-house, and supplement the lodgings with free meals. If a man comes when it is cold and asks admission to the almshouse, take him in, give him comfortable shelter for the winter, and then, when spring comes, let him depart. This was the method employed in mediæval monasteries, and is still more or less practised in most of our American cities. The trouble with this method is that "we can have as many tramps as we will pay for." A Western farm-hand once gave an account of his experience during three months when he had wandered about with tramps as a tramp. After telling of the way in which he got a living, and of the many sharp practices resorted to, he concluded in a meditative and almost puzzled way, " Oh, it was a good deal of fun, but somehow or other I didn't like it." He had stood at the parting of the ways. It had been in his power to become a laborer or to become a tramp, and he chose the better part. He now has considerable property and a family. Now, if the persons to whom he applied had been a little more liberal and equally thoughtless, if the jails to which he was liable to have been committed had been a little more comfortable, if in the cities he happened to visit he had found a few more institutions for furnishing free lodgings and free soup, his choice might have been different. His case is not a typical one, for the average man does not decide thus consciously. He drifts into the life of vagabondage through following the line of least resistance. But, however unconscious of the decision the average wanderer may be, he makes it surely and too often fatally. As in the other cases, indiscriminate giving is to be deplored, not so much because it wastes money, as because it corrupts men.

A modification and improvement of this method is to give indiscriminately, but never to give at all without applying the work-test. It is substantially the method of the English Casual Ward. The Boston Wayfarers' Lodge is the best example of this plan in the United States.

On reviewing the three methods of dealing with the homeless poor already mentioned, it is apparent that each is adapted to certain classes of applicants; some

UNEMPLOYED AND HOMELESS POOR. 189

should be given direct relief, some should be punished, and some should be sent to other places. There are tramps and tramps; any method that enables us to deal with them properly must enable us to discriminate.

The machinery necessary for dealing properly with the problem of the homeless poor has been set up in comparatively few places, although it can be adapted to both large and small communities with comparative ease. It consists of an institution or place where the work-test can be rigidly applied, and where a man can earn his support pending an investigation of his case. Secondly, it includes facilities for giving meals and lodgings; thirdly, facilities for bathing and for disinfecting clothing; and fourthly, some person to investigate the case of each applicant thoroughly, and to act as circumstances require. Philadelphia was one of the first of American cities where the machinery described was operated successfully; the Society for Organizing Charity of that city established friendly inns and provident woodyards, and a special office for dealing with cases of non-residents. The station-houses were emptied, and the police referred all applicants for lodgings to the society.

In Philadelphia an applicant to the agent for the care of non-residents is first asked to state his case. If he claims to have a residence, or to be able to get work somewhere else, or if he admits having relatives and friends elsewhere, or whatever may be his story, he is sent to the woodyard to earn his living while it is being investigated. No man is assisted to leave the city unless it appears on some authority, additional to his own, that he would be better off in the place to which he is sent. Many men, after telling their story and taking the card which would admit them to the lodging-house and woodyard, never present it. Some are conscious that their story would not bear investigation, and some do not care to work while it is being investigated. All cases of honest destitution, whether the applicant be a boy, a man, or a woman, are dealt with in the same kindly but thorough-going fashion; and the result is help for the deserving, and disappointment for the loafer and impostor.

In Boston there is the lodging-house and the woodyard, but no attempt at investigation; the men drift through the institution, and no one attends to their needs beyond the giving of the temporary relief. In New Haven Mr. Preston of the Organized Charities Association has improved upon the Philadelphia plan. The woodyard is open in the evening, so that a man can always work in advance of getting relief, and the men work according to a certain stent, instead of by the hour as in Philadelphia. Here also the investigation is very thorough, and many cases of wanderers returned to places where they could be finally provided for might be told. In Washington the District government opened a municipal lodging-house in January, 1893. At that time there were about 150 men per night sleeping in the station-houses. It was a specially cold time; and as the municipal lodging-house could not accommodate more than fifty, it was feared that it would be over-full at once. But the woodyard was kept open for workers in the evening, the men were made to saw by the piece and not by time-work, and the institution during the whole remainder of the winter never had as many lodgers as it could accommodate, although the station-houses were completely closed to lodgers.[1] Neither has it been full

[1] On a cold night in February, 1892, I made the round of the station-houses and free lodging-houses in Washington. A friend who went with me wrote a description of what we saw for the Washington *Post*, and I give some extracts as affording a sort of snap-shot photograph of trampery in an American city. "The Seventh precinct was the first station visited; and its lodgers' room may be taken as a type, for, with trifling differences of ventilation, none of them too good, the stations provided the same accommodations.

"'Only six in to-night,' said the clerk; 'bad nights bring us from eight to twelve. Like to take a look at them?'

"The room was bare, the walls were whitewashed and reasonably clean, and the six lodgers were picturesquely disposed on the 'bench,' a platform about three feet high and six feet wide, running the width of the room, and inclined at a slight angle to raise the sleepers' heads. The only preparation for bed seemed to be for the lodger to kick off his shoes and wrap his head in his coat. Why this was done was not apparent, nor could any one explain; but at most of the stations the sleepers' heads were closely swathed — possibly to keep out the air, which was very foul.

"'It is easy,' said the sergeant, 'to tell the honest man in hard luck from the regular tramp or rounder. When we meet with the former, we do the best we can for him, give him a blanket, and sometimes find him something to eat in the morning. But the regulars get short commons. If they come too often, we "vag" them — send them down to the farm — and this they don't like, for it means steady work for their board and lodging; but they divide up in gangs, and work the city by sections. There are nine precincts; and by working each of them for a couple of nights, they are forgotten at one before they make the rounds of the rest. Some of the faces are very familiar, and we often get hold of cases that have been working the town ever since I have been on the force, and that's twenty-three years; but they don't age much, hold their own remarkably well, considering the life they lead.

"'You can't treat them kindly, or they will take advantage of it. For some time the Georgetown College and the convent were in the habit of having a daily distribution of food during the winter, but the vags got on to it and went up there in gangs. At the convent, where there were only women to deal with them, they got disorderly, and several times tried to raise a row. But we were notified; so we laid

during the present winter. The same experiment was tried in Baltimore during the winter of 1893-4 with exactly similar results.[1]

Many, especially those engaged in the agitation for

for them, and one morning brought fifteen down here and sent the most of them to the farm. Now the college makes those who get food work for it by chopping wood and doing odd jobs around the grounds.'

"The Night Lodging-House, 312 Twelfth Street, was the next place visited. This institution has been in operation for more than twelve years. It is supported by private subscription and a small appropriation from Congress, and is open through the winter months only. It can accommodate thirty men with a clean cot, sheets, and blanket for each. On coming in the men are given a supper of good soup and bread. They bathe and receive a clean night-shirt in exchange for their clothes, which are stored in a separate room till morning. For breakfast they get bread and coffee; and, unless the weather is very bad, leave the house at eight o'clock. The house is perfectly free, and a man is given a room for but three nights.

"'We have only ten to-night,' said the superintendent. 'Turned off eight on account of vermin.'

"'Where do they go?'

"'Next door; same place we send any that are troublesome.'

"'Next door' was the First precinct. 'We are medium full to-night,' said the clerk there. 'Sixteen in there,' and he opened the door to the lodgers' room. The 'bench' was packed with men lying upon edge to save space. The floor was likewise full; and where the seventeenth man, who came in just then — came in on one leg and a crutch — was to sleep was a mystery. The air was better than in the Seventh precinct, but it would hardly support combustion.

"'They keep coming in up till one or two o'clock,' said the station-keeper. 'We never vag them. There are very few women among the applicants, and when there are we turn them over to the matron.'

"'Have you any way of washing the men or devitalizing their clothing?'

"'No, and don't want to have. They overrun you if you treat them too well. The janitor cleans up the place in the morning, and salts it down with insect powder. That's all we can do.'

"The round-up for the entire city showed 68 lodgers in the station-houses, and 37 in three free lodging-houses, or a total of 105."

[1] See circular issued by the Central Relief Committee.

the establishment of municipal lodging-houses such as those described, have thought that the whole tramp problem would be solved by their institution; but there are certain difficulties attendant upon their management, not usually reckoned with. In the first place, it is almost impossible to find anything that is really profitable for the men to do. If they saw wood, they come in competition with steam-saws, and if they break stone, with steam stone-crushers. In Washington it was found that it cost eighty cents more per cord to supply the District with sawed wood from the yard in connection with the municipal lodging-house than it did to get sawed wood direct from the contractor. This was in part because of the nature of laws regarding the letting of contracts in the District, but in no place is it possible to have men earn much by hand-sawing. The Philadelphia society finds continual difficulty in disposing of its wood supply in competition with the regular dealers; and in New Haven the wood-sawing department only pays the running expenses of the yard, and for the meal and lodging tickets which the men are given. No careful calculation has been made in Boston to ascertain what profit, if any, is made in the woodyard. Where, as in Washington, every stick of wood that a man saws costs the District a little more than if the man did nothing at all, we have manifestly not reached any real solution of the difficulty. It is just this impossibility of finding remunerative work for labor which is on the whole incompetent that has induced the English workhouses to give pure task-work to the inmates of their casual wards. But work which is avowedly task-work is not only unprofitable, but it is almost as degrading to the man who does it as to receive relief for which he makes no return. Its only justification is its deterrent influence. It is profitable because it reduces the number of applicants. Where woodyards have been made to pay expenses, as with the Appleton Homes in Boston, it is because some man has donated to the work sufficient managerial ability to make up for the poor quality of the labor and methods used.

Another reason why the lodging-house and woodyard does not solve all the difficulty, is that its management seems to have an inveterate tendency to become mechanical. Interest is lost in the individuals; and they are ground through the regular routine without any real attempt being made to get hold of the helpable, and to punish habitual and degraded vagrants. As a consequence, there comes to be a very considerable army of intermittently drunken loafers who rely upon the lodging-house and woodyard as a place where they can always get something to eat and a lodging for the night. They are not unwilling to work for a short time and in a perfunctory way. The multiplication of this class, or at least the toleration of it as it multiplies, is said to be one of the serious evils connected with the Naturalverpflegungsstatsionen in Germany.[1] Where small account

[1] Labor Colonies in Germany and Holland: German and Dutch experiments in the matter of relieving the unemployed are too instructive to be passed by with only the brief reference proper to them in the text.

Experiments on behalf of the unemployed group themselves roughly in three or possibly four classes. First, those based on the assumption that the unemployed are efficient workmen whom circumstances have deprived of work; they are designed to tide over the temporary difficulty by relief or relief in work, and the finding of regular work for the man. Second, those based on the assumption

is taken of individuals, men can come repeatedly to the lodging-house in spite of a rule limiting their residence there to not more than three days at any one time.

The chief advantage of the woodyard and lodging-house arrangement is that it gives the citizens of the locality an opportunity to refuse all unknown applicants for relief, and to send them to the lodging-house. More than that, if there be but one of these lodging-houses in

that the unemployed are many of them not efficient, but may be trained back into efficiency, and providing for this attempt. Third, those based on the assumption that many of the unemployed are incurably inefficient as far as ordinary industry is concerned, but may be so organized on a farm colony as to be self-supporting. These three classes of benevolent effort develop one after the other as experience accumulates in a given locality. Each succeeds in curing dependency in some cases; but finally there is a residuum of persons who cannot be made self-supporting by any education or organization, and these call for a fourth class of institution — the farm colony which does not pretend to be self-supporting. This, however, is virtually an almshouse. Most American experiments are of the first class, the German Labor Colonies are of the second, and the Dutch Free Home Labor Colonies are of the third, while the Dutch Beggar Colonies are of the fourth.

During the early years of the last decade, the number of beggars and vagabonds in Germany seemed to be steadily increasing. Indiscriminate giving on the part of individuals was very general, the excuse for it being that there was no other way to keep men from starving. Von Bodelschwingh, a Protestant minister interested in the management of an institution for the care of epileptics, began to make experiments at this institution in the direction of giving relief only in return for work done. As long as this rule could be followed, it was found that the number of applicants decreased, while their character improved. On certain waste but redeemable land, situated not far from the highway between Berlin and Cologne, and about ten miles from the manufacturing town of Bielefeld, Pastor von Bodelschwingh secured the establishment of the first Laborers' Colony, Wilhelmsdorf, which was opened in March, 1882. The primary object of the colony was announced to be " to employ at agricultural or other labor, until such time as regular positions could be found for them, all

a city, or if those that exist co-operate one with another, it is possible to stop that drifting about from one place to another in the same town, which enables a vagrant to stay there through the whole winter. This centralization was one of the very best things resulting from the establishment of the municipal lodging-house in Washington.

The machinery described is necessary machinery; but

men, of whatever religion or rank, who were able and willing to work." The second object was to deprive all vagabonds who would not work (arbeitsscheue Vagabunden) of their stock excuse for begging — the claim, that is, that they could find no work.

Twenty-four colonies organized in a similar way and for similar purposes are now in existence, with possible accommodations for nearly twenty-eight hundred laborers. The expenses of maintaining the colonies are usually met by voluntary contributions from private persons; but public subventions, oftenest in the form of a non-interest bearing loan, are not infrequent. The influence of the church, both in raising the funds and in the management of the colonies, is very marked. They are established from "free compassion," and it is held that neither the church nor the state should be organically connected with their management. Men are admitted without regard to their moral deserts or past record.

It was originally thought that the colonies would afford an opportunity to unemployed but willing and capable men, to earn a living and a respectable outfit of clothes preparatory to obtaining some permanent position in the regular industries of the time. The matter of entrance and departure was accordingly left very much as the individual beneficiary desired to arrange it. The large proportion of re-admissions indicates that this freedom is being abused by habitual vagabonds. This conclusion is confirmed by a further study of the inmates. Berthold's tables are for the two years ending March 31, 1889. During this time 20 colonies were in operation, to which there were 13,575 admissions; but, by excluding the repeated names, it is found that only 10,403 different men were thus aided. The applicants are for the most part industrially worthless or of little value. Three-fourths of them have already been in correctional institutions. A considerable number are advanced in years; few have thoroughly learned any trade; and many, while willing to work for a time, will

UNEMPLOYED AND HOMELESS POOR. 197

it will not run itself, and it will not solve the tramp problem. It gives the basis for proper action, but does not insure it. As already suggested, proper action can come only after there has been a thorough discrimination between cases. Proper dealing with the tramp problem in the United States is for the most part impossible until we have reformed our infamous system of county jails. The basis of all charitable work for the

not work steadily when subjected to the temptations of ordinary life. Of the 10,403 persons admitted during the two years, the facts regarding precedent imprisonments were obtained in 10,037 cases. The following condensed table arranges these facts according to the number of times each person was admitted to the colonies:—

Times Admitted to the Colonies.	Never in a Correctional Institution (per cent).	Had been in a Correctional Institution one or more times (per cent).	Total of Different Persons.
1	27.2	72.8	6,013
2	17.7	82.3	2,142
3	17.2	82.8	985
4	14.7	85.3	462
5	16.4	83.6	231
6	15.3	84.7	118
7	8.9	91.1	56
8	25.0	75.0	12
9	...	100.0	9
10	25.0	75.0	4
11	...	100.0	4
12	...	100.0	1
All persons.	23.1	76.9	10,037

The proportion of criminals and misdemeanants here shown is about the same as that given in tables previously published.

A review of the reasons of departure of those leaving the colonies for a series of years does not show a satisfactory tendency. Of those leaving all the colonies in 1885-86, work was found for 27.4; 1886-87, 24.7; 1887-89, 20.8. On the other hand, there was a proportional in-

198 AMERICAN CHARITIES.

homeless poor, should be a carefully drawn statute providing for the commitment of all the habitual vagrants and drunkards under indeterminate sentence to houses of correction. In the houses of correction they should be put at hard labor, and not let out until some evidence of reformation is given. At present, a man who is sentenced for vagrancy is usually sent for from ten to ninety days to a warm and pleasant jail, where he can play

crease in the number of those who left at their own request, almost all of whom returned to a life of vagabondage. The percentages of this class for the same periods were as follows: 54.1, 57.8, 60.4. The proportion of those who left on account of drunkenness, laziness, or bad conduct, is nearly constant for the three periods. Of the 11,849 departures from the colonies, 913, or 7.7 per cent, took place within seven days after admission. It is further shown that the demand for admission increases faster than the number of places available: —

Year.	No. of Colonies.	Applicants Admitted.	Applicants Refused Admission.	Applicants Refused because of Lack of Room.	Places Available.
1888	20	5,802	1,691	. . .	2,312
1889	21	6,594	2,252	1,054	2,477
1890	21	6,962	4,690	3,558	2,603

This rapid increase in the number of applicants for whom places could not be provided, together with the large number of re-admissions, and the unsatisfactory showing as to the cause of departure, seem to indicate that the colonies are training a class of men to accept the conditions of colony life as a permanent thing. The labor-test is not sufficiently deterrent; but, with intervals of wandering freedom and probable debauch, these "colony bummers" are willing to spend their lives in the various colonies.

The Dutch Free Home Labor Colonies were established in 1818. General van den Bosch had become convinced, from a knowledge of certain Chinese colonies in Java, of the practicability of employing poor or pauper laborers in fertilizing and cultivating barren soils; and he believed that in this way able-bodied indigent persons of good character might be made self-sustaining, provided funds could be obtained

cards, chew tobacco, discuss crime, and tell indecent stories with his peers. To threaten a vagabond with arrest under such circumstances, is merely to promise to do him a favor.

If there were the proper punitive machinery for removing these worthless vagabonds from the consideration of the charitable, it would next be necessary to have properly organized institutions to care for the young, the

to purchase the waste land, and to maintain the families until it became productive. The movement was popular, and the support generous. Several free colonies were undertaken; the first, largest, and most enduring being that of Frederiksoord, on the heath land between the provinces of Drenthe, Friesland, and Over-ijssel. The establishment of the beggar colonies, which are semi-penal settlements, began in 1820, the two largest being Ommerschans and Veenhuizen. The interesting history of these colonies from the beginning cannot be here given. They went more and more deeply in debt until 1859, when the free and beggar colonies were put under separate management and the public authorities came to the financial relief of the *Maatschappij van Weldadigheid* (Society for Benevolence). The net gift of the State to the association amounted to about 5,535,000 gilders.

As it is in the nature of the colony that it should be a home, but few new families can be received. As a matter of fact, less than half a dozen are admitted annually. The number of colonists has decreased from 2,007 in 1873 to 1,789 at the close of 1886. Between the energetic poor, who refuse to go to the colony, and the abject beggars, who will not be received, the number of available recruits is small, and apparently decreasing.

The beggar colonies are semi-penal settlements, managed and supported since 1859 by the government. A person convicted of begging is sentenced for a short term to jail and in addition is sent to the colony for about three years. Some are also admitted on request, and some confirmed drunkards are also sent to the colonies. The population of the beggar colonies is about 3,000, many of the inmates being too old to work, and many too feeble and sick. The annual net cost of maintenance is 350,000 guilders, out of which hospitals are maintained, officers and soldiers are paid, books are purchased for the free library, and Protestant and Catholic clergymen and their churches are supported. Farm workshops are operated; but work is much

sick, the aged, and the otherwise incapable. This would very greatly reduce the number with whom the superintendent of the lodging-house would have to deal, and if he were a man of sound sympathies and sound judgment, and were put in a position where the time at his disposal was adequate for the work, he could then discriminate intelligently between the different applicants and do the right thing by each. It is quite certain that hampered by the fear of "competing with honest labor." It is hard to find enough work to keep all busy, and therefore clumsy machines and processes are used to make work. Besides support, the workers receive small wages, graded according to efficiency. Two-thirds of this they may spend, receiving the rest on dismissal. While the inmates are sentenced for definite terms, many of them like the freedom from care in the life of the colony, and are so expert at getting recommitted that they are practically inmates for life.

Experts agree that the colonists are not self-supporting in either the free or the beggar colonies. Those who are predisposed in favor of them are prone to say that, if certain mistakes had not been made, they would have been financially, as well as otherwise, successful. It need only be answered that mistakes are such a constant factor in all industrial enterprises, that it is necessary to allow for them in making calculations.

Both in Germany and Holland the deterrent influence of the experiments has been more beneficial than their positive results. "To farm waste land with bad labor" has not been found directly profitable.

A bibliography of Labor Colonies, prepared by Professor James Manor, is to be found in the Appendix to the English Labour Department Report on the "Unemployed." The report also contains a full account of the colonies. A small monthly periodical is published by Bertelsman, at Gaederbaum, as an organ of the Colony Association. Berthold, "Statistik der deutschen Arbeiter-Kolonien" (Berlin, 1891) is a valuable scientific study. Willink, "Dutch Home Labour Colonies" (London, 1889) is a careful piece of work. Some accessible review articles describing these or the English Salvation Army experiments are as follows: Earl of Meaty, *Nineteenth Century*, vol. xxix., pp. 73–89; Moore, *Contemporary Review*, March, 1893; Peabody, *Forum*, Feb., 1892; Mavor, *Journal of Political Economy*, Dec., 1893; Warner, *Quarterly Journal of Economics*, vol. v., pp. 1, *et seq.*

there are resources sufficient in almost any American community to deal with the problem of the homeless poor efficiently and completely, if they could only be organized so as to meet the genuine needs. The trouble has been that here, as in England, we have vacillated between excessive severity and excessive leniency, oftener erring on the latter side than on the former, until the tramp has become an institution, and appears to think that he has an inalienable right to life, liberty, and the pursuit of vagabondage.

CHAPTER IX.

DEPENDENT CHILDREN.

[Hart, " Economic Aspect of the Child Problem," N. C. C., 1892, pp. 191-204; the best brief survey of the problem, including the care of defective and delinquent children. "Report of the Committee on the History of Child Saving," special volume, N. C. C., 1893. The different methods of caring for dependent children in use in the United States are given by persons closely identified with the work which they respectively describe. Riis, " Children of the Poor," is concerned chiefly with the children of New York City, the conditions of life and work for them. Brace, " Dangerous Classes of New York," deals largely with the work of the New York Children's Aid Society. Florence Davenport-Hill, " Children of the State," gives English experience; chap. vii., " State Children in the United States." Mrs. C. R. Lowell, Report on " The Care of Dependent Children in the City of New York and Elsewhere," to the New York State Board of Charities, 23d An. Rep., pp. 175-259. Conference on the Care of Dependent and Delinquent Children in New York, Nov., 1893. "Massachusetts' Care of Dependent and Delinquent Children." (Published by Massachusetts Board of Managers, World's Fair, 1893. Part of it included in " History of Child Saving," pp. 54-68.) A great many papers on the subject have been submitted to the N. C. C., but the publications mentioned cover the ground quite thoroughly.]

AT the Denver Conference of Charities, Mr. Hart of the Minnesota State Board of Charities and Corrections estimated the number of dependent children in the United States to be 74,000. The expenditures for buildings and "plant" used in taking care of these children he put at $40,000,000, and the annual expenditure for maintenance in all forms at $9,500,000. About 9,000 persons were supposed to be employed as care-takers.[1] Unless the Eleventh Census secures more reliable returns than were obtained in 1880, this estimate by a careful man is more trustworthy than the formal tabulation of incomplete or careless reports. In this department of charitable activity, it is not wise to leave wholly out of view the nominally correctional work; and so mention should be made of Mr. Hart's further estimate that there were 15,000 [2] inmates of juvenile reformatories costing $10,000,000, and entailing an annual average charge for maintenance of $2,000,000.

The work for dependent children is the most hopeful branch of charitable endeavor in that it affords more possibilities of constructive work than any other line. When Charles L. Brace, the elder, was a young man, his first association with benevolent undertakings was in work for the adult vagabonds and loafers whom he found in the lower districts of New York. A little experience with these persons was enough to discourage him thoroughly, and it was not until he turned to the work of caring for neglected children that he felt sure of the helpfulness of his efforts. In work for the aged, the sick, the defective, even for the unemployed, one is conscious that for the individuals dealt with there is no possibility of any high measure of success. There is little else possible than to make the best of unfortunate circumstances, to deal with palliatives, to brighten the individual lives, and to prevent misfortune from spreading. With children, on the other hand, especially for the

[1] N. C. C., 1892, p. 193.
[2] This was probably taken from Census Bulletin No. 72 (published May 27, 1891) where the exact number is given as 14,846. As reformatories are public institutions the census figures are approximately correct.

quite young and tolerably healthy, there is a possibility of more positive results. The young life contains within itself the principle of growth, and may be enabled to expand into something actively useful. But if the work for children has thus its specially hopeful side, it has also its corresponding dangers, and imposes upon those who would undertake it a responsibility such as has no exact counterpart in other departments. I have talked with those who chose work for the incurable or the aged because they felt that in this the responsibility of a day's work ended with the day. If an old person, querulous and miserable, had been made somewhat less unhappy for a time, that modicum of benefit was at least secure. With children they were haunted by the feeling that the days of comfort afforded might be not a blessing but a curse. When the life of a dependent child is misdirected the misfortune entailed upon the individual and the community is far reaching. Fifty years hence many of the 74,000 children now dependent will still be suffering from or profiting by the training that charity affords them.

The care of destitute infants (children under two years of age) is sharply distinguished from the care of older dependent children. Among the former the death-rate is the principal index of success or failure, while among the latter the death-rate is always low and the attention must be given to evidences of right or wrong development afforded by the character and subsequent careers of the children.

In a great majority of cases, it can matter but little to the individual infant whether it is murdered outright or is placed in a foundling hospital — death comes only a little sooner in one case than in the other. This fact, that foundling hospitals are, for the most part, places where infants die, is not sufficiently appreciated by the public. A death-rate of 97 per cent per annum for children under three years of age is not uncommon.[1] The printed reports of institutions for infants usually do not give the number of deaths. One foundling hospital, the president of which was a prominent physician, stated in each annual report that the death-rate was comparatively low. When the president was asked what the exact death-rate was, he admitted that he did not know, and would not know how to compute one. It was found that the average number of inmates in this institution was thirty, and the number of deaths in the preceding year had been forty-five. In an institution where no exact death-rate was computed, a study of the books brought out the following facts: Between July 1 and December 1, 1891, twenty-three children had been admitted; up to July 1, 1892, four of these children had been given in adoption, one was still in the institution, and eighteen had died.[2] Twenty-eight infants were consigned one after another by a public official to a private institution administered by a religious order, and they all died.

Of course this high death-rate comes in part from the bad condition of the children when received. They are often marasmic, rachitic, syphilitic, half dead from drugging or neglect, or from ante-natal or post-natal

[1] N. C. C., 1889, p. 1, gives an instance.
[2] The best way of computing a death-rate for institutions for children, as in the case of hospitals for the sick, is to find the ratio of deaths to the whole number disposed of, or perhaps to find of the whole number received how many attain the age of three years.

abuse. Yet this does not explain entirely the high death-rate common to institutions, as is shown by the fact that strong, thriving babies droop and die in them, and by the further fact that improved methods of caring for these same children bring down the death-rate to almost that of the average population for corresponding ages.[1] The high death-rate where children are cared for in institutions often results from positive neglect. A baby, if not attended to, gets into a very bad condition in a very short time. A woman who has from four to eight babies to take care of is apt to become neglectful. It is possible to clean them up for visiting day, or the inspection of directors or supervisors, but to keep them all clean and comfortable through twenty-four hours of the day, seven days in the week, and fifty-two weeks in the year, is another matter. Frequently they are left to lie in their cribs scalded by urine and in a miserable plight generally. The attendants, being assigned more work than they can do, settle into the conviction that it does not much matter whether they do anything at all or not. If attendants are hired, it is difficult to get the best class of help for such work. If they are members of a religious order the chances of self-devotion are better; but the Sisters are often ignorant and tolerably selfish women, and are usually overworked. Even when the infants are not neglected, and when, apparently, the attendants do everything possible for their comfort, the death-rate is still high. It is not possible to raise babies by wholesale. The institution baby lacks, and must lack, that affectionate handling which gives exercise to the baby muscles, and the zest

---

[1] N. C. C., 1889, p. 1.

to infant existence which makes it worth while for the child to live. Though the ward of an asylum be flooded with sunlight, as it frequently is not, and though the bed be clean and dry, as it generally is not, yet there still is lacking the light and warmth of affection and the comforts of personal attention.[1]

Feeding the children is another difficulty. The doctors do their best in recommending sterilized foods of all kinds and descriptions, but the infants still insist on dying. One institution in a Southern State, under the care of Sisters of Charity, undertook as a last resort to

---

[1] In Paris, so long as the *Enfants Trouvés* were kept for a considerable time in a reception hospital, the mortality was high. In 1830 Mrs. Fletcher reports that about 9,000 new-born infants were received. Those living at the end of three days after the reception were sent to the country, but one-third died before the time of departure arrived. "Yet each infant had its separate crib, and the extreme of neatness pervaded the wards." Quoted in "Children of the State," p. 285. Mrs. Fletcher describes the constant wailing of the children in the wards, and the extreme and cheerful composure of the clean and pleasant-faced Sisters of Charity as they watched the agonies of dying infants. The authors of the work add (p. 286), "Our own memory is haunted . . . by an agonized face, gasping out its last breath, alone on its bed of perfect purity and neatness in the children's branch of a destitute asylum in Australia, closed now, thank God, by the extension of boarding-out. It was not lack of proper nourishment solely to which these tragedies were due. It is now understood that the multiplied presence of babies is fatal to each other; while to most the personal warmth and cherishing of the mother's arms are as essential as food to their existence." On the same point Dr. Parry says: "The most healthy and carefully attended infant always has about it a faint, unpleasant odor. If a large number are confined together this is materially increased, and when it is mingled with other effluvia it becomes almost insupportable; and if general hospitals are difficult to keep pure and well ventilated, infant asylums are more so. The last difficulty is augmented by the peculiar susceptibility of young children to cold, which makes the ventilation of such institutions a matter of extreme importance." "Infant Mortality," p. 21.

keep goats for the children to nurse, but with no good results. Many institutions admit a woman with a baby on condition that she shall nurse that and another. This is usually hard on the other baby, and the presence of a large number of these mothers under one roof makes administration very difficult.[1] Others board the infants out with wet nurses. This is the method in the New York Hospital for foundlings under Sister Irene.[2] Where there is a large and healthy laboring-class this plan works very well. It is the method pursued in Paris, where the infants are sent out into the country, chiefly with the wives of peasants. In the Southern States suitable wet nurses can often only be found among the colored people.[3] The Massachusetts State Board of Lunacy and Charity, following the example of the Massachusetts Infant Asylum, boards out infants in the country villages about Boston, placing them with women who bring them up by artificial feeding. About ten dollars per month is paid for the board of each child, and clothing is furnished by the officials. By

[1] In Naples, 1800–1822, there was an infant asylum containing about 300 nurses and 600 children. At the end of the first nine years of the experiment, out of 2,259 infants received, 1,831 had died. "Children of the State," p. 300.

[2] The following table shows the results at this institution:

	1890.	1891.	1892.	1893.
Number of children cared for	2,789	2,751	2,891	2,962
Number of deaths	549	553	611	596
Death-rate	19.13	20.10	21.13	20.10

It is not stated how many of those cared for were over three years of age.

[3] Colored women usually refuse to take any but white children to nurse.

carefully selecting the families, by subsequent visitation and frequent calls, at both stated and unexpected times, and by keeping constantly subject to summons a physician working on a salary paid by the State, it has been found possible to bring the death-rate among these children to about the same figure as that of children of similar age in the ordinary population.[1]

One who has had considerable experience with the placing out of infants in this way, gives it as his opinion that a foundling hospital is the most useless institution in the world. He says that an efficient children's aid society, or an efficient public official, would always know of homes in which infants could be received temporarily, and from which they could be placed in families that would care for them indefinitely, if properly paid. He maintains that even as a place of reception the "institution" is needless.

Next to the actual preservation of the life of the child, the most important question connected with the

[1] The Massachusetts Infant Asylum began operations in 1869, and has received about 2,000 inmates. They receive no child over nine months old, and dispose of the children when they reach the age of two. The death-rate among this class of dependents before they began operations had been about ninety in a hundred. They have devoted themselves especially to the work of devising ways to save the lives of these children. Their plan now is to board out about three-fourths of the babies, and to keep the others, usually in the care of wet nurses, in an institution especially designed for the purpose. In the early years, when occupying an ordinary house and employing only a few wet nurses, the death-rate, obtained by comparing the total number of different children in charge of the asylum during the year with the total number of deaths, ranged from 26 to 45. Under the newer methods this rate has been reduced to 5, and even less. Even when the State Board was sending a large number of foundlings the death-rate was never higher than 16, and sometimes went as low as 8.

care of destitute infants is upon what conditions they shall be received. The mediæval device long used in France, and perhaps still used there in some parts of the country, consisted of a double cradle. When the child had been placed in the cradle on the outside of the building, the contrivance was revolved, ringing a bell as it turned. By this process the child was placed in the institution, and another cradle was waiting at once for the next comer. The purpose of these "*tours*" was to make it so easy to get rid of babies that there might be no temptation to infanticide. The agitation for the abolition of this system of admission was bitterly resisted, Lamartine speaking of it as a case of "figures *vs.* humanity." When the *tours* had been suppressed in some of the departments, attention was called to the fact that infanticide increased thereafter. But further examination of the statistics showed that infanticide had also increased in those departments where the *tours* were still in operation; in fact, it had increased faster in the latter than in the former. This last mentioned fact seems to reflect the actual results of such appliances, and of all instances of laxness in receiving unwanted children from parents. Its indirect influence is so to promote disregard of parental ties and infant life that more children are murdered outright than where it is less easy for parents to get rid of offspring. This conclusion, which seems to be tolerably well established, is sufficient in itself, without resort to the common plea that easy disposal of offspring promotes illegitimacy, and without reference to the money cost of the laxer methods. It is not, as Lamartine said, a case of "figures *vs.* humanity," but rational and helpful sympathy *vs.* diseased and mischievous sympathy.

The Foundling Asylum of the Sisters of Charity in the city of New York (now the New York Foundling Hospital), under Sister Irene, affords the best known American example of facilities offered for the abandonment of infants. A cradle was formerly placed in the vestibule, in which infants could be placed without observation from those inside. At last, however, they began to come two or three in a single night;[1] so now the cradle is put inside the door, and an applicant must ring the bell. If a mother brings her child, she is asked to stay and nurse her child and another. If she refuses, she is allowed to depart without further question, leaving the infant. Perhaps a majority of foundling hospitals in the United States make no adequate investigation and keep no adequate record of the parentage of children received. There are some cases where any investigation must be fruitless; but the experience of the Pennsylvania Children's Aid Society and the Massachusetts State Board of Lunacy and Charity proves that if trouble enough is taken, thorough investigations usually bring out some helpful facts, and that such a course is not only wise but kindly. It has a bad effect upon all concerned, for a woman or a man to be able to dispose of a baby "and no questions asked."[2]

Many infant asylums are also maternity hospitals. If not, the mother passes quite quickly from the institution where the child is born to the institution where

---

[1] The first year 1,399 babies were placed in the crib. Mrs. Bouvier, New York Conference on Child-Caring, pp. 71–2.

[2] Massachusetts, within the last few years, has passed very radical legislation designed to suppress "baby-farming." Persons making a business of boarding infants for pay are required to report to the State Board of Lunacy and Charity, and to submit to its supervision.

she gives it up. She either deserts it at once, or promises and intends to do something for its support. This promise it is usually not possible for her to keep, and very commonly she loses her desire to keep it.

In most cases it is quite certain that to enable a mother to leave her infant is a gratuitous mistake. Even if the child be illegitimate, her maternal instincts are the best thing about her. She is salvable through these, or probably not at all. To give her facilities for deadening these instincts is to do her final harm. I call it a gratuitous blunder, because experience has shown that with a little kindly aid she can be enabled to keep the child and support herself and it. At the worst she can enter an institution for a time, and nurse her child and another. But experiments in the cities of Boston and Philadelphia have shown that suitable service places in the country can be found to which destitute mothers may go, taking their children with them. "The demand for this class of help usually exceeds the supply," and in Philadelphia between four and five hundred mothers with their children are yearly sent to situations in the country.[1] If judiciously placed, a majority of these women give satisfaction to their employers, and are satisfied themselves. It is said that they do as well as those who take situations without children, and in many instances they are more reliable for help in the country. Of course a destitute woman with no one to help her support her child has not an easy life before her; but, on the whole, life will be hap-

---

[1] State Charities Record, March, 1892; also, New York Conference on the Care of Dependent and Delinquent Children, Nov. 1893, pp. 77-82.

pier and healthier in every way if she is aided in keeping her child, than if she is aided in getting rid of it.

Children over two years of age live quite persistently. Therefore, as regards these, we do not need to examine so closely the death-rate, for they may be very improperly cared for and the death-rate still be low. The first question of importance regarding them is upon what terms they shall be received and supported as dependants.

The rules of private institutions for receiving children are very various, and often very erratic. Sometimes illegitimacy is a prerequisite. One endowed institution required that a child should be the legitimate offspring of parents both of whom had been members of the Presbyterian Church, and one or both of whom were dead. In some institutions children are received temporarily, and in others they are not admitted unless the natural parents give up all title to them. The rules of admission to private institutions are usually lax in practice if not in form; but they are nowhere so lax as in those States where the managers admit the child, and the State or city government is then constrained by law to pay for its maintenance without question. The financial aspects of this system will be considered later, but here must be noted its extreme perniciousness as regards the children. New York and California are the States most notorious for their recklessness in this matter.

Two things are necessary in order that agencies for the care of children may avoid the evil of encouraging the temporary or permanent abandonment of children. The first is, that the case of every child received must be thoroughly investigated by some competent agent; and the second is, that when relatives give up a child to be a dependant, they must give up all title to it. Guardianship should be vested completely in the agency that takes care of the child.

As to the first point, most private institutions for children are unduly negligent. It frequently happens that children are received through the influence of some member of the board of managers, or by a sympathetic matron, until the institution is overcrowded, and cases far more deserving of care then go unprovided for. Even where the matron or a member of the board of managers tries to make an investigation, it is work in which such a person is not an expert, and it is too often ill done. The business of deciding when children ought to be taken from parents, or received from parents, is becoming a specialty by itself; and the societies for the protection of children and children's aid societies ought to be asked to investigate all doubtful cases. So grave is the abuse of receiving children too readily, and so great is the injury to the children themselves when so received, that Mr. Randall of Michigan, and other men identified with the most progressive work for children, hold that no child should be placed in an institution except on judicial approval, and a finding that the given child is delinquent or dependent.[1] This rule they would have applied to institutions wholly supported by private funds, as well as to public institutions and private institutions receiving public subsidies.

The second rule, namely, that when parents or relatives leave a child to be supported by charitable agency, they should lose all title to it, seems a hard

---

[1] "History of Child Saving," p. xiii.

one, yet in the great majority of cases it is thoroughly salutary. Perhaps the rule of the Children's Home of Cincinnati, which refuses to receive a child for more than two weeks without having the guardianship of the child vested in the Home, affords as much latitude as ought to be given. It is urged that parents are after all the best guardians of their children, and if the time ever comes when they can take care of their own it is better that the children be returned. But experience shows that it has a bad effect on parents as parents to get rid of the care of their children for a time, and that they spoil the life of a child by selfishly taking it home when they think it is old enough to be of service.[1] Parents who cannot support their children usually have not the capacity required to bring up a child in a healthful way and in a healthful environment. Besides this, the privilege of temporarily disposing of a child is frequently the means of bringing about its permanent abandonment.[2] As affection wanes in consequence of absence, parents that would have found some way to support their children rather than give them up in the first instance, gradually accustom themselves to the idea of abandoning their offspring.

A stock instance of the effect of removing children from institutions to families, with the result that the natural parents will lose sight of and title to them, is that of the Union Temporary Home in Philadelphia. After thirty-one years of work, it was decided to close the Home and put the children out to board. Out of

---

[1] Miss Davenport-Hill lays especial stress upon the evil of allowing the natural parents to claim their children after something has been done for their betterment in a charitable institution.

[2] N. C. C., 1881, p. 282.

70 children, the parents of all but 9 were able to take good care of them themselves, and of the rest 3 found a way before final arrangements were made.[1] The diminution in the number of dependent children is especially large where the law provides that guardianship shall be vested in the State, or a board of children's guardians, in the cases of all children for whose support public money is given. At Washington, D.C., there were about 600 children in institutions receiving public money. A board of children's guardians was established under a law providing that the dependency of each child should be ascertained by a court, and the guardianship of a child then vested in the board of guardians. While the law as planned was not carried out, it became evident that, were it so carried out, there would not be more than 150 dependent children in the district. In the early seventies, two States awoke to the fact that they were disgraced by the presence of a large number of children in the county poorhouses. One State, Michigan, had about 600 persons under sixteen years of age in such institutions;[2] and New York, the other State referred to, had 2,179 in poorhouses.[3] Both State legislatures received reports showing the degrading influence of almshouse life upon the children, and giving pitiful instances of resulting disease and degeneration.[4]

[1] Cited by Mrs. Lowell in her Report on the Care of Dependent Children to the New York Board of Charities, 1889, p. 202. Also by Riis, " Children of the Poor," pp. 282-5.
[2] " History of Child Saving," p. 205.
[3] Tenth Annual Report N. Y. Board of Charities, p. 102.
[4] " In one of the county houses, three small children were found in a desolate room, one perishing with fever-sore, and the other two taking care of the sick one." Report Michigan Board of Charities and Corrections, 1874, p. 132. See also, Letchworth, " History of Child Saving," p. 178.

DEPENDENT CHILDREN. 217

In 1874 Michigan established a State Public School at Coldwater, and provided, first, that children adjudged dependent should be sent there, and subsequently placed in private families as soon as possible; second, that after an order is made to commit a child to the State Public School, "the parents of said child shall be released from all parental duties toward and responsibility for such child, and shall thereafter have no right over or to the custody, services, or earnings of such child, except in cases where the said Board has, as herein provided for, restored the child to its parents." The result of this system in Michigan has been that, whereas in 1874 she had 600 dependent children supported by public authorities, or one dependent child for each 2,223 inhabitants, she now has 300, or one in each 7,256 inhabitants. While the population increased sixty per cent, the number of dependent children decreased fifty per cent. Not only is this true, but the children that have passed under her care to Dec. 31, 1892 (3,317), have been well cared for, and, as a rule, restored to the normal population of the State.[1]

New York took a different course. In 1875 she passed the so-called "Children's Law," which forbade the keeping of children between the ages of two and sixteen years in the almshouses. It further provided that a dependent child should be committed, if possible, to an institution controlled by the same religious faith as that of its parents, and that the county should pay the child's

---

[1] See "History of Child Saving," pp. 213-14. The Michigan system has been repeatedly described at the National Conference of Charities. See "Ten Years of Child Saving Work in Michigan," by J. N. Foster, superintendent of the State Public School, N. C. C., 1884, pp. 132-42.

board. The legal guardianship of the child was not mentioned, and so remained with the parents, if it had any. In addition to this, special acts were subsequently passed enabling certain large institutions in New York City to receive children at will, and collect from the county two dollars per week for the care of each. It only remains to contrast present conditions in New York with those in Michigan. On Oct. 31, 1892, there were in the city and county almshouses of the State of New York, 963 children, many of these, however, being crippled, diseased, or under two years of age.[1] Besides this, there were in the private institutions of the State, but supported chiefly by the cities and counties, an army of 24,074 children. In these private institutions alone, there was one dependent child to each 270 persons in the State.[2] If we include the almshouse children, the proportion of dependent children to the population is one to 260.

After the question of receiving children and their guardianship, the next most important question concerns their classification. This matter should precede the decision as to the method of care, as it will often

[1] Twenty-Fifth Annual Report N. Y. State Board of Charities, Tables 9 and 13.

[2] Letchworth in "History of Child Saving," p. 182. See also Tables 19 and 21 in Twenty-fifth Annual Report N. Y. State Board of Charities (1891). The cost of these children to the tax-payers of the state for the fiscal year ending Sept. 30, 1892, was $2,019,342.94. Mr. Letchworth does not think that the Children's Law itself or alone produced these results, but does not specify what he considers the cause to have been. The subject was discussed in all its bearings at the Conference on the Care of Dependent and Delinquent Children in New York. This is the latest and best authority on the subject. See especially the last paper in the volume of the proceedings, on "The Public Support of Dependent Children in Private Institutions."

modify it. In the first place, we are compelled to set apart those who are distinctly unsound in body or mind. The sick must be remanded to hospital care or homes for incurables; cripples preferably to special institutions, and the feeble-minded and epileptic to institutions designed for them. There ought to be this separation of the unsound from the sound, but it is easier to say that classification is needed than to do the classifying. Every children's hospital has inmates that are well enough to be discharged, but within a month after discharge are likely to be sick enough to be readmitted. In making a personal investigation of 611 inmates in eleven institutions for children, I found 32 that had some marked mental defect or nervous disease, such as epilepsy or paralysis. Besides this, 92 of the children were markedly defective or diseased. Not many cripples were found, but many afflicted with severe forms of scrofula and other varieties of practically incurable blood-poisoning. That is, one out of six of these children was distinctly unwell, mentally or physically.[1]

While it is necessary not only to separate the sound from the unsound, to further classify those adjudged healthy is similarly important and difficult. First are the depraved, subdivided into criminals, misdemeanants, and unmanageables. These are usually spoken of as "delinquents," and the reform school is prescribed. As a rule, they must be so classed, and cannot be considered here, though their proper care is one of the most impor-

---

[1] This, of course, does not include those children that were suffering from such ailments, common to institution life, as mild skin disease, sore eyes, etc. See Report Supt. of Charities for District of Columbia, 1892, p. 28.

tant problems in applied sociology. On the average, they probably have more vitality in them than the other classes of dependent children, and frequently the overt act that brings them before the court is the result of an accident. The child that has actually committed arson, theft, or assault may be not essentially different from a playmate that has not done these particular things. It has consequently come to be the rule in progressive States to give the courts wide discretion in the commitment of juvenile delinquents. They may be sent to reform schools, to charitable institutions, or consigned to the care of children's aid societies or boards of guardians. In many cases it has been found possible to board actual delinquents in private families with good results.[1]

After the delinquents, come the dependent children proper, made up of the neglected, abused, abandoned, and otherwise parentless, and the children of utterly destitute parents. While a few delinquent children are placed in the care of charitable agencies with good results, it is far commoner for simply destitute children to be sent to correctional institutions with very dubious results. The laws of most States provide a definition for vagrancy that is broad enough to include almost any neglected child, and further provide that vagrants or children that wander about and beg from door to door may be sent to reform schools. Another elastic provision is that regarding "incorrigibles." If the parent sees fit to swear that the child is incorrigible, the court has very little option in many States, but must commit such child to the reform school. In several institutions visited, fully half the children seem to be

[1] N. C. C., 1891, pp. 136-45.

neglected and abandoned, rather than juvenile delinquents. Mixed with the more depraved who properly belong to the school, the chances for these boys and girls to come to the best that they were capable of is not good. The classification at exactly this point — the separation of the depraved from the merely destitute — is an essential element in the wise handling of the neglected and destitute children of any State or locality.

In the classification of destitute children, it will be noticed that orphans and half-orphans have not been included, a distinction which is more commonly made, perhaps, than any other; and yet for purposes of care it has very little significance. The child that must be taken from its parents is parentless, and it is of very little significance so far as the child itself is concerned whether its parents are dead or not. The distinction between orphans and half-orphans, which is recognized by the laws of California and other States in providing money for private institutions, and which is usually recognized in the administration of private institutions, is simply a device by which the managers of an institution save themselves the trouble of examining into individual cases. The distinction is made because it is easy to make, and they feel that they must draw the line somewhere. It is, however, of comparatively little consequence for our present purposes, and can only be of use in studying causes of dependency among children.

What has been said regarding classification shows the great importance of the work of the children's aid societies and the societies for the protection of children from cruelty and immorality. They are, or should be, specialists in exactly this work of classification. It is their business to understand the character of the children and the possibilities of the situation; and wherever their work is done with conscientious intelligence, the courts cannot do better than to take their advice in disposing of destitute or delinquent children. In many cases it may be found that institution life of any sort is unnecessary; and where it is necessary, the institution should be chosen with distinct reference to the individual child.[1]

After the matters of reception, guardianship, and classification are disposed of, the final matter of importance is the method of providing for dependent children. Broadly speaking, there are two systems; the first is the institution plan, and the second is the plan of placing out.

Without the figures of the Eleventh Census at hand, it is impossible to tell how large a proportion of the dependent children of the country is in institutions; but it is a comparatively large number. To build institutions for

[1] It has not been deemed necessary to call attention to the need of classifying dependent children according to sex, as this is usually done. One unfortunate failure to make classification is in reform schools, where the boys and girls sometimes are in the same institution. Under good administration, however, as in the New York Catholic Protectory, it is not impossible to secure satisfactory results where both sexes are in one institution. There are certain factitious classifications, as by the religious faith of the parents, with which the scientific student of the problem is sometimes inclined to lose all patience; and yet the desire to have such classifications and the belief of the community in their wisdom must be reckoned with. The courts usually try, either under statutory provision or without it, to send a child to an institution managed by the same religious sect as that to which the parents belong. This should never be done unless all other requirements of good classification can be met at the same time. The rules of admission of many private institutions establish arbitrary rules of classification; and these lines, running across those of rational classification, bring about unfortunate complications.

children has been the common and obvious thing to do in providing for them. The institution is preferred by parents, because they know where the child is, and can usually visit it, and frequently can retain the right to take it back again when they will. Institutions are also in favor with the benevolent, because the work done is so manifest. A hundred or more children, prepared for the occasion, make an attractive sight to the board of directors or to visitors. Buildings are obvious, and the money that goes into them takes a concrete form gratifying to the contributors. The churches prefer such life for the children dependent upon them, because the children can be so easily isolated from teachings other than their own. There is opportunity for catechetical instruction. In New York City all the institutions having more than a thousand children are of a distinctly religious character.[1]

On the whole, institutions are preferred by the children themselves, at least after they have been in them for some time. They do not feel at home outside of the sheltering walls, and shrink from the rough contact of ordinary life. In many institutions former inmates keep returning again and again, either seeking work or begging to be taken back, because it is the life they are used to, and the only one for which they are fitted. I have known matrons to suggest that after orphan asy-

---

[1] Foundling Asylum of the Sisters of Charity, N.Y. . . . 1,744
　Mission of the Immaculate Virgin, N.Y. 1,882
　Missionary Sister of Third Order of St. Francis, N.Y. . 1,145
　New York Catholic Protectory 2,374
　Orphans' Home and Asylum of the Holy Church, Brooklyn, E.D. 1,136
(Annual Report State Board of Charities, 1892, Table No. 21.)

lums there ought to be other custodial institutions to take adults of either sex and give them shelter for the remainder of their lives.

The institution, commending itself in interest to these various parties, has necessarily had a greater development than the placing-out system. Besides, there are many things to be said in its favor by those who have a really disinterested wish to benefit the dependents. The children receive many negative benefits. They are not cold, nor dirty, nor neglected, nor hungry, nor abused, — that is, if the management is good. The grosser forms of profanity and vice can be restrained; their attendance on school exercises is entirely regular, as are also their hours of sleep and eating. But admitting these advantages, we have said about all that is favorable to institution life for children. The congregating of them together, which we found in the case of infants to result in high mortality, results in the case of older children in a low vitality. Even a small institution is different from a large family. In the latter the children are of different ages; they have different opportunities for amusement — one imitates the other. In even a small institution, one with only eight or ten children, they are apt to be of about the same age, none of them especially ambitious, and with their opportunities for self-education very limited. In the large caravansaries, where hundreds or even thousands of children are congregated, their non-development is very apparent. The fundamental fault is, perhaps, that life is made too easy. A child ought to have more opportunities of hurting himself, or getting dirty, or being insubordinate, than can possibly be accorded to him here. It is a pitiful sight to see a hundred children together, and none of them making a fuss. The discipline that would make a good soldier ruins a child. It is fatal to him to march in platoons, to play only at the word of command. As a matron in South Australia says, "They [the children] never grow up properly if you have a lot of them together. I would never have children of two or three years of age there; for if they get into an institution they never develop into anything: they only grow up into half-idiotic men and women. However good a nurse you have, she cannot draw out the intelligence of every child, and nurse it as it would be nursed in a home. . . . We have only five now, and they are as bright again as when we had twenty."[1]

How is a child to learn to use matches if he lives in a building with steam heat and electric light? How will the child learn to cook in the ordinary home where nothing but great ranges are used for cooking? How learn to wash under ordinary circumstances where the laundry does work for one or two hundred people? What experience can a boy have here that would qualify him to bring in wood? How learn to carry water where there is nothing to do but turn the stopcock? How will a child learn to tell the time of day where everything moves at the stroke of a bell or the word of command? How obtain any appreciation whatever of the value of money when everything comes to him as if the world had been arranged to provide him with each thing that he needs and just as he needs it? There is, in fact, no proper development of the child's inventiveness or individuality, or even of

[1] "Children of the State," p. 235.

his ambitions. A hundred institution children deluged with toys at Christmas enjoy them less, and feel less gratitude, than the children of the individual home who have learned to long for things, and learned to know in some sort what it costs to provide them.

The fact already mentioned, that the child is never quite ready to leave the institution, tells strongly against this method. The neglect of superintendents to follow the subsequent careers of the children, and make careful statements of how they turn out, while readily explained, is very unfortunate. It is a well-known fact with institutions receiving older children — those of ten or twelve years of age — that inmates who have gone through a previous institution experience cannot hold their own with those who come direct from the slums. Children who have grown up in infant asylums to the age of ten must be classed with children of from six to eight, who even then go by them in classes and at work. I have known the matron to ask all those who had come from another institution for younger children to step out of line; and they were distinctly flabby and under-vitalized as compared with the others. As the matron herself remarked, "They are so good for nothing!"

A great part of the evils of institution life come from the mingling of individuals, none of whom have a very good heredity behind them, and some of whom have inherited weak constitutions and bad moral tendencies. It is a continual fight on the part of matrons to repress skin diseases and sore eyes; and these contagious diseases are but typical of the contagious vices which are not so obvious, but more to be dreaded. That institution life is partly faulty because of the low grade of children who are received, and who bring about degeneration in each other, is proved by the experience of institutions that have introduced an element of artificial selection, which separates the low from the more highly organized. At Girard College and at the McDonogh School, where the attempt is made to get boys from respectable families, and where any boy who cannot carry his studies or will not obey the rules, is promptly dismissed, there has obtained an *esprit du corps*, an ambition, among the inmates, which is utterly impossible in those institutions that take all comers, without reference to capacity. Especially at the McDonogh School, where boys are admitted only on competitive examination and where admission is a prize worth working for, the whole atmosphere of the place shows the difference. Some of the most capable and ambitious young men in Baltimore come from that school.

It should also be said that institution life has been greatly improved by the introduction of kindergarten work for the smaller children, and industrial training for those of maturer years. But the trouble is, that in the great majority of cases, the expense of giving such work properly leads to the mere pretence of giving it, — going through the motions of industrial training without the spirit of it, or managing a kindergarten in a way that makes the child completely dependent upon somebody else for all its possibilities of play and enjoyment. It is not sufficiently understood that a poor kindergarten stultifies the child, and that manual training which is not well conducted has no virtues in it.

Another way in which institution life is improved is by sending the children out to the public schools. In relatively small institutions this is possible, and very desirable. It gives the child that contact with others which he needs. It is a common practice among Hebrews, unknown among the Catholics, and only practised occasionally by Protestant and "non-sectarian" managers.

Over against the institution plan of caring for dependent children is the plan of placing them in private families, with or without the payment of board. There are two tolerably distinct methods of procedure in this work. By one, the children are sent to a great distance, and given but little subsequent supervision — that is the so-called "emigration plan;" and by the other they are placed within easy reach of the agency having them in charge, and subsequent supervision is systematic and constant.

In London a large number of children are sent to the colonies. The emigration bureau operated in connection with Dr. Bernardo's Homes sends about five hundred children per year to Canada; and some of these no doubt find their way to the United States. The plan is to drop the child amid new surroundings, as carefully as is conveniently possible, and then to keep only so much track of him as is necessary to show to contributors or others that a goodly proportion of cases turn out well. The child is simply given one more chance to sink or swim. It is found that foster parents are more readily obtained for children coming from a distance, probably because it is less likely that the natural parents will tamper with them.[1]

---

[1] Alexander Johnson of Indiana: "It is a striking fact that a much better class of citizens will accept the children brought from Boston than will accept children from our asylums in their own county." — *Charities Review*, vol. ii., p. 220.

In the United States the greatest agency for emigrating children to the West is the Children's Aid Society of New York, founded by Charles L. Brace in 1853. Up to 1892, they had emigrated 84,318 children, of whom 51,427 were boys, and 32,891 were girls. Some of these were not sent to a great distance, nearly 39,000 of them being placed in the State of New York, 4,149 in New Jersey, etc. The Western States receiving the largest number were Illinois, to which 7,366 were sent; Iowa, 4,852; Missouri, 4,835; Indiana, 3,782; Kansas, 3,310; Michigan, 2,900; Minnesota, 2,448.[1] The work of this society very well illustrates the advantages and the limitations of the emigration plan. Its great number of children were placed out at an average expense of about ten dollars per child, and much less care was taken in placing and supervising in the early years than have since been found necessary in order to reconcile the States to the reception of the children. Professor White describes the methods used with two groups of children sent to Kansas. The first were placed in Kansas in 1867. Many of the boys were over fourteen years of age. They were carelessly placed, and most of them did not remain long. Not one of this party now resides in the county in which he was originally placed, and only two are known to live in Kansas. On the other hand, the party placed in Kansas in 1884, consisting of children much younger on the average, were placed with greater care, and the results have been far more satisfactory. The society's statement for all the children

---

[1] "History of Child Saving," p. 30. See also pamphlet published by the Society, 1893, "The Children's Aid Society of New York, Its History, Plan, and Results."

placed in Kansas is as follows: "The total number of children placed in homes among the residents of Kansas is 960, of which number 129, or about 13.43 per cent, were girls. Ninety-four, or 9.79 per cent, have no records. Nearly all of these were large boys and girls who were placed early in the history of the society; 32, or 1.56 per cent, are known to have died; 95, or 9.89 per cent, left their homes within the first few years; 23, or 2.39 per cent, have bad records; 64, or 6.66 per cent, have poor records; 212, or 22.08 per cent, have very fair records; 425, or 44.27 per cent, have excellent records. The average age of the children was 12.3 years; 84 per cent of those under eight years have done well.[1]

Hastings H. Hart of the Minnesota State Board of Corrections and Charities has investigated the results of the children placed in Minnesota by the Children's Aid Society of New York, and finds that the methods of placing were frequently too inexpensive and incautious; and while for the most part the society took care of children that did not turn out well, this was not true in all cases. In some cases they were placed in families so destitute as to be receiving public assistance, and other unsatisfactory placements were made. "From our experience," says Mr. Hart, "we are positive in the opinion that children above the age of twelve years ought not to be sent West by the Children's Aid Society. In this opinion I understand that the officers of the society concur. Secretary Brace says: 'The emigration plan must be conducted with careful judgment, and be applied so far as practicable to children under say fourteen years of age.' If the society would adhere to the wise rule laid down,

[1] *Charities Review*, vol. ii., p. 225.

we should have little cause for complaint. Our examination shows," concludes Mr. Hart, "with reference to children under thirteen years of age, that nine-tenths remain, four-fifths are doing well, and all incorrigibles are cared for by the society. If properly placed, faithfully supervised, we are willing to take our full share of these younger children in Minnesota."[1]

All investigations of the emigration system have not been as careful and impartial as the two made by Professor White and Mr. Hart from which I have quoted. Consequently, at the National Conferences of Charity and elsewhere there have been bitter attacks upon the society for flooding the West with dependent children, and filling Western reformatories and prisons as a result.[2] Whether justly or not, the authorities in the Western States are for the most part disinclined to welcome these children, and the territory within which they can be placed is gradually becoming more limited.

The placing-out system, properly so called, — that is, the placing of children where they are easily accessible to the agency responsible for them, — has been practised for a long time by the officers of the Poor Law Unions of England and of American towns and counties. Children were simply kept in the almshouses until old enough so that somebody would take them. Mr. Folks, in writing of this system of disposing of pauper children in Pennsylvania, says that in many cases the directors of the poor of the different counties do not know how many chil-

---

[1] N. C. C., 1884, pp. 149, 150. In the article referred to, Mr. Hart gives very complete tables of results, and an uncolored and interesting account of the methods used in placing children.

[2] N. C. C., 1887, pp. 293-297.

dren they are responsible for, and their records hardly show how many have been placed out. One record simply showed that a certain child had been given to "Mr. Jones, who lives just over the hill."[1] This, of course, is placing-out at its worst, especially if it be not resorted to until the children have been spoiled by almshouse or asylum life. Institutions must find some way to dispose of their children when the time comes for them to leave; and frequently a matron or manager of an institution is prejudiced against the placing-out system because he finds it so difficult to provide places for them. He forgets that he is not an expert in this branch of his work; that he does it during some slack season in a hurried way, and without the skill that comes from practice. Such placers-out of children frequently say that the older the children are, the better; and it is doubtless true that the older ones are less likely to be foisted back upon the institution; but it is because they are more likely to wander away and bring up in a reform school, house of correction, or prison. It is one of the things to be especially charged against institutions for children, that their methods of sociological bookkeeping are so limited that they cannot tell how the children with whose lives they have tinkered turn out; yet this, as Mr. Folks well urges, is the only real test of the results.

Placing-out as a speciality has been carried to its most satisfactory results by such public institutions as the State Board of Lunacy and Charity in Massachusetts, and the State School for Dependent Children at Coldwater, Mich., and by such private associations as the Children's Aid Society of Massachusetts, and the Child-

[1] "History of Child Saving," p. 144.

ren's Aid Society of Pennsylvania. With these agencies " the setting of the solitary in families" is a business. The following description, taken not literally, but in substance, from Mr. Folks's article on "Child Saving Work in Pennsylvania,"[1] will give the best idea of how this system operates. The Children's Aid Society of Pennsylvania consists of a central society, with county committees in each county of the State, or in as many of them as efficient committees can be maintained, who have received from the directors of the poor or others, dependent children, whom they place at once in families. Usually they are placed in the county where they become dependent; but when the children are particularly troublesome, or relatives interfere, or the family name is unfavorably known in the locality, the main office often removes the child to a distant part of the State. A large proportion of the children are placed in Pennsylvania, but a considerable number also in adjoining States. The work of the main office is conducted under the supervision of the managers by a corps of eight salaried officials, two of whom are men. One assistant gives her whole time to the problem of homeless mothers with young children, providing for them service places to which they can take their children. Four workers are travelling almost constantly, investigating families who have applied for children, visiting children who have been placed out, or taking children to and from their homes. Having relied so largely upon the family plan, the society has given much attention to the elaboration of the details of its administration, and has thrown around it every possible safeguard. Its investi-

---

[1] "History of Child Saving," pp. 146, 147.

gation of a family is systematic and exhaustive, and is carefully recorded. The applicant fills out a blank containing twenty-six questions relating to the various phases of the family life, as church relations, distance from school, size of farm, occupation, number of members of family, with their ages, etc. A study of this return usually reveals the real motive of the application, and gives the data for an opinion as to the *material* fitness of the family. Their moral fitness is ascertained by sending a list of questions to six of the neighbors, stating that their replies are confidential, and that the appeal to them is not known to the applicant. A personal visit completes the investigation. After the child is placed out, his welfare is ascertained and protected by from one to five personal and unannounced visits each year, by a monthly report from the teacher of the public schools, and a quarterly report from the pastor. The society uses neither indenture nor written agreement, the terms being perfectly flexible, and subject to change from year to year to suit the circumstances of each individual case. This society considers institutions for normal children needless, and has even had good success in boarding out juvenile delinquents received from the courts. A similar work has been done by the Massachusetts Children's Aid Society, which has one or two home-like institutions where abnormal children are placed until they can be fitted into a proper home.[1]

[1] A summary account of the Massachusetts Society as a placing-out agency is herewith reproduced from the charts prepared by it for the charities' exhibit of the Chicago Exposition : —

Terms on which children are placed: $2.50 per week, and clothing for children under one year. $2.00 per week, and clothing for children

DEPENDENT CHILDREN. 235

Michigan and Massachusetts are the two States whose public officials have done most notable work in placing out. The results in Michigan have already been referred to in contrast with the results of another system in the State of New York. From the State School at Coldwater the children are sent to homes in various parts of the State, where the visitors look after their interests, and where they are visited by the representative of the State School from time to time. It has been found possible to reincorporate all normal children with the population very speedily. The number at the State school is not as large now as formerly. This system

over one year until placed free. Free usually when about twelve years of age. Wages when worth them, usually at fourteen to sixteen years. Collecting board from parents and book-keeping take one person's time. Children attend public schools; boarded children full time, other children as required by law; (thirty weeks per year until fourteen years old in Massachusetts, twenty-six weeks in Vermont, and sixteen weeks in other New England States), and as much longer as can be obtained.

Condition on which children are placed: Applicants must have some adequate means of support besides board of children. No other children are to be taken from public or private agencies. One child, as a rule, placed in a family; sometimes two, if of same sex, but very different ages; brothers and sisters generally placed together.

Children must attend church and Sunday-school and public schools if of suitable age, eat at same table, and receive same care, discipline, and kindness as would children of the family. Families to consider all information about children strictly confidential. Responsibility of family for child's entire moral, religious, physical, and mental training constantly emphasized, also frequent consultation with visitor on the subject.

Supervision: Three paid visitors and twelve volunteers. Average cost of placing a child and supervision for a year, $26, excluding board and clothing. I. Visiting. Visitor accompanies child when placed. Points covered in visits to children: Food, clothing, sleeping arrangements, cleanliness, neatness, schooling, church attendance, reading, companions, amusements, punishments, training in house or

was to have been copied in Wisconsin; but there the influence of the private institutions has compelled a compromise between the system of State placing-out and the New York system of child storage. The same unfortunate condition of contending systems obtains in the District of Columbia; but in Minnesota, the Michigan system has been completely introduced, and is completely successful.[1]

In Ohio there is a system of county homes, from farm work, adaptability of child to family, its happiness, special failings or habits, progress in study, work, and character. II. Reports required. If children are taken free of charge, family reports every two months; if boarded, every month. Statements required at regular intervals in regard to clothing, attendance and progress at school, and wages. Children, if old enough, write to visitor once a month.

Children in charge within the year Oct. 1, 1892, to Oct. 1, 1894.

	FREE.	BOARDED.	WAGES.	TOTAL.
Destitute, Exposed and Untrained	61	218	15	294
Wayward Girls	14	13	9	36
Wayward Boys from Training School,	93	8	67	168
TOTALS	168	239	91	498

BOARDED CHILDREN.	COST OF BOARD AND CLOTHING FOR BOARDED CHILDREN FROM OCT. 1, 1891, TO OCT. 1, 1892.
Total 239	
Supported entirely by parents or relatives 91	Total $13,781
Supported partly by parents or relatives. 61	Paid by Child. Aid Society, 6,227
Supported entirely by charity 87	Paid by other Public or Private Charity 1,155
	Paid by parents or relatives, 6,398

[1] On State Public Schools for Dependent Children, see G. A. Merrill, "History of Child Saving," p. 204. On Massachusetts System, see Mrs. Richardson, *ib.*, pp. 54-68. These are the last and best accounts. The various systems have been described repeatedly at the National Conferences of Charities, in papers which those especially interested in the matter will perhaps be glad to consult.

which children are placed out; and the one criticism which advocates of placing out might pass upon that work is, that there is a slight tendency for the children to accumulate in the homes, instead of being promptly reincorporated with the general population. The commissioners serve without compensation. The almshouses have there been emptied of children, and a large number of unsalaried officials fill the honor offices by which the institutions are managed. A detailed statement of the Ohio county homes for dependent children will be found in Mr. Hathaway's article in the "History of Child Saving."

On the whole, the placing-out system deserves the commendation it has received from the most advanced specialists. If administered " with an adequate supply of eternal vigilance," it is economical, kindly, and efficient. If badly administered, it leads to very obvious abuses; but at its best it is the best system. In the conclusion of this chapter, attention should be again called to the fact that it is less in child-caring than in child-saving work that really helpful results are to be found. Newsboys' lodging-houses, industrial schools, reading-rooms, home libraries, and the countless agencies for benefiting the street Arab and making a man of him, carried on by the New York Children's Aid Society and the Massachusetts Children's Aid Society, and similar organizations, are doing a work which we commend, but neglect, — the work of prevention. The same is true of the societies for the protection of children from cruelty and immorality; and, as we noted under the head of classification, it is necessary that these specialist organizations should be called in to classify and assign to the proper child-caring agency the children that are to be dependent. It is to these two classes of organizations also that we must look for help in the proper discharge of children from dependency; and it is especially to them that we look for a system of sociological book-keeping that will enable us to tell with definiteness what is being accomplished — how the children "turn out." There is no better fund of raw material for sociological study than the great records of the children's aid societies and other advanced child-caring agencies of the United States. From such records we may expect some time to draw a partial answer to the question, " Whither is philanthropy leading us ?"

CHAPTER X.

THE DESTITUTE SICK.

[The only authority that need be cited on the subject of this chapter is the monumental volume of over 700 pages on "Hospitals, Dispensaries, and Nursing," published by Section III. of the International Congress of Charities, Correction, and Philanthropy, held at Chicago, 1893. (Hopkins Press, Baltimore, 1894.) The volume is edited by Dr. John S. Billings and Dr. Henry M. Hurd, and eminent specialists of nearly all countries have contributed papers. A few of the papers are printed in German and a few in French.]

PREVIOUS to the appearance of the final report of the Eleventh Census on the dependent classes, there is no way of estimating accurately the number of the destitute sick provided for in the United States. It is simply known that within the last twenty years the hospitals of the country have had a very rapid development, coming in part from the influx of the foreign population accustomed to seek hospital service,[1] in part from the increasing density of population, but very largely, without doubt, from the increased efficiency of the hospitals. Formerly a hospital was regarded as a place that every one would stay away from if he could. It was a place where the shattered wrecks of armies must be taken, where the homeless stranger must seek refuge if overtaken by sickness, and where the abjectly destitute must necessarily be cared for. But of late the improvements in medical art, and especially in surgical processes, have

---

[1] See Billings, "Hospitals," p. 2.

enabled hospitals to render better service than can be given even in the homes of the well-to-do; and, as a consequence, there has been a greatly increased demand for accommodations for pay patients, and with the growth of every hospital has come also the growth of free wards. The increase in the number of free beds, and the increase in efficiency, have rendered the poorer classes less disinclined to seek refuge in the hospital, and especially to resort for free consultation and medicine to the dispensaries. Even if we knew how many patients had been sheltered by the hospitals of the United States, it would be a task of great difficulty to find out how many of the beds were really free to those filling them. There are those who believe that eventually hospital service will be free to all willing to accept of it at public expense, just as for the insane, hospital service or asylum care is now free to all willing to accept of it in Minnesota, and ostensibly in some other States; or as education, including support, is free in many States to all defectives.

As indicating the extent of the burden which is now imposed upon tax-payers for the maintenance of medical charities, the author has collated with some care from the official reports, verified in some instances by correspondence and personal visitation, the public expenditure for medical charities in ten American cities.

It will be seen that during the year to which the figures refer for the different cities, the expense has been from a little less than 11 to a little more than 63 cents per capita for medical charities, the average being 31.09 cents; but in any one of the cities named the amount stated in no wise represents the total expenditure for the

TABLE XXVII.

Public Expenditures for Medical Charities in Ten American Cities.

CITY.	POPULATION (Census of 1890).	FISCAL YEAR.	AMOUNT.	PER CAPITA.
Brooklyn	806,343	1889–90	$196,115.61	$0.2432
St. Louis	451,770	1889–90	140,773.43	.3116
Boston [1]	448,477	1890	188,177.88	.4195
Baltimore	434,439	1891	111,790.00	.2573
Cincinnati	296,908	1890 or '91	110,162.92	.3710
Buffalo	255,664	1891	67,650.00	.2646
Minneapolis	164,738	1890	17,842.64	.1083
St. Paul	133,156	1890	27,269.02	.2074
Indianapolis	105,436	1891	29,170.00	.2767
Washington	230,392	1890–91	145,625.00	.6320
ALL TEN CITIES	3,327,323	. . . .	$1,034,576.50	.31093

[1] The figures for Boston cover the expenditures for the City Hospital only. Since the table has passed from under my hands I learn that there are expenditures on the part of the State for medical charities which serve the poor of Boston, and the per capita might possibly be as high as that of Washington if all the items could be included. However, the service is of a much higher grade than that given in Washington, costing nearly twice as much per patient per week.

relief of the destitute sick. The proceeds of endowments and private contributions are not taken into view at all.

The American hospitals are so careless in making up their reports, that it is frequently impossible to glean the facts important in estimating their efficiency. The expenditures per patient in a hospital are usually large for the small institutions, and relatively small for the large institutions, but normally depend chiefly upon the character of the cases treated, and especially whether the cases are chronic or acute. It is therefore desirable that the following items should find a place in the reports of a given hospital : —

1. The average daily number of patients, or the total number of days' service rendered during the year. Many hospital reports give the number of patients treated, but no data to determine the daily average number of patients.

2. The number of different patients treated during the year.

3. The longest time any one patient has remained in the institution, and how many, if any, have been there during the whole year. Also, the average length of time patients remain. This is to indicate whether the hospital is serving chronic or acute cases, an item of great importance in estimating the proper cost.

4. The ratio of deaths to the whole number disposed of. The death-rate is a thing about which competing institutions wrangle a great deal. The ratio is frequently given to the whole number of patients, which is not as fair as the method just indicated. It is sometimes given to the number of days' service rendered, which is meaningless, because many of the cases may be chronic. But even when the death-rate is given as suggested above, it may or may not indicate good management of the hospital. Its significance is still ambiguous, for it may be kept down by refusing to receive all cases where the prognosis is death.[1] This policy, except possibly in certain special

[1] Lord Cathcart remarks that moribund cases stand a doubtful chance, or no chance, of being taken to the great voluntary hospitals of London. "Hospitals," p. 13.

institutions, is condemnable, because hospitals for the poor should be among other things comfortable places for people to die in. The refusal of doctors to perform operations that are dangerous, but are yet in the interests of the patients, may also keep down the death-rate, but not indicate efficiency.

The cost of hospital construction is thus stated in a table prepared by Dr. Aucker of St. Paul: —

TABLE XXVIII.

CONSTRUCTION COST OF CERTAIN HOSPITALS.

(N. C. C., 1888, p. 184.)

HOSPITAL.	SQUARE FEET OF FLOOR PER BED.	CUBIC FEET OF SPACE PER BED.	LINEAL FEET OF WALL SPACE PER BED.	SQUARE FEET OF WINDOW SPACE PER BED.	COST PER BED.
Johns Hopkins, Baltimore	103	1,675	7.7	28	$4,330
St. Thomas, England	125	1,886	8.0	15	3,460
City, New York	94	1,300	4.0	20	3,100
Herbert, England	87	1,200	7.4	19	1,750
City, Boston	100	1,400	6.6	28	1,425
City, St. Paul	108	1,512	7.8	28	750

The care of the sick, especially in the wards of a great hospital, is something that appeals very directly to the sympathies, and a large amount of voluntary contributions can usually be relied upon to support such institutions. Besides this, they usually serve a purpose in the education of medical students and young physicians, and almost invariably a purpose in building up the reputation of the physicians and surgeons in charge of them. There are cases, indeed, where the gratuitous treatment of all applicants has in it no element of charity, the clinic being worth more to the school than it costs. Advertisements are frequently kept in the dailies of a large city, announcing free dentistry to all who care to receive it. The person responding to such an advertisement will be attended to by a probably skilful student, under the guidance of the professor in a school of dentistry; and the opportunity of educating the student is fully equivalent to the services rendered. A lecturer or manager of a clinic of a medical school frequently pays a patient a considerable amount for the privilege of showing some operation or disease to the class. This is not only free treatment, but pay was given for the privilege of treating.

Not less than three strong motives, therefore, contribute to the development of medical charities, — the desire to aid the destitute, the desire to educate students and build up medical reputations, and the desire to protect the public health. The latter has often been the leading cause of public appropriations for medical charities. A few hospitals decline to admit students to their advantages; but the uniform testimony of medical experts seems to be that the teaching hospitals render better service than the non-teaching institutions.[1]

In order that there may be no clash between the officers in charge, each medical school usually desires to control its own hospital, and the officers in charge of a

---

[1] "Hospitals," pp. 5, 6. An eminent specialist speaks in the following enthusiastic strain of the services rendered by a certain hospital to the medical school: "Annually opening its exhaustless treasuries of disease to crowds of educated, zealous inquirers after medical knowledge."

THE DESTITUTE SICK.   245

given hospital usually wish to be connected with some one medical school. The great public hospitals arrange as well as they can to give the facilities of their wards to the medical schools of the locality in which they operate.

The qualification for admission to a hospital as such is disease. For admission to a free bed, there should be the additional qualification of destitution; but this latter point is usually not insisted upon. The competition of medical schools, or schools of medicine, and of individual institutions, is usually so great that no one willing to put up with the inconvenience, and to take the risks of free hospital treatment, is refused.[1] People enter hospitals as

[1] Nearly all the medical journals attack spasmodically the tendency of physicians to promote themselves by gratuitous service for hospitals or dispensaries. The low price for admission to the pay wards of a hospital frequently angers the medical profession more than the gratuitous services rendered. The Johns Hopkins Hospital, both by gratuitous services at its dispensary when first opened, and by low rates of admission to its wards, brought down upon itself a great amount of adverse criticism. Many tolerably eminent specialists in neighboring cities lost their patients because they drifted away to the Hopkins Hospital for critical operations and the subsequent nursing. Along with this, the young practitioners in the neighborhood found that the class that they had expected to serve went, almost without exception, to the out-patient department of the great hospital in which they had confidence, and at which there was no charge. There was formed, in consequence, an organization known as the United States Medical Practitioners' Protective Alliance, which does not appear, however, to have extended its operations much beyond Maryland. The English experience in this matter is very instructive. The *Medical Times* has said that "the amount of gratuitous work done by the profession in no way raises it in public estimation. It is well known that it is not performed from motives of charity, but from the position that is gained by being attached to a hospital staff, and the hope of a good practice accruing therefrom." The British Medical Journal says " Hospitals compete with each other as to the number of patients, without regard to the fitness of the cases or the position of

pay-patients only if they wish some special advantages or privileges. That people are admitted to free beds without investigation is especially true in those places where the private institutions admit patients for whom the municipality or county pays the bills. This is the system in vogue in Baltimore and Brooklyn, and other large cities where the subsidy system obtains. In Buffalo there has been a much more careful arrangement, by which it is required that any one admitted to a free bed at the expense of the State must secure a permit either from the Health Department or the poor-law officers. An agent of the Health Department goes through the hospital wards weekly or semi-monthly, to see what patients paid for by the public can be properly discharged, or if chronic cases can properly be remanded to the almshouse. The city of Buffalo or the county pays a certain rate per week for the care of patients which it sends to the various hospitals. The per capita expenditure in Buffalo for medical charities is about 26.5 cents; while in Washington, where the looser system prevails, it is 63.2 cents.[1]

Within the hospital the lines of authority should be as distinctly traceable as possible. The various depart-

the applicants." In the Children's Hospital of London, where the rule was adopted of referring all applicants to the Charity Organization Society, and where no patients were excluded provided that the parents were making less than 30 shillings a week, there was found an abuse-rate of 57 per cent. In the London hospital, when an inspector was appointed for the out-door patients, there was a reduction in twelve months of 7,311 patients, which brought about a saving of some $7,000 in one year to the charity. At this hospital the abuse-rate was about 50 per cent. See Rentoul, " Voluntary Medical Charities."

[1] See Table XXVII.

ments of administration are: first, the purely business side, the getting of supplies, keeping of books, etc.; second, the housekeeping; third, the nursing; and fourth, the medical work. All of these should be under the care of a single superintendent, who may or may not be a physician. In public institutions the great problem of management is to keep out politics.[1] The evil conditions to which a great hospital may be brought by the reign of ward politics was formerly perfectly illustrated in the Bellevue Hospital, New York, and now, perhaps, is best illustrated in the Cook County Hospital of Chicago. At the International Congress of Charities, Dr. Burdett of London said that the management of the institution, except among the nurses, was characterized by an absence of all conscience. He added, "I have never seen anything in the whole course of my experience, and I have visited hospitals in every country in the world, including Russia, which has gone so straight to my heart, which has been so appalling and awful, as what I saw in my visit to the Cook County Hospital."[2] At this hospital the officers are appointed by the County Board of Supervisors. They are appointed for purely political reasons, and usually change every year. At San Francisco the conditions are equally bad. St. Paul is practically free from the curse of politics, and Cincinnati is between the two. The Philadelphia hospital has been redeemed from the "political buzzards" by the reform of the State government under the Bullitt Bill.

The question of politics brings us to the question of

---

[1] See the account of Philadelphia Hospital, by Richard Wood, "Hospitals," pp. 58, *et seq.*

[2] "Hospitals," p. 708.

private *versus* public control of hospitals. American cities have done comparatively little in establishing municipal hospitals as compared with their activity in other lines of development. In the smaller towns the cheapest way is to subsidize private hospitals; and this is the system which has been resorted to, and which has fastened itself upon even large cities like Brooklyn and Baltimore. About the only public hospital that is maintained in many of our large cities is that in connection with the almshouse, where chronic cases are received on the general principle of almshouse management, that all who cannot go anywhere else can go there. These almshouse infirmaries frequently develop into what are really large general hospitals. There is needed in all the cities better co-ordination of all the medical charities; and yet it is one of the most difficult things to bring about, because of individual, medical, and religious rivalries. The best method seems to be for the city itself to establish a large general hospital, which shall be as well managed as the character of the municipality or county will allow, and to which the various medical schools shall be admitted as may be compatible with good service to the inmates. This hospital should be kept as large as is necessary to provide for the destitute sick. Then, if medical schools, or churches, or individuals desire to establish special additional hospitals, they should do so at their own expense.

The dispensary is the most efficient engine of hospital extension; and therefore, where we have competing institutions, it is a department that develops first and fastest, and is the most complained about by rivals. Among those rivals must be classed the junior members of the medical profession. Dr. Savage estimated that in the city of New York there are between 300,000 and 350,000 patients treated gratis at the dispensaries annually, or one in four persons of the tenement-house population. A writer in the *Evening Post*, also cited by Dr. Savage, puts the estimate at 628,286, from which he deducts 178,057 duplications, leaving a net number of 452,529 distinct individuals receiving dispensary aid during the year. The figures for some of the leading New York hospitals are given in a table borrowed from Dr. Savage : —

TABLE XXIX.

STATISTICS SHOWING WORK OF GENERAL DISPENSARIES OF NEW YORK.

NAME.	PATIENTS AT DISPENSARY.	PATIENTS AT HOME.	TOTAL NEW PATIENTS.	CONSULTATIONS.	PRESCRIPTIONS.	SENT TO HOSPITALS.
New York	42,912	3,570	48,482	123,025	115,162	906
Good Samaritan (Eastern)	89,116	6,117	95,233	148,018	107,808	581
Northern	11,516	3,582	15,098	. . . .	22,524	205
Demilt	25,254	4,857	30,111	71,300	59,704	142
Northwestern	25,920	4,043	29,963	. . . .	74,866	94
Northeastern	18,299	3,395	21,694	. . . .	59,141	37
Harlem	2,357	286	2,643	6,795	64,154	17
Manhattan	. . . .	. . .	3,857	4,130	3,437	. .
German	. . . .	. . .	28,232	71,584	45,846	. .

All statistics on this subject, however, are difficult to make definite, because there are so many duplications between different institutions and in the same institution. Some dispensaries count their patients over again every month, so that one man attending the dispensary all the year would be counted as twelve patients. One woman has been known to be attending four different clinics in the same dispensary, so she would count as four different cases.

Wherever a considerable number of dispensary cases are investigated to ascertain whether or not the patients are destitute, a tolerably high abuse-rate is found. Some of these, as ascertained in England, have already been given. Dr. Savage gives the following account of certain investigations in New York City: "In the most attractive dispensary of the city, possessing an elegant building, a complete equipment, and high-grade physicians, the patients are largely of a class one might judge able to compensate a physician. The Charity Organization investigated 1,500 cases selected out of 35,000 applicants. The answer was that about one-fourth were able to pay, another fourth had given a wrong address (possibly from an aversion to its being known that they had applied for dispensary aid, or because they resided out of the city), and the remaining half were recommended as worthy of medical charity by reason of poverty. For another dispensary the same society made investigation of 212 cases, and returned answer that 55 were able to pay, 58 were not found at the address given, 18 information not conclusive, and 81 unable to pay. These referred cases were deemed questionable out of nearly 30,000 patients." [1]

Dr. Savage doubts, however, whether the abuse has a

'Hospitals," note, p. 644.

sufficiently bad effect so that any very severe measure should be taken to correct it. This is a matter on which physicians differ widely. Charity experts usually consider that this free medical service has a very bad effect upon the applicants. The Charity Organization Society of London has waged a long and apparently losing fight against it. The Charity Organization Societies of the United States have investigated cases whenever referred to them; but, for the most part, hospitals do not want the cases investigated — they are glad to take all that come. Sir Morrell Mackenzie gave it as his opinion that the out-patient department of a great hospital was the greatest pauperizing agency existing in England. Lord Cathcart, who served on the Lords' Committee on Hospitals, thinks the effect has not been nearly as bad as supposed, and that the matter had better be left to limit itself. "The out-patient department, however well managed," he says, "is a social test in itself, — the crowds, long waits, unpleasant neighbors, crying and irritable children. There is also some little risk of looking in with one complaint and coming out with another." [1]

In England provident dispensaries have been organ-

[1] At the Joshua Hopkins Hospital a small charge is made for medicines, and patients usually wish to pay. One who had inquired carefully about this institution, says he thinks the abuse-rate very small. One physician who had had experience in both classes of dispensaries, stated that where the patients paid for the medicines, the medicines did them a great deal more good than where they got them free. This at first sight seems absurd; but on further consideration it appears that the patients take more care to follow directions, and in other ways to put themselves in a position to profit by their outlay. Where the medicines are given absolutely free they are sometimes thrown away outright, if the taste does not suit, or the person happens to choose to go to another dispensary.

ized to a considerable extent, at which, in consideration of the deposit of a weekly or monthly sum, medical attendance and medicine are provided. There has not been very much done in the line of provident dispensaries in this country; but the various mutual benevolent orders, and the relief associations of the railroads and some other corporations, provide medical attendance in consequence of stated contributions per month.

American municipalities vary widely in the public provision which they make for sending medical relief to the destitute sick in their own homes. In some cities there are ward physicians, or district physicians, or, as they are usually called by the beneficiaries, "poor-doctors," who are paid from $10 to $50 per month to respond to all calls for gratuitous treatment. These positions are eagerly sought after by certain junior members of the medical profession, and apparently would be if no salary were paid at all. In Philadelphia, where the rate of pay was cut in half, the number of applicants remained as great as before. In Cincinnati, where the pay is $25 per month, the office is political spoils, and the incumbents change with the change of party. In Washington, where the pay is $40 a month, the applicants are not apparently more numerous nor more eager for the place than in cities where the pay is only $10 per month. In cities like New York, where there are no public physicians to the poor, the gap is filled by private benevolence, the large dispensaries, and the gratuitous services of the medical profession.

Nursing as a form of medical and charitable service existed before many of the other branches of these arts.

Within the last two or three decades it has had a new access of usefulness through the advances in medicine and surgery, and from the knowledge that has been obtained of the sources of disease and the methods of antiseptic and aseptic treatment, as well as in consequence of the cultivation of nursing as a specialty.

There are substantially three types of hospitals as far as regards nursing: first, those with paid or "professional" nurses; second, those where the nursing is done by pupils under trained supervision; and third, those where the nursing is done by members of the religious orders. In certain hospitals, usually those under public management, the nursing is done by persons who are paid a small amount and keep their positions from year to year, or as long as politics allow. This, on the whole, is the cheaper form of getting the service; but the service is not nearly so good. The class of persons that will work at this occupation continuously for a small salary is distinctly poor; and usually a hospital relying upon this system drifts into the policy of employing inmates to do the nursing. The nursing in an almshouse hospital is usually of this kind, more or less capable inmates being paid small amounts to assume the responsibility and work of nurses.

The second method of securing the necessary service is by pupil nurses, serving a novitiate usually of two years, and receiving only enough to support them. The nurses may come in from an outside training-school, or the training-school may be a branch of the hospital administration. In either case, the special work of nursing must be under one experienced person, who has full control of the *personnel* of the nursing-force, and is distinctly responsible for this branch of the work.

The system of pupil-nursing secures a much higher grade of applicants for positions; and while the necessity of continually dealing with new nurses causes the medical officials to grumble from time to time, yet most efficient service can be got by this method if there is a sufficient force of trained head nurses.

So far as some of our large public hospitals are concerned, the greatest blessing that has come from the introduction of training-school nurses has been in the reaction upon the general administration of the institutions. Bellevue Hospital in New York City is the most conspicuous example of such improvement. The report of the special committee of the State Charities Aid Association appointed to take measures in regard to the erection of a new Bellevue Hospital, showed that by the reports of the old hospital during the 18 months from January, 1872, to June, 1873, the number of surgical amputations, not including fingers and toes, was 58, of which there were 30 recoveries and 28 deaths. Of 5 hand amputations, 2 recovered and 3 died. Of leg amputations, including the knee-joint, there were 28, of which 15 recovered and 13 died. Of 8 foot amputations, 4 recovered and 4 died. During the year 1870, there were in the hospital 1,071 deaths, or 12.2 per cent of all patients treated. In this 1,071 deaths, there were 69 cases of hospital poisons, or 6.44 per cent. In 1871 the statistics regarding deaths were substantially the same. Out of 376 confinements, there were 33 deaths from puerperal fever, or 8.7 per cent of all women confined. During the spring of 1874, puerperal fever at Bellevue Hospital became epidemic, and reached the height of nearly two deaths out of every five women delivered.[1] In addition to the number of patients dying from hospital poisons, there was also a large number of cases of gangrene, erysipelas, exhaustion, etc., to which hospital poisons may have been tributary.[2] The nursing was done largely by persons sent from the poorhouse or the house of correction. At the Charity Hospital in New York City, the report of 1874 describes the following condition of the fever ward for forty beds: "The only nurse was a woman from the workhouse, under a six months' sentence for drunkenness. . . . There were no chairs with backs in the hospital; rude wooden benches were the only seats, and the only pillows were chopped straw. The only bathing conveniences consisted of one tin basin, a piece of soap, and a ragged bit of cloth, passed from bed to bed. It was the opinion of the committee that the larger part of the patients in this hospital were hungry every night."

The introduction of trained and pupil nurses was not the only force operating for reform, but it was a powerful one. From the reformed institution have gone out and go out annually women trained to the work of nursing, many of whom are called to be head nurses and superintendents in other institutions.[3]

In the third class of hospitals the nursing is done by members of the religious orders. Such institutions are usually owned by the orders themselves, and the Sister

[1] Third Annual Report of N. Y. State Charities Aid Association, p. 23.
[2] See report cited, pp. 10–12.
[3] It is to be hoped that the Cook County Hospital in Chicago will be regenerated through similar influences.

Superior is at the head of the administration.[1] Such hospitals are frequently subsidized by the municipalities; but it is rare with us, though common in Europe, for a religious order to be given charge of the nursing in a public institution.

Physicians and surgeons, according to individual experience, vary in their estimates of the relative efficiency of Sisters or others as nurses. One surgeon of wide experience tells the author that Sisters were never properly trained as nurses; and another, that none but those animated by religious zeal ever had enough devotion to make the best nurses. Both statements, as made, may be taken to be false. Some of the orders take great pains in the training of their novices. It will be interesting to see, as time goes on, whether persons of sufficient intelligence and education to make the best modern nurses will continue to enter the religious orders; and, on the other hand, whether "cash payment" and simple devotion to duty will give the entire reliability which is needed in the nurse at all times and places.[2]

---

[1] When the author asked one Sister Superior how the medical staff was chosen, she said, "Oh, at the beginning of each year I send them notice of their appointment, and then they get together and confirm it."

[2] For an account of the training of male and female nurses in the Catholic Orders, see Dr. Köllen, "Hospitals," pp. 473-477. Dr. Köllen thinks the religious orders make unrivalled nurses. He says, after describing the work, "The soil upon which these fruits have ripened, and from which the members of the orders, even after their training, draw strength and enthusiasm for their lives so full of pain and self-sacrifice, is the strict and uniform care of the spiritual life, and that complete devotion of one's entire existence to suffering humanity, from the love of God, based upon the evangelical rules of the Catholic creed." Since 1877 the hospitals of Paris have been transferred from the religious orders to lay pupil nurses. Professor La Fort, who writes

Standing between the religious orders of the Catholic Church and the paid nurses of the training-schools are the orders of deaconesses of the Protestant denominations. Their work is particularly for the poor. In this country these orders have not as yet taken up hospital work to any notable extent. They differ from the Catholic orders in that the vows are taken for only a limited period of years, whereas, after the novitiate of four or five years, a member of a Catholic order takes the vows for life. Members of the deaconess orders also retain the title to private property, and do not cut themselves off from their relatives, if they have any.

This mention of the orders of deaconesses brings us to a late development in nursing-work for the poor, namely, the so-called "district nursing," which is simply the gratuitous nursing of the sick poor in their homes. Such care of the poor has long been given by the Sisters of Charity and the *Sœurs de Bon Secours* of the Catholic Church, who have attended to it with a devotion and an amount of personal sympathy that is hardly paralleled. In the United States salaried nurses to the poor were first employed, at least to any considerable extent, by a religious society — the Woman's Branch of the New York City Mission and Tract Society. The first experiments were made in 1877. The nurse receives from $40 to $50 per month. She passes from home to home,

---

an article for the volume on "Hospitals" describing this change, was formerly in favor of the *laicization* of the hospitals, but in this article is emphatically against it. His account, however, shows that a very different class of persons were drawn upon for the pupil nurses from that which turns to this business in the Unted States. The suggestion has been made in some cases that the Sisters give up their patients as hopeless too soon.

doing what is necessary for the sick; and the influence of her example of cleanliness, order, and wise-doing is frequently contagious. "Almost every day," says Miss Summerville, "I find some former patient carrying out many of the simple directions that have been given during some former sickness."[1]

The public authorities in this country have not, as a rule, introduced gratuitous nursing as an adjunct to the work of gratuitous medical service to the poor, rendered through the physicians in the pay of the municipality; but this is an advance that will probably come, as it has in Paris and other European cities.[2]

In nursing, more distinctly than in almost any other line of benevolent work, is seen the sacrifice of capable people to the incapable. Nurses, especially pupil and paid nurses, are frequently overworked, and the members of religious orders also break down at an early age. The death-rate among all classes of nurses is very high.

---

[1] For an account of a day's work of one of these salaried nurses to the poor, see "Hospitals," pp. 541-543.

[2] The development of district nursing on the one hand, and the prices charged by successful trained nurses to private patients on the other hand, have led to the remark that no one can afford to have a trained nurse except a millionaire or a pauper. With a view to providing nurses for the middle class, the Dubois Fund in New York and the Creerar Fund in Illinois have been established to pay part of the wages of nurses, so that those who can afford to pay a little may have them. In Philadelphia, the District Nursing Association collects carfare from the patients whenever possible, and also furnishes nurses at cheap rates for those not able to pay the full fee usually charged by nurses. In this way the association is very largely self-sustaining. In Chicago almost nothing has been done in the way of meeting expenses from the contributions of beneficiaries. It costs in England about $400 per annum to provide a trained nurse to the poor, and in Chicago about $900. An endowment yielding this amount will therefore pay a nurse in perpetuity.

It should be seen by those in authority that strong, capable women are not killed off gratuitously by overwork which could be avoided. The conditions of their lives must be as health-giving and as health-preserving as possible; and whether they are members of a religious order or the salaried servants of a society, they must have opportunities of recruiting their strength, and so of preserving their usefulness.

CHAPTER XI.

THE INSANE.

[The official reports of most use are: U. S. Census, 1880 and 1890, as far as published; Reports of the State Boards of Charities, and of the State Commissions in Lunacy. Next to official documents in value are the Proceedings of the National Association of Medical Officers of Institutions for the Insane, and the papers presented to the National Conference of Charities. The latter treat the subject best in its social, economic, and administrative aspects. The best single paper for the general reader among those published by the Conference is that of C. Eugene Riggs, " Progress of the Care of the Insane in the Last Twenty Years," N. C. C., 1893, pp. 222-262. Of especial value also is the Committee Report on " The Commitment and Detention of the Insane," N. C. C., 1888, pp. 25-68. The early reforms in the care of the insane in the United States are interestingly described in the " Life of Dorothea Lynde Dix."

ACCORDING to Census Bulletin No. 62 there were, during the year 1889, in public and private institutions for the insane of the United States, 97,535 inmates, showing an increase during the nine years from 1881 of 41,330, or 73.53 per cent. The population during the decade had increased but 24.53 per cent. In 1889 there were 1.56 insane persons in each thousand of the population. The figures do not indicate an increase of insanity in the country, but rather that institution treatment had come to be accepted by a much larger number of the insane, or by their guardians on their behalf. Further than this, each succeeding census comes more nearly to getting all the figures regarding the special classes investigated, and the increase is therefore statistical, but not actual.

The better way to estimate regarding increase of insanity is to take figures from a single State, that have been collected with care and on a uniform system during a series of years. The annual census of the insane of New York, as prepared for the State Board of Charities, shows an increase during the 12 years ending Oct. 1, 1892, of 7,920, or an annual increase of 660. At the beginning of the period the insane numbered one to each 533 of the population, and in 1892, one to each 373 of the population. The increase of the population from 1880 to 1892 was 28 per cent, while the increase in the number of the insane during the same period was 83 per cent.[1] In the public institutions of Massachusetts the number of insane has increased from 1,795 in 1867 to 5,268 in Sept. 30, 1893. During these 27 years, therefore, the average annual increase has been 128.6, or 3.7 per cent, an increase which is distinctly greater than the increase in the ordinary population in the same State at the same time.[2]

Even in the case of a single State where the methods of collecting statistics have been tolerably uniform, a large part of the increase is accounted for by the fact that the definition of insanity has broadened, and many who are now classified as insane would some years ago have simply attracted attention as being queer or perverse. For comparison as between two countries, it is very important to know whether idiots and feeble-minded are classed among the insane; but, in fact, comparison between different countries are full of statistical

---

[1] Report New York State Board of Charities, 1892, pp. 24, 25.
[2] Annual Report State Board of Lunacy and Charity, 1893, Table 18.

quicksands, in which none but an expert can find footing.

Granting an increase, which experts seem to agree has actually taken place, not only in the number of persons classed as insane, but in the number actually suffering from a diseased mental condition of given severity, the explanations that are offered for this increase are many. While some of them are discouraging as to the outlook for the race, others are not.

1. The humane treatment of the insane has tended to lessen the death-rate among them. Gathered together into institutions where the sanitation is good, as a rule, the food nourishing, and the care watchful and kindly, there is a larger quantity of life falling to the lot of the insane population than would formerly have come to them. Their numbers increase because each remains longer upon the scene.

2. Medical skill is learning to control many of the contagious diseases and acute fevers. The consequent prolongation of life, that is the result in the population as a whole, has tended to allow larger numbers of comparatively weak constitutions to come to the period of life when degeneration of the nervous or vascular system takes place. This is held to account in part, not only for the increase in the number of the insane, but also for the increased number of persons who die from cancer and from diseases of degeneration.

3. Another explanation that is frequently given is the great amount of foreign immigration, and the character of the immigrants. A certain, or rather an uncertain, number of paupers, lunatics, and imbeciles have undoubtedly been foisted upon us by Europe. Besides this, the

complete change of conditions, climate, and associations seems to have unsettled the minds of many foreigners on coming to this country.

4. The over-tension of modern life, which is spoken of by some as if it were wholly responsible for the increase in the number of the insane, has undoubtedly had much to do with the increase in insanity.

5. The climatic influence of the country, with sharp extremes of heat and cold, and the dry atmosphere permitting rapid evaporation from the body, is held by many physicians to tend to the unbalancing of the nervous system.

6. Dr. Pliny Earle maintains that insanity is, as a whole, really becoming more and more an incurable disease. He says, "If it be true, as reported by Feuchtersleben, and doubtless no one will deny its truth, that in the progress of the last few centuries, as civilization has advanced and the habits of the race have been consequently modified, disease has left its strongholds in the fleshy and muscular tissues and at length seated itself in the nervous system, it follows as a necessary consequence, that, by the continuation of the cause of this change, the diseases of the nerves and brain must become more and more permanent."

7. Especially among the more highly organized individuals the burdens which modern life puts upon the reasoning powers is out of all proportion to that which was placed upon them a few decades ago. We challenge custom, we question our instincts, we are sceptical where we used to have faith. In matters, for instance, such as the relation of man to the church, and of the sexes to each other, we now believe that reason should be con-

stantly compelled to act. We have put upon the minds of the present generation great burdens, which those minds are not sufficiently well-developed and well-organized to bear.[1]

Much lurid poetry and fiction have been produced having for their basis the unjust commitment of sane persons as insane; and, on the other hand, many papers have been written by physicians and others showing the danger of allowing insane persons to be too long without asylum restraint, and of the injustice that comes from making it too difficult to secure judgment of insanity and subsequent commitment and detention. Probably the danger of the commitment of sane persons has been greatly over-estimated. The Earl of Shaftesbury, who was chairman of the English Commission in Lunacy for fifty years, stated that, though the number of certificates that had passed through their office was more than 185,-000, there was not one person who was not shown by good *prima facie* evidence to be in need of care and treatment. Drs. Ordroneaux and Smith, who were State commissioners in New York from 1873 to 1888, stated that, during the fifteen years of their term of service, no case of illegal detention has occurred in the State; and the inspector of hospitals, Massachusetts, made a similar statement.[2]

In most instances there are two things to be decided: first, whether a person is legally insane and in need of asylum treatment, or the control of a guardian, and

---

[1] It may even perhaps be said that rationalizing the instinct of charity is putting an added burden upon the minds of the most intelligent part of the population, and may weary to the point of injuring brains already taxed by hard thought on a multitude of problems.

[2] Dr. Riggs, N. C. C., 1893, p. 227.

second, whether or not he or his relatives should be compelled to support him. The first of these decisions, that as to sanity, is primarily a medical question; the old method was to treat it as a legal one. The person "charged" with insanity was brought personally into court and tried before a jury. In the District of Columbia, Illinois, and Colorado, jury trial is obligatory in all cases, and the presence of the patient at the trial is demanded. This system is properly characterized by Dr. Riggs as barbarous. At the same time, there is a judicial element in the matter which requires that the cases should be passed upon by a court; and the more progressive States provide that all commitments shall be recorded in the Court of Records, but that the testimony upon which the action is based shall for the most part be that of medical experts. It is simply necessary that adequate publicity should be provided for, and that an adequate amount of expert testimony should determine the question.

The whole matter of the commitment and detention of the insane was thoroughly worked over by a committee of the National Conference of Charities which reported at Buffalo in 1888, and whose work has resulted in palpable advancement in this matter in New York and other States.

The detention of the insane is another matter when it is necessary to protect the interests at once of the community and of the inmates. It is a matter on which the inmates will usually differ in opinion from the superintendent of the institution, and it has not been found easy to work out rules that guarantee against all abuses. In the main, the right of correspondence should remain with the patients, the letters that they write being read by the superintendent or his representative, and any which are not forwarded being filed for the inspection of directors or other supervisors of the institution.[1]

Where the insane who are committed and detained are classified according as they or their relatives can or cannot pay for their support, the adjudication of this matter must usually rest with the overseers of the poor. There is likely to be a good deal of care exercised where the expense of maintenance is left to the towns and counties. Where the State maintains both the acute and the chronic insane, the drift is in the direction of giving free support to all insane persons, whether of the well-to-do classes or not. This is the avowed policy of Minnesota, and is practically the outcome of loose legislation in California.

Under the head of commitment and detention, must be mentioned the matter of proper escort of the insane from the place of family residence to the hospital or asylum to which they are committed. In most States this matter is left to the sheriff, a relic of the time

---

[1] When Nelly Bly, in the interests of a New York paper, got herself committed to the Flatbush Insane Asylum on Long Island, she gave it as her opinion that it would have been impossible to get out without help from the outside, although after she had once been committed she dropped all affectation of insanity or peculiarity. She resented certain indignities of the treatment to herself and others, and this was taken by the authorities to be evidence of derangement. At the outset, however, in order to secure commitment, she had acted in a way that could be explained on no other hypothesis than that of insanity. She had deliberately misled the medical authorities, and they could have had no reason to think that a person who had acted as she did could be sane.

when only the legal aspects of the matter were considered by the courts. In other States the asylums are expected to send proper attendants to take the inmates to the institution, and a few States, as for instance Michigan, provide that the county shall send a female attendant with every female patient, unless accompanied by her husband, father, brother, or son. The recent State Care Act of New York provides for female escort for females, and attaches a penalty for its non-observance.[1]

The history of the treatment of the insane is ordinarily divided into three periods: the first, that of neglect, when the insane were only dealt with in case they were dangerous, and when they were treated as witches or wild animals; the second, the era of detention, when they were treated under such laws as the English Vagrancy Act; and third, the present era, when insanity is recognized as "a disease and not a doom."[2] In this country, during the early part of the present century, the English precedents were followed, and the precedents rather of the earlier than of the passing period.

[1] For a summary of State laws regarding the proper escort of insane females, see the Report of the Board of Public Charities, Committee on Lunacy, Pennsylvania, 1892, p. 16.

[2] Very different thoughts are brought to our minds by the two words "Bethlehem" and "Bedlam." Yet the second is only a corruption of the first; and the miserable associations that it recalls are connected with it because in a "hospital" founded in 1247, by the order of "St. Mary of Bethlem" (or Bethlehem), the insane were treated or mistreated during three centuries. Hodder's Life of the Earl of Shaftesbury, vol. i., pp. 90 ff., gives a good summary of the history of the treatment of the insane. For the influence of the church upon the treatment of insanity, see Andrew D. White, "Demoniacal Possession and Insanity, and Diabolism and Hysteria," *Popular Science Monthly*, February, March, May, and June, 1889.

In New York, the law provided for the detention of the insane by chains if necessary. Dorothea Lynde Dix, who, in the middle of this century, visited a large number of places for the care of the insane, was compelled to tell a most grievous tale of abuse and barbarity. Even with the establishment of the State Boards of Charity in the more progressive States in the middle of sixties and early seventies, the condition of things was hardly better. The reports of the early seventies, describing the condition of the insane in the town and county almshouses, give accounts of barbarities as hideous as any unearthed fifty years earlier in England, or described by Miss Dix in this country.[1] The thing that had been accomplished by her agitation had been the establishment of many rather large asylums, in some of which the treatment was decidedly good; but a great proportion of the insane remained under the mistreatment of the local poorhouses.

English critics of American institutions claimed that our superintendents of institutions for the insane were far behind the times, because they would not commit themselves to the dogma of entire non-restraint; but careful foreign investigators who visited this country found that in the larger asylums there was as little restraint as obtained at the same time in England. Our superintendents simply would not pledge themselves to dispense with a style of treatment which they thought, like any other drastic remedy, might be called for in certain cases. At the same time, they did not use restraint to

[1] For description of present abuses under almshouse care, see example of Illinois, cited above, p. 104, and Reports of the Maryland Lunacy Commission, especially the 8th, p. 38.

any definitely mischievous extent. The early State asylums had been comparatively small, designed for not more than 300 persons. In the later sixties and early seventies, the agitation for the removal of the insane from county to State care resulted in the building of mammoth institutions, capable of accommodating in some cases as many as 2,000 patients. Williard Asylum, in New York, is typical of this class. Expense was also incurred in the most reckless way in building these great institutions. In some cases there was an expenditure for building and plant amounting to a cost per capita of from $1,000 to $3,000, or even more, while, as Dr. Wilbur pointed out in 1878, the cost of the most expensive hotels probably did not exceed $1,500 per capita. These great caravansaries filled up, and still the counties had a large number of the insane. At the opening of Williard Asylum in 1869, there were 1,500 insane persons in New York State in county care. Six years later it was reported by the State Board that Williard Asylum was full, and that there were still 1,300 remaining in county institutions.

It was further found that the very large institutions were not answering their purposes, because their size made the individualization of cases difficult or impossible, and there was a sort of contagion of insanity resulting from the presence of such large numbers of lunatics on a small area. Later there has come a tendency to build cottages grouped about a central administrative and hospital building, where families of the insane in the care of proper housekeepers and attendants can live in relative seclusion. Kankakee, Ill., is probably the best illustration of this system of construction. To save expense, however, the legislature has insisted on making the "cottages" much larger than was desired by those having an interest in this new development.

The colony plan consists in making the cottages small and scattering them over a large estate. This is being tried at Kalamazoo, Mich. The great difficulty is to provide cheap and adequate facilities for water, drainage, and heat. This difficulty can probably be overcome with the advance of the mechanical arts, just as the disadvantages of scattered buildings on the cottage plan have been very largely overcome at the present time. For both systems, of course, pneumatic tubes, telephones, and electric lighting give great facility for centralizing the administration.

With this modification in the methods of building large institutions for the care of the insane, the tendency to remand all this class of dependents to the State has been greatly strengthened; and New York has finally accomplished what its State Board of Charities and State Charities Aid Association had agitated for during many years — the transfer of all insane from county to State care, except in the two counties of Kings and New York. This brings better treatment and larger expense, and has been the system adopted by the Western States almost without exception.

Wisconsin prides herself on having devised a method of county care under State supervision. Whenever cure or improvement is considered possible, the patients are sent to a State hospital under the charge of specialists. Chronic cases not needing special restraint or care are sent back to the county after hospital treatment can benefit them no farther; but no county is allowed to care for its own insane unless the plans of its almshouse buildings and the management of that institution are approved by the State Board of Charities. If so approved, there is a small weekly per capita allowance from the State treasury to the county that cares for its own insane. If not approved, at any time the State Board has the power to transfer all the insane belonging to the county to State institutions or the almshouse asylums of other counties, and collect the bill for their maintenance from the county to which they belong. Thus it is to the interest of the county to care for its own insane and to care for them properly.

The idea of segregation and of special provision for the harmless chronic insane has been carried to the point of boarding selected cases of the insane in families. This has been experimented upon in Massachusetts. The amount paid for the board, together with the cost of the necessary visiting, makes it not much more economical than asylum care, although it is much more satisfactory for selected cases. There are those who hope that, as with children the placing-out system may supplant the institution system, so with the insane it may be possible to board larger numbers of them, and incorporate them thus in the ordinary population. In Scotland this system has been developed much farther than in this country. The advancement along this line seems to be very nearly at a standstill in Massachusetts; and other States have not followed her example, as other States have not followed the example of Wisconsin in county care under State supervision.

The cost of county or township care for the insane ranges all the way from nearly nothing to about $150 per annum, while under State care the expense ranges from about $150 per annum to $300.

Patients are probably cared for to a decreasing extent in private institutions. Some of the gravest abuses, as in Pennsylvania, have grown up in these private homes or retreats. In several medical schools lecturers on mental diseases say that, as a rule, commitment to a public institution is safer than to a private institution, unless the character of the man in charge is very well known.

After the classification by sex, and in the South by color,[1] the next great line of division among the insane which specialists have attempted to make has been between acute, or possibly curable, and the chronic, or probably incurable cases. As one superintendent remarks, "You cannot do too much for a man if you can thereby cure him." In order to make cure as likely as possible, it is desirable that institutions should be small, the number of attendants large and of good character, and all the conditions of life as nearly like those of a normal home as possible. To provide such facilities as these with the purpose of curative treatment is expensive; while, on the other hand, to take adequate care of the chronic or probably incurable insane requires a comparatively small per capita expenditure, and experts have constantly agitated for the separation of the two classes. But there has hardly been a proposal to establish an asylum for the chronic insane, or the matter has hardly ever come up in the National Conferences of Charities, without some would-be orator objecting to the erection of any institution over the door of which must be written, "Farewell to hope, all ye who enter here."

[1] See Report Md. Lunacy Com., 8, pp. 43, 44.

For this reason the asylum at Agnews, California, intended and planned by the architect for the care of the chronic insane, has been compelled to depart from this intention, and to care for all classes of the insane in large wards, and under conditions not most favorable to cure. Each asylum in the State of California receives all classes without regard to their character as curable or incurable. The compromise results in proper treatment for neither class. In the States where this classification between institutions has been measurably maintained, it results in very considerable saving, and in considerably better treatment for the curable insane. At the same time insanity is not usually a curable disease. Even in the best managed institutions, and those receiving the likeliest class of patients, less than thirty per cent permanently recover. The statement of Dr. Thurnam, an English expert, made many years ago, based on the experience of forty-four years at the York Retreat, still comes nearer the truth than the more sanguine predictions of later authorities. Dr. Thurnam says: "In round numbers, of ten persons attacked by insanity, five recover, and five die sooner or later during the first attack. Of the five who recover, not more than two remain well during the rest of their lives; the other three sustain subsequent attacks, during which at least two of them die."

After the separation of the curable from the incurable, in order to provide for the proper care of each, the next most important classification is, perhaps, into the criminal and the non-criminal insane; that is, those having dangerous or criminal instincts and those who do not have them. Some States have treated the criminal insane as criminals, and provided for them in branch penitentiaries. Others have treated them as insane, and put them into the same institution with other persons of that class, sometimes to the danger and often to the disgust of such other patients and their friends and relatives. The best policy, and the one adopted by the progressive States, is to have a separate asylum for the criminal insane.[1]

Another essential to the proper classification is the separation from the insane of those who are epileptics, and also the distinctly feeble-minded. The class of epileptics, especially, is a great annoyance both to the inmates and managers of institutions for the insane, as they require special treatment which they can properly have only in a special institution. Beyond these distinctions which obtain as between institutions, there must further be a classification of the insane in any given institution to bring together those that do not vex or excite one another, and to segregate the filthy and the unmanageable. It is one of the defects of very large institutions that have been erected in some States, that the wards are too large to make possible proper classification, and consequent individualization of cases.

No mention can here be made of the improvement in the treatment of the insane which comes only through

---

[1] At Broadmoor, England, is an asylum designed for the criminal insane. Of its 500 inmates, 90 have murdered their own children, 300 have either committed murder or attempted to do so. In this whole institution, designed as it is for the most dangerous classes of lunatics, no mechanical restraint is resorted to, no fetters, no strait waistcoats, no leg locks or straps. The nearest approach to this species of restraint is to force the patient into a padded room, with no furniture but a bed on the floor.

an improvement in the personnel of the institution, through freedom from spoils politics, through the introduction of civil service reform, through the activity of clubs of men connected with each institution organized for their mutual improvement, and through the development of training-schools for attendants upon the insane. It is by these and other agencies that the present great advancement is being made along the lines of greater wisdom in treatment, greater kindness in control, and greater freedom within the bounds of safety for the insane.

CHAPTER XII.

THE FEEBLE-MINDED AND ANALOGOUSLY DEGENERATE CLASSES.

[Howe, "Report on Idiocy in Massachusetts" (Boston, 1848) is valuable but not easily accessible. The " Proceedings of the Association of Medical Officers of American Institutions for Idiotic and Feeble-minded Persons " (sessions held since 1876) contain much useful material. Dr. Kerlin's papers, read before the National Conference of Charities, are valuable, especially the first one, 1884. Dr. Fernald reviewed the progress of twenty years at the Chicago Conference (1893, pp. 203–221). The subject has been treated at each Conference since 1884.]

THE term feeble-minded is now used to cover all grades of idiocy and imbecility, from the child that is simply dull and incapable of profiting by the ordinary school, to the gelatinous mass that simply eats and lives. If it is difficult to give an exact definition of insanity, it is manifestly even more difficult to give an exact definition of feeble-mindedness. Some have been hardy enough to say that we are all more or less insane, and it would be still easier to assert that we are all more or less feeble-minded. The class to which the technical term is applied may be expected to increase as specialists improve their acquaintance with the different symptons of feeble-mindedness. For this reason, as in the case of the insane, the census figures bearing upon the subject indicate a rate of increase out of all proportion, probably, to any actual increase of the condition of feeble-mindedness in the population. The

THE DEGENERATE CLASSES. 277

census of 1890 shows a total of 95,571 idiotic and feeble-minded persons in the United States. It is certain that this enumeration does not include nearly all. Of the whole number, but 6,315 were in special institutions for feeble-minded. A list of the leading public or semi-public institutions for this class is herewith reproduced from Dr. Fernald's paper read at the Twentieth National Conference of Charities at Chicago.[1]

The buildings and grounds for these institutions alone required an outlay of about four millions, and an annual expenditure for these classes of defectives amounting to over one million.[2] It will thus be seen that the feeble-minded are next to the insane in the number to be provided for, but that provision for them has only begun.

As to the classes of the population in which they are found, in 1848 in Massachusetts, out of 574 idiots examined by Dr. S. G. Howe or his assistants, 220 were supported by the town or State, 20 had property of their own, and 26 belonged to wealthy families.[3] In Pennsylvania, in 1871, there were about 3,500 feeble-minded children. Of these, 717 were in families of ample ability to furnish support; 604 in families of moderate circumstances (they could hardly pay the rates usually charged at private institutions); 1,619 were in poor families, who would be unable to pay for their support away from home, yet would be unwilling to relieve themselves of a painful burden by casting their children on the county; 560 were in homes of the most degraded character, or at public expense in almshouses.[4]

[1] N. C. C., 1893, p. 214.
[2] Dr. Fernald, N. C. C., 1893, p. 215.
[3] Report on Idiocy, 1884, p. 23.
[4] Dr Kerlin, N. C. C., 1884, p. 247.

TABLE XXX.

INSTITUTIONS FOR THE FEEBLE-MINDED.

NAME.	LOCATION.	DATE OF ORGANIZATION.	CAPACITY.
California Home for Care and Training of Feeble-Minded Children	Glen Ellen	1885	259
Connecticut School for Imbeciles	Lakeville	1852	130
Illinois Asylum for Feeble-Minded Children	Lincoln	1865	536
Indiana School for Feeble-Minded Youth	Fort Wayne	1879	421
Iowa Institution for Feeble-Minded Children	Glenwood	1876	456
Kansas State Asylum for Idiotic and Imbecile Youth	Winfield	1880	102
Kentucky Institution for Ed. and Training of Feeble-Minded Children	Frankfort	1860	156
Maryland Asylum and Training-School for the Feeble-Minded	Owing's Mills	1888	40
Massachusetts School for the Feeble-Minded	Waltham	1848	450
Minnesota School for the Feeble-Minded	Faribault	1879	332
Nebraska Institution for Feeble-Minded Youth	Beatrice	1887	154
New York State Institution for Feeble-Minded Children	Syracuse	1850	502
New York State Custodial Asylum for Feeble-Minded Women	Newark	1885	345
Randall's Island Hospital and School	New York Harbor	1870	364
New Jersey Home for the Education and Care of Feeble-Minded Children	Vineland	1888	154
New Jersey State Institution for Feeble-Minded Women	Vineland	1886	65
Ohio Institution for the Education of Feeble-Minded Youth	Columbus	1857	822
Pennsylvania Training-School for Feeble-Minded Children	Elwyn	1853	851
Washington School for Defective Youth	Vancouver	1892	25

In this particular class, which is commonly of very degenerate stock, or made up of degenerate individuals, a study of the cases of feeble-mindedness or idiocy will give much help in the appreciation of the general causes of pauperism. It therefore seems advisable to inquire what has been ascertained in this matter, although we have not considered the causes of dependency in other groups. The report of Dr. S. G. Howe already quoted was concerned especially with the causes of idiocy in Massachusetts; and as it was made at a time precedent to the large foreign immigration, which in Dr. Kerlin's opinion increased the number of feeble-minded in Pennsylvania, the causes of idiocy then found are such as might be considered indigenous. Dr. Howe had a feeling that idiocy could not have been in the plan of nature, or, as he says, "It was hard to believe it to be in the order of Providence that the earth should always be cumbered with so many creatures in human shape but without the light of human reason. . . . Where there was so much suffering there must have been sin."[1] Entering upon the investigation with this bias, we may presume that he emphasized as fully as the facts warranted, but assuredly not more than he considered them to warrant, personal and moral causes of idiocy. As to heredity, the table already given in Chapter III. states the results in full. "Out of 420 cases of congenital idiocy examined, some information was obtained respecting the progenitors of 359. In all these cases save only four, it is found that one or both of the immediate progenitors of the unfortunate sufferers had in some way widely departed from the normal condition of health,

[1] Pages 3, 4.

and violated natural laws; that is to say, one or the other or both of them were very unhealthy or scrofulous, or they were hereditarily disposed to affections of the brain, causing occasional insanity, or they had intermarried with blood relatives, or they had been intemperate, or had been guilty of sexual excesses which impaired their constitutions. More fully itemized, the causes indicated in the foregoing paragraph are: 1, low condition of the physical organization of one or both parents; 2, intemperance; 3, self-abuse, probably more important than intemperance; 4, intermarriage of blood relatives (on this last point the report says that one-twentieth of the idiots examined were the offspring of the marriage of blood relatives; in 17 families, the heads of which being blood relatives intermarried, there were born 95 children, of whom 44 were idiotic, 12 were scrofulous and puny, one was deaf, and one was a dwarf); 5, attempts to procure abortion — frequently cases were found where all the children of a woman were sound except one upon whom abortion was attempted, and that an idiot."[1] Further indications of the bodily condition of idiotic persons examined by Dr. Howe and his assistants are given in the table reproduced on following page.

The origin of the work of training the feeble-minded has two sources; one the school, and one the hospital; it lies between the department of education and the department of medicine. The schools for the deaf and blind found themselves asked to educate children that were also feeble-minded, and hospitals for the insane were asked to treat a large number of imbeciles. The educational element was at first most strongly devel-

[1] Pages 79–90.

TABLE XXXI.[1]

SHOWING THE BODILY CONDITION OF 574 IDIOTIC PERSONS.

DEFORMITY.	CONGENTAL IDIOCY.	IDIOCY SUPERVENED.	TOTAL.
Blindness or deformity of the eyes	15	6	21
Deafness	12	1	13
Deformity of mouth or nose	22	1	23
Deformity of hands or feet	51	3	54
Torpor of feeling	11	3	14
Paralysis in some or all parts	83	13	96
Insatiably gluttonous	218	62	280
Known to practise masturbation frequently —			
Males	59	57	116
Females	43	32	75
Total	102	89	191
Subject to fits	92	33	125
Use of tobacco at once brings on convulsions	1	2	3
Anger at once produces violent convulsions and insensibility	6	1	7
Anger causes spasms or less violent fits	19	3	22
Fright causes faintness, nausea, and vomiting	7	0	7
Supposed to have been injured by use of calomel	0	8	8
Supposed to have been injured by use of opium	0	5	5

[1] Dr. S. G. Howe's Report, Table No. III., p. 44 of tables.

oped. Hopes were entertained of making 50 or 75 per cent of the feeble-minded self-supporting; but that optimistic view had to be modified, and it is now seen that not more than 10 or 15 per cent can be made self-supporting in the sense that they can return to an independent life in the ordinary population.[2] The educational side was well illustrated by the exhibit made at

[2] Dr. Fernald, N. C. C., 1893, p. 217.

Chicago and Nashville of the work done by inmates of institutions for the feeble-minded.

The medical side of the work has been especially considered by the Association of Medical Officers of American Institutions for Idiotic and Feeble-minded Persons, which held its first meeting during the centennial year, 1876, at the institution for the feeble-minded at Elwyn. At the annual meetings different medical aspects of the matter are discussed, and surgical remedies for feeble-mindedness proposed.

On the side of philanthropy the matter has been discussed at most of the national conferences since 1884. At that conference Dr. Kerlin mildly rebuked the conference for its preceding neglect of this branch of work, and it was there introduced by a paper that showed conclusively that it must receive a progressively large share of attention from a body concerned with general philanthropy.

The classification of feeble-minded persons, and the treatment possible for them, can best be described by an extended extract from Dr. Kerlin's paper, read to the Conference of Charities at St. Louis:[1] —

"It has been convenient to group the chief varieties or grades of idiocy under the following syllabus: —

GROUPS.
1. *Idiocy.*
   (a) Apathetic.
   (b) Excitable.
2. *Idio-imbeciles.*
3. *Imbeciles.*
   (a) Lower grade.
   (b) Middle grade.
   (c) High grade.
4. *Juvenile Insanity.*

[1] N. C. C., 1884, pp. 248-251.

"To aid description, imagine that you walk through a considerable range of separated buildings, allowing me to select the types of the seven or eight grades we shall encounter in as many localities.

"Here, in a large, airy, sunny room, lying on couches or advanced to rocking-chairs, is the saddest and lowest group. You are likely to stop before its type, a helpless, gelatinoid creature, ten years of age, so limp and structureless that, in the language of the nurse, 'he doubles in three like a clothes-horse when lifted from his bed.' The only noise that interests him is that of a bell. The only object he ever seems to look at is his hand. He cries when he is hungry. He enjoys being held and rocked, and shows actual delight when bathed. With his great, luminous, soft jet eyes, he reminds one of a seal. Perhaps his intelligence is rather below that of a trained seal. It is certainly not that of a babe four weeks old. He is a profound idiot, with epileptic complication. Near by is another of the same age, mute, dwarfed, and helpless. She actuates nothing. Her only expression of common wants is a low moan or cry; but she rewards the faithful nurse by a smile, recognizing the epithet 'baby,' which has been applied to her. She sleeps well, and enjoys her bath.

"Excitable idiots are not so common as the apathetic. They usually die early from exhaustion, or, less happily, sink into apathetic forms; but there is a group in every large asylum of this class, taxing the ingenuity of their present care-takers, after wasting the best life of their families.

"The temptation for their extinction rises to the lips of the careless, forgetful how far such practice would be from all moral or judicial right, how revolting to every religious sentiment, and contradictory to every logical principle.

"So we have them with us, although so little of us. Annie F., the saddest type, aged eight years, mute, wild, and vicious, biting any one whom she can reach, with a nervousness in the act that suggests its irresponsibility; darting to an open window to throw herself headlong below, her glittering eyes, tensely drawn lips, and sudden pallors indicating the pain and commotion of her poor and worried brain. How fittingly and terribly does this disturbed life project itself from its ante-natal unrest — an unwilling and unhappy conception, for the destruction of which the mother's stormiest passions had unceasingly but unavailingly contended! And there are a few others as sad, exciting wonder why they continue to live, and greater wonder how the home and the neighborhood tolerated for years their cries, discordant noises, and uncouthness.

"Advanced beyond these apathetic and excitable idiots, we find an intermediate group, the idio-imbeciles. Many have the facial appearance, the deformed heads, the dwarfishness of body, the narrow buccal arches, the imperfect teeth, of very imperfect creatures, but there is dawning intelligence. Taken from their isolation, they feebly grasp, through their shyness and sensitiveness, for the better things about them. Expecting them to do little or nothing, the trainer is daily sustained by successes, and goes on hopefully introducing most of them to a higher grade, — that of the lowest forms of imbecility; and here we discover the strongest individuality, so that it is quite impossible to select a type. T. T., age twelve, will illustrate as well as any. He is a microcephalic paralytic imbecile of low grade; articulation quite imperfect; sense of sight and hearing good; hand well formed; imitation above the grade in which he is placed; cruel in his disposition; showing discrimination, analysis, and candor, when he says he 'likes to wear heavy boots — good to kick boys with.' He is the better of two similarly malformed and imbecile brothers now living. In this lowest plane of imbecility will be found many mutes who are yet possessed of perfect hearing, ready appreciation of language, and often dexterous finger and hand capacity. Under special training in articulation and the inspiring effect of concert recitation and song, they come to the partial possession of speech. They rarely become perfect in speech. As their capacity is gradually developed, they are carried forward into the higher ranks, to become our most interesting children. The idiocy or imbecility displayed by them is, as often as not, the effect of their isolation. The brighter children of the family outgrow them. They betake themselves to solitary lives and belittling occupations, until the range of their intelligence becomes very limited. They are the Kaspar Hausers of our community.

"Advancing into another apartment, the fifth and sixth of the series through which you must imagine yourselves to have been led, we find the middle-grade imbeciles of a congregate family. They are orderly and neat at their school tables, because, from habit training, they have become so. They are patient under the discipline of light work, many of them becoming useful drudges and domestic servants. They crowd forward into our great laundry, where, commencing with the folding of our table napkins, they come to dispute with one another for the use of the ironing-table or power-mangle. The tone of the place being industry, they creep out of their sloth and indolence to keep lagging steps with the crowd that carries them forward.

"The unfairness of applying to the highest grade, or indeed to any grade of imbecile children, the word 'idiot,' in any other than its generic sense, will occur to any sympathetic and thinking person, as he steps across the threshold of the class-room or calisthenium devoted to the higher grades of our defective children.

"The mental deficiency or deviation is often so slight, or the imperfection is found in such a limited range, perhaps involving only the power to form a judgment of values, or a judgment of social proprieties, or a judgment of moral risk, or a judgment of the prevalent wickedness outside of asylums, that it may seem strange that several of these boys and girls should be under the care of an institution of this character.

"In this first rank are often found children who have been typical cases of idiocy from deprivation, who, under the advantages of educational influences especially adapted to the infirmity, rise to the first rank, many to become self-supporting under kindly guidance, but who, left to themselves, sink lower in their enforced isolation."

From this account one gets something of the feeling that comes with a visit to a well-managed institution for the feeble-minded. Nothing is more repulsive than neglected or untrained idiots; but, on the contrary, nothing gives higher ideas of the possibilities of kindness and intelligence in training all grades of the degenerate, than a visit to an institution managed like that at Elwyn, of which some idea is given by Dr. Kerlin's description. One comes to realize the educational value to the community of such kindly care, and the truth of the statement that kindness is its own reward, to society or to the individual.

The custodial care of the feeble-minded has thus far been undertaken by the managers of the schools for the feeble-minded, it being found that, under wise administration, the adult imbeciles could be useful in the work of the institution; and it being better, therefore, to introduce the colony plan with appropriate segregation of classes, than to establish other new institutions for the custodial care of adults. For instance, at Elwyn, it was found that many feeble-minded women had a liking for children, and that they could be distinctly serviceable in taking care of the young children in the school department, a work which made them happier, and benefited their own malady as far as anything could. "It is not," as Dr. Knight says, "legislatures to the contrary notwithstanding, because the managers of these institutions wish to build up a great institution, but because by the colony plan a larger share of service can be rendered than by splitting one institution into several new ones." New York, however, has established special custodial homes for adult idiots and a home for feeble-minded women, and New Jersey has recently followed the example. It remains to be seen whether, as in the case of the insane, specialists will conclude that classification should be maintained as between institutions, or whether it should be carried on in large institutions on the colony plan. With the plan of detached buildings for different classes, the dependants can be provided for at an expense of about $400 per patient for construction, which is much less than the construction cost heretofore thought necessary for the insane. At the Pennsylvania institution, which now contains nearly 1,000 inmates, the annual per capita expense has been reduced from $300 per inmate to a little over $100. Dr. Doren of Ohio, after an experience of thirty years in this work, has offered, if the State will give him a thousand acres of land, to care for every custodial case in Ohio, without expense to the State.[1]

That custodial care for most grades of the feeble-minded will come to be increasingly demanded cannot be doubted. It has been later in coming than the custodial care of the chronic insane, because the latter are more actively and obviously mischievous to society; but whenever the importance of human selection becomes better understood, the custodial care throughout life of the feeble-minded of both sexes will be demanded.[2]

[1] N. C. C., 1893, p. 219. Those who are acquainted with the difficulty of making a farm productive by incapable labor will be surprised at Dr. Doren's confidence. It is possible that he could make good his boast, but hardly possible that many men could be expected to follow such an example. An amount of managerial ability having a commercial value of many thousand dollars per annum would have to be put into such an institution in order to make it self-supporting.

[2] As a concrete illustration of the need of custodial care for feeble-minded, may be given the case of a woman in California, several of whose children had been transferred from the almshouse to the school for feeble-minded, until finally Dr. Osborn prevailed upon the local authorities to send the woman herself, and she is now contented and useful in the institution. Another case is given by Dr. Fernald, N. C. C., 1893, pp. 212, 213, as follows: "A feeble-minded girl of the higher grade was accepted as a pupil in the Massachusetts School for the Feeble-minded when she was fifteen years of age. At the last moment the mother refused to send her to the school, as she 'could

The latest differentiation in the care of the classes mentally or nervously diseased is in providing special custodial homes for epileptics. It had for a long time been found that in both homes for the feeble-minded and hospitals for the insane, the presence of epileptics was unfortunate from the standpoint of the other patients, while at the same time the special attention that they needed could not be given them. Therefore, at all the large institutions, special wards or buildings were provided where those subject to epileptic seizures might be properly provided for. This was also much more satisfactory to the epileptics themselves, as many of them in the intervals between attacks were fully conscious of their whereabouts, and had well-ordered minds. It is consequently directly in the line of further classification that institutions should be established for the care of epileptics alone, although some of the specialists in the care of the feeble-minded express their doubt as to the wisdom of this course.[1] Ohio was the first State to establish a home for epileptics, and the example has

not bear the disgrace of publicly admitting she had a feeble-minded child.' Ten years later the girl was committed to the institution by the court, after she had given birth to six illegitimate children, four of whom were still living and all feeble-minded. The city where she lived had supported her at the almshouse for a period of several months at each confinement, had been compelled to assume the burden of the lifelong support of her progeny, and finally decided to place her in permanent custody. Her mother had died broken-hearted several years previously."

[1] Particularly Dr. Kerlin, Association of Medical Officers of Institutions for Feeble-minded Persons, 1892, p. 284. He says, "I have nowhere seen that any special advantages are claimed for this separate care of the epileptics; the argument that they are an affliction to those not affected by these symptoms, is answered in the proposal to so classify them in separate buildings as shall benefit them and spare those whom they disturb."

been followed in New York. The Ohio Act was passed in April, 1890, and an institution has been erected and opened at Gallipolis. The Report of the State Board previous to the opening of this institution showed that there were in the State in the asylums for the insane 273 epileptics, and in the county infirmaries or almshouses 449, making a total of 722.

To some it may seem improper to treat of the care of inebriates in the same chapter with the care of the feeble-minded; but there is a growing tendency to consider habitual drunkenness a disease, or at least as resulting in diseased conditions, which must have medical treatment — reducing persons to a mental condition which demands custodial care. The neuroses resulting from or in habitual drunkenness have been studied of late, and one thing at least is manifest: The system of short term commitments for drunkenness in the county jails or in the houses of correction has no curative effect whatever. The person who has been convicted ten times for drunkenness and is convicted again is sentenced by the judge with the perfect knowledge on the part of the latter that no good will result, except that the person will be kept from bothering the community during the time of the sentence, and that he will come out of jail as likely to offend against the law as before he was committed. In some cases as many as one hundred and twenty commitments have been registered against a single person. By alternating jails and almshouses in order to secure a change of diet and associates, the habitual vagabond drunkard is enabled to recuperate his shattered forces at the expense of the community, and prolong his life and evil influences indefinitely.

The first State to establish a home for the inebriate was Massachusetts. Judging from the report of the board for 1893 this is by no means a success as yet. The act establishing the Massachusetts Hospital for Dipsomaniacs and Inebriates was passed in 1889. An eminent board of directors was named, of which Francis A. Walker of Boston was chairman. An original appropriation of $150,000 was made, and special appropriations for land and equipments amounting to over $32,000 have since been made. The hospital was opened Feb. 6, 1893. "This hospital was designed for the restraint of excessive drinkers during a period of time assumed to be sufficient for an attempt to bring their physical and mental condition up to a point which would enable them to resist a craving for drink, and successfully to contend with the evil influences sure to surround them on their discharge." [1]

Curiously enough the superintendent of the Foxborough Hospital has no power to compel inmates to work, though this is the best remedial agency known for the disease treated. Further than this, courts have shown great looseness in committing persons to the hospital as inebriates. The institution is not a place for the idle, disorderly, or vicious classes, but was planned rather for those whose lives, apart from that habit, had been decent and without scandal to the communities in which they lived.[2] Yet the courts have sent a number of inmates who, by their disorderly or criminal habits and tendencies, imperil the success of the humane venture of the State. It is recommended by the State Board of

[1] Report of Board of Lunacy and Charity, 1893, p.85.
[2] Ib., p. 87.

Lunacy and Charity that the officials in charge of the hospital should have the power to refuse persons committed by the courts, if they are palpably not adapted to the institution. Manifestly such an institution as this must have some way of securing the inmates for which it is intended and none others; and at least it must not be made what its enemies have called it, "a place for coddling drunkards."

Analogous to the institution for inebriates would be one where persons convicted of habitual offences against chastity might be committed for treatment and especially for detention. In case cure or reform, whichever we choose to call it, should prove to be impossible, they could then be detained during the remainder of their natural lives, working for their own support in a colony. New York has at present a custodial home for feeble-minded women. Such a place as the one just suggested has been advocated by Mrs. Lowell from the Conference of 1879 down to the present. Short commitments for this class of offences are manifestly as futile as in the case of habitual drunkards. Further than this, this class of persons are especially subject to disorders analogous to feeble-mindedness; and in all institutions for wayward girls the number verging upon feeble-mindedness is found to be especially large. The managers of reformatories and refuges for fallen women frequently complain that those who come to them need hospital treatment and prolonged detention. This the custodial home could give.

There is also need of custodial institutions for male offenders against chastity, nothing at present being done, perhaps because any treatment with the present punitive and reformatory machinery would be so manifestly futile. With proper custodial homes for persons of these classes of both sexes, we could begin to segregate and thereby sterilize a large number of those who have proved themselves by their conduct to belong to the class of the unfit.

CHAPTER XIII.

FURTHER DIFFERENTIATION AND SUMMARY.

WE have now examined the methods in vogue of caring for the different classes of dependents so far as these classes have become distinct enough to require special institutions supported in whole or in part by public money. From the almshouse, or from the poor relieved in their homes, there has been a constant drafting off of the specialized classes; and this process is undoubtedly to go still farther.

While the almshouse is, as a rule, the best place that public authorities yet consent to provide for the aged poor of good character, there have grown up in all centres of population a considerable number of private homes for the aged, usually managed by churches. Admission to these is generally obtained by the payment of a sum down which insures care during life. It is really a life annuity for somewhat less than its money value. One hundred to six hundred dollars is the sum charged, and persons are usually not admitted under sixty years of age. Sometimes the age limit is still higher. Frequently there is a provision that persons must be members of a particular denomination; sometimes the homes are established for a particular class, as for the wives of deceased ministers, and so on. Friends often contribute the admission fee for a deserving person, and obtain a place for him. Very frequently they are used as a means of providing a safe and comfortable place for the aged having a little property, or possibly a pension, who have no relatives with whom they can live, and who have not property enough to support them outside such an institution. When well managed, these homes furnish a very satisfactory way of providing for the aged of good character, and prevent the possibility of their degradation to the almshouse.

The Catholic Order of the Little Sisters of the Poor maintains in various large cities homes for the aged, to which persons are admitted without regard to creed or character, if only they are amenable to the rules of the house after admission. These homes are supported entirely by the Sisters, who beg from door to door, and from office to office, and go at the close of business to the markets and stores to collect the refuse or whatever may be given by the owners; and who further collect from hotels, restaurants, and private dwellings the broken victuals and other material that can be used. These homes are models of order. The Sisters, most of whom come from France, where is them other house of the order, have perfect control of the very querulous and often exacting inmates, whom they speak of as " the children."

There has lately developed a tendency for these institutions, including the homes of the Little Sisters of the Poor, to ask for public appropriations. This may possibly be the beginning of a new classification among those formerly sent to the almshouse, — a tendency to support those of good character in special homes receiving public subsidies, and on the other hand, to leave those of degenerate character to be provided for in the almshouse. A wiser way would seem to be that here-

FURTHER DIFFERENTIATION AND SUMMARY. 295

tofore suggested: Draft off those of bad character to special institutions, and leave the almshouse as a home for the unfortunate.[1]

On the side of medical charities, we may expect the development of special homes for incurables, of which there are now a considerable number maintained by private benevolence. The almshouse is still about the only home for incurables which the public maintains, though private institutions of the kind are sometimes subsidized. There may also eventually be special institutions

[1] The very serious agitation in England for a system of relief for the aged more honorable than that afforded by the poor-law authorities has crystallized about the idea of old-age pensions. It seemed likely for a time to carry everything before it. Canon Blakesly of the church, Charles Booth the statistician, and Joseph Chamberlain the politician, each had plans to propose for the endowment of old age. The agitation at present seems to have lost some of its force, but will probably come up again in other forms until something results from it. No analogous agitation has taken place in the United States; but it is likely enough that if successful in England, it will be transferred to the United States. We already have in California what amounts to a pension for the aged. The State law provides that any institution maintaining persons over 60 years of age shall receive for each such person an annual allowance of $100 per year. (Institutions owning property worth $15,000 or more, and supporting at least ten inmates aged 60 years or over, are entitled to $100 per year for each inmate. Statutes and Amendments to Codes, 1883, pp. 380-382.) This applies to the county almshouses and public institutions as well as to private charities. It thus comes about that county officials can admit old people to the benefits of the institution and the bill will be paid by the State. There is sometimes even a profit. On the explanation of the county officials, it was shown to the State authorities that many old people might just as well be given their $100 in their homes as to be compelled to take up their residence in the almshouse. This was assented to; and it thus comes about that there is an old-age pension in California, which can be obtained from the county authorities, but is paid by the State. As soon as the law has brought about some of the results that must spring from its operation, it will no doubt be repealed.

for special incurable diseases. Another subdivision in medical charities, following European example, will doubtless be "lock-hospitals," for the treatment of venereal diseases.

For some adults of the defective classes, the blind and the deaf and dumb, it is already apparent that permanent homes will be needed, since all of them cannot be rendered self-dependent. Iowa has such a home for the adult blind, and a number of other institutions might be named.

Most of the classes of which we have treated in Part II. are fully dependent, and many of them are chronic cases. Except among dependent children, the cure of dependency is the exception rather than the rule. There is, however, throughout the whole country, and especially in the large cities, a vast amount of relief work done by individuals, churches, and benevolent organizations which has for its particular purpose the saving of individuals and families from crossing the pauper line. Most of the work of the charity organization societies comes under this head. It is dealing with incipient dependency, attempting to treat the cases at an early stage of development so that chronicity may be avoided. Different individuals dealt with may belong to any of the classes for which special provision is now made, but at the critical time of their experience it is sought to give them aid that will save them from dependency. This work will be especially dealt with in Part IV. of the present volume.

Finally, it must be repeated that the greatest blessing which could come to our charitable work in the way of further differentiation and better classification would be improvements in our judicial and punitive machinery.

An inefficient police department and vulgar and corrupt police courts are the greatest "cross" that an active worker for the poor in many of our large cities has to bear. No thorough-going reforms in work for the poor can be perfected until the system of jails, reformatories, and prisons is reformed.

On reviewing what has been said regarding the dependent classes, we find that from the primitive institution, the almshouse hospital, or the hospital almshouse, there have developed a dozen or more special institutions for the care of the different classes of unfortunates. It is differentiation and intergradation analogous to that which has gone on in modern industry. This specializing and classifying, however, may result in a mechanical treatment, not as helpful as the earlier individualizing of cases and the treatment of each on its own merits. If extended classification results simply in a herding together of a large number of similarily defective persons who are treated as a class, fed as a class, drugged as a class, and buried as a class, we shall have a specialization which eliminates human sympathy, and makes charity something mechanical and uncharitable. If, on the other hand, fuller classification results in the fuller individualizing of cases and the adaptation to each of the best agencies of modern science and modern sympathy for care and cure, then the development has been one not only toward wiser sympathy, but deeper sympathy, and has prepared the way for a fuller development of the changes already in progress. In other words, our modern highly deferentiated methods of treating the dependent classes bring with them a possibility, but not a guaranty, of better service.

PART III.

PHILANTHROPIC FINANCIERING.

PART III.

PHILANTHROPIC FINANCIERING.

CHAPTER XIV.

PUBLIC CHARITIES.[1]

It is asserted from time to time that public charities are not charities at all. The excuse for the assertion is that the tax-payer does not contribute his money from motives of benevolence, the hired official does not disburse it because he pities the beneficiaries, and the latter receive it with no sense of gratitude. It is not benevolence, but the motive of preserving the public health and the public peace that maintains public institutions for the relief of the destitute. The reply is that benevolence is present as a motive in supporting public charities. The tax-payers submit to an increase of burdens partly because they sympathize with distress, and are anxious to have it relieved. The question is one of definition simply, and it is now necessary to explain the meaning in which certain words are used. The writers cited in the present chapter do not agree one with another in the meaning they attach to elementary terms.

---

[1] In this and in all but two of the succeeding chapters the amount of existing literature bearing directly upon the subjects treated is so small that the foot-notes are a sufficient guide to it. A bibliographical note is therefore not inserted at the beginning of each chapter.

By "charities," as the term is used in the title of this chapter and in this volume, are meant all those institutions and agencies which give direct material aid to the poor as such. On the one hand, this leaves out of view all purely educational institutions, because the aid given is not material. According to English usage and according to legal usage in this country, an educational institution, unless supported by the fees of the pupils, is a "charity." A prominent American within the last fifteen years has asserted that a free soup-house and a free school are based upon the same principle. He is wrong, because there are dangers inherent in the gifts of free food which do not inhere in the gift of free education. Benevolence may set aside the rule that if a man will not work neither shall he eat, but not the rule that if a man will not study neither shall he learn. The beneficiary can get no advantage without personal effort from free tuition; he is, therefore, not exposed in the same way as is the recipient of material relief to the danger of degradation.

In educational institutions for the defective classes material relief, free board and lodging, is given to the pupils not able to pay, along with free tuition. This, in our opinion, makes such institutions charities to a certain extent, although they protest against being so classed, and wish to be considered purely educational. For administrative reasons, however, the supervision of them is usually given to the State Board of Charities. The educational element in their work so far overshadows the relief-giving element that they have only been incidentally referred to in this book.

The definition of charities given, while a little

broader than some would wish it, is narrower than the general application of the term. For instance, strictly taken, it would exclude institutions for the care of the insane, where, as in Minnesota, any citizen is entitled to gratuitous treatment and care, irrespective of ability to pay. In such a case the poor are given direct material relief in the form of board and lodging and medicine, but they do not receive it as being indigent. The State relieves the insane as insane, not as poor. The same would apply to hospitals such as those recommended by Havelock Ellis, maintained for the treatment of all disease at the expense of the State. It applies, too, to those institutions for defectives in which tuition, including board and lodging, is absolutely free to all comers irrespective of ability to pay. But still it may be said that, whether ostensibly or not, it is the desire to relieve the poor that primarily influences legislation of this sort. Although the poor are not nominally relieved as such, yet in fact they are so, since they make up a very large proportion of those receiving gratuitous treatment. In other words, the charitable element in the institution has not been eliminated by being hidden, and the need of insisting upon this is that the dangers of direct material relief are not eliminated either. Those institutions that give board and lodging and all the care that this implies to their beneficiaries must be classed, for administrative purposes at least, as charities, and are so considered in the present volume.

By " public charities" is meant those institutions or agencies which are entirely controlled by the state in any of its branches, federal, State, county, township, or municipality. The distinction is a legal one, and is perfectly simple. A public corporation is one existing under the authority of the state, and which the state can modify or abolish at will. Frequently great private charities, as Girard College or the Johns Hopkins Hospital, are spoken of as quasi-public institutions. They serve the public indeed, and the wealth which they administer might be considered as affected by a public use in the same sense as wealth owned by a railroad company; but their charters are contracts with the state and cannot be arbitrarily modified by it. By "public funds" are meant such funds as are derived from the revenues of the state in any of its branches. They are usually the proceeds of taxation.[1]

There have been many searches for the principle upon which the state has acted and should act in taking upon itself work for the relief of the poor. In Europe, the Teutonic countries have usually guaranteed relief to all citizens, while the Latin countries have not done so; and yet this fundamental difference is not shown in any very great differences in the character of their relief-work. Those who have argued that to guarantee relief was fatal to the independence of a people, and would induce all to become paupers, have been shown that under proper administration this is not true; since the condition of the pauper, while he may be saved from starvation, can be made very much less agreeable than that of the independent workman. Scanning the history of the different countries, especially of our own, the prin-

---

[1] Alex. Johnson, in his article on "Some Incidentals of Quasi-Public Charities," uses the term "public" in a sense somewhat different from that outlined for use in the text. There is one clear distinction between public and private institutions which can be made and ought continuously to be made.

ciple that underlies the assumption of relief-work by the state seems to be this: Whenever a community has been educated up to such a point that it insists on a large amount of relief-work being done, and when the methods of doing it have been reduced to a routine, then the state has been asked to undertake the work, and relieve private benevolence of the burden. This we have seen in the care of the insane, the education of the deaf and dumb and the blind, and the education of the feebleminded. In the matter of caring for inebriates, the experiment is now in progress under private management, and it is not yet clear that the time has come for the state to take hold. Relief work is adapted to administration by the state in proportion as it can be reduced to a routine, and in proportion as it requires very large expenditures to which all taxpayers can properly be asked to contribute. The state is not inventive, its agencies are not adaptable and flexible; but it is capable of doing a large, expensive work when the methods for doing it are sufficiently elaborated. The administration of out-door relief is dangerous for the state to undertake, for the simple reason that it never can be reduced to a routine.

The advantages of public support for charitable institutions are briefly as follows: —

1. The income can be absolutely depended upon, and may be made adequate. During an industrial depression there is no shrinking of revenue, as is sometimes the case in private charities, and an amount adequate to the work may always be reckoned upon.

2. There is greater publicity in a public institution. The records will ordinarily be fuller and more open

to inspection. The press is freer to expose abuses. The checks of public opinion are consequently more easily applied. The whole aim and purpose of a public institution may be modified whenever the people of a community see that modification is desirable. While not flexible in little things — the small points of administration — a system of public charities is frequently more susceptible of large adaptation than a system supported by endowments and private contributions.

3. Under a just system of taxation all persons are compelled to contribute according to their ability. The stingy man is not allowed to thrive at the expense of his benevolent neighbor. The law is primarily an agency for bringing up the laggards in the march of progress; and when the community on the average wants benevolent work done, this is the method of pushing forward those who hang back.

The chief disadvantages of public relief are the following: —

1. It is necessarily more impersonal and mechanical than that of private charities or of individual action. There is less kindness on the part of the giver, and less gratitude on the part of the receiver; and yet many cases occur where those who have received aid from the State have done so with thankfulness, and with a feeling of gratitude to the community as a whole for providing the means of relief.

2. There is possibly some tendency to claim public relief as a right, and for the indolent and incapable to throw themselves flat upon it. This feeling will always assert itself whenever it is given an opportunity to do so. In the case of public charities it can be checked,

as already indicated, by leading the pauper to feel that, while he can claim relief as a right, he cannot claim as a right relief enough to make him nearly so comfortable as the man who is self-dependent.

3. In public charities officialism is even more pronounced than under private management. The degradation of character of the man on a salary set to the work of relieving the poor has been called one of the most discouraging things in connection with relief-work, and perhaps it is especially true that public officials are likely to become hard and unsympathetic.

4. It is possible to do so much relief-work, that while one set of persons is relieved, another will be taxed across the pauper line. This was palpably the case in England before the reform of the poor-law in 1834. Our own expenditures for charitable institutions have seldom reached the sums that make it possible to demonstrate the connection between the difficulties falling to the lot of the struggling, self-dependent members of the community, and the increase of taxation for the benefit of the destitute. But under our chaotic system of taxation it is usually true that the burden of supporting the State tends to diffuse itself along the lines of the least resistance; consequently, money which is raised for the relief of the poor may come out of pockets that can ill spare it.

5. The final disadvantage of public institutions for the relief of destitution is the weightiest, at least in the United States. The disadvantage referred to is that the blight of partisan politics and gratuitously awkward administration often falls upon the work. City and county politics seem to degrade public charities even more than other branches of the local administration.

Charitable institutions are spoils of an insignificant character, thrown frequently to the less deserving among the henchmen of the successful political bosses. The managing boards of the hospital and almshouse are not content with appointing the superintendent, and leaving the responsibility of minor appointments to him, but make a complete list of employees, and force the superintendent to accept them. Frequently, says Mr. Low, where a board is divided, the majority meet and apportion the appointments among themselves, and then vote them through as the nominations of a caucus. "This, more than anything else, accounts for the frequency of inharmonious boards."[1] The benevolent of a community can

[1] N. C. C., 1888, p. 166-167. In the same connection Mr. Low gives the following example: ten thousand like it could be collected had we access to the inside history of the administration of local charities. "In the city of Brooklyn, there is an institution known as the Truant Home. The superintendent and other officers in this institution are appointed by the vote of the common council, without nomination by the mayor. Among the officers to be appointed is the farmer; and at one time, when the appointment had been made, the farmer turned out to be a hatter. He had supposed himself entirely equal to the duties of drawing the salary, and this he presumed would be the limit of what he had to do. When he discovered that the duties of the farmer included taking care of a cow and the raising of vegetables, he sent in his resignation without delay. In this connection, it transpired that all places in the gift of the common council were filled in the following way: The members of the board, comprising the majority, held a caucus, and by mutual agreement or by lot parcelled out the places among the different members of the majority. Consequently, when this farmer resigned, the individual alderman to whom the appointment was held to belong — I ask you to notice the word — selected another friend, this time not to be daunted by the idea of taking care of a cow, and upon his nomination this friend was immediately confirmed by the board of aldermen." As one out of the numberless illustrations of the way in which politics affect the distribution of public out-door relief, see Mr. Lockwood's remarks about Cleveland, ib., pp. 445, 446.

usually not do a better thing than to mingle in local politics enough to see that the local charities are not treated as spoils.

State institutions have been comparatively free from this blight; although politics have exiled men like Gundry from Ohio, and Drs. Gillette, Dewey, and Wines from Illinois. Politics also abolished the Board of Charities and Reform in Wisconsin, and substituted the Board of Control, with salaries for all members. Mr. Craig states that in New York charitable institutions have been comparatively free from the blight of partisan politics, although the same cannot be said of the prisons. In Ohio, the State board has taken advanced ground in this matter, and is recommending the appointment of bi-partisan boards, with the introduction of civil-service examinations for the filling of minor places.[1] The bi-partisan board is by many not considered a remedy. The city and county of New York gives many examples of the futility of this device as a means of eliminating politics. In Indiana the political spoliation of the charitable institutions, and the resultant disgust of the intelligent part of the community, has had influence, close observers believe, in turning the tide of election at one or two critical times. The State Board of Charity there succeeded, without any positive law on the subject, in securing the introduction of civil-service methods in the selection of minor employees in many State institutions.[2]

Both in this country and abroad the administration of

[1] See Ohio Board of State Charities, Report for 1891, pp. 9-13.

[2] The State universities are kept "out of politics" without the adoption of any formal civil service reform rules. It is apparently because large numbers of the influential classes are interested in their efficiency.

charities has been very greatly improved by the extension of the system of honor offices. These are offices in which no salary is paid the incumbent. The best and most efficient of our State Boards of Charity have members holding by this tenure. The directors, where there are special boards for the local hospitals and almshouses and other institutions, are frequently of this class. The only danger is that these boards, whose principal function is to select the salaried superintendent of the institutions over which they have control, or, in the case of State boards, a salaried secretary to do the work, will degenerate into mere engines of the political boss, to be used by him in the distribution of spoils. Yet the danger of this is much less with unsalaried than with salaried boards; and their further function of supervision and advisory interference with the management, are usually more developed, provided that the members receive no salary. It is frequently found possible to secure for such boards the services of some of the best men and women in the community; and, where it is possible, it is usually better that both men and women should be upon each board. Appointment seems, as a rule, to secure better members than election. The term of office should be of considerable length, the members going out in rotation. It is through the development of a system of honor offices that out-door relief in Germany has been robbed of its dangers, and it will be in part by the extension of the honor-office system in this country that the spirit of willingness to serve the State may be developed.

On the whole, there seems to be an improvement in the administrative sense of our people, and an appreciation of the fact that administration as such must be taken out of politics so far as possible. Any considerable improvement in our public charities depends upon this improvement. As a people, we have boasted loud and long about our achievements in the development of constitutional law; it is time for us to stop bragging, and humbly to take up the study of the science and art of administration.

In each commonwealth the fabric of the public charitable institutions rests upon the quicksands of the poor-law, which few study and probably none understand. It was said of the English poor-law, by the commission appointed to investigate its workings, that there was scarcely one statute connected with the administration of poor-relief which had produced the effect designed by the legislature, and that the majority of them had created new evils and aggravated those which they were intended to prevent.[1] The same is substantially true in many of our own States, and especially in the older commonwealths, such as New York and Pennsylvania, where the legislatures have not been careful to repeal existing legislation when enacting new laws. The result is a tangle of statutes which cannot be rationally interpreted because they have no rational basis. The courts construe them from time to time, because they must, and not because they know how. The fact that, after years of giving out-door relief in Brooklyn, the whole system was decided to be illegal, shows the unsubstantial nature of the foundation upon which our system of poor-relief sometimes rests.

In the Eastern States the English example has been followed, and laws regarding settlement are very com-

[1] Nicholls, "History of Poor Laws," vol. ii., p. 259.

plicated. The State Board of Lunacy and Charities in Massachusetts is busied to a very considerable extent in deciding where the burden of providing for particular persons should rest, whether upon the town, county, or State. In the Western States, while there may be a law defining residence, and another providing that only residents shall be relieved, these laws are almost never heeded. A dependant passes from township to township, from county to county, and from State to State, expecting to be relieved wherever he happens to need relief. It is a loose system; but it may be doubted whether the old system of settlements, as now administered in Massachusetts, is susceptible of adaptation to times when the mobility of the population is so enormously increased by facilities for transportation. The looseness of the San Francisco almshouse, which has received a Canadian pauper direct from the vessel on which he came to the State, appears to be carrying the matter too far; but we, doubtless, should not go back to a system of settlement laws like those formerly obtaining in England. A well-administered system of charities — that is, a system which aims at cure as well as relief, and which succeeds in making the condition of the willing pauper much less satisfactory than that of the self-dependent man — will probably not attract people from any great distance. The cure for migration is in the proper administration of local charities. This does not apply to the international migration of paupers, which has been but inadequately dealt with by our federal government, nor to assisted migration — the foisting of dependants upon one political unit by another.[1]

[1] See committee report on "Immigration and Interstate Migration," N. C. C., 1892, pp. 76-87. A federal law is suggested.

Closely connected with the subject of settlement is the matter of adjusting public burdens as between the various political units. The economical way is to make the locality bear all the burden, because then those who pay the taxes administer the relief, and are directly interested in keeping the amount as small as possible. This is the old English system. It has broken down in the case of the special classes of defectives, — the insane, etc., — because there were not enough of each class in a given township or county to enable that political unit to provide for them properly. They were therefore gathered under State control, and at first the cost of supporting them was assessed upon the county or township from which they came. The difficulty of collecting these assessments, together with the fact that the local desire to save money resulted too often in the denial of relief needed, has led to the removal of an increasing number to the support of the State at purely State expense. The county is then anxious to foist as many of its dependants upon the State as possible, since it does not feel the added burden of State taxation. Where the education of defectives, the care of children, the care of the insane, have all been transferred to the State, where, as in Pennsylvania, the State subsidizes many local hospitals, and where, as in California, the State pays for the care of a large number of the aged, little is left for the local political units. For the sake of securing better service, we have sacrificed the possibility of economy inherent in local administration of relief-work; and it does not seem likely that we will revert to the earlier principle, because to do so must usually be at the cost of less adequate relief.

There will come a time, however, when the enormous expense arising from the system of State-administered charities will be no longer bearable, and we shall have to seek methods of economy in the administration of these institutions. In some places, where the accumulation of expenses for these purposes has been recklessly allowed to increase for years, the legislature has finally had a spasm of economy, and made a horizonal reduction to the injury of the service and the distress of many inmates. More commonly the State has undertaken to do a thing, for instance, to care for the insane, and then has not done it, the appropriations necessary for carrying out the plans not being made. Economy by either of these methods is distinctly wasteful as well as brutal; and it is to be hoped that the pressure of large expenditures for charities will eventually force attention to the prevention of pauperism, and an attempt to remove its causes, instead of forcing reversion to the policy of letting suffering go unrelieved.

CHAPTER XV.

PRIVATE CHARITIES.

By private charities we understand those that in their management are independent of the authority of the State, except that the same, as private individuals, may be subject to its general police and supervisory powers. A private charity may, or may not, receive public money in the form of a subsidy. Other funds come either from voluntary contributions, or from the proceeds of legacies or endowments. We concern ourselves here chiefly with the first-mentioned method of obtaining money.

We have already adverted in Chapter I. to the influence of the ancient and mediæval church in securing the bestowal of alms. The art of inducing men to give has been practised ever since charity began, and at all times one of its most constant features has been religious or ecclesiastical influence. The motive of the giver frequently deteriorated, and became the selfish one of securing merit for himself, instead of the unselfish one of benefiting the one to whom alms was given.[1]

[1] See Ashley in "Economic History," vol. ii., p. 331. He quotes Crowley, who, he says, was a man not without some power of observation, but who, after describing the tricks of beggars counterfeiting diverse maladies, tells his readers, —

"Yet cease not to give to all,
Without any regard,
Though the beggars be wicked,
Thou shalt have thy reward."

The old abuses of ecclesiastical charity have been sufficiently raked over, and do not need to be recounted here. Those interested in see-

At the present time, it is still the church that is the most powerful agent in inducing people to give.[1] Whether charities are identified with any particular denomination or not, it is usually, though of course not uniformly, the people of the churches that support them; and of all the churches the one that still induces the largest amount of giving in proportion to the means of those who give, is no doubt the Roman Catholic. This is the church which has succeeded best in inducing people to give not only money, but service. The religious orders of the Roman Catholic Church are still unequalled in the amount of this kind of contribution to the care of the poor.[2] The orders that have had the largest development in the United States are the Sisters of Charity; certain of the teaching orders, which serve chiefly in charitable institutions; the Little Sisters of the Poor, who maintain homes for the aged; the *Sœurs de Bon Secours*, who nurse the poor in their own homes. The order best known is that of the Sisters of Charity, who conduct almost any form of work that seems to

ing what can be said on the other side will do well to examine Baluffi, "The Charity of the Church a Proof of Her Divinity," translated by Gargan, 1885, a Catholic work; Uhlhorn's "Christian Charity in the Ancient, Mediæval, and Modern Church," three volumes, one to each period, of which the first has been translated. It is a work called out in part by the harsh review of ecclesiastical charity by Emminghaus, in "Das Armenwesen und die Armengesetzgebung in Europäischen Staaten." Chas. L. Brace's work, "Gesta Christi," is chiefly concerned with tracing the beneficial influence of the church in humane progress.

[1] The church charities of Baltimore, exclusive of religious missions, have an annual expenditure of about $230,597. See report C. O. S., 1892.

[2] See the paper on Catholic charities by Bishop Ireland, read at the Conference of Charities, 1886, pp. 38-47.

need doing, according to the needs of the locality to which they are sent. In the building up of hospitals, the nursing orders of the Catholic Church have been particularly successful; and their personal devotion leads them to render especially important service in times of pestilence.

Of Protestant denominations, there are few in the large cities, where destitution is a problem, that have not done something for the care of the poor. The preventive and educational work, in proportion to other kinds, has been more largely undertaken by the Unitarians than by any other denomination. The great hospitals are likely to be supported by whatever denomination has the largest wealthy membership in any large city. There has been a great increase in the beneficial activity of the various churches within the last ten or fifteen years.

An unfortunate feature of the work of American churches is interdenominational competition, which induces many of them to develop their charities as engines of church extension. This can be, and sometimes is, carried so far as to make their charities a nuisance. The condition of things does not, however, seem to be worse than in countries having a single church. In the latter, ecclesiastical orders within the church compete one with another.

Next after religious influence, pure and simple, the most powerful of the secondary motives that induce men to give money for charitable purposes is possibly social influence. Many of the large charities of our cities are officered, so far as boards of management are concerned, by fashionable or otherwise influential people;

and to contribute to the charities of the locality [1] is one of the means by which social advancement is secured. A long chapter, and conceivably one of some value, might be written on the methods of raising money for charities by means of balls, entertainments, oyster suppers, and other devices for inveigling money from the pockets of those who would not otherwise contribute the same amounts. Such enterprises must be judged each on its own merits. The end does not justify the means; the means must justify themselves. A lottery is pernicious, though managed by a church for the benefit of a charity. A voting contest is usually vulgar and mischievous in its results, no matter what institution may be the beneficiary. Ostentation and extravagance at a charity ball are just as condemnable as at any other place, possibly more so. Wheedling and teasing are no more pleasant for a charitable purpose than for any other. On the other hand, any occasion which has sufficient results in instruction or healthful social recreation to justify the expense is justified irrespective of its motive.[2]

A third influence that is brought to bear in order to secure contributions for private charities is that of persistent teasing or other skilled solicitation on

---

[1] A man who makes excellent public addresses on the subject of charity organization once remarked privately of a particular association that he did not believe its work was good, but it was as much as one's social position was worth not to contribute to it.

[2] It has been suggested that the small affairs where women contribute the things sold, and then induce their husbands, relatives, and friends to buy, indicate an unsatisfactory condition of financial servitude on the part of the women, who can get money to contribute only in this indirect way.

the part of paid collectors working on a commission.[1]

Finally, the most powerful motive that influences contributions to private charities is that of benevolence, properly so-called. It is not more certain that there are large sums seeking investment in ordinary industry than it is that there are large sums which the holders would gladly give for the promotion of the public good, if they could find ways of bestowing such sums that they were sure would result in helpfulness.[2] In order to obtain possession of a portion of this really large fund which is intelligently given or intelligently withheld, the managers of a charity must not only do thoroughly good work, but must contrive to let it be known that they are doing such work. The methods of philanthropic advertising, using the word advertising in a distinctly honorable sense, are various. The best introduction that a charity can have to the benevolent people of the community is the gradual diffusion from one intelligent person to another of the opinion that the charity is in fact doing something that is worth while. Beyond this, most of the non-sectarian charities and those operating under the guidance of Protestant denominations issue annual reports. As a rule, it does not pay a society to economize by a failure to publish such a report. In order to reach the most influential

---

[1] See Johnson, "Charities Review, vol. i., pp. 152, 153, where some examples are given of fraudulent collections, and others of charities that got but a small portion of the money subscribed.

[2] It was upon this motive that Mr. Brace relied almost exclusively in securing support for the Children's Aid Society of New York. It is now one of the most liberally supported private charities in the United States.

members of the community, it must be well prepared, well printed, and discreetly distributed. Many societies publish their own condemnation in their annual reports, and many more fail to publish anything that commends them to the intelligent part of the community. The perpetual re-using of stereotyped phrases, the filling up a report with the cant of philanthropy, and having the reports year in and year out substantially in the same form, from which the essential facts regarding efficiency are omitted, brands the society as unprogressive and unsatisfactory. In addition to the annual reports, a great many societies issue circulars, and even periodicals, explaining their work as it develops. Great use is also made of the daily and weekly press, but this is frequently not as wisely used as would be for the good of the institutions. What the daily press wants is news; and there is usually, or at least there should usually be, a considerable amount of news about the development of any large charity. To offer this in a way that makes it available for the daily press, is to offer exactly the material which will do the most good when printed. It is of no advantage to a paper, nor to an institution sending the copy, to print a "lot of gush" about some charity. The editor does not want it for the simple reason that he knows it will not be read; and if he inserts it at all it is under personal pressure, and although he is conscious that its insertion is a mistake. I have known papers to take ill-prepared copy from a charitable institution, and charge a certain amount per column for inserting it; while, when the same material was put in different shape, and prepared in a way to make it attractive to the general public, they were willing to pay as much per column for the copy as they had formerly charged.[1]

In order to commend the work of a charity to the favor of the most intelligent part of a community, it is essential that no attempt should be made to do the work too cheaply. "Cheap and nasty" is a phrase that can be applied to charities as well as to merchandise. Just as a physician cannot afford to begin practice without a proper preparation for his work, and without the facilities in the way of library, instruments, and office that are necessary in order to do his work well, so a charity will not, even from the financial side, find it wise to undertake to do for seven thousand dollars a work that can only properly be done for ten thousand. It is usually easier to manage the finances of a society that insists on having a revenue adequate to the work that it is doing — that would in fact go out of existence rather than proceed otherwise — than it is to manage the finances of a society that consents to half do its work because of an inadequate income.

The advantages of private charities over public ones are that they afford on the average a somewhat larger share of personal sympathy, that their benefits cannot logically be claimed as a right (although they often are so claimed), that they do not oppress the poor by increasing taxation, and that they are supposed to bring a somewhat smaller degree of degradation to the recipient of relief. The disadvantages of this style of support are that it sometimes leads charities to resort to sensationalism to obtain contributions, that it some-

---

[1] Catholic charities very rarely publish reports, unless required to do so because they receive public money or for some similar reason. An exception is the Society of St. Vincent de Paul.

times results in undue plutocratic influence in the administration of the funds,[1] and that in some cases the amount obtained is inadequate to the work that should be done. This last was probably what led to the break-down of private relief at Elberfeld, and compelled the substitution of public relief. It is not found, however, as a rule in this country, that the funds shrink during times of depression so as to make contributions less when the need is greatest. This is a danger often anticipated without cause. It should be said, also, that where private charities have developed to a very large extent they are as mechanical and as badly administered as public charities, and it is less easy to reform them. This was the case in France before the Revolution, and in Italy before the recent secularization of charities. It is just as possible to pauperize a population through private charities as through public ones, as the example of Italy especially proves. Usually, however, when great abuses grow up in connection with charities, it is because they are heavily endowed; and this subject is to be treated in the next chapter.

In conclusion, it can only be reiterated that private charities are especially useful along lines of philanthropic experimentation. People with ideas in advance of those of the general community can find through private charities an opportunity to experiment, and, by results, to satisfy the community as a whole of the need and of the possibility of doing a certain work. Private charities are not suited to the administration of large funds, and the doing of a large volume of work, unless they are made amenable to state regulation.

---

[1] Contributors to the English "voluntary" hospital sometimes have an undue influence in deciding who shall be admitted.

ENDOWMENTS. 323

CHAPTER XVI.

ENDOWMENTS.

[Hobhouse, "The Dead Hand" (London, 1880); Kenney "Endowed Charities" (London, 1880). These two books describe English experience forcibly and with considerable completeness, and present the arguments for the restriction, supervision, and revision of endowments. A brief account of the official literature on the subject is given later on in a foot-note. Chalmer, "On Endowments" (Glasgow, 1827), chiefly literary and ecclesiastical; Fitch, "Endowments" (College Association of Pennsylvania, Philadelphia, 1888), a very forcible address; Nitti, "Poor Relief in Italy," *Economic Review*, vol. ii., pp. 1–24; Johnson, *Charities Review*, vol. i., pp. 152–159.]

WHEN those who support a charity find it difficult to raise the funds they need, and are weary with unsuccessful applications for contributions; when, further, they dislike to turn to the public treasury because of the stigma attaching to public relief, their wish is apt to be that their charity were adequately endowed. Then, they think, they could give their whole time to the administration of the funds, instead of giving so much of it to securing funds. It seems as though their hands would be free for very large usefulness, and the benefits of the institution might be indefinitely extended. It consequently happens that the annual reports of nearly every charitable association which is supported by voluntary contributions contain, in a conspicuous place, a form of bequest by means of which any one so inclined may, without inconvenience, insert a provision in his will, leaving property to this particular charity. There is also a feeling in the community that one who leaves his wealth to charity has done a commendable thing, and there is a great tendency in the older portions of the country for endowments to accumulate rapidly. Nothing is done to discourage the movement on account of the feeling that it should be as untrammelled as possible. Yet no other country has ever permitted entire freedom in the granting of charitable bequests without finding, in the course of years, or of centuries at most, that the wealth of the country was coming to be too largely administered by the "dead hand." In the United States there are special dangers in laxness in this matter, by reason of the provision of our federal Constitution which forbids States to pass laws impairing the obligation of contracts. This makes it especially difficult for us to modify the system that is now developing. In England, whenever Parliament sees fit to change the administration of an endowment, or even to sequester its revenue for other purposes than those of the testator, Parliament can do as it will; but that is out of the question with the State legislatures in this country. If a charitable establishment has a charter in which the State has not reserved the right to amend or repeal it, then, under the Dartmouth College decision, that charter is a contract with the State, which the latter cannot alter without the consent of the corporation.[1]

[1] The Dartmouth College decision was reported in 4 Wheat., 516, et seq.; also in 1 N. H., 111. The legislature of New Hampshire had attempted to modify the corporation of Dartmouth College by changing the number of its trustees and in other ways. The Supreme Court of the State decided that this was possible without the consent of the old Board of Trustees. The Supreme Court of the United States reversed the decision, holding that the charter was a contract

ENDOWMENTS.

We are not, of course, likely to have a dangerously large amount of property devoted to charitable uses very soon, but it is better, as those who have studied the subject know, and as any one must see on reflection, that we should make rules for the right development at the beginning, rather than be compelled to remove a mountain of abuses after they have accumulated. Owners of property frequently feel as if they had a "natural right" to provide for its bestowal in perpetuity. Exactly why people should expect to be allowed to manage their property after they are dead and can no longer use it themselves, it is hard to see; at least, it is hard to see why a community should think itself bound to accord them the privilege that is to make them legislators in

between the State and the corporation, and could not be altered without the consent of the later, on account of the provision of the federal Constitution which forbids any legislature to pass laws impairing the obligation of contracts. Art. I., Sec. 10. The decision has been extensively undermined in the case of railroads and other corporations considered to be of a quasi-public nature, by the ruling in Munn vs. Ill., in which it was held that the legislature had the power to regulate the administration of property affected by a public use. Later decisions have modified this by giving to courts the right to say what "regulation" is "reasonable." So far as eleemosynary corporations are concerned, the Dartmouth College decision has not been modified to any appreciable extent; but it has been rendered nugatory for corporations created since the time it came to be appreciated, by the insertion in a large number of State constitutions of the provision that all charters granted under general or special acts shall be subject to amendment or repeal by the State. This makes the power of amendment or repeal a reservation on the part of the State included in the contract. Whether the decision of the Supreme Court of the United States was good law or not, it was certainly a mistake from an economic standpoint. As Cooley says in effect, it has been found that there is less danger in granting to legislatures the power of amendment and repeal of charters, than there is in giving to legislatures power to grant charters which are irrepealable.

perpetuity, regarding the disposition of a certain amount of wealth, which they happen at the time of death to possess. One feeling may perhaps be that the person who leaves money to charity acts only from commendable motives, and that his will should therefore be respected. But even if it were true that they always acted from good motives, it would have to be remembered that "hell is paved with good intentions," or, as the Bible puts it, "There is a way which seemeth right unto a man, but the end thereof is death."

But their motives are not always commendable. Hobhouse gives the following analysis of the motives of decedents who leave money to charity.[1]

1. Love of power, ostentation, and vanity. 2. Superstition. The influence of this extends far beyond the Catholic Church, and leads people who have done little good in their lives to attempt to do a great deal by the disposition of their wealth after they can no longer control it personally. 3. Spite. "An appreciable number of men," says Hobhouse, "and perhaps more women, especially those who are childless and have been teased by expectant legatees, are on bad terms with their relatives. Now, the only way to disinherit your legal heirs is to give your property to some one else; what, then, so obvious as to give it to charity?" 4. A fourth cause, which Hobhouse thinks is far inferior in extent of operation to the first two mentioned, is the honest belief on the part of founders that their disposition of property is best calculated to benefit their country. This is patriotism, or philanthropy, or public spirit.[2]

[1] Hobhouse, "The Dead Hand," pp. 15-20.
[2] Ib., p. 18. "As in other departments of life so in this, the vulgar are influenced by vulgar motives. If a man makes his gift by will,

But without regard to the motives, it is found that judgment is very fallible, that, at least, it is seldom adequate to provide what will be wise for future generations. Dr. Fitch quotes a paragraph from an article contributed by Turgot to the French "Encyclopédie" in 1757, which sets out very strikingly the difficulties that must be encountered by one who tries to be wise for all time to come: "The testator," he says, "is apt to be ignorant of the nature of the problem he desires to solve and of the best way of solving it. He is seldom gifted with a wise foresight of the future and of its wants. He puts into his deed of gift theories, projects, and restrictions which are found by his successors to be utterly unworkable. He seeks to propagate opinions which posterity disbelieves and does not want. He takes elaborate precautions against dangers which never arise. He omits to guard against others which a little experience shows to be serious and inevitable. He assumes that his own convictions and his own enthusiasm will be transmitted to subsequent generations of trustees and governors, when, in fact, he is only placing in their way a sore temptation, at best to negligence and insincerity, at worst to positive malversation and corruption." [1]

i.e., out of other people's pockets instead of his own; if we find him stipulating for benefits to his own soul; making provisions to perpetuate his own name or arms or tomb; devising solemn oaths to deter men from altering his arrangements; in such cases, whatever fine words he may have used, we may be sure he was really thinking more of himself than of his fellow-creatures. Now, most private foundations have one or more of the latter class of characteristics. For that reason I attribute but a minor place to the influence of patriotism or public spirit."

[1] Proceedings of the Second Annual Convention of the College Association of Pennsylvania, Dr. J. G. Fitch, "Endowments," pp. 20, 21.

In England it has been found that in many parishes rents are increased by the fact that those who live in these particular parishes can obtain doles from the great endowments. As a consequence, a pauper population is attracted to the place, and the poor-law rates are higher than where there are no endowments at all. Many dole-giving endowments have also been established in the United States which are having, in so far as their extent makes it possible, exactly the same influence.[1]

But irrespective of their motives, or the wisdom of testators, endowments are not likely to accomplish as much good as is expected of them because the character of boards of management is not all that could be desired, and because of a tendency to officialism, which develops when any society finds its economic existence assured.

The expenses of administration very frequently eat up the greater part of the income. While this is not the worst possible result, it still indicates in many cases a waste of the income consumed.[2]

---

[1] In San Francisco a large swarm of widows with children are drawn to the mayor's office every year to get a share in an annual allowance of about $2,000 to be distributed among them from the proceeds of an endowment. Those who are successful receive about $2.00 each, and every one who applies for the dole is inevitably degraded. This is a typical example of this sort of bequest.

[2] Mr. Johnson, in the article referred to, points presumably to Girard College as an example of extravagance in the administration of a charitable trust. At this college, which is really an industrial school for boys, according to the account of it given by Mr. Alden, "History of Child Saving," pp. 70-75, about three million have been spent on the construction of buildings which are of white marble. "The central or main building is the finest specimen of pure Greek architecture in America." The endowment fund of this institution is now considerably over $15,000,000 (Johnson estimates it at $20,000,-000), yielding a gross annual revenue of about $1,500,000. There are less than 1,600 boys in attendance, about 150 leaving "College" each

ENDOWMENTS. 329

Boards of management are usually co-optative, and tend to be made up of old persons, often not particularly wise or progressive in the administration of the funds given to them. The habit of leaving funds to be distributed by public authorities is not as common in this country as in England, and not as common in the West as in the East. The character of efficient societies commonly declines when they became considerably endowed. They illustrate over again the truth of that saying of Emerson's which paupers are often said to especially exemplify, "men are as lazy as they dare to be." [1]

Three things are necessary in the proper regulation of the endowments.

1. The restriction of endowments. Our law at pres-

---

year. By comparison of such figures as these with those of the great universities, it will be seen that an enormous amount of money is invested in the education of comparatively few boys. One of the absurdities likely to cluster about endowments is found in connection with Girard College. "No minister of any sect is *ever* to be admitted within the premises, as the founder wished to 'keep the tender minds of the orphans who are to derive advantage from this bequest free from the excitement which clashing doctrines or sectarian controversy are apt to produce.'" Johnson, in the article quoted, recalls Dickens's description of "a place for the entertainment of 'seven poor travellers'" at Rochester, England. The accommodations for the keeper had improved, and those for the travellers had gradually deteriorated; and it was in contemplation, when he visited it, to build a shed outside for the travellers, and then the keeper would have a comfortable house, and those whom the house was built for would be entirely out of it. At the time of his visit only about one-thirtieth of the annual revenue was expended on the purposes commemorated in the inscription over the door, the rest being handsomely laid out in chancery, law expenses, collectorship, receivership, poundage, and other expenses of management highly complimentary to the importance of the seven poor travellers." *Charities Review*, vol. i., p. 156.

[1] Alex. Johnson in the *Charities Review*, vol. i., pp. 156, 157.

ent declares endowments invalid for superstitious or immoral purposes. This is a limitation left over from the time of the Reformation. It was established especially to prevent perpetual payments for prayers for the dead. Surely we have advanced far enough at the present time so that foundations for the distribution of indiscriminate doles might also be prohibited. As the problems of poor-relief are better worked out, there should be some authority to pass upon the wisdom of endowments, and to allow them to take effect or not according as public interests would or would not be served.[1]

2. There must be a public supervision of endowments. This is necessary to prevent abuses from which inmates or institutions may suffer, as well as to prevent the misapplication of funds, and their use by private parties. There are very few States in this country that have any provision for visitation of endowed institutions. The English law, that the founder and his heirs and assigns shall be the visitors, obtains; but this visitation is not adequate, and should be supplemented by that of some responsible public official. The State Board of Charities is the proper authority where such a board exists.

3. It is necessary to provide for the revision of endowments. Times change. An endowment providing for the ransom of the captives of the North African pirates may have benefited some individuals for a time after it was made, but to provide for a similar expenditure in perpetuity was an absurdity. An endowment

---

[1] In New Haven an endowment was left providing for a dole to be given through the city authorities. They at first decided to decline it: but this decision was reversed, and the charity is now administered as contemplated by the testator.

for superannuated wool-carders continued to support warden and bedesmen long after wool-carding had ceased to be an occupation. An endowment of 1683 for seven poor old men of the Protestant religion in the Asylum of the County of Cork, that had been soldiers and were unable to work, is handed down to a time when sufficient Protestant soldiers cannot be found in Cork to exhaust the income of the charity, and there is at present an accumulated fund of £2,300. There is a fund in Stirling worth £5,400 a year, which was given when certain trades and crafts possessed a monopoly in the town, for the indigent members of these guilds. The income of the charity became so great that it was distributed among the members of the guild irrespective of poverty and even of residence. In 1869 it was found that of the 412 members, 369 were recipients of the charity, and some of these were soldiers in Australia. Endowments for teaching children to card, spin, and knit are of small use at the present time, or a foundation for the supply of spinning-wheels is not of any particular value.[1] Changes in religion, politics, and knowledge, as well as in industry, leave old endowments supporting something that is useless or worse, and there must be public authority for revising them.

Limitations upon the powers of testators will not lessen the amount that is given in charity eventually. They may keep a man whose motive is vanity, who is set in his own way and wishes to perpetuate his own will, from giving money to charities. He will see that public officials may interfere with his plans or whims.

[1] For the foregoing and other examples of futile or mischievous charities, see Kenny, "Endowed Charities," pp. 160 ff.

But those whose aim in leaving wealth is to benefit their fellows will look upon it as an advantage that, if their ideas are found not to be sound with the passage of years, there will be public authorities having power to modify and make useful their bequests.[1]

[1] Fitch, in his article on "Endowments," gives the following instance: "In 1869, when I was engaged on a special Parliamentary inquiry into the condition of education in Birmingham, the late Sir Josiah Mason said he should like to show me over his orphanage which he had then very recently founded; and he described to me the very bountiful provision he had made for the future maintenance or this institution. He also told me what schemes he then had in his mind for the endowment of the great Science College which has since been established. I said to him then, 'Are you not afraid of leaving such large bequests to posterity when you see the modern tendency to overhaul and revise the wills of founders?' He replied, 'That is the very reason why I feel such confidence in leaving these sums of money; if it were not that public authorities are likely to be vigilant, and to correct any mistake that I make, and to take care to keep these institutions in full working efficiency, I should feel very much hesitation in leaving such large sums to my successors.' It was in this spirit that in the following year, 1870, he introduced into his deed of foundation for the Science College this provision: 'Provided, always, that it shall be lawful for the said Josiah Mason at any time during his life, and after his decease for the trustees, within two years after the expiration of every successive period of fifteen years, to alter or vary the trusts or provisions herein contained in all or any of the following particulars.' Then he enumerates every one of the particulars, except the general object of the foundation, namely, the improvement of scientific instruction."

As an example of what a country comes to with the lapse of time, we may turn to England. The great endowments of the monasteries, with their dole-giving features, were secularized by Henry VIII. at the time of the Reformation. The opinion has already been cited that the property was of more use in the hands of dissolute favorites of the king than in that of the monks. Bequests of land were strictly limited by subsequent legislation, and endowments for superstitious uses were forbidden, and in many ways the power of bequests was greatly restricted; but when Lord Brougham, among his many other agitations during the first quarter of this century, got a commission

ENDOWMENTS. 333

to investigate endowed charities, it was found to be a gigantic task even to enumerate them. The commission worked from 1818 to 1837; and the results of this research were published in 38 folio volumes, consisting of some 25,000 pages, describing 28,820 charities, with an aggregate income of £1,200,000, compiled at a cost of more than a quarter of a million. (See Kenny on " Endowed Charities," p. 135.) A general digest of this great report was published in 1867-76 by the Charity Commissioners. The gross income from endowments as given in this register was:

From land	£1,558,251
From personalty	640,213
Total	£2,198,464

The land held by them included 523,311 acres. The income was devoted to the various forms of charity in the following proportion:

Education	£666,863
Apprenticing and advancement	87,865
Clergy and lecturers	90,843
Church purposes	112,895
Nonconformist churches and ministers	38,832
Parochial and other public uses	66,875
Almshouses and pensions	552,119
Medical hospitals and dispensaries	199,140
Distribution amongst the poor	383,029

The income includes no estimate of the prospective increment in the lands held by the charities, nor upon the buildings and other leases, nor of the values of the land and buildings kept for occupation as charitable premises. The universities, some large school foundations, and cathedral foundations are also omitted. Finally, a considerable number of charities probably escaped enumeration, as new ones are continually turning up which had not previously been tabulated.

The proper administration of such a great block of wealth as this is manifestly of the utmost importance to the community; and if it goes in mischievous doles, or is consumed in useless administration, the community ought to have the power to interfere and modify the administration and purposes of the endowments.

CHAPTER XVII.

PUBLIC SUBSIDIES TO PRIVATE CHARITIES.[1]

WHEN contributions are hard to get, when fairs and balls no longer net large sums, and when endowments are slow to come, the managers of private charities frequently turn to the public authorities and ask for a contribution from the public revenues. On the other hand, when local or State legislatures see the annual appropriation bills increasing too rapidly, and when they see existing public institutions made political spoils, and the administration wasteful and inefficient, they are apt to think of giving a subsidy to some private institution, instead of providing for more public buildings and more public officials. The former course is cheaper at the time, and seems to promise better administration.

Between the problem of public *versus* sectarian schools on the one hand, and of governmental control of private business corporations on the other, — allied to both but identical with neither, — is this problem of granting or of not granting public subsidies to private charitable corporations. It is related to the school question not only because the care of dependent and deliquent children by sectarian institutions involves their education in the faith of a

[1] In some of its parts this chapter is identical with a paper read by the author at the International Conference at Chicago in 1893, and published in the volume of the Reports of that Congress devoted to the " Organization of Charities."

sect, but because there is reason to believe that the subsidizing of sectarian charities has been resorted to with the conscious purpose of evading, and perhaps of undermining, the laws that forbid public aid to sectarian schools. It is related to the problem of governmental control of private corporations, not only by the fact that the legal questions involved are frequently the same, but by the further fact that the methods used by eleemosynary corporations to secure public subsidies frequently remind us of the methods used by money-making corporations to secure legislative favors.

On Feb. 2, 1893, while the Senate of the United States was sitting as town council for the City of Washington, a member moved to amend the appropriation bill by inserting a proviso that almshouse inmates or other paupers and destitute persons who might be a charge upon the public should be turned over to any private institution that would contract to provide for them at ten per cent less than they were then costing the District. Senator Call, who introduced the amendment, explained that it was in lieu of one which had been rejected at the previous session of Congress, whereby he had sought to have $40,000 of public money given to the Little Sisters of the Poor, to enable them to build an addition to their Home for the Aged. He defended the original proposal on the ground that this sisterhood cared for the aged poor better and more cheaply than the almshouse, and that the existence of their institution had saved to the taxpayers of the District in the last twenty years a sum believed to be not less than $300,000. It was not a novel plea; for Congress had already appropriated, since 1874, $55,000 to aid the Home for the Aged of the Little Sisters of the Poor; and each year the District appropriation bill had included subsidies for a large number of private charitable institutions, some of them avowedly under sectarian management and others not. How far the tendency to grant public subsidies to private charities had gone in the District of Columbia is in some sort indicated by the following table:

DISTRICT OF COLUMBIA APPROPRIATIONS FOR PUBLIC AS COMPARED WITH PRIVATE CHARITIES.

	NUMBER OF INSTITUTIONS.		APPROPRIATION FOR MAINTENANCE.		
	1880.	1892.	1880.	1892.	INCREASE.
Public . .	7	8	$78,048.82	$119,475.05	160%
Private . .	8	28	46,500.00	117,630.00	253%
TOTALS .	. . .	. . .	$124,548.82	$237,105.50	

	APPROPRIATIONS 13 YEARS, 1880-92.		
	CONSTRUCTION.	MAINTENANCE.	CONSTRUCTION AND MAINTENANCE.
Public . . .	$155,130.70	$1,296,125.95	$1,351,256.65
Private . . .	300,812.53	840,940.00	1,141,752.53
TOTALS. . .	$455,943.23	$2,137,065.95	$2,493,009.18

From this table it will be seen that the amount given for maintenance to private charitable institutions at the beginning of the period was a little less than one-third of the whole amount, while at the close of the period it is a little less than one-half. The most surprising fact, however, is that the District had given to private institutions nearly twice as much money to be used in acquiring real estate and erecting buildings as it had granted to its own public institutions. Were we to deduct a sum of $66,900 charged to the workhouse, a purely correctional branch of the so-called Washington Asylum, it would appear that more than three-fourths of the money appropriated for permanent improvements in charitable institutions was given to private corporations.

The government of the District of Columbia is, of course, in many respects unique; but this tendency to vote public money to private charities is by no means peculiar to it. The best known example of persistence in the policy of reckless subsidies to private institutions is that of New York. A single institution in this State, officered by a religious order, receives from the city government more than $260,000 per year. A list of over two hundred private institutions for orphan children and the friendless in New York State shows that, of their total revenue, but $1,225,104.69 was derived from legacies, donations, and private contributions, while more than twice as much, namely $2,664,614.40, came from the tax-payers of the State, the counties, and the cities. A great part of the money handed over for disbursement to private institutions goes for the support of dependent children.[1]

According to Mrs. Josephine Shaw Lowell, the administrative results of this policy in New York City have been to build up the private eleemosynary institutions of the State at the expense of the public ones. She gives the following statement covering a series of years to show this:

Year.	Population.	For Prisoners and Public Paupers.	For Paupers in Private Institutions.	Total.
1850	515,547	$421,882	$9,863	$431,745
1860	813,669	746,549	128,850	875,399
1870	942,292	1,355,615	334,828	1,690,443
1880	1,206,577	1,348,383	1,414,257	2,761,640
1890	1,600,000	1,949,100	1,845,872	3,794,972

[1] See Chapter IX.

The appropriations for 1890 to private institutions fall under three heads:

For defectives, sick and vicious	$ 133,565
For children admitted by managers	1,081,746
For board of children committed by magistrates	630,561
Total	$1,845,872

After showing how ruthlessly the estimates for the public charities were cut by the Board of Estimate and Control, she says: "The point to which I wish to call attention is that the city continues, at the bidding of the Legislature, to pay, without protest, year by year, increasing sums for the support of public dependents under care of private persons in private institutions, many of whom, but for this provision, would probably not be dependent at all, while at the same time the public dependents under the care of public officers in public institutions are housed in buildings which are in danger of falling down and are a discredit to the city."[1]

In 1889 the Legislature of Pennsylvania appointed a special committee, which investigated very fully the management of the charitable and correctional institutions of the State, and especially the methods employed by such institutions in securing public appropriations. The constitution of Pennsylvania forbids the granting of public funds to "sectarian" institutions; but the word "sectarian" is not defined, and the report of the committee shows a strong tendency to increase the number and amount of the State subsidies granted to private charities. This tendency is characterized as an "insidious danger." The committee tabulated the

---

[1] State Charities Record, April, 1891.

expenditures during a series of years for charitable and correctional purposes, amounting to about $37,000,000, and found that nearly a third of it went to private institutions. The report says:

"The remarkable increase during the last few years in the number of institutions receiving aid from the State is confined in great part to the so-called private charities, or private hospitals, homes for the destitute, and to miscellaneous charities. A proportionate increase will soon render the commonwealth a contributor to the funds of every charitable institution in the State."

The fact mentioned above, that there is no generally recognized definition of the word "sectarian" is noteworthy. There are few institutions that will admit its applicability to themselves, and there are few to which it is not applied by some one. The author has been gravely assured that an institution entirely administered by the oath-bound members of a religious order was not sectarian for two reasons: first, because it admitted beneficiaries without regard to religious faith, and second, because there was a Presbyterian minister on its board of trustees — a purely ornamental body. On the other hand, an institution having among its managers representatives of all the religious denominations except one, is apt to be regarded as "sectarian" by that one. Many institutions having no trace of sectarianism in charter, constitution, or by-laws, are yet administered in the interests of a sect. A willingness to admit beneficiaries of all denominations is frequently less an evidence of non-sectarianism than of a tendency to make proselytes. Much might be said in favor of the idea that all private institutions are sectarian, when not in a religious, then in a medical or social sense. Public aid to a hospital may help to build up a medical school or a school of medicine just as surely as aid to an infant asylum may be used to build up a church. Social rivalries may stimulate people in pushing charities just as much as inter-denominational competition.

In States where a constitutional limitation forbids the voting of public money to " sectarian " institutions, members of the Protestant denominations seek to have this clause so interpreted as to exclude the institutions officered by the Roman Catholic orders, while charitable enterprises in which they are themselves interested are nominally unsectarian. The Catholics try to evade the constitutional limitation by disingenuous and unfair subterfuges, usually successful; and the Protestants, with characteristic short-sightedness, encourage such a course by their own eagerness to secure public money for the private institutions in which they are themselves interested. There is a logical and manifest distinction between public and private institutions. With the former the government owns the property, and can modify or abolish the institution at will. In the case of the latter the property is owned by a private corporation, usually self-perpetuating, its charter is a contract with the State that granted it, and the fact that it is a "private" institution protects it in a great measure from criticism. In Pennsylvania it is found that such institutions tend more and more to be managed by a few persons who really choose their successors, and the State which grants them millions has not even the membership vote of a private individual who pays one, two, or three dollars annually as dues. Just before the advent of a superintendent of charities in the District of Columbia, a Congressional committeeman thus described the attitude of subsidized institutions towards the government :

"There is a universal feeling that, while Congress must furnish the money, each society must have absolute control of the expenditures; and none of them are willing to submit to any visitation or control of such expenditures, or even any auditing of the accounts. The beginning and end of their connection with Congress, in their eyes, seems to be, 'Give each one of us so much money, and let us do what we please with it'"

This fact, that there is a clear-cut distinction between public and private charities, but none between sectarian and non-sectarian charities, is one that those who shudder at every symptom of public aid to sectarian schools would do well to recognize. Protestants are willing to tease legislators for public money on behalf of a hospital or an orphan asylum in which they are interested, urging that it is "doing good," and that it is preventing crime and pauperism, and so saving money to the tax-payers. They do not see, or will not acknowledge, that the same could be said of a parochial school, and that the claim which they set up that their own institution is "non-sectarian" is equivocal and unfair, and one which in practice the courts have never been able to make definite.

A tendency could hardly have gone as far as has that to grant public subsidies to private charities, without there were in favor of it many considerations of great force, either apparent or real. As favoring this policy, the consideration which is first and foremost in the minds of "practical" people is the matter of economy. Especially where the number of dependants in a given class is small, it is cheaper to hire them cared for than to establish an institution for them. This is the reason that in most small towns a private hospital is subsidized instead of one being erected at public expense; but, when we find a great city like Brooklyn depending entirely on subsidized hospitals for the care of its sick poor, this argument is inapplicable. Economy, however, may result from other causes, as when the private institutions are administered by religious orders, the members of which receive no pay except their support. In almost every branch of philanthropic work Roman Catholic institutions can underbid competitors, so to speak, because of the great organizations of teachers and nurses and administrators whose gratuitous services they can command; and if the State is to sublet its relief on the contract system, it is hard to see why those who can bid low should not get the contracts. In reformatory institutions, those under private management have an advantage over those managed by public officials in that the former are able to keep the inmates busy at remunerative employment with less opposition from outside trade organizations. A public reformatory for girls that should keep its inmates busy with work from a great shirt factory, would be sure to be attacked on the ground of its competing with poor sewing women; but such employment in private institutions, even those receiving public subsidies, is quite common. Even in institutions not officered by members of a religious order, the salaries are apt to be lower and all the items of expense to be more closely scrutinized than in a public institution. Add to all this the further fact that frequently private contributors aid in the support of a private institution, and we see how great may be its advantage on the side of economy. To the real economies of this method of operation should be added the apparent economies when a private institution is willing to make a very low bid, to make great temporary sacrifices, in order to get the subsidy system introduced — in order to establish connections between itself and the public treasury. "At first," said a United States senator, speaking of the charities of the District of Columbia, "at first they thrust in only the nose of the camel."

Secondly, it is urged that private institutions, especially those for dependent and delinquent children, have a better effect upon the inmates than can public institutions.[1] For one thing, dogmatic religious instruction can be given. For another, the spirit of self-sacrifice that pervades a private institution has a good effect upon the inmates, and is contrasted with the cold and officialed administration of the public institutions. Connected with this, as also with the matter of economy, is the fact that boards of trustees and of lady managers and visitors give freely of their time and energy and sympathy in aid of private undertakings.

Thirdly, it is urged that, by subsidizing private institutions, we free them from the blight of partisan politics and the spoils system. The miserable political jobbery connected with so many almshouses and insane asylums and other public charitable institutions is pointed out, and we are asked to shield as many as possible of the State's dependants from similar evils. In the matter of educating the blind and the deaf and the dumb, the private institutions managed by close corporations or by

[1] This is the principal point in Judge Richard Prendergast's plea for public subsidies to private charities, N. C. C., 1886, pp. 161-167.

corporations of contributing members are thought to have been more successful than public institutions for similar purposes. The specialists needed to conduct them properly prefer to work for a private corporation, as their tenure is more secure, and it is easier to map out and pursue a policy of steady development and improvement. At the same time it should be said that one of the institutions which the committee of the Pennsylvania legislature found most secretive and least well conducted was a private school for the blind sustained by public subsidies.

A fourth consideration is, that by means of subsidies we aid the poor without attaching to them the stigma of pauperism. A home for the aged is more respectable than an almshouse, and a private protectory or industrial school is supposed not to discredit the inmates as much as a public reform school.

But this last mentioned consideration brings us to a turning-point for it is urged against such subsidies as well as in favor of them. It is urged that private institutions receiving public money promote pauperism by disguising it. Children who would support aged parents rather than allow them to go to the almshouse, desert them promptly when some provision is made for them that is ostensibly more honorable. An illustration is afforded by the case of an abandoned woman who supported her mother for years rather than permit her to go to the poorhouse, but who was trying all the while to get her admitted to a "private" home for the aged. Parents unload their children upon the community more recklessly when they know that such children will be provided for in private orphan asylums or protectories, where the religious training that the parents prefer will be given them. And thus we reach the first great objection to granting public subsidies to private charities. While it may be cheaper to provide thus for each dependant during a year, yet the number of dependants increases so rapidly that eventually the charge upon the public is greater than if the alternative policy were pursued. The results are most astounding, where, as in the case of dependent children in New York, the managers of each institution are free to admit children and have them charged to the community. In New York City any one of many private institutions can receive any child, either temporarily or permanently, and collect a stated amount per week from the local authorities. For a large institution, there is a profit in taking care of children at the rates fixed. The larger the institution the greater the per capita profit. "A study of the reports made by these institutions to the State Board of Charities shows that at least nine of the twenty-three institutions received more money from the public funds during the year ending Oct. 1, 1892, than was expended by them during the same period for the maintenance of all the children in the institutions (including some for whom the city does not make per capita payments, but whom, as is thus shown, it does nevertheless actually support); the excess of appropriations from the public treasury over the cost of maintenance of the children varied in different institutions from $63 in one institution to $24,300 in another; the total excess of appropriations from the public funds over the cost of maintenance being in these nine institutions $65,498."[1] As the children are

[1] New York Conference on Child Caring, 1893, p. 164.

to be educated in the same religious faith as the parents, and as the parents can claim their child again at will, self-interest imposes on neither the parents nor the institution any hindrance to the unloading of children upon the public. Under this system New York City has one dependent child in each hundred of the population, and the State one dependent child in each 260 of the population. Seth Low gives an example of two children in Brooklyn who had property in their own right, and whose mother also kept a shop in Jersey City. Mr. Riis tells of a public official drawing a salary from the city, which not only enabled him to support his family, but to gratify rather expensive private tastes, whose boy was being cared for at public expense.[1] Only about twenty per cent of these children in New York are orphans; and a very large number of them, as soon as they become old enough to be of use are "returned to relatives or friends." "That is," comments Mrs. Lowell, "to the persons who had given them up to be paupers."[2] The superintendent of the Juvenile Asylum, which contains an average of a thousand children, said that three-fourths of them could not be sent to free homes in the West, because their relatives would not consent to their going.[3] "Child Storage at Public Expense" has been suggested as an appropriate sign to be placed over the entrances to the great New York caravansaries for dependent children.

Where public officials alone have the right to commit

[1] "Children of the Poor," pp. 280–281.

[2] Twenty-third Annual Report New York State Board of Charities, 1889, p. 201.

[3] Anna T. Wilson, "Some Arguments for the Boarding-out of Dependent Children in the State of New York." Quoted by Riis.

children or others to the subsidized institutions a check is put upon reckless admissions. But even under this system, there is danger that many will be charged to the public who would never have sought admission to a public institution. In Illinois the constitution forbids public grants to sectarian institutions; but a law was framed providing that a county court might adjudge a girl to be a dependant, commit her to an industrial school, and that school should then be entitled to receive ten dollars a month for her "tuition, care, and maintenance," besides an allowance for clothing. After the passage of this act the Chicago Industrial School for Girls was incorporated. Of the nine incorporators and directors, seven were officers and managers of the House of the Good Shepherd; and all the girls committed under the act to the Chicago Industrial School for Girls were placed either in the House of the Good Shepherd or in St. Joseph's Orphan Asylum, both Catholic institutions. Questions as to the legality of such arrangement brought the matter into court; and during the trial it transpired that about seventy-three girls who were committed to the Chicago Industrial School for Girls by the county court were already in the House of the Good Shepherd and the St. Joseph Orphan Asylum at the time of such commitments. "In other words, being already inmates of the institutions, they were taken to the county court and adjudged to be dependent girls, and at once returned to those institutions, and thereafter the county was charged with $10 per month for tuition for each of them, and $15 or $20 or $25 for clothing for each of them." The courts at first decided that the Chicago Industrial School was a "sectarian" institution, and the payment of the money therefore illegal; but the institution has since found a way to evade the constitutional limitation. This is a very good example of the unsubstantial nature of the barrier which such a constitutional limitation forms.

In Maryland the juvenile reformatories of rival faiths are so anxious to secure inmates that the courts are criticised by each side for committing an unduly large number of children to the other institutions. A lobbyist opposing a bill before the New York legislature, urged that it should not pass because it would reduce the number of inmates in an institution in which he was interested, and which was just building large extensions. The anxiety of a doctor to fill up any hospital in which he is interested is well known, and it has been openly charged in a leading medical journal that the managers of dispensaries and hospitals are the beneficiaries of the well-intended philanthropy which supports them rather than the poor for whom they are intended. The average dispensary makes no attempt to determine the ability of an applicant to pay, and the most reckless competition for patients exists between them. When the new superintendent of charities for the District of Columbia called at dispensaries where he was unknown, offers were twice made to prescribe for him out of hand, although he made no attempt to appear especially unwell or impecunious. The success of the subsidy system as regards institutions for the education of the blind and the deaf and the dumb seems to come from the fact that in this particular work the number of possible beneficiaries is strictly and obviously limited.

In the second place, the argument from economy in

support of the subsidy system is negatived by the fact that under this system there must be so many duplicate institutions. In Maryland, for instance, there are two reformatories for boys within a mile of each other, and two for girls, both in Baltimore. Catholics manage one pair of institutions, and private Protestant corporations the other. Besides this inevitable line of cleavage between Protestants and Catholics, there are various causes of institutional fission resulting from medical or social sectarianism. Many charitable institutions have been established less from brotherly love than from a quarrel in the board of managers in an older institution. This, together with the influence of individual ambitions, has led especially to the establishment of a great number of medical charities. When the public begins to grant such favors, it is hard to draw a line. As a United States senator once said in speaking of the situation in the District, —

"The very fact that Congress makes these appropriations has caused, to a great degree, the multiplication of the organizations. A few people getting together who are desirous of doing charitable work, or who have discovered some special need, or who are dissatisfied with some feature of some existing institution, instead of adding to or modifying such an institution, will start a new one, because they can appeal directly to Congress for the money necessary to begin it, and can base their claim on the ground that they are just as good as some other association already on the list."

A third reason for objecting to the subsidies we are considering is, that when voting upon them the legislator must resist special pressure. He has not a clear-cut question of a given service to be rendered balanced by a given expenditure, but it becomes partly a question of offending or favoring some sect or nationality. The contention that the subsidy system takes the charitable institutions out of politics seems to be unsound. On the contrary, it drags them into politics in a new and unfortunate way, — in a way that is found in practice to give great scope to log-rolling and kindred expedients. Many who will not do anything else for a charitable institution are willing to bully a legislator on its behalf, though this is probably not common. Most of the lobbyists are sincere even to fanaticism, but their view of the situation is terribly one-sided. It had come to pass that when the District of Columbia appropriation bill was under consideration, and in the haste of the last days of the session, the Congressional committee rooms would be full of the representatives of the various charities, both men and women, intent upon getting the largest share possible. There was neither time, nor ability, nor opportunity on the part of the committee to come to any intelligent conclusion. Often those applicants most skilled or most personally attractive were most successful, and sometimes the committees were obliged to average their gifts. After such a policy has been entered upon, it cannot be altered without injury to great vested interests, and without giving offence to large and powerful constituencies.

A fourth objection to the subsidy system of supporting charities is that it tends to dry up the sources of private benevolence. Individual contributors dislike to have their mites lost in the abundance of a public appropriation. Almost without exception those institutions that have received public aid the longest and the most constantly receive least from private contributors.

In looking up the history of a considerable number of institutions, it was found that, after the public became a contributor, private contributions fell off from year to year, not only relatively, but absolutely, and in some cases ceased altogether.

Mrs. Lowell states that, of the 18,900 children supported by charity in New York City, 2,700, or one-seventh, are supported in private institutions at private expense (14 per cent of the total expenditure), and that 1,200 are supported at public expense in public institutions. Of the total expenses for all purposes of the twenty-three institutions caring for the remaining 15,000, 8.8 per cent is contributed by private benevolence. From this it appears that 21 per cent of the expense of caring for dependent children is borne by private benevolence, while 79 per cent is borne by the city. In Philadelphia, under a different system, the proportion borne by private benevolence is 97 per cent.[1] In New York one institution, that received in 1892 $250,000 from the city, received from private sources less than $500; and in the case of twelve institutions the receipts from private sources were less than 5 per cent of the total expenditure.[2]

Commissioner Bolles of Pennsylvania says: —

"The State by appropriating so generally is drying up the interest of individuals in organized charities. Our people have acquired great wealth, and their sympathies should be cultivated in every possible manner. The State can never do, through its long perfunctory arm, acts of mercy with the same degree of kindly interest as individuals, who live nearer the scene of relief, and who have a more distinct interest in the sufferers."

[1] See Conference on Care of Dependent and Delinquent Children, New York, 1893, pp. 164, 165.
[2] Ib., p. 165.

This brings us to a fifth reason for objecting to the granting of public subsidies to private charities. It frequently does positive harm to a charitable institution, and sometimes wholly destroys its usefulness. An institution that receives no public money is freer in all its operations, and is more highly valued by those who sustain and manage it. The beneficiaries also feel differently toward their benefactors. When visiting one subsidized institution the request was made that nothing should be said before the inmates that would inform them that the institution received any public money. One could understand the wish, and presume that the inmates would work more faithfully, be more grateful for favors received, and finally "turn out better," because they were kept in ignorance of the fact. Yet we may doubt the possibility or propriety of thus using public money, and at the same time trying to conceal the fact of doing so. By no hocus-pocus of subsidy-granting can we make taxation do the work of self-sacrifice.

It should be remarked that the several States and municipalities have entered upon this policy of subsidizing private charities without deciding to do so, and even without perceiving that a decision was called for. Each request for a subsidy has been treated as a matter of administrative detail, involving no principle, and not significant as a precedent. The resultant system, as it is applied to the care of dependent children in New York City, is about as business-like as though the city should try to get its streets paved by announcing that any regularly incorporated association that should pave a given number of square yards of street — location, time, and method to be decided by itself — should receive a given amount from the public treasury. The Washington system is theoretically looser, but practically not so bad. It is as though private associations were allowed to do paving at their own discretion, and then, on coming to Congress and teasing with sufficient skill and pertinacity, they should be given subsidies on the general theory that they were "doing good" and rendering " public service."

This is subsidy granting at its worst. At its best, the government must attend to three things: First, on behalf of the poor as well as the tax-payers, it must provide for the thorough inspection of subsidized institutions, and the systematic auditing of their accounts. This work cannot be done by grand juries, or legislative committees, or *ex-officio* inspectors, who may from time to time thrust their inexperienced noses into matters which they know nothing about. The work of inspection must be done by some thoroughly experienced and otherwise suitable administrative officer, who is definitely responsible for the thoroughness of his work. Second, the State must keep in the hands of its own officials the right of deciding what persons shall be admitted to the benefits for which it pays, and how long each person may continue to receive those benefits. If it pays for beds in a hospital, one of its own officials should have entire control of admitting and discharging the patients cared for. This is necessary in order that "there may be some gauge of indigency, and some assurance that the gauge will be used." Third, subsidies should only be granted on the principle of specific payment for specific work. When any one of these three conditions is lacking, the policy of subsidy granting is necessarily pernicious.

But even at its best, and with these safeguards, the policy of granting public subsidies to private charities is one of doubtful expediency. There is ground for thinking that, if the State is too big and awkward to do a given work, it is also too big and awkward to decide properly whom it shall subsidize in order to get the work done. All that can be said against subsidies in general can be said against this form of subsidies, and more; because here we have to deal with religious, medical, and social sectarianism, and because we are giving over the defenceless to the care of the irresponsible. As a transition policy for growing communities, or for new and developing varieties of benevolent work, it may possibly have its place; but it should never be entered on inadvertently, for while all its advantages and economies are greatest at the beginning, the disadvantages and dangers of it increase as time goes on. Those who would entirely avoid establishing any precedent whatever for the voting of public money to private schools can take properly but one course. That course is consistent opposition to any and all public subsidies to private charities.

PART IV.

THE SUPERVISION, ORGANIZATION, AND BETTERMENT OF CHARITIES.

PART IV

THE CLASSIFICATION, ORGANIZATION, AND DEPLOYMENT OF QUALITIES

PART IV.

THE SUPERVISION, ORGANIZATION, AND BETTERMENT OF CHARITIES.

CHAPTER XVIII.

SUPERVISORY AGENCIES

One who has read the chapters of Part III. may have thought that they were largely occupied with telling how things should not be done, — with locating pitfalls rather than with mapping safe highways. It is not intended, however, to give any dark view of the possibilities of successful work for the relief of the poor by public, private, or endowed charities. If the map of the field shows difficulties, it is only because the difficulties are there, and an accurate map must show them. It is not a pleasant task to indicate where the pitfall is, but it is much better than to allow the traveller to find it through accident. It is next in order, however, to indicate the methods by which improvements are and may be introduced, and by which it may be brought about that benevolence shall be more constantly beneficent.

The charities of a given locality which should for useful result be systematically directed to the accomplishment of their common purposes, are usually a chaos, a patchwork of survivals, or products of contending political, religious, and medical factions, a curious compound, in which a strong ingredient is ignorance perpetuated by heedlessness. Individually they have originated as needs arose, or were supposed to have arisen, in a given locality, and in small communities, where ignorance of what was already being done could not exist; this has given them a sufficient degree of co-ordination. Public charities themselves are frequently organized on no system; they develop without any thought of how they should develop. Like Topsy, they simply "grow." Public out-door relief is frequently the incidental work of county supervisors to whom the position of supervisor comes as an incident in the performance of more important political or business functions. The almshouse is an institution to be favored or economized upon, according as its superintendent has or has not a political "pull." The insane are in almshouses or jails, according as provision has or has not been made for them by the State, and are taken care of as the personal characteristics of the different sheriffs or superintendents of the almshouse may determine. Dependent children are neglected by public officials or striven for by denominational organizations, and the other classes that need relief are treated or not, according as the contending influence of self-sacrifice in many forms, and selfishness in many forms, work out their good or bad results. State charities are often but little better. Busy legislators pass laws regarding charities heedlessly, or heedlessly refuse to pass them. Systems of care for the insane or for other defective classes are entered upon and partially inaugurated, and then with or without reason, abandoned. In all institutions, furthermore, there is a possibility of mismanagement through individual bad character or lack of sense. Beyond this, each manager of an individual institution is so interested in securing additions that are needed, or a new water supply, or something else that costs money, that he very possibly neglects to examine the conditions upon which dependants are admitted, or to take any wide view of the purpose of his institution and the extent to which it is fulfilling that purpose.

Yet it is manifest that not only must palpable evils be checked, but that there must be some way of organizing and co-ordinating the efforts of all the charities of a given State, if they are to work out any valuable results. There must be some power outside of them which is interested not only in the details of their administration, but in their general plan and purpose. A man cannot supervise himself with satisfactory results to the public, and an institution frequently does not understand its proper relation to others at work in the same field.

Soon after the conclusion of the Civil War, there was a movement in some of the older and wealthier States to establish public supervisory agencies known as State Boards of Charities. This was part of the general tendency to amplify and improve the administrative machinery of our State governments. The creation of boards or commissions for the care of the public health, the collection of statistics regarding labor, and similar purposes, were inaugurated at this time.[1] The first board for the supervision of charities was established in Massachusetts in 1863, and Ohio and New York followed

[1] See W. F. Willoughby, " State Activities and Politics," Papers American Historical Association, vol. v., 1891.

with similar boards in 1867. Illinois, Pennsylvania, and Rhode Island established boards in 1869. We now have nineteen States with organizations of this character.[1] Most of the boards established in later years, for instance, since 1880, have been in the new States of the West; and the movement for their establishment seems to have come to a standstill in States that were in full operation at the close of the war. Indiana, however, established a board in 1889.

In the main, these State Boards of Charities are of two general types, one having the powers of supervision and report only, and the other having powers of control over the charitable institutions of the State. Typical boards with the latter method of organization are now found in Rhode Island, Kansas, and Wisconsin. Boards with executive powers are usually made up of salaried members, limited in number, — usually not more than six, — who are the trustees of the public charitable institutions which they inspect, and of which they appoint superintendents and other officers. Boards without executive power are usually composed of honor officers. The number is sometimes considerable, as in the case of New York, where one member is appointed from each judicial district in the State. These unsalaried boards, with powers of supervision and report only, are necessarily made up of persons willing to give to the work a considerable amount of time for no other return than the possible payment of their expenses. Each board, as a rule, appoints a salaried secretary who is a permanent officer, or should be permanent, and who attends to the

---

[1] See the list of members of the State Boards, N. C. C., 1893, pp. 467–469.

routine work of the office. These secretaries of State Boards of Charities have been the moving force in organizing the National Conferences of Charities, and many of them are as eminent specialists as this country has produced. It has usually been found easier to keep politics out of these unsalaried boards. The supervisory board in the case of Wisconsin has been abolished to make way for politically appointed receivers of salaries. In Illinois an eminent specialist has been removed from the position of secretary for political reasons only. As a rule, however, there is "not enough in it" to induce politicians to make much of a fight to secure control of one of these advisory boards. They consequently have a greater degree of stability, and from this fact they have a much greater influence. Where officials are changing very frequently, as is the case with our State legislators, and for the most part with our State executive officers, a group of men whose position is relatively permanent, and who from year to year accumulate experience, and clarify their ideas as to what is necessary, can carry out plans of reform that would be impossible to a rapidly rotating board, even assuming that its members were of equal ability and devotion.

This does not imply that certain executive duties, such as the removal of foreign paupers from the State, as in New York and Massachusetts, and the care of certain classes of dependants, as in the case of dependent children in Massachusetts, and the removal of the insane from hospital to hospital within the State, as in Illinois and elsewhere, may not be ingrafted upon advisory boards without changing their general character. In some States, where it seems best to centralize the executive control of certain large classes of institutions, as of those for the insane, additional commissions have been created to discharge these executive functions. This is the case in New York. But over all such executive boards, there should still obtain the power of the Board of Charities to investigate and report upon everything in the line of charities within the State. A board with powers of supervision and report only is much freer in giving its opinion as to needed changes than one having executive powers. For instance, in the matter of applying to the legislature for appropriations, an executive board must subordinate everything to securing enough money to carry the institution through the fiscal period in prospect. They will usually have occasion also to make applications for extensions, and increased appropriations for other purposes. They cannot risk these important matters by recommending reforms which might antagonize certain interests, and raise up for them opponents in the legislature or about it. A board with powers of supervision and report only, is not limited in any of these matters. If it sees a reform or co-ordination possible in the charities of the State, it can recommend an improvement, even at the risk of offending influential persons, and stand out for specific reforms without endangering current appropriations. Furthermore, an unsalaried board is more likely to stand well with successive legislatures than is a set of men who get their living out of the business; and their recommendations for increased appropriations in which they have no personal interest will have more weight with many legislators than the persistent application of those whose support comes from the appropriations that they ask for. A board with powers of supervision and report only is consequently a benefit to institutions as well as a check upon them; for it can further their growth, and stand as a guaranty of honest administration, which helps them in the opinion of the community. There are two reasons why all charitable institutions, especially public institutions, should be carefully supervised and reported upon. One is that abuses may exist in such institutions, and another is that they may not. In the first place, it is for the protection of the beneficiaries and the public that supervision is desirable; and in the second place, it is for the protection of the institutions and the managers from unfounded suspicions that supervision is useful. It enables the institutions to be above suspicion, which is out of the question unless there is some disinterested supervisory power over them.

One valuable service which has been rendered by the State Boards of Charities has been to raise the standard of service of the county and township charities. The managers of these, especially in the rural counties, are usually persons of honest intention, but with small information concerning the duties put upon them. It is therefore possible through visiting, correspondence, and suggestion to place at their disposal the hard-earned experience of other communities, and to make it possible for them, without additional expense, to do an increasingly satisfactory work. In the matter of approving plans for county jails and almshouses, which is frequently given into the hands of the State board, the very fact that the plans must be submitted to the State board will frequently lead to greater care in drawing them than would otherwise be used. Many of the State boards have published for the guidance of county officials designs of the best and most economical forms of construction to be used in caring for the various classes of dependants. Sometimes a county, as Marion County in Indiana, sends a committee of its county officials travelling over the country at public expense to see the best jails and to get ideas on the construction of such edifices before building. But besides the expense involved in this, the wandering investigators may miss the most essential points in what they should see and learn, while the State Board of Charities, having representatives from year to year in the National Conference of Charities, having available in its libraries the reports of other boards, and the reports of the various conferences, having also the experience of all the counties of the State for its own information, and a knowledge of what is done in distant cities, can frequently, by pointing to certain publications, or offering certain plans, give county officials assistance in the construction and administration of charities which it would otherwise cost them large sums to seek out.

In one important particular the powers of supervision and report with which American State Boards of Charities are endowed are as a rule defective. That is, they are not given sufficient power to supervise the administration of purely private charities, and to regulate the administration of endowments. The New York Board has powers of visitation over private charitable corporations, with power to inspect and examine officials under oath, to collect statistics, and to report to the legislature. By the Act of 1883 the certified consent of the board is required as a condition precedent to the incorporation of any further orphan asylums or institutions for the care of children.[1] A few other States give their respective boards supervision of particular species of private institutions. The Massachusetts body has the care and maintenance of indigent and neglected children boarded in private families, as well as the supervision of delinquent children in the State schools, the care of insane patients in private families, and the supervision of insane patients in private asylums, as well as public hospitals. The Connecticut Board visits incorporated hospitals; the Illinois Board can inspect and report upon private insane asylums, and upon the State Industrial School for Boys and Girls which has been authorized by the government to receive inmates committed by the courts; but it has no further jurisdiction over charitable corporations, though by the courtesy of their managers it occasionally makes returns respecting them in its annual reports. In Colorado and Montana charitable institutions of a private nature receiving public aid are within the jurisdiction of the board.[2] The power of the New York Board to " visit " purely private institutions has recently been used in preparing a Directory of the Charities of the State of New York, which is of the very greatest value in giving an idea of the charities of the State as they actually exist. The mere collection and publication of these facts gives a view of the situation not otherwise obtainable. It is to the State Boards of Charities that the power should be given, in all States having such boards, to restrict, supervise, and revise endowments for charitable purposes.

[1] N. C. C., 1893, p. 41.   [2] Ib., 1893, pp. 41–42.

Testators should be made to feel that there is an authority that can insure the public against injuries from foolish or obsolete endowments, directing the money left for charities to wise purposes according to time and place.

Radiating from the State Boards of Charities are certain delegated visitorial powers bestowed upon appointees in the various counties and localities of the State. A local representative of a State board is expected to visit county institutions, and call to the attention of the board anything that seems to be amiss. In Ohio the Board of County Visitors is appointed by the Court of Common Pleas. This county board consists of six persons, three men and three women, and not more than three of each party; and they are required to visit all places of charity and correction in the county where they live. They have power to visit such institutions at least four times during the year; in fact, they make many more visits. They report to the Court of Common Pleas once a year, and they send a report also to the State Board of Charities. They have special powers regarding any child likely to be sent to reformatories through the courts. These Boards of County Visitors, and other officials interested in the administration of relief, have held two annual conferences, which have done much to clarify the problems attending the work of their members. The members of the boards are appointed for two years, and two members go out each year. Judges are said to take a great interest in these matters.[1] In States where there is an active State

---

[1] Gen. Brinkerhoff's remarks, published in "Organization of Charities" (International Congress of Charities, Chicago, 1893), pp. 32–33.

board, but where the law does not provide for unsalaried visitors in this formal way, a considerable number of persons are in fact interested in local charities; and their visiting is made effective in the introduction of reforms through their correspondence and intercourse with the State board. Conferences of the superintendents of the poor are also frequently held under the auspices of the State board, as in Michigan, Wisconsin, and Indiana. The value of official boards has been greatly enhanced by the large number of people they have been able to interest in the administration of the public charities.

In two States, New York and New Jersey, there have grown up associations for the voluntary unofficial supervision of public charitable institutions in co-operation with the official boards. The State Charities Aid Association of New York was organized in 1872, with the object of bringing about reforms in the poorhouses, the almshouses, and the State charitable institutions of New York, through the active interest of an organized body of voluntary visitors, acting in co-operation with and as an aid to the local administration of these institutions and the official State boards of supervision. Upon the nomination of the State Charities Aid Association, through its board of managers, district supreme courts are authorized to grant to the visitors of the association orders enabling them to visit, inspect, and examine on behalf of the association any of the public charitable institutions owned by the State, county, township or city, the poorhouses and almshouses within the State of New York, such visitors to be responsible to the counties from which these institutions receive their inmates. The association reports annually to the State Board of Charities and the State Commission in Lunacy upon matters relative to the institutions subject respectively to the inspection and control of these two official bodies.[1] A similar organization was created in New Jersey in 1881, and worked in a single county until 1886. In that year its activities were extended to the whole State, and ten counties of the State are now included in its organization.[2]

The New York Association has a central board of managers, largely of New York City, and county visiting committees in all parts of the State where people of the respective localities can be got to take an interest in the work of the association. The paid secretary of the association visits these corresponding boards once a year, and if possible goes with the members to inspect the different county institutions. The association is supported entirely through voluntary contributions. The expenditures are not heavy, only about $10,000 per year. There is a salaried secretary and assistant secretary. The association declares that it will not receive any money from public sources, as it wishes to be independent of all outside influence. A considerable proportion of its expenditures are for publications. It prints quite an elaborate report each year, and various pamphlets appear from time to time bearing upon pressing problems in the administration of the relief-work of the State.

Such an agency as this would manifestly be a nuisance

[1] See article by Miss L. Schuyler, read at the International Congress of Charities, 1893, published in "Charity Organization" volume of the proceedings, p. 57. An appendix gives the text of the organic act of the association.

[2] See article by Mrs. Williamson, International Congress of Charities, 1893, "Charity Organization" volume, pp. 72-76.

unless wisely managed, and would result in legalized meddling. But actually the association has secured very large results through its voluntary inspection of public institutions. In her paper at Chicago, Miss Schuyler enumerated the following reforms as being traceable very largely to the influence of the association: —

1. A higher standard of care has been introduced into every almshouse in the State. This includes many minor points.

2. A training-school for nurses was established in 1873 at Bellevue Hospital. The results of this movement have been already commented upon in the chapter on medical charities.

3. In 1874 the Hospital Book and Newspaper Society was established to provide reading-matter for the inmates of hospitals.

4. In 1875 the farming out of the poor was abolished.

5. In some counties of the State the establishment of temporary homes for children was secured through the activity of the local visiting committees.

6. The Tramp Act was passed in 1880, which abolished a condition of things which had made it to the pecuniary interest of the overseers of the poor to encourage vagrancy.

7. In 1882 a society for instruction in "First Aid to the Injured" was established through the influence of the hospital committee of the association.

8. The training of nurses for the insane has been introduced.

9. A permissive act authorizing municipal lodging-houses in New York City was passed in 1886. The association is now trying to secure a mandatory instead of a permissive act.

10. Largely with the help of the association the State Care for the Insane Act of 1890 and the State Care Appropriation Act of 1891 were passed, assuring the removal of the insane from the unsuitable county almshouse.

This record of "things done" shows the possibilities of this type of voluntary organization under wise management. It has been frequently suggested that some organization similar to this might be established in States having no board of charities, as a means of educating people up to the point where a State board could be safely created. No such experiment as this is known to have been made; and it would only be feasible in case there were a group of persons with considerable wealth, considerable leisure, and a vast amount of intelligence and tact, who were willing to give their time to it.

The class of public institutions that need the most supervision, and ordinarily get the least of it, are those of our large cities. Ordinarily, if there is a city department, it is an executive department, subject to the influences of politics, and not gifted with the power of supervising itself satisfactorily. In Boston, in 1892, Mayor Matthews appointed a committee of private citizens to visit and report upon charitable institutions of that city for his information and that of the public. A most valuable report was prepared, from which quotations have already been made in the course of this volume. Among other things the committee recommended that an ordinance be passed providing for the appointment by the mayor of a permanent committee of visitors, men and women, for terms varying from three to five years. The committee further recommended that these visitors should have full power to inspect institutions, but no executive powers and no salaries. This, it will be seen, is a provision for a municipal board of charities with power of supervision and report only. A second committee was appointed by Mayor Matthews the succeeding year, in accordance with an ordinance passed as recommended.[1]

[1] Commissioner Douglas of the District of Columbia appointed an extra-legal board of visitors for the Washington Asylum, the Almshouse, and the House of Correction; but the author does not know that the practice has been continued there. It is one of the best methods of improving the charities of our large cities to have such a board of visitors established.

CHAPTER XIX.

THE ORGANIZATION OF CHARITIES.

In its widest sense the organization of charities includes work already described. It is the purpose of a State Board of Charities to organize and co-ordinate the public institutions. It is the purpose of a body like the State Charities Aid Association to see that public charities work together for good. But in its technical meaning the term "charity organization" has come to be applied to the organization of all charities of a locality, either public or private, especially the charities of our large cities. It is this particular work that has been described at the National Conferences of Charities since 1880 under the heading of "charity organization."

If the charities of a State are chaotic, the charities of a large city are still more so. When we take up a directory of charities prepared by one of the American societies, and find a table of contents classifying the various agencies in the city, the first impression that we may get is that there is something systematic about the actual charitable system of the locality. Take, for instance, the classification of charities arranged according to the Table of Contents of the Baltimore Directory which is as follows:

  A. Relief of the Sick.
    1. Hospitals.
      a. General.
      b. Special.

TABLE XXXII.
SUMMARY OF INCOME AND PERSONAL SERVICE ACCOUNTS OF FIFTY-FIVE CHARITY ORGANIZATION SOCIETIES.

CITY OR TOWN.	ADMINISTRATIVE OFFICERS.				PAID OFFICERS OR AGENTS.				FRIENDLY VISITORS.				INCOME.		INVESTED FUNDS.
	MEN.		WOMEN.		MEN.		WOMEN.		MEN.		WOMEN.		1882.	1892.	1892.
	1882.	1892.	1882.	1892.	1882.	1892.	1882.	1892.	1882.	1892.	1882.	1892.			
Albany	4	4	...	...	1	1	...	...	...	5	...	21	$600.00	$1,022.00	
Auburn, Me.	...	...	...	...	...	1	...	...	...	...	...	34	...	150.00	$180.00
Baltimore, Md.	11	41	...	8	1	1	2	11	...	41	...	195	1,345.00	6,533.00	1,000.00
Bangor, Me.	...	...	...	5	...	...	...	...	...	...	14	18	...	101.41	
Boston, Mass.	87	94	117	185	3	...	11	22	...	84	*642	683	11,282.63	17,444.28	{ 25,650.00 11,000.00 in Building.
Bridgeport, Conn.	...	...	...	8	...	...	...	...	...	40	...	...	...	...	
Brooklyn, N. Y.	...	...	...	...	1	5	1	6	...	113	...	*532	2,026.93	20,035.00	
Bryn Mawr, Pa.	...	...	...	...	...	3	...	...	...	...	...	17	...	(91),580.00	
Buffalo, N. Y.	43	51	...	28	2	5	...	2	...	...	...	12	3,443.00	6,734.57	308,872.99
Burlington, Ia.	...	2	...	2	...	...	...	1	...	...	...	*70	...	167.00	
Castleton, S. I., N. Y.	...	...	...	12	...	...	...	1	...	...	...	48	...	408.99	
Charleston, S. C.	...	...	...	...	...	...	...	1	...	...	...	12	...	875.00	5,000.00
Cincinnati, O.	21	13	24	15	5	8	4	3	30	70	35	145	11,968.23	8,154.71	
Cleveland, O.	...	29	...	8	...	2	...	2	...	...	...	*75	...	9,000.00	
Davenport, Ia.	...	19	...	9	...	...	...	1	...	...	...	...	...	600.00	
Denver, Col.	...	*13	...	...	...	1	...	3	...	30	...	30	...	23,000.00	
Detroit, Mich.	...	3	...	...	...	2	...	...	...	50	...	75	...	2,300.00	
Hartford, Conn.	...	40	...	4	...	1	...	...	...	...	...	...	...	1,000.00	
Indianapolis, Ind.	40	30	...	16	1	1	1	5	...	...	...	...	1,200.00	6,025.00	
Kansas City, Mo.	...	...	...	...	...	...	...	...	...	...	...	...	2,215.99	6,202.69	
Lawrence, Mass.	...	60	...	...	...	1	...	...	...	...	...	20	2,584.43	3,050.48	
Lincoln, Neb.	...	22	...	3	...	2	...	1	...	...	...	45	...	888.67	1,025.00
Lynn, Mass.	...	5	...	7	...	...	...	1	...	...	...	25	...	1,100.00	
Milwaukee, Wis.	28	31	1	5	1	1	1	1	...	...	...	...	2,470.00	3,690.00	750.00
Minneapolis, Minn.	...	5	...	...	...	1	...	3	...	2	...	98	...	6,500.00	700.00
Newark, N. J.	15	30	4	4	1	1	4	3	...	...	75	100	2,160.00	3,300.00	
New Brunswick, N. J.	...	13	...	13	...	...	1	1	...	...	*46	*50	...	336.00	
Newburg, N. Y.	...	8	...	13	...	...	...	1	...	4	...	25	...	1,291.25	58.56
New Haven, Conn.	17	41	4	6	2	2	1	1	...	...	...	7	16	2,018.38	4,705.61	8,500.00
Newport, R. I.	10	13	4	3	...	...	1	1	...	3	...	13	...	1,000.00	
Newton, Mass.	...	12	...	9	...	...	...	1	...	...	17	29	...	816.00	
New York City	21	54	2	8	4	9	6	31	...	...	235	218	15,537.00	40,926.00	41,351.00 + ¼ Charities Bldg. $150,000
Omaha, Neb.	...	...	...	...	...	3	...	...	...	5	...	135	...	4,300.00	
Orange, N. J.	...	...	...	...	...	...	...	...	...	...	38	60	946.19	1,424.17	
Pawtucket, R. I.	...	7	...	14	...	1	...	...	...	...	...	34	...	1,300.00	500.00
Philadelphia, Pa.	...	34	...	2	...	14	...	13	...	...	...	...	†24,437.28	47,850.95	
Plainfield, N. J.	...	23	...	26	1	1	1	1	...	...	59	51	22,164.83	2,393.83	
Portland, Me.	...	...	...	...	...	...	...	1	...	...	80	30	...	...	
Portland, Ore.	...	9	...	...	3	3	...	1	...	15	...	25	...	7,723.05	
Providence, R. I.	...	...	...	...	1	1	...	...	...	...	...	...	...	2,000.00	
Pueblo, Col.	...	7	1	2	...	...	1	2	...	7	8	19	...	...	
Richmond, Ind.	...	...	...	25	...	...	...	1	...	...	...	...	...	...	
Rochester, N. Y.	...	3	...	1	...	...	...	3	...	...	...	100	...	2,000.00	
Salem, Mass.	...	5	...	4	...	...	...	1	...	...	...	53	...	1,000.00	400.00
Salem, N. J.	...	...	3	4	...	...	...	...	...	...	33	25	219.69	282.84	
San Francisco, Cal.	...	112	...	25	...	1	...	2	...	3	...	12	...	4,189.99	
Seattle, Wash.	...	...	...	...	...	1	...	...	...	...	...	107	...	2,500.00	
Syracuse, N. Y.	...	9	...	2	1	2	1	1	...	21	...	28	...	2,348.75	
Taunton, Mass.	...	14	...	8	...	...	...	1	...	...	...	18	...	700.00	
Tivoli, N. Y.	...	...	...	10	...	...	...	...	...	...	...	8	...	200.00	
Trenton, N. J.	...	...	...	4	...	...	...	1	...	...	...	13	...	2,172.58	
Waterbury, Conn.	...	5	...	...	...	2	...	...	...	...	...	91	...	...	
Wilmington, Del.	...	12	...	13	...	...	...	2	...	2	...	86	...	4,667.42	
Worcester, Mass.	...	...	...	...	...	...	...	2	...	1	...	53	...	...	
Yonkers, N. Y., report of '91	...	...	...	...	...	...	...	...	...	...	...	...	...	829.44	
TOTAL	297	763	160	511	24	77	36	135	30	456	1,329	3,534	$86,019.58	$263,421.39	$409,037.55
INCREASE		156 %.		219 %.	220 %.		275 %.		1,400 %.		165 %.			206 %.	
						253 %.				260 %.					

* No distinction of sex is made in the returns. In this table Administrative Officers have been credited to Men and Friendly Visitors to Women, where the returns make no distinction, because these are the sexes that predominate in those sorts of service.

† Contributions to Ward Associations only. The contributions to the Central Treasury not returned, but probably about $15,000.

THE ORGANIZATION OF CHARITIES. 373

 2. Dispensaries.
  a. General.
  b. Special.
 3. Nurses.
 4. Convalescent homes.
 5. Fresh air excursions.
 6. Visiting and relieving the sick.

B. TEMPORARY RELIEF OF THE NEEDY.
 1. Shelter and lodging.
 2. Food, clothing, and fuel.
 3. Sewing-machines.
 4. Employment.
 5. Foreigners and their descendants.
 6. Day nurseries.
 7. Protection of children.
 8. Transportation.
 9. Free burial.

C. CONTINUOUS OR PERMANENT RELIEF OF THE NEEDY OR DEFECTIVE.
 1. Homes (institutional).
  a. For adults.
  b. For incurables.
  c. For children.
 2. Homes found in families.
 3. Schools.
  a. For the blind.
  b. For the deaf mutes.
  c. For the feeble-minded.
 4. Insane hospitals or asylums.
 5. Pensions.

D. REFORMATORY.

E. CO-OPERATIVE HOMES.

F. PROVIDENT AND BENEVOLENT (mutual benefit).

G. EDUCATIONAL AND MORAL.

It might appear from this that every need was provided for, and that the field was adequately covered,

But a fairer view of the actual situation in a modern city, Baltimore or other, would be given by scanning a list of the charities arranged without reference to purpose. By running through the names of one or two hundred charities thrown together helter-skelter, one would come to realize the chaotic nature of relief-work in a modern city. A poor person in need of relief does not usually have a directory of charities in his library, and may be referred from agency to agency without being able to find the relief he needs, which all the while is waiting for him. In Baltimore, for instance, it will be found that there are societies to relieve any need whatever of particular classes of persons. The Hebrew Benevolent will do this for Israelites, the German Society for Germans, the St. Andrew's Society for the Scotch, the denominational societies for those of their faith and for an undetermined number of outsiders. On the other hand, there are societies that will relieve any person whatever in some particular way. The Poor Association will give coal and groceries to any applicant it considers worthy, without regard to religion, race, or color. The dispensaries will give medicine, the sewing-societies clothing, and so on. It will be noticed that the lines of activity intersect. The classification by race overlaps that by religion, while the classification by needs overlies them both, and several agencies for the same sort of work are superimposed upon the others, while unlimited claims upon individual benevolence supplement or duplicate the whole. Suppose the case of a German Lutheran who is in need of one thing, say fuel. There are four organizations to which he may properly apply: 1, The German Society; 2, his church; 3, the Poor Association; 4, the police-station. If he is sick, the Indigent Sick Society may also aid; if a soldier, he may apply to the Confederate Relief Society or the Grand Army of the Republic; if his children go to a Methodist Sunday-school, help may be had from that source; if a Roman Catholic, he may also apply to the Society of St. Vincent de Paul; and finally, if he is just out of jail, the Prisoner's Aid Association may help. All this, of course, does not include what he may obtain from private individuals.

When a couple of begging children ring a door-bell in Baltimore, and ask for help, the one who answers will find, if he or she treats the case as thoroughly as it should be treated, that half the different kinds of charitable institutions in the city must be utilized, and several branches of the civil government set in motion, before one can unwind to its final links the chain of poverty and of incipient degradation that holds the youthful beggars. In such a case the agent of the Charity Organization Society has had recourse to the following agencies: The Society for the Protection of Children, the Poor Association, a church with which the parents had nominal connection, a dispensary for the sick mother, the police and the police court to compel the father to do his duty more fully, and a friendly visitor to advise with and encourage the mother and her girls. Now, it was not only desirable, but necessary, that all these agencies should work together heartily, in order to do what needed doing in the case. Proper aid to many destitute families involves a much wider circle of co-operation; and if we consider not special cases, but charitable work in general, we find that not one of the agencies can properly isolate itself; no modern charity liveth to itself alone.

In the fifties there had been organized in nearly all large cities in the United States general relief-giving societies, usually going under the title of " Societies for the Improvement of the Condition of the Poor." The " Boston Provident " belongs to this class. As indicated by the name, these societies held before themselves the highest purposes that benevolent people could seek to accomplish. In fact, most of their announced objects agree quite closely with those of the most modern societies. It was their purpose to find work for all willing to do it, to investigate all cases thoroughly, to raise the needy above the need of relief, and incidentally to relieve directly such want as seemed to require it. But as these Societies for the Improvement of the Condition of the Poor were dispensers of material aid, this function, as Mr. Kellogg puts it, submerged all others, " and they sank into the sea of almsgiving." Their work was done more or less well; but there is a general agreement that twenty years ago private almsgiving in American cities, for the most part through organized and even incorporated societies, was profuse and chaotic, while still not meeting the demands made upon it. It was dispensed in tantalizing doles miserably inadequate for effectual succor where the need was genuine, and dealt out broadcast among criminals and impudent beggars.[1] Public relief, at the same time, was in an unsatisfactory condition, out-door relief being administered with especial recklessness, and frequently tainted by political

---

[1] Kellogg, " Charity Organization in the United States," N. C. C., 1893, pp. 53, 54.

THE ORGANIZATION OF CHARITIES. 377

corruption. The old movement for the betterment of charities had substantially come to a standstill. While profession was still made of doing all that was needed, the energies of the societies were absorbed in giving direct relief. The tendency that has frequently been commented upon, of the charity worker tending to be dominated by details, so busy with immediate needs that he has not time to prevent their recurrence, had largely neutralized the beneficial effects of the Societies for the Improvement of the Condition of the Poor.[1]

The movement for charity organization had its origin in London in 1868, and was introduced into this country about ten years later, being copied direct from London at a number of independent points, such as Buffalo, Boston, and Philadelphia. After the trial of a society with similar purposes at Germantown, Pennsylvania, and certain tentative and unsatisfactory experiments in clearing-house registration of relief work in New York and Boston, the first real Charity Organization Society was established in Buffalo, in December, 1877. The Rev. S. H. Gurteen, an English clergyman, who had been active in the London society, was the moving force in the inau-

---

[1] The author once followed through with considerable care the annual reports of one of these Societies for the Improvement of the Condition of the Poor, interested to notice how from year to year the reports changed. One thing that seemed to serve as an index to the changing efficiency of the society was the statement regarding the number of persons for whom work was found. This item gradually dropped out of their reports altogether. Instead appeared sensational appeals for funds and descriptions of need in special cases. The large number relieved annually was especially dwelt upon; but the inadequacy of the relief given, while not dwelt upon, was manifest from the figures.

guration of this enterprise.[1] Boston, Philadelphia, and New Haven established similar societies in 1878, and Cincinnati, Brooklyn, and Indianapolis followed in 1879. The society in New York was not organized until 1882, when the initiative in the matter was taken by the State Board of Charities, which adopted the following resolutions: —

"*Whereas*, There are in the City of New York a large number of independent societies engaged in teaching and relieving the poor of the city in their own homes, and

"*Whereas*, There is at present no system of co-operation by which these societies can receive definite mutual information in regard to the work of each other, and

"*Whereas*, Without some such system it is impossible that much of their effort should not be wasted, and even do harm by encouraging pauperism and imposture, therefore,

"*Resolved*, That the Commissioners of New York City are hereby appointed a committee to take such steps as they may deem wise, to inaugurate a system of MUTUAL HELP AND CO-OPERATION between such societies."

"In accordance with this resolution, the New York City members of the State Board of Charities invited citizens, representing as far as possible all portions of the community, to assist in organizing this society, under a carefully prepared constitution, and to act as a Provisional Central Council until their successors should have been chosen by the society at large, at its first annual meeting. The Society was thus formed Jan. 26, 1882."[2]

In nearly every instance the motives leading to these

---

[1] Gurteen's work on "Charity Organization," a volume containing certain papers prepared by him on different phases of the subject is still the best explanatory volume to put into the hands of a person unacquainted with the work. It is unfortunately out of print.

[2] New York Directory of Charities, 1892, pp. 1, 2.

THE ORGANIZATION OF CHARITIES. 379

organizations is declared to be "discontent with the prodigality and inefficiency of public relief, and the chaotic state of private charity." Twenty-two of the associations organized at these or later dates report that "voluntary charity was lavish, uninformed, and aimless, with no concert of action; two that it was variable, and therefore unreliable; one that it was impeded by discouragement; and one that it did not exist in the community."[1] The same impulse that established the new societies abolished out-door relief in Brooklyn and Philadelphia, and greatly reduced it in Buffalo and Indianapolis. The growth of the movement is roughly outlined by the insertion of the accompanying table, which gives for the fifty-five societies reporting to the Committee of the National Conference in 1893 a summary of income and personal service accounts.

In order to afford as concise a view as possible of charity organization, there is given in tabular form, on the following page, a statement of the objects, methods, and machinery of the societies undertaking such work.[2]

To accomplish the first three objects may be described as the essential or constituent functions of Charity Organization Societies. The remaining five objects are usually kept in view, but not invariably so. The several societies vary much more as to the machinery than as to purposes.

---

[1] Kellogg, as above, p. 61.

[2] One of the most arduous duties connected with being an officer of a Charity Organization Society is to reply to the casual uninformed inquirer who asks, "Well, what does your society do?" One begins by saying that his society does not give material relief of any sort, and this is apt to astonish the questioner so much that he may have the patience to listen to a necessarily long explanation of the purposes and methods of the society.

TABLE XXXIII.

THE ORGANIZATION OF CHARITIES.

OBJECTS.	METHODS.	MACHINERY.
1. Co-operation between all charitable agencies of a given locality, and the best co-ordination of their efforts.	1. Comparison of relief records of the several agencies and mutual acquaintance of workers.	1. A card or other alphabetical catalogue of cases at a central office and frequent conferences of workers.
2. Accurate knowledge of all cases treated.	2. Thorough investigation, followed by careful registration.	2. Paid agents assisted by volunteer visitors, and elaborate case records either at central or branch offices.
3. To find prompt and adequate relief for all that should have it.	3. Bringing each case to the attention of appropriate relief agencies willing to aid.	3. Correspondence, personal interviews, sometimes a "Golden Book," or even a relief-fund (wisdom of this last questioned).
4. Exposure of impostors and prevention of wilful idleness.	4. After investigation, notification in all cases of those likely to be deceived, and, where feasible, arrest of impostors and professional beggars. Worktest.	4. Paid agents, sometimes (especially for this work) publication of a "cautionary list," information to all asking for it in specific cases, woodyard.

5. To find work for all able and willing to do anything.	5. Employment agency, wood-yard, stone-breaking, laundries, rag-sorting, etc.
6. Establishment of relations of personal interest and sympathy between the poor and the well-to-do.	6. Organization of corps of volunteer visitors who are not almsgivers, working under the guidance of paid agents.
7. Prevention of pauperism.	7. Kindergarten night-schools, industrial schools, penny provident funds, provident dispensaries, fuel funds, etc.
8. Collection and diffusion of knowledge on all subjects connected with the administration of charities.	8. Board meetings, annual meetings, conferences, lecture courses, periodicals.

5. To provide regular work where possible and relief-work when necessary.	
6. Friendly visiting.	
7. By above means and by special educational and provident schemes.	
8. Discussion, public meetings, publication.	

Taking up *seriatim* the objects and methods of the Charity Organization Societies of the United States, it may be seen that the fundamental thought is the co-operation of all charitable agencies of a given locality, and the best co-ordination of their efforts. In order to secure this, it is usually requested that the societies, so far as practicable, furnish records of the relief-work done by each, so that the accounts may be compared and the overlapping of relief prevented. The Charity Organization Society maintains at its central office an alphabetical list of all cases that have received relief from any reporting agency whatever, or that have been investigated by itself; and this comparative catalogue of work done is a treasure-house of facts for the guidance of those engaged in the work to be done. The New York society has a register giving some account of 170,000 families, or parts of families. While this is the largest consolidated list in the country, yet the central office catalogues of Boston, Philadelphia, and Baltimore contain a very large number of cases. These are so arranged that any case can be referred to at once, and the person charitably interested in that case can get a reply regarding it from the society by return mail. This clearing-house function of the Charity Organization Society is the first and perhaps the most fundamental one, and the one most clearly stated in the name which the societies adopted. Yet efficient co-operation in this matter on the part of all relieving agencies has been one of the most difficult results to secure. In some cities it has dwindled to almost nothing, in others it is very complete. Public officials in some of the cities co-operate fully, and, as in Buffalo, submit all cases to

THE ORGANIZATION OF CHARITIES. 383

which they give out-door relief, to the investigation of the society.

A second fundamental object of the Charity Organization Society, which is partly attained by the methods taken to secure co-operation and prevent the over-lapping of relief, is an accurate knowledge of all cases treated. Besides consulting the records of co-operating societies, this is to be gotten by thorough investigation, followed by careful registration. The old relief societies frequently depended upon the memory of the paid agent for the facts regarding different families aided; but the Charity Organization Society wishes to have records preserved with a thoroughness that can only be obtained by writing, and extending beyond the lifetime of any one individual. Investigation is not merely for the prevention of fraud, but is an essential pre-requisite of the proper treatment of cases needing relief. The giving of money or supplies is merely one form of prescribing for a case of destitution, and an investigation is as essential in dealing with the case as a diagnosis in a case of sickness with which a physician deals. The table on following page reports the varying forms of treatment deemed desirable by the Charity Organization Societies in over 74,000 cases coming under their observation in 1892.

The third function of a Charity Organization Society is to find prompt and adequate relief for all that should have it. The society is an animated directory of charities of the locality in which it works. No one is turned away from the office of the society with the statement, "Your need is none of our business;" for the society makes it its business to see that each need is brought to the attention of the proper agency. If no agency exists, a benevolent

TABLE XXXIV.

Treatment Desirable in 74,704 Cases.

TREATMENT.	NUMBER.	PERCENTAGES.[1]
Number treated	74,704	
Continuous relief	3,562	4.76
Temporary relief	18,558	24.84
Needing work rather than alms	11,989	16.05
Not relieved, having relatives	2,534	3.39
Not relieved, having vicious habits	7,719	10.33
Placed in institutions	1,182	1.58
Placed in charge of churches or societies	5,768	7.72
Placed in charge of police	572	.76
Aid procured from municipality or state	668	.89
Aid procured from churches and societies	8,408	11.13
Aid procured from individuals	4,931	6.60
Aided by loans	596	.80
Employment secured	13,477	18.04
Applicants' resources developed	46	.06
Removed to relatives or new situations	490	.65
Brought to self-maintenance (estimated)	1,524	2.04
Unclassified		

[1] Some of the totals in this column contain duplications of cases.

individual (called in Boston a " B. I.") can usually be found to give the relief required; and this bringing together of the giver and the receiver under wise guidance is one of the best results of charity organization. In discharging this function of finding prompt and fitting relief for each case of need, some societies have been led to start relief-funds of their own. When the first of these organizations were formed, the antagonism of the old relief-giving societies was frequently aroused; for the latter thought they saw in the new movement a likelihood of the duplication of their own efforts, which would be mischievous in its influence on the poor, and embarrassing when appeals were made to contributors. It was partly because of this position on the part of the established societies that many of the new organizations started out as non-relief-giving charitable agencies, in this matter breaking with English tradition, and making a new departure in charity work. Experience seems to have shown that this abstention from relief-giving has been the very best thing to allay the jealousy of older societies; and not only this, but that it has been the salvation of Charity Organization Societies, preserving them for the higher purposes which they had in view. A Charity Organization Society with a relief-fund must necessarily compete in its appeals to contributors with other organizations giving direct relief to the poor. These organizations are consequently jealous of it, and do not co-operate willingly, either in aiding cases it brings to their attention, or in giving to it and obtaining from it information of common advantage. It thus drifts into a condition where it is simply one of several relieving agencies.

Further than this, the public is used to organizations of the relief-giving type; and when it hears of the Charity Organization Society, it simply shrugs its shoulders and thinks, "Well, there's another one." On the contrary, when a society starts out announcing that its work is to benefit the poor, but that it does not give alms in any form, its very existence has an educational influence of great value in the community. People ask at once, "If you do not give relief, what do you do?" and then they can be induced to look over the long list of things other than relief giving that need doing. Besides this, the older societies were continually hampered by criticisms upon them on account of the amount spent in administration. "How much does it cost to give away a dollar?" was asked again and again of their solicitors. If it was shown that twenty, thirty, or fifty per cent of the contributions went for the payment of administrative expenses, a person when approached might object, saying that he could give his money away more cheaply than that himself. Since Charity Organization Societies have no relief-fund whatever, all this comparison of expenses for administration with relief is obviated. If asked how much is spent for purposes of administration the answer is, "All," and this has a good tonic effect upon both the questioner and the representative of the society. The former begins to see that helpfulness means more than almsgiving; and the latter realizes that if he is going to win the support of the public for his work, that work must be really and demonstrably useful. Somewhat less than half the societies of the country have relief-funds of their own. Philadelphia is the largest city in which the society for organizing charity has the relief feature largely developed. Here it was considered necessary to do this work in order to secure the abolition of public out-door relief; but the result of the compromise has been unfortunate so far as organization work is concerned. Most of the relief-giving organization societies are in small places where the problems are comparatively simple.[1]

[1] The author's personal experience in the administrative work of a Charity Organization Society has convinced him, somewhat to his own surprise, that such a society ought never to have a relief-fund. Such a fund at once saps the energy and ingenuity of agents and visitors in treating cases and securing co-operation. It also makes it more difficult for them to obtain co-operation, even if they try equally hard.

THE ORGANIZATION OF CHARITIES. 387

The fourth function mentioned in the tabular view, the exposure of impostors, and the prevention of wilful idleness, is frequently over-emphasized in describing the purposes of a Charity Organization Society. People look upon the society as merely an anti-mendicity league, a detective society for preventing imposition, and bringing swindlers to justice. The society is consequently regarded as bloodless, cold, and uncharitable, doing a work which may be necessary, but is certainly ungracious, and that does not appeal to the actively benevolent. As shown in Appendix G to Mr. Kellogg's report, the societies of the country have suppressed nearly 1,000 street beggars and impostors during the year 1892, and have detected over 100 fraudulent schemes. A society in a large city like New York or Chicago has much of this work to do, especially the detection of fraudulent charities. In smaller places there are not many fraudulent charitable enterprises, but there are always dishonest begging letter writers, and dishonest beggars from door to door. To give their contributors and co-operating agencies knowledge of these, several of the societies publish a cautionary list containing a description of dishonest applicants for relief, with their various *aliases* so far as known. The New York Society has carried farthest the special work of dealing with street beggars, employing two agents for that purpose, who aid, warn, expose, or arrest, as circumstances may seem to require in each case. This work of freeing the streets of mendicants is very much limited by the practice in most cities of giving licenses for petty peddling on the streets, or for operating musical instruments of the hand-organ type. In order to prevent wilful idleness most of the societies provide a work-test for both men and women, or one is operated by a co-operating association available for the use of the society.

Closely connected with the work of preventing wilful idleness is that of finding work for all able and willing to do anything. The woodyard and laundry may serve as work-tests, but they cannot give steady and profitable employment to all those desiring work. Each Charity Organization Society is, consequently, an employment agency, dealing for the most part and in ordinary times with the semi-capable, with those who from some perversion of character or defect of mind or body cannot fit themselves into the industries of the time, but may be able to do certain things if those things are sought out and brought to their attention. Many of those with whom the society deals are able-bodied, but not able-minded; or they may be both strong and intelligent, but not reliable. There are comparatively few cases where there is not some limitation of capacity more than that belonging to the average person. When the Bureau of Charities in Brooklyn was in charge of the late Mr. Buzelle, it had a reputation of being peculiarly successful in finding suitable work for everybody that was willing to work. It was said that if a woman without character and without skill could pick black rags from white ones, and was willing to do it, she could be given work; and if she was improvable, different grades of work would be found for her until finally she was taught something that would make her self-supporting. The same was true, though not in so complete a way, of the agencies for giving work to men. If it transpired that a given individual of either sex was not improvable,

THE ORGANIZATION OF CHARITIES. 389

such a person was made to see that the best place for him to obtain relief was at the almshouse. The success of a society in finding employment for these semi-capable applicants for work is a very good gauge of its efficiency. Nothing but perpetual effort and constant exercise of ingenuity can give success in this line.

The sixth enumerated function of the Charity Organization Society is to establish relations of personal interest and sympathy between the poor and the well-to-do. This is sought to be accomplished through what is technically known as " friendly visiting," volunteer visitors being secured who are willing to go to the poor as friends, and not as almsgivers. Preferably each friendly visitor has but one, or at most but two, cases, and the relation is made as permanent as possible. There are many instances where for years the same visitor has gone to the same family, and genuine personal attachments have been formed. Visitors should never be almsgivers; for in that case the poor look upon them as persons from whom something is to be gotten, and, on the other hand, if empowered to give relief, the visitor fails to invent methods of rendering the better service that is needed in order to cure poverty.[1] The work of friendly visiting is declared by the most advanced societies to be the heart of the work. The motto, "Not alms, but a

---

[1] A worker among the London poor who went into certain districts as a volunteer sanitary officer, trying to secure better sanitation in the tenement houses visited, established very satisfactory relations of personal friendship and regard with the population. When later he went into the same district as a distributer of the great Mansion House fund, he found that the whole attitude of the population toward him had changed for the worse. He was then one from whom something was to be obtained, and was despised by the better class and fawned upon by those anxious to obtain relief.

friend," first adopted in Boston, has come to be the motto of many of the societies. The work is developed under great discouragements in most of our large cities, especially in New York, where the long distances to be covered by the one going to the poorer districts, and the shifting nature of the indigent population, make it very hard to establish permanent relations of friendship, or even of acquaintance. Success, however, has been reached in Boston, even in districts where there is not one resident that could be called upon as a friendly visitor, and where many of those who do the visiting travel from the suburban towns to reach the field of work.

The influence of the visiting upon the poor may be excellent, but there can be no doubt that one of its very greatest benefits is upon the visitors. It is a method by which we may hope to reach "the upper classes." In all large cities there are places which, though not far from the well-to-do geographically, are likely to be completely forgotten. Balzac said of Paris that there were streets and alleys of which the upper classes knew no more than a man knows what is going on in his pancreas. This is not as true as it was when Balzac said it; but if it is less true, it is because the great associations of volunteer workers have been looking into these different parts of the city, and taking an interest in the people that live and die there. There is no education in charitable work so good as that which comes to the friendly visitor. Becoming interested in one family, he is likely to be led out into an interest in all branches of city government, and of the county and State government as well, and may even have his attention drawn to the need of federal prevention of undesirable immigration. He who takes an interest in trying to cure poverty in a single case will soon come to find that nothing in politics or industry is foreign to him.

The seventh function of the Charity Organization Society has been enumerated as the prevention of pauperism. This is sought to be accomplished by all the means that have been indicated for the furtherance of the other specific purposes of the society. But many organizations go further and seek to establish special branches likely to assail pauperism in its causes. The Crèche, or day nursery, at which working mothers can leave their children during the day, has been established in several cities, notably in Buffalo. The kindergarten movement for poor children, or in connection with the public schools, has had the active assistance of charity organizationists. Cooking-schools, sewing-schools, trade-schools, and laundries for the education of the workers have been established, as well as different varieties of savings-funds. Several of these funds operate with a system of stamp deposits, some of them being through collections made from house to house by the friendly visitors. The New York Society has been especially active in the pushing of stamp deposit funds, having established 206 stations, with 26,732 depositors, and over $15,000 on deposit. In Boston and Baltimore provident schemes of a similar character have been established, but not under the Charity Organizations Societies, though cooperating with them. Fuel funds, by means of which summer savings can secure winter delivery of coal at summer prices, have been established by some of the societies. The rule of nearly all the societies is not to undertake these special schemes if some independent organization can be found that will push them. They are desirable things that the charity organizationist wishes to see established, but they are not undertaken by the society itself except when necessary. Frequently such new enterprises start in connection with the society, and are then graduated into independent life.

The eighth and last function of the Charity Organization Society is the diffusion of knowledge on all subjects connected with the administration of charities. No progressive society neglects this function. Public meetings, conferences of visitors, lecture courses, and, in the case of four societies at least, the publication of periodicals which undertake to further these purposes of educating the community into wiser methods of charitable effort, are the agencies employed. In Appendix L to Mr. Kellogg's report at Chicago will be found a bibliography comprising more than a hundred titles of the pamphlets and other publications issued by the societies of the country.[1] Their annual reports themselves are educational literature of high value, giving detailed accounts of cases, and explaining the countless things, not to be summarized, which are necessary in wisely aiding the poor.

Finally, it should be observed that the charity organizationist, properly so-called, is essentially a man who will not consent to be buried under details. Neither the

[1] N. C. C., 1893. Most of the societies of the country are very liberal in sending to all requesting them their annual reports and the pamphlets which they have issued for gratuitous distribution. The societies of Baltimore, Boston, and New York are especially generous in this manner, and have been applied to by almost every place intending to start a new society on charity organization lines.

work of friendly visiting, nor the pushing of penny provident schemes, nor the operation of a woodyard, and, most of all, not the giving of relief, will he allow to distract him from a survey of the whole field, and from the endeavor to improve by better co-ordination the charitable efforts of the community. He is determined that the field shall be covered with some measure of adequacy, and that charitable forces shall not be wasted in competitive and misdirected efforts. For this reason the movement, which perhaps it is no longer proper to call new, has drawn to itself some of the most active and intelligent workers for the poor in the whole country; and at the National Conference the section on charity organization has secured an amount of attention out of all proportion to the extent of the funds used by these societies, and the number of persons interested in them. It is the only section of the National Conference that has set itself with earnestness to gather statistics as to the causes of destitution. If the persons concerned are loyal to present principles, they will continue to have a part in the development of new ideals and better methods of service.

CHAPTER XX.

CERTAIN HOPEFUL TENDENCIES.

Those who juggle with the word charity find it easy to prove that there has been no progress in charity since the early days. They can point to manifestations of a sentiment as pure and unselfish as is humanly describable on the part of the early Christian and of the pre-Christian pagans; and then can point to our modern charities with their material aid, their admixture of self-seeking, and all their defects, and ask us to note how charity has degenerated. They call attention to the fact that the King James translators of the New Testament could use the word charity in the thirteenth chapter of 1st Corinthians, while those who made the new translation substituted the word love. This last suggestion contains the explanation of the whole controversy. It is a matter of words and definitions. The word charity has several meanings, and it is by playing fast and loose with these that the case is made out against modern charity.

With a calculus of the sentiments we have nothing at present to do. Presumably thirst is the same to-day as in the time of Gideon, but when his soldiers drank they lapped from the hand or bowed themselves to the stream. The modern city must have water-works. So though benevolence or charity-in-the-sense-of-love be the same yesterday, to-day, and forever, yet the social machinery

CERTAIN HOPEFUL TENDENCIES. 395

for making benevolence beneficent changes with the changing times. It is with the machinery of benevolence that we are especially concerned, and at present with practicable improvements.

Even when attention is confined to charities, in the sense of the word defined for use in this volume, it is not so easy to be sure of progress. Institutions, localities, and nations have their ups and downs in the matter. Good systems break down because weakly administered, and bad systems work very well in the hands of the exceptionally honest and capable.[1] Wise observations regarding charity have been made so often during so long a time, the literature of the subject so bristles with opinions and expositions that should have clarified the subject and insured improvement, that one who has reviewed that literature, especially that which has been written within the last one hundred years, can hardly be otherwise than discouraged by what appears to be a lack of verifiable progress. Where so many good suggestions have fallen flat, and people have so persisted in making mistakes, it seems almost a hopeless task to strive for betterment. Many are inclined to conclude with the Preacher that "The thing that hath been, it is that which shall be; and that which is done is that which shall be done," and that there is nothing really new in the matter of charity. It is hoped that each chapter of this volume contains some evidence of the unsound-

---

[1] Lecky, European Morals, vol. ii., pp. 92-93. "It will continue to be found that the Protestant lady working in her parish, by the simple force of common sense and by a scrupulous and minute attention to the condition and character of those whom she relieves, is unconsciously illustrating with perfect accuracy the enlightened charity of Malthus."

ness of the view described, and in conclusion certain hopeful tendencies in the development of modern charities will be enumerated.

1. There is an element of progress in the very weight of the burden that charity is imposing upon modern communities. This burden already amounts to about one hundred million dollars per year in the United States. It may seem at first that one must be forced far afield for his hopeful tendencies who gives this as the first. Indeed, to "point with pride" to the large burden imposed by charitable institutions, frequently indicates ignorance rather than information on the subject. Yet in this burden there is a justification of healthful hope. It is found in the fact that the burden is becoming so heavy that its weight will compel attention to better methods, especially to curative and preventive methods. It is not an unhopeful fact that we are coming to a point where we can no longer put aside our duties. We must become wiser or be crushed. Aside from this rather grim reason for hopefulness, the weight of the burden more or less voluntarily assumed, is further encouraging because symptomatic of the widening and deepening of the altruistic instincts, and it roughly gauges a growing recognition of the solidarity of society.

2. Closely connected with the weight of the financial burden of charities, is the burden of responsibility for bad social conditions imposed upon large numbers of the influential classes. From interest in persons they have passed to interest in institutions. We often hear of the necessity of getting past the institution to the individual poor person, treating him as his special needs demand and as personal sympathy may dictate. But

there is a reverse process of equal importance to the right development of modern philanthropy. It is that by which charitable workers interested in a poor person come to see the necessity of improving institutions affecting the life of the poor, either those having their origin in politics or in industry, or in other social adjustments. The lady referred to by Lecky, who is operating so wisely by force of her own instincts and common sense, may succeed well enough in the country parish, and in a population not more fully organized than that of the rural districts; but in large cities one can hardly become interested in the cure of poverty in any given case, without also coming to have a lively interest in the betterment of city government, the improvement of sanitary legislation, and, finally, even a lively concern for federal legislation on the subject of divorce, or some other topic that would have appeared at the beginning equally far from the work of relieving the poor. An active charity organization society loses many of its friendly visitors from the fact that through their interest in cases they come to have an interest in institutions, and pass from the work of caring for the one to the work of reforming the other. To those who think that this is a loss, and that such persons have been turned aside from the work of real charity to something entirely different, it may be said that the interest in the institution, and willingness to guide it along lines of right development are absolutely essential, not only to the improvement of modern charities, but to the preservation of society. Institutions have heretofore grown through the operation of unconscious forces. They are now so complex and so highly developed, that their further growth must be consciously guided to wise ends, or they will be sources of social disease. This improvement of social conditions through the influence of those having a personal interest in the poor is best illustrated in the large cities, because there institutions are most typically modern, life is intensest, and the necessity of right action is most imperative.

Whenever a system of honor offices obtains, a large number of the influential class become interested in the administration of public charities. Inevitably there results a betterment of political institutions and often a modification of industrial conditions. A concern for the improvement of all social and industrial conditions is at once evidence and source of a desire to do preventive rather than relief work. Of late years there has been much demand for charity to do exactly this — to deal with causes rather than results. But to a great extent charitable institutions are still in the condition of half-capable business men who cannot be said to manage their business, but who rather let their business manage them, being driven so hard by attention to details that they have not time properly to organize and direct their work. While all agree in the truth of the statement that "a fence at the top of a precipice is better than an ambulance at the bottom," or with the more usual proverbial sayings which embody the same truth, yet they are so busy picking up the fallen that they do not get time to prevent others from falling. As already noticed, it is one of the peculiar merits of the charity organizationists that they will not allow themselves to be buried under details. They insist on surveying the whole field, and it is for this reason that so many of their workers combine an interest in individuals with an even more hopeful interest in the reform of social conditions. Many are impatient because workers in charities do not move faster in this direction. Organized labor is continually scolding at the short-sighted philanthropists.[1] Some of those living at social settlements in the United States find it particularly hard to be patient with those administering the charities, because the latter have such small concern for the causes of distress, and for its prevention. But while our charities may not be moving as fast in this desirable direction as many wish, they are probably moving faster, more perceptibly, than ever before. This cannot be doubted by one who turns the pages of the proceedings of the National Conference of Charities, or of the local conferences held in States like Indiana, Ohio, and Michigan, or of the local conference at Baltimore in 1877, or of the New England Conference of Charities, or of the Conferences on Child-Caring held in Boston, Philadelphia, and New York. The interest of the influential classes in all departments of social reform is being re-enforced by that of the various associations, both scientific and popular, for the study of the social sciences.

3. This suggests the help that modern charitable work is receiving from science and scientific methods. So long as the work of aiding the poor remains an art only, having its origin in instinct and its encouragement in super-rational or non-rational sanctions, a lack of verifiable progress is to be expected. Such was the case in the art of healing, as well as the art of nursing.

[1] One labor paper speaks of "a poverty which the bell-punch charity of organized, big-wig circumlocution societies cannot cure."

That charities will be improved through the help of science is stoutly denied by many who resent the application of scientific methods to this field of effort as something necessarily cold-blooded or unkind. Especially has the poor old science of political economy been hated by the philanthropist. After attending several sessions of a Conference of Charities, an American minister of the gospel preached a sermon on the general subject of charity in which he made use of the following modification of a scripture text: "Pure religion and undefiled before God and the Father is this: to visit the fatherless and the widows in their affliction, and to keep yourselves unspotted from political economy." The London Charity Organization Society is believed by many to have suffered from the dry rot of a political economy of untruthful narrowness. The biological sciences are also held to be inimical to benevolent work, it being thought that they teach that the unfit are only subjects for extermination.

It may be admitted at once that the scientist, in dealing with social problems, is in danger of taking the view that human suffering is of no consequence. He has learned to know that much suffering is curative in its influence; and if he jumps to the conclusion that all suffering is curative or of no consequence, he has taken a position which the instincts of those with whom and for whom he would work will never sanction. It is a position also that is scientifically false, and he only gets his deserts if he finds himself discredited. There is a time when science must be very modest, when its premises are not undisputed, and its deductions are consequently to be used with caution. All the social sciences are at present in this condition. Yet science is nothing but organized common-sense, and is always a more or less helpful agency in guiding the hand of art. Its conclusions "improve gradually and become good for something." They are at least safer than individual impressions, and are useful to correct human instincts and render them more sane and healthful. At last there comes a time when the hypotheses of a science are so well verified and its conclusions so clearly established that they can be followed with comparatively little caution, as now in the science and art of navigation. The art of nursing, and its improvement through the help of the science of bacteriology, offers an excellent example of the manner in which an art, presupposing sympathy in the one practising it, can yet be improved by the help of science. No one appreciates more fully than the ideal physician and the capable nurse the non-material aids to health. Drugs cannot take the place of hope, nor sterilized poultices the place of sympathy. Many of the component parts of gentleness are non-material, and acquired skill is no substitute for conscientiousness. But it remains true that it is science upon which medicine and nursing have drawn for help in the art of healing, and thereby made it more certain and more satisfactory in its results. The social sciences are even less certain in their conclusions than the medical sciences; but after this is admitted, it is still true that they are helpful if not taken for more than they are worth. The tendency to use them wisely is one of the most hopeful signs in modern charitable work, and contains the best possible guaranty of substantial and persistent progress.

4. So far has the helpfulness of science to philan-

thropy been recognized, that considerable didactic instruction is now given in that branch of social science to which the awkward but not inappropriate name of philanthropology may be applied. In nearly a dozen of the colleges and universities of the United States more or less elaborate courses are offered in this study.[1] Fully half of the men who have been engaged in this instruction are those who have had some practical experience in the administration of charities. On the other hand, a very considerable number of young men and women, who have recently gone into the new profession of charitable work, have received instruction in these branches, or at least in the general principles of social science, during a university course. It is possibly suggestive that the newest of our universities — the University of Chicago — has done the first work in preparing a textbook on Dependants, Defectives, and Delinquents. The recent text by Small and Vincent, from the same institution, "An Introduction to the Study of Society," does far more than Dr. Henderson's to clarify the subject of social pathology, and to put it in right relations to the other branches of social science. The present volume is itself the outgrowth of teaching philanthropology; and, during its preparation, the various classes of interested students whom the author has faced have been constantly in his mind.

5. As charities become complex, and as social science and philanthropology come to be better understood, and consequently more and more useful, it is found that the

[1] See an article by the author, "Philanthropology in American Colleges," being his report as Secretary of Section VII. of the International Congress of Charities, Correction, and Philanthropy, held at Chicago, 1893. (Baltimore, Hopkins Press, 1894.)

man with definite preparation for charitable work has an advantage over a man of similar ability not specially prepared. The development of a new profession is manifestly under way. As yet preparation is obtained mainly through experience, as doctors of medicine used to obtain their training by being in the office of an established practitioner; but this condition of things will be progressively modified in one line of practice as it has been in the other.

Among salaried employees of charitable societies, Mr. Folks finds three tolerably distinct types: the first is the man considerably past middle age, who has outlived his usefulness in any other line, and who, by reason of his unusual goodness, is supposed to be an acceptable alms distributer. In the second type, the great excellency lies in clerical ability; work for a charitable agency is the same as work for a dry-goods firm, a grain warehouse, or a street-cleaning department, except that the wages are somewhat less. The third type differs from the other two in that the man considers the work a profession. "This means that he takes up philanthropy as other men take up journalism, law, theology, or medicine. He does his work because it is to him the most inviting field of service."[1] As yet those who belong to the third class have commonly had no preparation especially designed to fit them for their work. They have turned from other professions to this new one because the work attracted them. Many have been ministers,

[1] See "College men in Benevolent Work," Proceedings of Section VII., International Congress of Charities, Correction, and Philanthropy, held at Chicago, 1893. (Baltimore, Hopkins Press, 1894.) To the same volume Miss Anna L. Dawes contributes a valuable paper on "The Need of a Training School for a New Profession."

many teachers, some journalists, and a few lawyers. Among the older men a majority had perhaps been fitted for the ministry, and among the younger men a considerable number are those who would have been ministers at an earlier time. This is decreasingly true, however. Especially among the young men and women studying social science in American colleges, there are many who would never have thought of becoming ministers or foreign missionaries, who yet turn to the work of the new profession as a field of congenial service.

Training in the new profession will be important and will guarantee success in proportion as the basis of philanthropy becomes scientific. So long as it is an art, pure and simple, with no formulated principles upon which to rest, those with an instinct for the work will succeed best in it; but when it shall come to the point where well-ordered information is useful and even indispensable, and the guidance of theory not to be despised, one who has systematically fitted himself for the work will have an advantage similar to that which the graduate of a good normal school has over the untrained applicant for a position as teacher. It is curious, that at the present time it is easier for a young man or woman who wishes to go as a foreign missionary to secure training, than for one who wishes to enlist in the temporal service of the poor of our own country.

Training should include both didactic instruction and practice under expert guidance. Yet most of those who offer themselves for the work have either had instruction without experience, or experience without instruction; either the theoretical or the practical side of their preparation is defective. Under such circumstances it is only those strong enough to secure preparatory training independently that are at all well fitted. More energy and ingenuity are required to fit a person for this work than for most other lines demanding a similar grade of ability.

The inadequate preparation and the small number of men engaging in the work is sufficiently explained by the low pay offered. Salaries for this profession are still graded according to the deserts of the first two classes of workers mentioned by Mr. Folks, and meagre salaries are even defended by people who ought to know better. Those who willingly contribute to the support of a six thousand dollar clergyman will frequently insist that fifteen hundred per year is ample for the paid secretary of a charitable society. One who enters this new profession must be willing, of course, to make sacrifices for the work; clergymen expect to bring to their work some measure of self-sacrifice, but that does not preclude the possibility of their being well paid. It is not a proof of selfishness that a minister allows Providence "to point with better pay where duty lies." A clergyman on ten thousand a year can render better service than one on a smaller salary. At the Congress of Charities, Mr. Folks well urged that the salaried agent of a charitable society ought not to allow others to assess his contribution to the work and collect it in advance, by requring him to work for excessively low wages. Dr. Walk spoke of his own experience at a time when a reputable paper of Philadelphia was willing to say that no man ought to take a salary from a charitable society unless he would himself otherwise be an object of charity. That time has past, though there is still much need for greater liberality in the matter of salaries. Many young men and women are ready to consecrate themselves to the work; but they are not ready, and ought not to be ready, to consecrate themselves on terms that make good work impossible. In addition to consecration and native intelligence, the successful paid charity worker must have a tolerably expensive education continuing through life, and the sound health that enables a man to preserve clear vision and undulled sympathies through years of harassing work. While in the service of the poor we may hope to secure consecration and possibly intelligence for nothing, education and health are things that cost money, and must be paid for.[1]

The considerations here urged are already accepted as sound by the more progressive leaders in charitable enterprises, especially in the large cities where expert service is most essential. In Boston there is a club that meets once a month, composed wholly of paid charity workers; and similar organizations are contemplated elsewhere. With a body of intelligent and specially trained experts, giving their time and energies to the right development of the various branches of charitable effort, definite and constant advances may be expected.

The tendencies here touched upon, towards extensive growth, towards social amelioration, towards the employment of scientific methods, towards the introduction

---

[1] The religious orders give professional service at small expense; but it remains to be seen whether these orders can attract persons of the right stamp for progressive work, which shall use all that is useful in science.

of courses in philanthropology in institutions of learning, and towards the development of a new profession, are all, with the exception of the first, of recent origin, and nevertheless of very demonstrable strength. They find their clearest expression in the conferences of charities, national and local. These gatherings are for the comparative study of charities, and the more extended application of whatever methods have been found best. The members have included many of the most intelligent salaried workers for charity and many of the most devoted volunteers. The State Boards of Charities have formed the nucleus of the National Conference, which originated, it should be noted, as a branch of the American Social Science Association. In all these gatherings there is an excellent spirit of catholicity, an earnest desire to know the best and hope the best, and to welcome all real help that any science or any religion can give.

APPENDIX.

INDEX.

Administration, improvement of charities, 310.
Aged, private homes for, 293, 294; pensions for, 295.
Almsgiving, see Charity.
Almshouse, fundamental institution, 139; local political unit for care of destitute, 140; usual character of, 141, 142; differentiation of inmates, 142, 143, 153 ; effect on children, 142; Rep. N. Y. State Board of Charities on, 146; intemperance among inmates, 147, 149; probable independence among inmates, 147; disgrace attaching to relief by, 150; abuses, 150–152; in San Francisco, 154; laxness regarding admission and discharge, 155; resort for tramps, 156; feeble-minded women in, 157; lack of work-test, 159.

Beggars, see Unemployed.
Bell, Prof. Alexander Graham, on Deaf Variety of Human Race, 74.

Benevolence usually instinct, 125; effect in race improvement, 126; effect of public subsidies on, 350, 351.
Besant, Annie, limitation of population, 67.
Billings, Dr. J. S., causes of degeneration, 56–58.
Böhmert, Dr. Victor, causes of poverty in Germany, 42.
Booth, Charles, causes of pauperism, 26; tabulation of contributory causes, 35, 36; intemperance, 65; stories of Stepney pauperism, 84, 85.
Brace, Charles L., dependent children, 203.
Brooklyn, out-door relief in, 168–171.

Carlyle on English poor-law, 16.
Castration a punishment, 133; as treatment for insanity and feeble-mindedness, 133; Dr. Kerlin on, 134.
Chalmers on charity, 14.
Charities, expenditures for medical, Table XXVII., 241;

definition, 301; public, definition, 303, 304; administration, 310; expense, 313, 314; private, definition, 315; advantages, 321; usefulness, 322; no recognized definition of sectarian, 339, 341; chaotic condition, 357; necessity of organization, 359; supervision of State boards, 359–366; visitorial powers of boards, 366; voluntary supervision of, 367; need of supervision, 370; classification, 372–376; movements for organization, 377–379; objects of organization, 380–393; co-operation, 382; National Conferences of, 379, 399, 407; hopeful tendencies, 394–407.

Charity, early, 4; motives, 5, 8; degeneration of ecclesiastical, 7, 9; influence of church, 7, 8, 11; a species of fire insurance, 8; indiscriminate, 8; state interference, 9, 10; Defoe on, 11; influence of economics, 11, 19; Ricci on, 12; influence of French Revolution, 12; Malthus on, 14; Chalmers on, 14; no use for, in United States, 20; influence in human selection, 118; Bagehot on, 118; as selective force, 126; effect on death-rate, 129; effect on birth-rate, 130; indiscriminate, as a method of dealing with the unemployed, 180, 181; social influence as motive, 317; religious motives, 316, 317; methods of raising money, 318, 319; benevolence as motive, 319, 320.

Charity Organization Societies, 27,000 cases investigated, 30; schedule of causes of poverty drawn up by, 33.

Children, effect of pauperism of parents, 53; weakness cause of incipient pauperism, 55; effect of intemperance of parents, 63–65; effect of immorality of parents, 70; influence of heredity and environment, 78–81; effect of almshouse, 139; number of dependent, 202, 203; mothers of destitute, 212; rules of institutions for receiving, 213–215; Union Temporary Home, 215; in almshouses, 216; state school for destitute, 217; classification of dependent, 218–222; delinquent, 219, 220; societies for protection, 221, 222; institution plan of providing for, 222–228; institutions for, of religious character, 223; industrial training for dependent, 227; placing out of dependent, 228, 231–233; in Canada, 228; in Pennsylvania, 233; in Massachusetts, 235; in Michigan, 235; in Wisconsin, 236; in

Minnesota, 236; in Ohio, 237; advantages of placing out, 230, 237; support of, in New York, 337, 345, 346; Mrs. J. S. Lowell on, 351; under two years, see Infants.

Children's Aid Society of New York, 229–230.

Children's Law of New York, 217.

Church, degeneration of charitable motives, 7, 8; influence on charity, 11; private outdoor relief given by, 175, 176; work in preventing pauperism, 296; influence on almsgiving, 316; kinds of giving, 315–320.

Connecticut law concerning tramps, 186, 187.

Contagious Diseases Acts in England, 69.

Co-operation of charitable agencies, 383.

Crime as an accompaniment of intemperance, 62.

Crooker on early charity, 4, 5.

Crusoe, Robinson, Number Two, 25, 26.

Dartmouth College decision, 324, 325.

Deaf, intermarriage of, 132.

Deafness, sign of degeneration, 74.

Defectives, permanent homes for adult, 296.

Defoe on charity, 11.

Degeneration, diagram of forces tending toward, 56; characteristics of individual tending toward, 60; intemperance as a cause, 60; immorality, 66; lack of judgment, 71; laziness, 72; idleness, 102; influence of heredity, 74; Dr. Strahan on diseases, 77; idiocy, a sign of, 78.

Dependents, marriage among, 133; differentiation of classes, 297.

Disease a force producing incapacity, 57; employment of women and children a cause, 101; produces poverty, 116.

Diseases of occupations, 99.

Dispensaries, means of hospital extension, 248; statistics showing work of New York, Table XXIX., 249; number of destitute cases, 250; free medical service, 251.

Dugdale on causes of pauperism, 55; on intemperance, 60, 61; on sexual immorality, 70, 71; Jukes an example of degeneration, 88–92; out-door relief, 173.

Dutch Free Home Labor Colonies, 198–200.

Economics, influence on charity, 11, 19; failure of, 20; renaissance in United States, 21.

Economists, struggle with philanthropists, 14; reform of poor-laws, 15; a g a i n s t Shaftesbury, 17.
Efficiency, standard rising, 96.
Emminghaus, ideal of ecclesiastical charity, 10; Protestant control of charity in Germany, 10.
Employment, lack of, cause of poverty, 39-41; comparison of races in, 47; for lack of, see Unemployed.
Endowments, motives for securing, 323, 324; laxness concerning, in United States, 324, 325; motives of persons making, 326-328; disadvantages of, 328; regulation of, 329-331; in England, 332, 333.
English Poor-Law, 11, 311; Malthus on, 13; Walker on, 15; Senior on, 15; Carlyle on, 16.
Environment a cause of degeneration, 87, 91.
Epileptics, institution for, 288; see Feeble-minded.
Factory legislation, 16-18.
Farr, Dr. William, mortality in occupations, 106, 108.
Feeble-minded, custodial care of, 131; number of, 277; in what classes found, 277; institutions for, Table XXX., 278; Dr. S. G. Howe on, 279, 280; work of training, 280-282; Table XXXI., showing bad condition of 574 idiotic persons, 281; classification of, 282-285; custodial care of, 286; epileptics should be separated from, 288.
Feeble-mindedness, definition of, 276.
Foundlings, see Infants.

Galton, Francis, on D'Alembert, 81; on heredity of English judges, 83, 84.
George, Henry, explanation of poverty, 24.
Girard College, selection in, 227; endowments of, 328, 329.
Grimshaw, Dr., statistics of class mortality, 113.

Hall, G. Stanley, imitation in children, 64.
Hart, Hastings H., on placing-out of children, 230.
Hatters, diseases of, 100.
Henderson on out-door relief, 165.
Heredity, influence of, toward degeneration, 74; methods of studying force of, 82; of English judges, 83, 84; Booth's stories of Stepney pauperism an illustration of, 84, 85; inmates of New York almshouses as illustration, 86; the Jukes, 88-92; the Ishmaelites, 92-94; at bottom biological, 119; best working

hypothesis in regard to, 121; a factor in determining character, 122; transmission of deafness by intermarriage, 132.

Hospitals, foundling, death rate in, 129; effect on morals of free, 131, 132; maternity, 211, 212; growth, 240; items necessary to report, 242, 243; cost of construction, Table XXVIII., 243; motives contributing to development, 244; gratuitous service of physicians, 245; qualifications for admission, 245, 246; departments of administration, 247; politics in, 247; public *vs.* private control, 248; nursing in, 253–257.

Howe on idiocy and intemperance, 62; influence of heredity on idiocy, 78; on idiocy, 279, 280.

Hubert-Valleroux, origin of French charities, 9.

Incurables, homes for, 295.

Idiocy, sign of degeneration, 78; see Feeble-minded.

Idleness, cause of degeneration, 102; produces inefficiency, 180.

Immorality, cause of degeneration, 66; effect on laborers, 68; effect on offspring, 70.

Impostors, exposure of, 387.

Incapacity, cause of poverty, 40, 55; result of disease, 57.

Industrial training for dependent children, 227.

Industry, development of modern, 96; organization a necessity, 97.

Inebriates, care of, 289–291.

Inebriety, see Intemperance.

Inefficiency produced by idleness, 180.

Infants in foundling hospitals, 205–210; death-rate of destitute, 205, 206; feeding of destitute, 207, 208; boarding out, 208, 209; Massachusetts Asylum, 209; facilities for abandoning, 210–212.

Insane, number of, 260–262; reasons for increase, 262–264; unjust commitment of sane, 264; methods of commitment, 265; detention, 265; escort to asylums, 266; history of treatment, 267–269; size and construction of buildings, 269; boarding out, 271; acute *vs.* chronic, 272; private institutions, 272; classification, 272–274; criminal, 274.

Institutions, for destitute children, 213; for dependent children, 222–228; advantages of public support for charitable, 305, 306; disadvantages, 306–309; politics in charitable, 309; difference between public and private,

340; effect on inmates of private, 343; duplication of, 348, 349; subsidized, 352; government supervision, 353.
Intemperance, cause of poverty, 38, 46; cause of degeneration, 60–62; crime as an accompaniment, 62; idiocy and, 62; in Norway, 63; effect on offspring, 63–65; effect in United States, 65; Booth on, 65; among almshouse inmates, 147, 149.

Jails, bad system of, in United States, 197.
Judgment, lack of, cause of degeneration, 71.

Kellogg, C. D., on need of relief among those applying, 30.
Kerlin, Dr., on castration as cure for vice, 134.
Kerr on intemperance, 62.
Körösi, Josef, statistics of occupational mortality, 104.

Labor Colonies, German, 194–198; bibliography, 200.
Laziness, cause of degeneration, 72.
Lewis, W. Bevan, crime as an accompaniment of intemperance, 62.
Licentiousness, institutions for persons committing habitual, 291.

Lodging-houses and woodyards for tramps, 187–201.
Low, Seth, on outdoor relief in Brooklyn, 168–171; appointments in public charitable institutions, 308.
Lowell, Mrs. Josephine Shaw, on feeble-minded women, 159; public subsidies to private charities, 337, 338; support of dependent children in New York City, 351.

Macaulay, on factory acts, 18.
McCulloch, Oscar C., the Ishmaelites an example of degeneration, 92–94.
McDonogh School, selection in, 227.
Malthus on English poor-law, 13; principle of population, 23; ridiculed by Henry George, 24.
Marriage encouraged among defectives, 133.
Marshall on out-door relief, 176.
Mortality of illegitimate children, 70; statistics show influence of occupation on health, 103–110; causes of higher rate among lower classes, 112, 113; class, shows degeneration, 112–116.

Norway, intemperance in, 63.
Newsholme, mortality in occupation, 108.

INDEX. 417

Nursing in hospitals, 253–257; by Roman Catholic orders, 256; district, 257, 258.

Occupation lessens capacity of individual by accidents, 97; disease begetting conditions, 99; mortality statistics, 103; Körösi's statistics of mortality, 104.

Occupations, Table XVII., mortality and morbidity, 105; mortality, Tables XVIII. and XIX., 106, 107; death-rate of males in different, Table XX., 109.

Offspring, of feeble-minded women, 157.

Old age, cause of pauperism, 39, 55.

Organization, development of industry compels, 97; charity, 377–379; objects of, 380.

Pauperism, effect of parents on children, 53; weakness a cause of, 55; Dugdale on causes of, 55; commonest exciting cause incapacity, 55; extermination not a remedy for, 128; promotion by private charities, 344.

Philadelphia, out-door relief in, 171.

Philanthropy, see Charity.

Philanthropists, struggle of, with economists, 15–18.

Political Economy, see Economics.

Politics, influence on public charitable institutions, 309; private institutions free from blight of, 343.

Poor, homeless, see Unemployed.

Poor-laws in United States, 311.

Poor-relief, see Charity.

Population, Annie Besant on limitation of, 67.

Pot-makers, diseases of, 100.

Poverty, causes of, 22–58; socialist's explanation of, 24; methods of ascertaining causes, 22, 23, 26, 27; analysis of causes, 28; case-counting as means of ascertaining causes, 29, 34; result of many causes, 35; sickness most constant cause, 40; Böhmert's statistics on causes, 42; tendency of different races toward, 45, 46; large family not a cause, 51; result of accidents, 98; produces disease, 116; prevention an object of Charity Organization Societies, 391.

Protestant Church, charitable work of, 315; interdenominational competition, 317.

Railways, accidents to employees of, 98.

Relief, unreliability of statistics on out-door, 162; out-door, in six States, Table XXVI., 164;

Mr. Sanborn on out-door, 165; out-door in Hartford, Ct., 165; out-door in New Haven, 165; Henderson on out-door, 165; reasons in favor of out-door, 166, 167; reasons against out-door, 167, 168; out-door in Brooklyn, 168–171; out-door in Boston, 171, 172; out-door in Brookline, Mass., 172; out-door in Wisconsin, 173; Dugdale on out-door, 173; out-door a question of administration, 174; private out-door, 175, 176; Marshall on out-door, 176; for the unemployed, 181; principles of State poor, 304, 305; functions of charity organization societies in supplying, 383–386.

Religion as motive to charity, 5, 12; influence on views regarding sanctity of human life, 126–128.

Rentoul on women's work, 101.

Ricci on charity, 12.

Ritchie on natural selection, 124.

Roman Catholic Church, charitable work of, 316.

Rousseau, state control of charity, 12.

Russell, Sir John, and factory acts, 17.

Sanborn on out-door relief, 165.

Self-seeking, motive to charity, 5, 6.

Selection, natural, 123; Ritchie on, 124; difference between instinctive and rational, 124; natural, instinctive, and rational defined, 125; human, a combination of, 125.

Selection, human, important in race improvement, 121; different from natural selection, 123; defined, 125.

Senior, on English poor-law, 15.

Sense and sympathy, inter-action of, 18, 19.

Settlement laws, 312.

Shaftesbury, and factory legislation, 17.

Shiftlessness as a cause of poverty, 38, 46.

Sick, number of destitute, 239; relief for destitute, at home, 252; nursing of destitute, at home, 257.

Sickness a cause of poverty, 40; comparison of races, 47.

Smith, Adam, on poor-relief, 13.

Societies, objects of charity organization, 380–393.

State control of charities in Scandinavia, 9; in England, 10; in France, 10; in Germany, 10.

State interference in charities, 9; no improvement, 11; in France, 12.

INDEX.

Steuart, Sir James, on poor relief, 13.

Strahan, Dr., on diseases of degeneration, 77.

Subsidies, abuse of public, 242–245; motives for public to private charities, 334; in Washington, D.C., 336; in New York, 337; Mrs. Lowell on, 337, 338; considerations in favor, 341–344; objections, 344–353; constitutional limitations, 349; difficulties in regard to appropriations, 350; effect on private benevolence, 350, 351; effect on institutions, 352; doubtful expediency of, 354.

Table I., 27,961 cases investigated by charity organization Societies, 30; II., decisions in the cases of 8,294 applicants for relief, 32; III., causes of poverty in Buffalo, 33; IV., causes of poverty as determined by case-counting (insert), facing 34; V., tabulation of contributory causes of poverty, 36; VI., dependent children in German cities, 43; VII., existing causes of dependence, New York almshouse inmates, 44; VIII., causes of poverty as indicating misconduct or misfortune (insert), facing 44; IX., causes of poverty among Americans and Germans, 49, 50; X., classification of cases in Boston and New York (insert), facing 50; XI., by nationalities and marital condition (insert), facing 52; XII., applicants in four cities by marital condition, 52; XIII., percentage of native white, colored, and foreign born among population as a whole, 54; XIV., tendency of deaf persons to transmit deafness, 75; XV., hereditary tendencies apparently affecting idiocy in Massachusetts, 79; XVI., statistical summary of the "Jukes" (insert), facing 90; XVII., mortality and morbidity in five occupations, 105; XVIII., mortality per 1,000 at six age-periods, 106; XIX., number living at stated ages out of 1,000 living at age 25, 107; XX., death-rate of males in different occupations, 109; XXI., class mortality, 112; XXII., annual rate of mortality in Dublin, 114; XXIII., burden-bearing power in various classes, 115; XXIV., children under ten years of age in almshouses, 144; XXV., paupers in almshouses, 1880 and 1890, 145; XXVI., out-door relief in six States, 164; XXVII., public expenditures for medical charities in ten American cities, 241; XXVIII., cost of construction of certain hospitals, 243; XXIX., statistics showing work of general dispensaries of New York, 249; XXX., institutions for feebleminded, 278; XXXI., showing the bodily condition of 574 idiotic persons, 281; XXXII., summary of income and personal service accounts of fifty-five Charity Organization Societies (insert), facing 372; XXXIII., organization of charities, 380; XXXIV., treatment desirable in 74,704 cases, 384.

Tendencies, hopeful, in financial burden of modern charity, 396; in responsibility for social conditions, 396-399; in help received from science, 399-401; in instruction in social science, 402; in development of social science as a profession, 402-406; in organization of sociological clubs, 406.

Tramp, see Unemployed.

Unemployed, number, 177-179, 181-183; classes, 179; idleness produces inefficiency, 180; principles of relief, 181; methods of dealing with tramps, 183-201; German labor colonies, 195-198; Dutch free home labor colonies, 198-200; bibliography of labor colonies, 200.

Vagrants, legal measures for, 198, 199.

Venereal disease as result of immorality, 68, 69.

Vice, state regulation, 69, 70. Sexual, see immorality.

Walker on English poor-law, 15.

Weismann, on transmission of acquired characteristics, 120-122.

Wilson on intemperance, 64.

Women and children, labor of, 101.

Women, placing out of destitute, 212.

Woodyards for tramps, 187-201.

Work-test in almshouses, 159-161; for tramps, 189-196.

BIBLIOGRAPHICAL INDEX.

ABBREVIATIONS: N.C.C., National Conference of Charities; I.C.C.C.P., International Congress of Charities, Correction, and Philanthropy (Chicago, 1893).

ABBOTT, LYMAN.
Art. "The Personal Problem of Charity." *Forum*, Feb., 1894.

ACTON, W.
Prostitution Considered. Churchill, London, 1870.

AMMON, OTTO.
Die natürliche Auslese beim Menschen. Fischer, Jena, 1893.

AMOS, SHELDON.
Prohibition, Regulation, and Licensing of Vice. Stevens & Sons, London, 1877.

ANCKER, ARTHUR B.
Art. "The Municipal Hospital," in N. C. C., 1888.

ANSELL, CHARLES, JR.
The Rate of Mortality, etc., in the Upper and Professional Classes. Layton, London.

ARLIDGE, J. T.
The Hygiene, Diseases, and Mortality of Occupations. Percival, London, 1892.

ASHLEY, W. J.
An Introduction to English Economic History and Theory. Putnams', New York, 1893.

BAGEHOT, WALTER. The Works of.
Published by Traveller's Insurance Company, Hartford, Conn., 1889. 5 vols.

BALUFFI, CARDINAL.
The Charity of the Church a Proof of her Divinity. Translated from the Italian. Gill, Dublin, 1885.

BEARD, GEORGE M.
Art. "Physical Future of the American People," in *Atlantic Monthly*, vol. xliii.

BELL, ALEXANDER GRAHAM.
Memoir upon the Formation of a Deaf Variety of the Human Race. National Academy of Sciences, 1884.
Marriage: an address to the Deaf. Volta Bureau, Washington, D.C., 1891.

BERTELSMAN, W.
"Die Arbeiter Colonie :"
a small monthly periodical
published at Gadderbaum.

BERTHOLD, G.
Statistik der Deutschen Arbeiter-Kolonien. Priber,
Berlin, 1891.

BILLINGS, DR. J. S.
On Vital and Medical Statistics, reprinted from the
Medical Record of Nov. 30,
Dec. 7 and 14, 1889. New
York, 1889.
Hospitals, Dispensaries,
and Nursing. Section III.,
I. C. C. C. P.

BÖHMERT, VICTOR.
Armenwesen in 77 Deutschen Städten. Dresden,
1886.

BOIES, HENRY M.
Prisoners and Paupers.
Putnams', New York, 1893.

BOOTH, CHARLES.
Pauperism and the Endowment of Old Age. Macmillan, London and New York,
1892.
Labour and Life of the
People. Williams & Norgate,
London, 1891. 3 vols.

BOOTH, GENERAL.
In Darkest England, and
the Way Out. Funk & Wagnalls, New York, 1890.

BRACE, CHARLES L.
The Dangerous Classes of
New York. Wynkoop, New
York, 1880.
Gesta Christi. Armstrong,
New York, 1882.

BRINKERHOFF, R.
Art. "Infirmary Building." N. C. C., 1879.

BUZELLE, GEORGE B.
Art. "Some Uses of Relief in Work," in *Charities
Review*, Vol. I.

CENSUS BULLETIN, No. 72.
May 27, 1891. "Inmates
of Juvenile Reformatories."

CENSUS, ELEVENTH.
Bulletins Nos. 90 and 154
on Almshouses in U. S.

CHALMERS, THOMAS.
On Endowments. Glasgow, 1827.
On Political Economy.
Appleton, New York, 1832.

CHARITIES REVIEW, VOL. II.
Art. "Relief in Work."

CHILDREN'S AID SOCIETY OF
NEW YORK (THE).
Its History, Plan, and Results. Published by the Society, 1893.

CLOSSON, CARLOS C.
Art. "The Unemployed
in American Cities," *Quarterly Journal of Economics*,
January and July, 1894.

CODMAN, MRS. JAMES M.
Art. "Public Out-door Relief." Brookline, Mass., N. C. C., 1891.

CONFERENCE (New York) ON THE CARE OF DEPENDENT AND DELINQUENT CHILDREN. Nov., 1893.

CROOKER, JOSEPH H.
Problems in American Society. Ellis, Boston, 1889.

CYCLOPÆDIA OF TEMPERANCE AND PROHIBITION.
Funk & Wagnalls, N.Y., 1891.

DARGUN, Dr. LOTHAR.
Egoismus und Altruismus in der Nationalökonomie. Duncker & Humblot, Leipzig, 1885.

DAVENPORT-HILL, FLORENCE.
Children of the State. Macmillan, London, 1889.

DAWES, ANNA L.
Art. "The Need of a Training School for a New Profession." Proceedings of Section VII., I. C. C. C. P.

DRUMMOND, HENRY.
Ch. "Parasitism" in Natural Law in the Spiritual World. Hodder, London, 1888.

DUGDALE, R. L.
Art. "Hereditary Pauperism." N. C. C., 1877.
"The Jukes." Putnams', New York, 1888.

EDEN, SIR F. M.
State of the Poor. 1797. 3 vols.

EMMINGHAUS, A.
Poor Relief in Different Parts of Europe. Stanford, London, 1873.

EXTRACTS from the information received as to the administration and operation of the Poor-Laws. B. Fellowes, London, 1833.

FARR, WILLIAM.
Vital Statistics. Stanford. London, 1885.

FAWCETT, HENRY.
Manual of Political Economy. Macmillan, London, 1883.

FITCH, J. G.
Address. "Endowments." Proceedings of the Second Annual Convention of the College Association of Pennsylvania. 1888.

FLYNT, J.
Art. "The City Tramp." *Century*, March, 1894.
"The Tramp at Home." *Century*, February, 1894.

FOLKS, HOMER.
　Art. "College Men in Benevolent Work." Proceedings of Section VII., I. C. C. C. P.

FOSTER, J. N.
　Art. "Ten Years of Child-Saving Work in Michigan." N. C. C., 1884.

FOWLE, T. W.
　The Poor Law. Macmillan, London and New York, 1890.

GALTON, FRANCIS.
　Hereditary Genius. Appleton, New York, 1871.
　Inquiries into Human Faculty. Macmillan, London, 1883.

GILES, H. H.
　Art. "Location, Construction, and Management of Poorhouses." N. C. C., 1884.

DE GRAFFENRIED, MISS CLARE.
　"Child Labor." Publications American Economic Association, Vol. V., No. 2.

GRIMSHAW, DR., Registrar-General of Ireland.
　Mortality Statistics, *British Medical Journal*. 1887. Vol. II.

GURTEEN, S. H.
　Charity Organization. By the author, Buffalo, 1882. (Out of Print.)

GUSTAFSON, A.
　The Foundation of Death. Hodder, London, 1888.

HART, HASTINGS H.
　Art. "Economic Aspect of the Child Problem." N. C. C., 1892.

HERMANN, EMANUEL.
　Wirthshaftliche economische Fragen und Probleme der Gegenwart. Winter, Leipzig, 1893.

HOBHOUSE, SIR ARTHUR.
　The Dead Hand. Chatto, London, 1880.

HOBSON, JOHN A.
　Problems of Poverty. Methuen, London, 1891.

HODDER, EDWIN.
　The Life and Work of the Seventh Earl of Shaftesbury. K. G. Cassell, London, 1886. 3 vols.

HOWE, DR. S. G.
　Report on Idiocy in Massachusetts. Coolidge, Boston, 1848.

IRELAND, RT. REV. JOHN.
　Art. "The System of Charities in the Catholic Church." N. C. C., 1886.

JEANS, VICTORINE.
　Factory Act Legislation. Unwin, London, 1892.

JEVONS, W. STANLEY.
　The State in Relation to Labour. Macmillan, London and New York, 1882.

JOHNSON, ALEXANDER.
Art. "Some Incidentals of Quasi-Public Charity." *Charities Review*, Vol. I. February, 1892.

JOYCE, GEORGE F.
Art. "Out-Door Relief in Brookline, Mass." Massachusetts Board of Managers, World's Fair, 1893.

KELLOGG, CHARLES D.
Art. "Charity Organization in the United States." N. C. C., 1893.
Bibliography of Charity Organization Societies of the United States. N. C. C., 1893. Appendix L.

KENNY, COURTNEY.
Endowed Charities. Reeves, London, 1880.

KERLIN, ISAAC N.
Art. "Provision for Idiotic and Feeble-Minded Children." N. C. C., 1884.

KERR, NORMAN.
Inebriety. Lewis, London, 1889.

KIDD, BENJAMIN.
Social Evolution. Macmillan, New York, 1894.

KÖRÖSI, JOSEF.
Die Hauptstadt Budapest. Puttkammer, Berlin, 1881.

LECKY, W. E. H.
History of European Morals. Appleton, New York, 1876. 2 vols.

LEE, JOSEPH.
Art. "Out-door Relief in Brookline." State Charities Record. April, 1892.

LEFFINGWELL, ALBERT.
Illegitimacy. Scribner, New York, 1892.

LOW, SETH.
Art. "The Problem of Pauperism in the Cities of Brooklyn and New York." N. C. C., 1879.
Art. "Out-door Relief in the United States." N. C. C., 1881.
Art. "Municipal Charities and Correction." N. C. C., 1888.

LOWELL, MRS. JOSEPHINE SHAW.
Art. "One Means of Preventing Pauperism." N. C. C., 1879.
Committee Report to New York State Board of Charities, 1884.
Art. "The Care of Dependent Children in New York and Elsewhere." Twenty-third Annual Report New York State Board of Charities, 1889.
Art. "Methods of Relief for the Unemployed." *Forum*, February, 1894.
Art. "The Economic and Moral Effects of Public Outdoor Relief." N. C. C., 1890.

Art. "Are Labor Colonies needed in the United States?" Vol., "Organization of Charities" (Section VI.), of I. C. C. C. P.

MACAULAY, T. B.
Speeches, Vol. II., "The Ten Hours Bill." Houghton, Boston, 1874.

McCOOK, J. J.
Art. "A Tramp Census and its Revelations." *Forum*, August, 1893.

McCULLOCH, OSCAR C.
Art. "The Tribe of Ishmael." N. C. C., 1888.

MACDONALD, ARTHUR.
Abnormal Man. U.S. Bureau of Education, Circular No. 4, 1893.

MALTHUS, T. R.
An Essay on the Principle of Population. Johnson, London, 1803.

MARSHALL, ALFRED.
Principles of Economics, Vol. I. Macmillan, London and New York, 1891.
Art. "The Poor Law in Relation to State-aided Persons." *Economic Journal*, Vol. II.

MARX, KARL.
Capital. Translated from the German edition. Appleton, New York, 1889.

MAVOR, JAMES.
Art. "German Labor Colonies and the Unemployed." *Journal of Political Economy*, December, 1893.

MEATH, EARL OF.
Art. "Labour Colonies in Germany," *Nineteenth Century*, Vol. XXIX.

MOORE, HAROLD E.
Art. "The Unemployed and the Land." *Contemporary Review*, March, 1893.

NASH, VAUGHAN.
Art. "The Home Office and the Deadly Trades." *Fortnightly Review*, February, 1893.

NEWSHOLME, ARTHUR.
The Elements of Vital Statistics. Swan Sonnenschein, London, 1889.

NEW YORK CHARITIES DIRECTORY.
Published by Charity Organization Society, New York, 1892.

NICHOLLS, SIR G.
History of the English Poor-Laws. Murray, London, 1854. 2 vols.

NITTI, FRANCESCO S.
Art. "Poor Relief in Italy." *Economic Review*, Vol. II., January, 1892

PATTEN, SIMON N.
    Art. "Economic Basis of Prohibition. *Annals American Academy*, Vol. II., July, 1891.
PEABODY, FRANCIS G.
    Art. "The German Labor-Colonies for Tramps." *Forum*, February, 1892.
PITMAN, ROBERT C.
    Alcohol and the State. National Temperance Society, New York, 1886.
PRENDERGAST, RICHARD.
    Art. "State Aid to Private Institutions." N. C. C., 1886.
PROCEEDINGS OF THE ASSOCIATION OF MEDICAL OFFICERS OF AMERICAN INSTITUTIONS FOR IDIOTIC AND FEEBLE-MINDED PERSONS.
    Lippincott, Philadelphia, 1889, 1891, 1892.
PROCEEDINGS OF THE NATIONAL CONFERENCE OF CHARITIES AND CORRECTION.
    Ellis, Boston, 1874-1893.
RENTOUL, ROBERT R.
    The Reform of our Voluntary Medical Charities. Ballière, London, 1891.
    The Dignity of Woman's Health. Churchill, London.
REPORT OF CHARITY ORGANIZATION SOCIETY OF BALTIMORE. 1892.

REPORT OF A CONFERENCE OF CHARITIES.
    Published by the Charity Organization Society of Baltimore, 1887.
REPORTS, —
    Charity Organization Societies.
    Report of Superintendent of Charities for District of Columbia. 1892.
    Report of First Indiana State Conference of Charities. Indianapolis, 1890.
    Report, Third Annual, of New York State Charities Association.
    Report, Tenth Annual, of New York State Board of Charities, 1877.
    Reports of Board of Public Charities of Pennsylvania, Harrisburg.
    Reports of Board of Charities and Reform, Wisconsin.
    Report of English Board of Trade-Labour Department on "Methods for Dealing with the Unemployed." London, 1893.
    Report of Commissioner of Labor (United States), 1886.
    Reports of New Jersey Bureau of Labor, 1889, 1890, 1891, on "Health and Trade Life of Workmen."
    Report of Ohio Bureau of Labor, 1890, 1891, 1893.

Report of a Special Committee of the Charity Organization Society on "The Homeless Poor of London." London, 1891.

Report of Massachusetts Bureau of Labor, 1879 and 1887, on Unemployed.

Reports, Consular, on "Vagrancy and Public Charities in Foreign Countries." Washington, 1892.

Reports of State Commissions in Lunacy.

Report of Massachusetts State Board of Lunacy and Charity, 1893.

Reports of Maryland Lunacy Commission.

Report of State Board of Control, Wisconsin, 1892.

Report on Public Institutions. Boston, Document 192, 1892.

Report of the Statistician of the Inter-State Commerce Commission, 1892.

Report of Committee on "Immigration and Interstate Migration." N. C. C., 1892, p. 76, et seq.

Report from His Majesty's Commissioners for Inquiring into the Administration and Practical Operation of the Poor-Laws. B. Fellowes, London, 1834.

Report of the Committee on the History of Child-Saving Work. Special volume of N. C. C., for contents, see Proceedings for 1893, p. 139, 1893.

Report on "The Advisability of Establishing a Workhouse." New Haven, Conn., 1887.

Report of the Special Committee on Out-Door Alms of the Town of Hartford, 1891. Hartford, Conn., 1891.

RIBTON-TURNER, C. J.
History of Vagrants and Vagrancy. Chapman and Hall, London, 1887.

RIGGS, C. EUGENE.
Art. "Progress in the Care of the Insane in the Last Twenty Years." N. C. C., 1893.

RIIS, JACOB A.
Children of the Poor. Scribner's, New York, 1892.

RITCHIE, DAVID G.
Darwinism and Politics. Swan Sonnenschein, London, 1889.
Problems of Poverty.
Art. "Pauperism in the Light of the Theory of Natural Selection." Proceedings, Sec. VII., I. C. C. C. P.

SANBORN, F. B.
Art. "Indoor and Outdoor Relief." N. C. C., 1890.

Art. "Management of Almshouses in New England." N. C. C., 1884.

SCHUYLER, LOUISA L.
Art. "The State Charities Aid Association of the State of New York." Vol., "Organization of Charities," of I. C. C. C. P.

SCOTT, BENJAMIN.
A State Iniquity. Kegan Paul, London, 1890.

SHURTLEFF, H. S.
Art. "State Care of Destitute Infants." N. C. C., 1889.

SMITH, STEPHEN.
Art. "Report on the Commitment and Detention of the Insane." N. C. C., 1888.

SPENCER, HERBERT.
Negative Beneficence and Positive Beneficence. Appleton, New York, 1893.
The Principles of Biology. Appleton, New York, 1891. 2 vols.

STATUTES and Amendments to Code of California. 1883.

STEAD, W. T.
Josephine Butler. Morgan & Scott, London, 1887.

STRAHAN, S. A. K.
Marriage and Disease. Appleton, New York, 1892.

UHLHORN, J. G. W.
Die christliche Liebesthätigkeit Seit der Reformation. Gundert, Stuttgart, 1890.
Die christliche Liebesthätigkeit im Mittelalter. Gundert, Stuttgart, 1884.
Christian Charity in the Ancient Church, translated from the German by Sophia Taylor. Clark, Edinburgh, 1883.
Art. "Armenwesen; Geschichte," in Handwörterbuch der Staatswissenschaften.

WALLACE, A. R.
Art. "Human Selection." *Popular Science Monthly*, Vol. XXXVIII.

WALKER, FRANCIS A.
Political Economy. Holt, New York, 1884.

WARD, LESTER F.
Psychic Factors of Civilization. Ginn, Boston, 1893.

WARNER, AMOS G.
Art. "Philanthropology in Educational Institutions." Report of Section VII., I. C. C. C. P.
Art. "Public Subsidies to Private Charities." Vol., "Organization of Charities," of I. C. C. C. P. Chicago, 1893.

Art. "Some Experiments on Behalf of the Unemployed." *Quarterly Journal of Economics*, Vol. V.
    Art. "Evolution of Charities." Publications of the Brooklyn Ethical Association.

WEISMANN, AUGUST.
    The Germ-Plasm. Scribner's, New York, 1893.

WHITE, ALFRED T.
    Art. "Labor Tests and Relief in Work in the United States." Vol., "Organization of Charities," of I. C. C. C. P.

WHITE, ANDREW D.
    Art. "Demoniacal Possession and Insanity." *Popular Science Monthly*, Vol. XXXIV., 1889.
    Art. "Diabolism and Hysteria." *Popular Science Monthly*, Vol. XXXV., 1889.

WILLIAMSON, MRS. EMILY E.
    Art. "State Charities Aid Association of New Jersey." Vol. "Organization of Charities," of I. C. C. C. P.

WILLARD, FRANCES E.
    Annual Addresses Before the W. C. T. U.

WILLINK, H. G.
    "Dutch Home Labour Colonies." Kegan Paul, London, 1889.

WILLOUGHBY, WILLIAM F.
    "Child Labor." Publications American Economic Association. Vol. V., No. 2.
    Art. "State Activities and Politics." Papers American Historical Association, 1891. Vol. V.

WILSON, GEORGE R.
    Drunkenness. Swan Sonnenschein, London, 1893.

WINES, FRED H.
    Art. "Causes of Pauperism and Crime." N. C. C., 1886.

WRIGHT, A. O.
    Art. "Employment in Poorhouses." N. C. C., 1889.

WRIGHT, J. F.
    Art. "Marriage Relationships in the Tribe of Ishmael." N. C. C., 1890, page 345.

POVERTY, U. S. A.
THE HISTORICAL RECORD
An Arno Press/New York Times Collection

Adams, Grace. **Workers on Relief.** 1939.

The Almshouse Experience: Collected Reports. 1821-1827.

Armstrong, Louise V. **We Too Are The People.** 1938.

Bloodworth, Jessie A. and Elizabeth J. Greenwood. **The Personal Side.** 1939.

Brunner, Edmund de S. and Irving Lorge. **Rural Trends in Depression Years: A Survey of Village-Centered Agricultural Communities, 1930-1936.** 1937.

Calkins, Raymond. **Substitutes for the Saloon: An Investigation Originally made for The Committee of Fifty.** 1919.

Cavan, Ruth Shonle and Katherine Howland Ranck. **The Family and the Depression: A Study of One Hundred Chicago Families.** 1938.

Chapin, Robert Coit. **The Standard of Living Among Workingmen's Families in New York City.** 1909.

The Charitable Impulse in Eighteenth Century America: Collected Papers. 1711-1797.

Children's Aid Society. **Children's Aid Society Annual Reports, 1-10.** February 1854-February 1863.

Conference on the Care of Dependent Children.
Proceedings of the Conference on the Care of Dependent Children. 1909.

Conyngton, Mary.
How to Help: A Manual of Practical Charity. 1909.

Devine, Edward T. **Misery and its Causes.** 1909.

Devine, Edward T. **Principles of Relief.** 1904.

Dix, Dorothea L.
On Behalf of the Insane Poor: Selected Reports. 1843-1852.

Douglas, Paul H.
Social Security in the United States: An Analysis and Appraisal of the Federal Social Security Act. 1936.

Farm Tenancy: Black and White. Two Reports. 1935, 1937.

Feder, Leah Hannah.
Unemployment Relief in Periods of Depression: A Study of Measures Adopted in Certain American Cities, 1857 through 1922. 1936.

Folks, Homer.
The Care of Destitute, Neglected, and Delinquent Children. 1900.

Guardians of the Poor.
A Compilation of the Poor Laws of the State of Pennsylvania from the Year 1700 to 1788, Inclusive. 1788.

Hart, Hastings, H.
Preventive Treatment of Neglected Children.
(Correction and Prevention, Vol. 4) 1910.

Herring, Harriet L.
Welfare Work in Mill Villages: The Story of Extra-Mill Activities in North Carolina. 1929.

The Jacksonians on the Poor: Collected Pamphlets.
1822-1844.

Karpf, Maurice J.
Jewish Community Organization in the United States. 1938.

Kellor, Frances A.
Out of Work: A Study of Unemployment. 1915.

Kirkpatrick, Ellis Lore.
The Farmer's Standard of Living. 1929.

Komarovsky, Mirra.
The Unemployed Man and His Family: The Effect of Unemployment Upon the Status of the Man in Fifty-Nine Families. 1940.

Leupp, Francis E. **The Indian and His Problem.** 1910.

Lowell, Josephine Shaw.
Public Relief and Private Charity. 1884.

More, Louise Bolard.
Wage Earners' Budgets: A Study of Standards and Cost of Living in New York City. 1907.

New York Association for Improving the Condition of the Poor.
AICP First Annual Reports Investigating Poverty. 1845-1853.

O'Grady, John.
Catholic Charities in the United States: History and Problems. 1930.

Raper, Arthur F.
Preface to Peasantry: A Tale of Two Black Belt Counties. 1936.

Raper, Arthur F. **Tenants of The Almighty.** 1943.

Richmond, Mary E.
What is Social Case Work? An Introductory Description. 1922.

Riis, Jacob A. **The Children of the Poor.** 1892.

Rural Poor in the Great Depression: Three Studies. 1938.

Sedgwick, Theodore.
Public and Private Economy: Part I. 1836.

Smith, Reginald Heber. **Justice and the Poor.** 1919.

Sutherland, Edwin H. and Harvey J. Locke.
Twenty Thousand Homeless Men: A Study of Unemployed Men in the Chicago Shelters. 1936.

Tuckerman, Joseph.
On the Elevation of the Poor: A Selection From His Reports as Minister at Large in Boston. 1874.

Warner, Amos G. **American Charities.** 1894.

Watson, Frank Dekker.
The Charity Organization Movement in the United States: A Study in American Philanthropy. 1922.

Woods, Robert A., et al. **The Poor in Great Cities.** 1895.